A BUFFALO 3-PIECE-SUIT EQUIPS YOU FOR ALL UK & ALPINE WINTER CONDITIONS, & HIMALAYAS TO 20,000 FT., FOR AROUND £200.   STRAIGHT UP!

BUFFALO
DOUBLE-P-SYSTEM
Clothing and Sleeping Bags Ltd.

- A Buffalo 3-pce-suit = Shirt, Trsrs or Salop's, Jckt, Hood.

- You can choose from 5 Shirts, 3 Salop's, Trs, 3 Jckts.

- You wear the suit next to the skin and don't need to carry spare clothing. Weight >2kg. (stick that in your pack).

- Totally condensation free.

- Comfortable 5 minutes after immersion in icy water.

- Shirt is windproof to 40 mph. Rainproof to 12mm per hour. Replaces up to 5 layers.

- Shirt + Jckt virtually windproof and rainproof.

- Write, Fax or Tel. for info and stockists.

2 Books of testimonials in each shop.

THE OLD DAIRY, BROADFIELD ROAD, SHEFFIELD S8 0XQ TEL. 0742 580 611 FAX. 0742 509 323

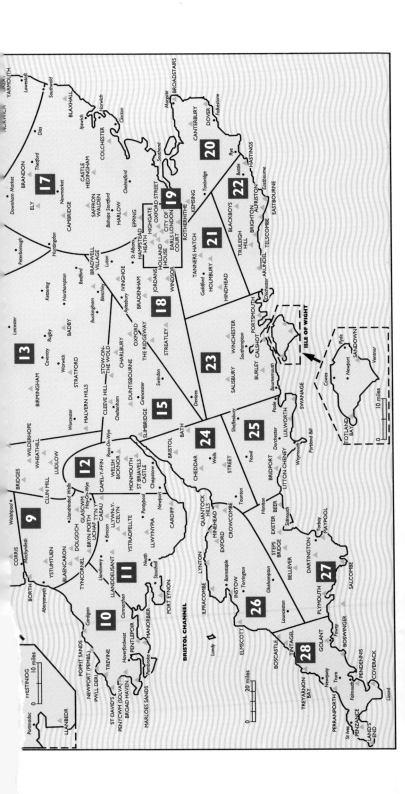

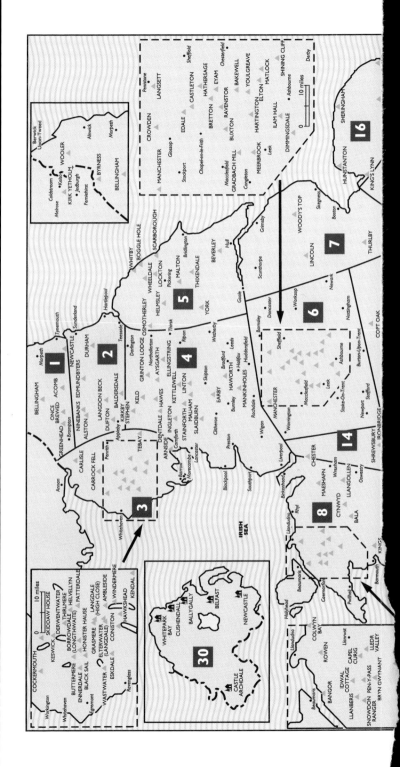

KEY TO SYMBOLS

Open (at the top of each Hostel entry)
Indicates the time the Hostel opens.
Hostels are also open 07.00 - 10.00 hrs.

(symbol) Telephone number

R-a-H Rent-a-Hostel scheme: Hostel available for
exclusive use during Winter months:
More details on page 7 or phone number
listed after **R-a-H** symbol

(symbol) Meals available

(symbol) Table licence available

GSC Self-catering facilities suitable for groups

(symbol) Full central heating

(symbol) Camping

(symbol) Games room

(symbol) Laundry facilities

(symbol) Secure lockers available

(symbol) Grounds available for games

(symbol) Suitable for wheelchairs

(symbol) No Smoking Hostel

S Shop at Youth Hostel

(symbol) Shop nearby

(symbol) Study room available

P Parking

BABA Available on the Book-a-Bed-Ahead scheme

IBN Hostel can be booked via International
Booking Network (see page 19)

(symbol) Number of rooms with **2 - 4 beds**

(symbol) Number of rooms with **5 - 8 beds**

(symbol) Number of rooms with **9 or more beds**

(symbol) Cycle hire at or near Hostel

(symbol) Horse riding

(symbol) Hill walking

(symbol) Watersports

(symbol) Rock sports

(symbol) Birdwatching

(symbol) Swimming

(symbol) Bus information

(symbol) Train information

(symbol) Ferry Information

(symbol) Tourist Information Centre

OS Ordnance Survey 1:50000 map

GR Grid reference

Bart Bartholomews 1:100000 map

DAYTIME ACCESS ARRANGEMENTS
BETWEEN 13.00 AND 17.00 HOURS

1 Simple shelter, WC where possible.

2 Good simple shelter, WC, luggage storage, booking
facility.

3 Good simple shelter, WC, luggage storage, booking
facility, often drinks machine.

4 Good simple shelter, WC, luggage storage, booking
facility, often drinks machine, staff on duty.

Opening Dates All dates inclusive.

Open . . . open every night between given
dates.

X . . . . except.

eg. . . . . . . Open X:Sun = Closed from 10.00 hrs
Sunday to 17.00 hrs Monday.

Contents

YHA NATIONAL OFFICE, 8 ST STEPHEN'S HILL, ST ALBANS, HERTS AL1 2DY

TEL: 01727 855215   FAX: 01727 844126

Membership Prices (from 1 January 1995)

UNDER 18	£3.00	
ADULT	£9.00	
FAMILY	£18.00	(for both parents, with children aged under 18 enrolled free)
	£9.00	(for a single parent family)
LIFE	£120.00	(or 5 annual covenanted Direct Debit payments of £28)

MEMBERSHIP PRICES ARE HELD FOR THE SECOND YEAR RUNNING!

Overnight Prices (from 1 March 1995)

(The scale for each Hostel is shown both in the index and under the individual Hostel entry.)

Scale	Under 18	Adult	Scale	Under 18	Adult
1	£3.60	£5.35	5	£5.35	£8.00
2	£4.00	£5.95	6	£5.95	£8.80
3	£4.45	£6.55	7	£6.55	£9.70
4	£4.85	£7.20	8	£7.20	£10.60

For London prices, look under individual Youth Hostel entries.

Meal Prices* (from 1 March 1995)

BREAKFAST	£2.70*
STANDARD PACKED LUNCH	£2.20
LARGE PACKED LUNCH	£3.00 (available at some Youth Hostels only)
EVENING MEAL	from £4.00

Camping Prices

The charge for camping at those Hostels where it is permitted is half the adult overnight fee for the Hostel per person regardless of the age of the camper(s).

PLEASE NOTE:

* Some Youth Hostels now offer an inclusive bed and breakfast package. Please see Hostel entries.

All prices stated within this Guide are current at the time of going to press. It is possible, however, that they may change during the year and it is a Condition of Booking that all persons are obliged to pay the charge current at the time of arrival. In circumstances where there has been an increase since booking, any additional charges will be payable to the Hostel staff on arrival.

YHA cannot accept liability for loss or damage to vehicles or their contents while parked at Youth Hostels.

Discover England & Wales with YHA

The Youth Hostels Association, a registered charity founded in 1930, aims: *"to help all, especially young people of limited means, to a greater knowledge, love and care of the countryside, particularly by providing Hostels or other simple accommodation for them in their travels, and thus to promote their health, rest and education."*

The Youth Hostels Association (YHA) has 240 places to stay in England and Wales, many in glorious town, coastal and countryside locations. The Youth Hostels are as individual as their visitors and vary from converted historic houses in our towns and cities to simple accommodation in remote, next-to-nature settings. Wherever you stay, you'll be free to discover the spectacular landscapes of England and Wales. Come by yourself, with friends or family — everyone's welcome!

When you stay at one of our Youth Hostels you can always be sure of friendly and helpful service from our staff. Accommodation is in comfortable bunk bedded rooms. Prices start from just £3.60 to stay the night and include bed linen and the use of all facilities — lounge, self-catering kitchen, plus drying rooms and cycle sheds. Many Youth Hostels have on-site parking and grounds available for recreation, as well as extras like a self-service laundry — look for the relevant symbols under the individual Hostel entries (you'll find a key to symbols on the inside map flap).

Most Youth Hostels also offer a full catering service, with prices starting from just £4.00 for a delicious three course evening meal (with a vegetarian option). Some Youth Hostels even have a table licence so adults can enjoy a drink of wine or beer with their meal!

Youth Hostels Association (England & Wales)

PATRON:
Her Majesty the Queen

PRESIDENT:
Dr David Bellamy

VICE PRESIDENTS:
Hedley Alcock, OBE
Chris Bonington, CBE
Len Clark, CBE
The Lord Lovell-Davis
Alun Michael, JP, MP
John Parfitt, CBE
John Patten

CHAIRMAN:
Derek Hanson

VICE-CHAIRMAN:
Chris Darmon

TREASURER:
Martin Green

ASSISTANT TREASURER:
John Hockey

CHIEF EXECUTIVE:
Colin Logan

YHA NATIONAL OFFICE:
YHA, Trevelyan House,
8 St Stephen's Hill, St Albans,
Herts AL1 2DY
Tel: 01727 855215
Fax: 01727 844126

YHA REGIONAL OFFICES:

▲ YHA Northern England, PO Box
11, Matlock, Derbyshire DE4 2XA
Tel: 01629 825850
Fax: 01629 824571

▲ YHA South England, 11B York
Road, Salisbury, Wiltshire SP2 7AP
Tel: 01722 337515
Fax: 01722 414027

▲ YHA Wales, 4th Floor, 1 Cathedral
Road, Cardiff CF1 9HA
Tel: 01222 396766
Fax: 01222 237817

▲ YHA Cities Division,
8 St Stephens's Hill, St Albans,
Herts AL1 2DY
Tel: 01727 855215
Fax: 01727 844126

Registered charity number: 301657

The Youth Hostels in this Guide are operated by YHA (England and Wales) Limited.

BARCLAYS

The bank has a long established tradition of supporting charitable and community causes and encouraging the development of young people plays an important part in our community programme. Therefore we are particularly pleased to be supporting the Youth Hostels Association in the production of this Accommodation Guide, which will benefit not only young people but also their families and friends.

As well as support for young people we also aim to improve the quality of life for elderly people and those who are concerned with the environment and funds are also targeted at employment training.

Sally Shire
Head of Community Enterprise Department
Barclays Bank PLC

How To Join YHA

You need to be a YHA member to stay at a Youth Hostel. Residents of England and Wales should just complete the membership form in this Guide (p.203). One year's YHA membership costs £9 for adults and £3 for under 18s.

If you're applying for family membership — £18 for one year or £9 if you're a one-parent family — please make sure you list the names of all adults and children in your family. Anyone aged under 18 is entitled to free membership when their parent(s) join and will receive their own card.

Groups can get hold of a Group/Organisation Card for just £10 which entitles all members of a group to use a Youth Hostel (for details fill in the coupon at the back of this Guide).

Overseas visitors can buy membership from the Youth Hostel Association of their home country. Alternatively, you can take out International Membership (£9) when you arrive at any Youth Hostel.

What You Get

Having a YHA membership card gives you access to hundreds of places to stay in England and Wales as well as over 5000 Youth Hostels worldwide. **It also means you can join a YHA Local Group and take part in Hostel-based activities while meeting new friends.**

In addition, YHA members will receive:

▲ regular copies of YHA's **Triangle** magazine (full of special offers and competitions as well as travel articles on the UK and abroad);

▲ the annual **YHA Accommodation Guide**

▲ a **Members Discount Book,** packed with discounts on travel, places of interest and outdoor gear.

You are also entitled to a ten per cent discount on most goods at YHA Adventure Shops (more details on p.197).

Other membership concessions include:

▲ Students aged 18 to 25 who are not travelling as part of a group will receive a £1.00 reduction on the Youth Hostel's overnight charge on production of a valid student card at the Hostel Reception.

Available at all Youth Hostels at all times.

▲ Adults who are YHA (England & Wales) members and who can provide proof that they receive means tested benefits related to low income will be charged the Under 18 rate for their overnight stay.

Available at all Youth Hostels at all times except in London. This concession is not applicable for Family Room or Family Annexe accommodation.

Not Just A Place To Stay

As well as providing safe, clean and comfortable accommodation for individuals, families and groups travelling on a budget, YHA membership also gives you a wide selection of holiday packages to choose from.

HOSTELLING WITH A GROUP

Youth Hostels are also available for group residentials, with many offering additional facilities for educational trips, such as leader rooms and class/meeting rooms (there may be a small extra charge). All-inclusive packages are also on offer which can include transport, itineraries, activities and excursions.

The YHA can give a helping hand to group holiday organisers by providing free planning visits. Group leaders are also entitled to free leader places on a one for ten ratio if their organisation has booked full board accommodation and paid in advance (subject to the booking conditions on our group booking form).

Several Hostels are suitable as conference and meeting venues — just look in the Additional Info section under individual Hostel entries.

If you would like to receive our free Groups Away colour brochure, simply fill in the coupon at the back of this Guide. For assistance in finding the most appropriate venue for your group's residential visit contact YHA Customer Services on 01727 845047.

RENT-A-HOSTEL

YHA's Rent-a-Hostel scheme — which runs from September to March each year — offers groups, families and friends the chance to take over an entire Youth Hostel, coming and going as they please. The minimum stay is two nights and the more people in your group the cheaper the price per person.

There are 52 Hostels on the scheme, ranging from cottages to farmhouses in some of the prettiest parts of England and Wales. Prices start from £126 for a two night break (no matter how many in your group) and can work out from as little as £3.50 per person. Look for the R-a-H symbol under individual entries.

For more details, simply fill in the coupon at the back of this Guide.

GREAT ESCAPES

More than 50 activity breaks — from walking, mountain biking and horse riding to caving, rock climbing and sand-yachting — are available on the YHA's Great Escapes programme. These special breaks, aimed at those who want to learn a new skill or brush up on existing ones, are held at locations throughout England and Wales — including our two specialist Activity Centres at Edale in the Peak District and Llangollen in North Wales (more details on the next pages).

If you would like to receive our free Great Escapes brochure, packed with adventure holidays for individuals, families and children, simply fill in the coupon at the back of this Guide.

YHA Local Groups

Joining a YHA Local Group is a good way to make new friends while enjoying everything from barbecues and slide shows to pony trekking and weekend walks. Local Groups also give you the chance to support YHA through a variety of volunteer activities. And with more than 100 Local Groups in England and Wales there's bound to be one near you!

If you'd like to find out more, just send off for our free leaflet (see coupon at the back of this Guide) which includes a full listing of Local Groups in England and Wales.

It's easy to join, rewarding and fun!

Activity Centres

YHA has two Activity Centres — Edale in Derbyshire and Llangollen on the Welsh Border — where many different activities can be enjoyed under the supervision of YHA's own qualified instructors.

The specialist courses, which last three, five or seven days, are pitched at several different levels to suit all abilities — ideal for children, adults, families and groups. The Centres also run multi-activity breaks where you can sample several activities in a weekend or longer.

Prices start from as little as £77 per person for a weekend break inclusive of all meals, accommodation, instruction, specialist equipment and one year's YHA membership (or renewal of existing membership).

ACTIVITIES ON OFFER

Abseiling

Archery

Adventure Course

Canoeing

Caving

Climbing

Gorge Scrambling

Hang Gliding (Edale only)

Hill Craft

Hill Walking

Jungle Run (Llangollen only)

Orienteering

Mountain Biking

Navigation

Night Hikes

Personal Development

Problem Solving

Pony Trekking

Road Cycling (Edale only)

Rifle Shooting (Llangollen only)

Sailing

Team Building

Windsurfing

CUSTOMER CARE & SAFETY

The YHA Activity Centres are respected providers of outdoor and adventure holidays. The Centres work within the stringent guidelines laid down by the governing bodies of each sport (such as the British Canoe Union and the Royal Yachting Association) and the recently issued Outdoor Adventure Activity Providers Code of Practice. The staff have a wide range of qualifications and experience and ensure that strict safety precautions are taken at all times. The Wales Tourist Board, which has set up a national scheme for the regulation and registration of Activity Centres, has accredited our Centre at Llangollen.

MORE DETAILS

To find out what's on offer at our Activity Centres, see the latest Great Escapes brochure — available by completing the coupon at the back of this Guide.

Llangollen Youth Hostel and Activity Centre.

Llangollen YHA Activity Centre, Tyndwr Hall, Tyndwr Road, Llangollen, Clwyd LL20 8AR

Tel: 01978 860330
Fax: 01978 861709

Edale YHA Activity Centre, Rowland Cote, Nether Booth, Edale, Sheffield S30 2ZH

Tel: 01433 670302
Fax: 01433 670243

Edale Youth Hostel and Activity Centre.

Stay With The Family

Youth hostelling is ideal for families — it offers good value accommodation and wholesome meals or self-catering facilities in locations which provide access to outdoor activities and attractions for all the family to enjoy.

Families are welcome at all Youth Hostels and you'll find a variety of accommodation to give you freedom and flexibility. You can make your own selections from the following:

FAMILY ANNEXES

Several Hostels have self-contained annexes which are fully equipped, offer self-catering facilities and all day access with a key. Annexes are usually booked for seven days at a weekly rate — turn the page for details.

Family Annexes are available for families with children aged three and over (though younger children may be accommodated at the Warden's discretion).

FAMILY ROOMS

More and more Youth Hostels have family rooms which offer a comfortable standard of accommodation, plus the freedom to come and go as you please during the day. Families are provided with their own key and the facilities will vary between Youth Hostels: some have en suite facilities and all are equipped with wash-basins, together with adequate storage space. Prices are charged per room per night — turn the page for details.

Family Rooms are available for families with children aged three and over (though younger children may be accommodated at the Warden's discretion).

FAMILY DORMITORIES

At Hostels which do not have these two categories of accommodation, families may be accommodated in small dormitories. Please check room sizes under the individual Hostel entries before contacting the Hostel direct. You'll be charged per person per night.

Family Dormitories are available for families with children aged five and over.

All our family accommodation is very popular so please book well in advance.

If you are unable to book a room for your family you can stay in traditional single sex rooms with other customers. There are, however, a few restrictions: Children need to be at least five years old. Children aged 5 - 8 must share the same dormitory as their parent or guardian of the same sex. Children aged 9 - 13 do not have to share the same room but they must be accompanied on their stay by a parent or responsible adult. Young people aged 14 or over can go hostelling on their own or with friends.

▲ **Family membership scheme:** when parent(s) join YHA, children under 18 are enrolled FREE and will receive their own membership cards.

▲ **Family membership discount on overnights:** All children hostelling with their parent(s) or guardian as part of the family membership scheme will receive a discount of £1.00 off the Under 18 overnight charge. We regret that this discount is not available for Family Rooms or Family Annexes.

HOSTEL	SEASON	2	3	4	5	6
NORTHUMBERLAND AND ROMAN WALL						
Once Brewed (p.25)	All year			£29.00	£34.00	£39.50
LAKE DISTRICT						
Ambleside (p.33)	All year	£19.50	£26.00	£32.00	£37.00	£42.50
Eskdale (p.39)	All year	£18.00		£29.00		£39.50
Grasmere BH (p.40)	All year	£18.00	£23.00	£29.00		
Hawkshead (p.41)	All year		£27.00	£36.00	£40.00	
Wastwater (p.47)	All year			£29.00		£39.50
Windermere (p.47)	All year		£22.50	£27.00		£36.00
YORKSHIRE DALES						
Aysgarth (p.49)	All year	£18.00	£22.50	£27.00	£31.00	£36.00
Kettlewell (p.53)	All year	£18.00	£22.50	£27.00		
Kirkby Stephen (p.54)	All year	£18.50		£27.00		
Malham (p.55)	All year	£19.50	£26.00	£32.00	£37.00	£42.50
YORKSHIRE WOLDS, MOORS & COAST						
Boggle Hole (p.58)	All year			£27.00		
Osmotherly (p.60)	All year	£18.00	£22.50	£27.00	£31.00	£36.00
York (p.63)	All year			£39.50 (B&B inc.)		£58.50 (B&B inc.)
PEAK DISTRICT & MANCHESTER						
Castleton (p.66)	All year	£16.00		£27.00		£38.00
Gradbach (p.70)	All year	£18.00	£23.00	£29.00	£34.00	£39.50
Hartington (p.70)	All year			£36.00		£50.00
Ilam (p.72)	All year			£36.00		£50.00
Manchester (p.74)	All year			£46.00 (B&B inc.)		£62.00 (B&B inc.)
Matlock (p.73)	All year	£19.50	£26.00	£32.00		£42.50
LINCOLNSHIRE						
Lincoln (p.78)	All year	£18.00	£22.50	£27.50		£37.00
Thurlby (p.78)	All year			£24.50		
NORTH WALES						
Bryn Gwynant (p.82)	All year		£23.00	£28.00		£38.00
Corris (p.85)	High (A)			£27.00	£31.00	£35.00
	Rest of year			£24.00	£28.00	£32.00
Kings (p.87)	All year				£27.00	£31.00
Llanbedr (p.87)	All year		£19.50	£23.00	£27.00	£31.00
Pen-y-Pass (p.91)	All year		£26.00	£31.00	£37.00	
MID WALES						
Borth (p.94)	All year			£28.00	£33.00	£37.50
WEST WALES						
Broad Haven (p.99)	High (A)		£26.50	£31.50	£37.00	£42.50
	Rest of year		£22.00	£27.00	£32.00	£37.50
Manorbier (p.99)	High (A)			£31.50	£37.00	£42.50
	Rest of year			£27.00	£32.00	£37.50
Penycwm (Solva) (p.101)	All year			£30.00	£32.50	£37.50
Trevine (p.103)	High (A)			£25.00	£29.50	£34.50
	Rest of year			£22.00	£25.50	£29.00

KEY: High (A) = 1 July-31 August   High (B) = 1 April - 31 October

HOSTEL	SEASON	Number of beds				
		2	3	4	5	6
BRECON BEACONS & SOUTH WALES						
Llanddeusant (p.106)	High (A)			£22.00	£26.00	£29.00
	Rest of year			£20.00	£23.50	£26.50
WYE VALLEY & FOREST OF DEAN						
Welsh Bicknor (p.112)	All year			£28.00	£33.00	£37.50
SHROPSHIRE & WELSH BORDERS						
Ludlow (p.120)	All year			£23.00		£32.00
COTSWOLDS						
Duntisbourne Abbots (p.124)	All year			£24.50	£29.00	
The Ridgeway (p.125)	All year			£30.50		
Slimbridge (p.125)	All year	£19.00		£30.50	£36.00	£41.50
NORFOLK COAST AND BROADS						
Great Yarmouth (p.128)	All year			£27.50		£37.00
Hunstanton (p.128)	High (A)	£25.00		£30.50		£41.50
	Rest of year	£22.50		£27.50		£37.00
Norwich (p.129)	All year	£17.50	£22.50	£27.50	£32.00	£37.00
Sheringham (p.130)	High (A)	£19.50	£25.00	£30.50		£41.50
	Rest of year	£18.00	£22.50	£27.50		£37.00
EAST ANGLIA						
Brandon (p.132)	All year			£27.50		£37.00
Cambridge (p.133)	All year		£33.00 (B&B inc.)	£42.00 (B&B inc.)	£51.00 (B&B inc.)	£63.00 (B&B inc.)
Castle Hedingham (p.133)	All year			£27.50		
CHILTERN HILLS						
Streatley on Thames (p.139)	All year			£27.50	£32.00	£37.00
LONDON						
City of London (p.142)	All year	£35.00 (B&B inc.)	£54.00 (B&B inc.)	£70.00 (B&B inc.)	£86.00 (B&B inc.)	£100.00 (B&B inc.)
Hampstead Heath (p.143)	High (B)	£29.00 (B&B inc.)	£43.00 (B&B inc.)	£58.00 (B&B inc.)	£72.00 (B&B inc.)	£86.00 (B&B inc.)
	Rest of year	£25.00 (B&B inc.)	£36.00 (B&B inc.)	£49.00 (B&B inc.)	£62.00 (B&B inc.)	£74.00 (B&B inc.)
Rotherhithe (p.145)	All year	£35.00 (B&B inc.)	£54.00 (B&B inc.)	£70.00 (B&B inc.)	£86.00 (B&B inc.)	£100.00 (B&B inc.)
KENT – GARDEN OF ENGLAND						
Broadstairs (p.147)	All year			£27.50		£37.00
Dover (p.148)	All year	£19.50		£30.50		£41.50
SURREY HILLS						
Holmbury St Mary (p.151)	All year	£18.00		£27.50		
SOUTH COAST						
Arundel (p.153)	All year			£24.50		
Hastings (p.155)	High (A)		£22.50	£27.50		£37.00
	Rest of year		£20.50	£24.50		£33.00
Truleigh Hill (p.156)	All year			£27.50		£37.00
NEW FOREST & ISLE OF WIGHT						
Burley (p.158)	High (A)			£30.50		£41.50
	Rest of year			£27.50		£37.00
Salisbury (p.159)	All year			£30.50		
Sandown (p.160)	High (A)					£38.50
	Rest of year					£33.50

KEY: High (A) = 1 July-31 August   High (B) = 1 April - 31 October

HOSTEL	SEASON	2	3	4	5	6
				Number of beds		
Totland Bay (p.161)	High (A)			£27.50	£32.50	£38.50
	Rest of year			£25.00	£29.50	£33.50

AVON & THE MENDIPS

HOSTEL	SEASON	2	3	4	5	6
Bristol (p.163)	All year	£19.50 (B&B inc.)		£39.00 (B&B inc.)		£59.50 (B&B inc.)
Cheddar (p.164)	All year	£15.00		£25.00		£35.00
Street (p.164)	All year		£20.50	£24.50	£29.00	

DORSET COAST

HOSTEL	SEASON	2	3	4	5	6
Bridport (p.166)	All year			£24.50		£33.00
Lulworth Cove (p.167)	High (A)			£27.50	£32.00	
	Rest of year			£24.50	£29.00	

NORTH DEVON, EXMOOR & THE QUANTOCKS

HOSTEL	SEASON	2	3	4	5	6
Exford (p.170)	All year	£18.00		£27.50	£32.00	£37.00
Ilfracombe (p.170)	All year	£18.00	£22.50	£27.50		£37.00
Instow (p.172)	All year			£26.50		
Minehead (p.173)	All year			£24.50		£33.00

SOUTH DEVON & DARTMOOR

HOSTEL	SEASON	2	3	4	5	6
Beer (p.175)	High (A)			£27.50		£37.00
	Rest of year			£24.50		£33.00
Bellever (p.175)	All year			£27.50		£37.00
Dartington (p.176)	High (A)			£27.50		£37.00
	Rest of year			£24.50		£33.00
Exeter (p.176)	High (A)	£19.50		£30.50		£41.50
	Rest of year	£18.00		£27.50		£37.00
Plymouth (p.177)	High (A)	£19.50	£25.00	£30.50	£36.00	£41.50
	Rest of year	£18.00	£22.50	£27.50	£32.00	£37.00

CORNWALL

HOSTEL	SEASON	2	3	4	5	6
Boswinger (p.180)	High (A)			£27.50		£37.00
	Rest of year			£24.50		£33.00
Coverack (p.181)	High (A)			£27.50		
	Rest of year			£24.50		
Golant (p.181)	All year	£19.50	£26.00	£31.00		£42.00

FAMILY ANNEXE PRICES

NORTH WALES

Cynwyd (p.85)	Price varies according to season – please enquire Tel: 01222 396766	From £85-£102 per week (sleeps 4 plus baby)

MID WALES

Bryn Poeth Uchaf (p.95)	Price varies according to season – please enquire Tel: 01222 396766	From £70-£87 per week (sleeps 4 plus baby)

WEST WALES

Manorbier (p.99) (3 units)	Price varies according to season – please enquire Tel: 01222 396766	From £130-£248 per week (sleeps 4 plus baby)
St David's (p.103)	Price varies according to season – please enquire Tel: 01222 396766	From £99-£160 per week (sleeps 4 plus baby)

CORNWALL

Boswinger (p.180)	High (A)	£175.00 per week
	Rest of year	£150.00 per week (sleeps 4)

KEY: High (A) = 1 July-31 August   High (B) = 1 April - 31 October

Here are some handy hints and advice to help make your stay as enjoyable as possible.

How to Book

The best way to be sure of your bed is to book in advance. Simply contact the Hostel direct by 'phone (Access and Visa credit cards accepted at most Hostels) or by letter with correct payment. It's usually a good idea to call before 10.00hrs or after 17.00hrs when Hostel staff can also take your meal orders too. Reservations which have been taken without pre-payment will only be held until 18.00hrs unless an alternative has been agreed.

Once on the hostelling trail you'll find that many Hostels will be able to book your next night for you at no extra cost — just look for the BABA sign under individual Hostel entries. You can also turn up at the Youth Hostel on the day (bring your membership card or join at the Hostel) but remember we cannot guarantee you a bed as at busy times we're often full!

What you need to know...

Most Hostels are open between 07.00hrs -10.00hrs and 17.00hrs - 23.00hrs. Several now open earlier (at 13.00hrs) or can offer some access during the afternoon. Most London Hostels offer 24hr access. Look under individual Hostel entries for details.

In the evenings you can check in until 22.30hrs. Youth Hostels are open until 23.00hrs and 'lights out' is usually at 23.30hrs. Some Youth Hostels are more flexible on these hours, especially those in towns and cities. Please check with the Hostel staff as you may not be able to get in if you arrive or return late.

For security reasons and to avoid disturbing other guests the Youth Hostel is closed until 07.00hrs, so even if it is a lovely morning please don't get up too soon! (If for any reason you need an early start, please discuss this with the Hostel staff. Packed breakfasts can be arranged at many Hostels). Please also bear in mind that most Hostel staff have their time off during the day, so try not to disturb them.

How To Find The Hostel

Under each Hostel entry there are clear instructions and/or a map giving the best routes to the Youth Hostel, as well as Ordnance Survey and Bartholomew map references and public transport details. As you get nearer to the Youth Hostel, you may see the following signs:

Brown and white pointer signs at road junctions

at the Hostel entrance

On Arrival

When you arrive, check in at the Hostel Reception where you will be given your room number. As well as our friendly staff who are always happy to help, Youth Hostels contain lots of useful information about the Hostel and what to do in the area.

You will stay in comfortable bunk bedded rooms sharing with people of the same sex unless you have made special arrangements in advance — for instance, families or groups of friends may be able to have their own private room (see p.10). More and more Youth Hostels now offer smaller rooms, often with their own washing facilities — check under individual entries. Otherwise you will find showers, toilets and washing facilities close to your room. Freshly laundered bed linen will be given to you. It is very important that this is used. Pillows, duvets and/or blankets are also provided.

Youth Hostels have self-catering kitchens (fully equipped with cooking facilities, pots, pans, crockery, cutlery and food storage) as well as small shops which sell non-perishable foodstuffs such as tinned foods (soup, meat, vegetables, fruit) tea, instant coffee, biscuits, chocolate, sweets and canned

drinks. Bread and milk will usually be available as well. Most Youth Hostels also provide a full meals service (look for the 🍽 symbol). Several Youth Hostels have table licences which means they are able to sell beer, wine and cider with meals. Otherwise alcohol should not be brought into the Hostel. The use of illegal drugs and other substances is also not permitted on Hostel premises. The Hostel staff will refuse admission to anyone under the influence of alcohol or drugs.

While many Hostels have areas specially set aside for smoking, there are also around 50 'No-Smoking' Hostels highlighted by the 🚭 symbol under individual entries.

At some smaller Hostels you may be asked to help the Hostel staff with simple household tasks like washing up. Please always clear up after yourself too.

Pets are not allowed in Youth Hostels, although special arrangements can be made for Guide Dogs for the Blind. Overnight grazing for horses can be arranged near 30 Hostels in northern England (leaflet available).

Facilities for People with Disabilities

Many Youth Hostels are in traditional buildings which may make access difficult for people in wheelchairs. Some Youth Hostels — like Broad Haven and Manorbier in Wales, Manchester, Sheringham in Norfolk, Wooler in Northumberland and Rotherhithe in London — have special facilities for people with disabilities (look for the 🦽 symbol under individual entries). Always contact the Hostel staff before booking to check that the facilities are suitable for your needs.

Camping (at permitted Hostels only)

YHA members who bring their own tents and bedding may camp in the grounds at Youth Hostels which display the Ⓐ symbol in the Guide.

The charge for camping is half the adult overnight fee for the Hostel per person regardless of the age of the camper(s). No price concessions are available.

Campers are strongly recommended to book ahead as Wardens may have to restrict numbers when Hostels are busy to avoid overloading facilities. Campers must register at the Hostel reception and present their YHA membership card before pitching their tent.

The charge for camping normally covers the use of Hostel washing, toilet, laundry/drying, self-catering and recreational facilities.

Campers must observe restrictions which may have to be imposed by Wardens in the interest of people staying in the Hostel.

No Hostel equipment may be taken out to the camping area. Campers may prefer to use their own cooking equipment especially when this would relieve crowding in the self-catering kitchens.

Watch Out

Although thefts at Youth Hostels are rare we advise you not to leave valuables and cash in dormitories or unattended during your stay. Some Youth Hostels now provide secure lockers for your belongings (see 🔐 symbol under individual entries).

YHA And The Environment

David Bellamy, the internationally famous environmentalist, is now in his 12th year as our President and takes an active interest in the work of the YHA.

YHA (England & Wales) has been an enthusiastic partner in the International Youth Hostelling movements' development of an

Environmental Charter which commits Youth Hostels around the world to a responsible approach to the environment. Practical work is undertaken in Hostel grounds and neighbourhood to create conservation areas and we try to reduce our effect on the environment by minimising waste and controlling its disposal.

To find out how members can help in this important work, contact: **John Kingsbury, the YHA's Countryside Officer, at YHA, 8 St Stephen's Hill, St Albans, Herts AL1 2DY.**

You can travel the world with a YHA membership which entitles you to stay at over 5000 Youth Hostels in 64 countries. Always look for the Hostelling International logo which assures you of safe, clean and comfortable accommodation all over the world.

HOSTELLING INTERNATIONAL

You can also book a bed ahead at key Hostels worldwide (see list below) by using the International Booking Network available from the following England and Wales Youth Hostels: all London YHs, Ambleside, Bath, Bristol, Cambridge, Canterbury, Cardiff, Dover, Oxford, Stratford-upon-Avon, Windsor and York — as well as from our Central Booking Offices (at 14 Southampton Street, Covent Garden, London. Tel: 0171 836 1036, Fax: 0171 836 6372 and 52 Grosvenor Gardens, Victoria, London. Tel: 0171 730 5769, Fax: 0171 730 5779).

AUSTRALIA Adelaide - South Australia Booking Centre*, Adelaide - Youth Hostel, Brisbane - Queensland Booking Centre*, Brisbane City, Melbourne - Victoria Booking Centre*, Melbourne-Queensberry Hill, Sydney - New South Wales Booking Centre*, Sydney-Glebe Point, Sydney-Hereford Lodge. **AUSTRIA** Salzburg Jugendgästehaus, Vienna - Central (ÖJHW) Booking Centre *, Vienna - IBN Austria (ÖJHV) Booking Centre*, Vienna - Brigettenau. **BELGIUM** Antwerp Booking Centre*, Antwerp, Bruges-Europa, Brussels-Jean Nihon, Brussels - Rue van Oost, Booking Centre*, Gent. **BRAZIL** Rio de Janeiro Booking Centre*, Rio de Janeiro Youth Hostel, Sao Paulo Booking Centre*. **CANADA** Banff International, Calgary International, Edmonton Hostel Shop Booking Centre*, Edmonton International, Halifax, Jasper - Whistler Mountain International, Montréal Tourism Jeunesse Booking Centre*, Montréal Youth Hostel, Ottawa Hostelling International Canada Booking Centre*, Ottawa International, Quebec - Centre Int. de Sejour, Toronto, Vancouver International. **COSTA RICA** San José. **DENMARK** Copenhagen - Amagar. **ENGLAND & WALES** Ambleside, Bath , Bristol, Cambridge, Canterbury, Cardiff, Dover, London - Booking Centre*, London - City of London, London - Earl's Court, London-Hampstead Heath, London - Highgate Village, London - Holland House, London - Oxford Street, London - Rotherhithe, Oxford, Stratford-upon-Avon, Windsor, York. **FINLAND** Helskini - Eurohostel. **FRANCE** Aix-en-Provence,

Arras, Boulogne - Opale AJ Booking Centre*, Boulogne-sur-Mer, Carcassonne, Chamonix, Grenoble - Echirolles, Lyon - Venissieux, Marseille - Bonneviene, Montpellier, Paris - Rue Pajol Booking Centre*, Paris - Cité des Sciences, Paris - Le d'Artagnan, Poitiers, Rennes, Strasbourg - Parc du Rhin, Strasbourg - René Casin. **GERMANY** Detmold - DJH Booking Centre, Düsseldorf, Munich-Neuhausen. **GREECE** Athens International. **HONG KONG** Hong Kong - Association Booking Centre*, Hong Kong Ma Wui Hall. **INDONESIA** Bali International. **NORTHERN IRELAND** Ballygally Belfast Central Booking Centre*, Belfast International Castle Archdale, Cushendall, Londonderry, Newcastle Omagh, Whitepark Bay. **REP. OF IRELAND** Dublin International. **ITALY** Florence, Genoa, Naples, Rome Booking Centre*, Rome, Salerno, Sorrento, Torino, Venice. **JAPAN** Beppu, Fukushima, Hakodate, Hamasaka - Hamasaka, Ise - Isheshima, Kanazawa - Kanazawa, Kawachi-nagano, Kita-kyushu, Kurashiki, Kusatsu, Kyoto Booking Centre*, Kyoto-Higashiyama, Kyoto-Kitayama, Kyoto-Utano, Mashu-ko, Matsue Lakeside, Matsyshima, Matsuyama, Muika machi, Nagasaki - Nagasaki, Nagoya - Aichi Booking Centre*, Nara - Nara-shi, Oga Seaside, Okinawa - City Front Harumi, Okinawa - Naha, Osaka Booking Centre*, Sendai - Dochuan, Shikotsu-ko, Shodoshima, Shuzenji - Shuzenji, Takeo, Tokushema, Tokyo - National Office Booking Centre*, Tokyo - Tokyo Association BookingCentre*, Tokyo-Yoyogi Booking Centre, Yokohama. **KENYA** Nairobi.

LUXEMBOURG Luxembourg City - Mansfeld. **NETHERLANDS** Amsterdam - Future Line Travel*, Amsterdam - Stadsdoelen, Amsterdam-Vondelpark, Rotterdam. **NEW ZEALAND** Auckland Travel Centre Booking Centre*, Auckland - City, Auckland - Parnell, Christchurch - Rolleston House, Wellington. **PORTUGAL** Lisbon. **SCOTLAND** Carbisdale Castle, Edinburgh Booking Centre*, Edinburgh - Bruntsfield, Edinburgh - Eglinton, Glasgow Booking Centre*, Glasgow, Stirling, Inverness. **SOUTH AFRICA** Durban - AWT Booking Centre, Johannesburg - AWT Booking Centre. **SPAIN** Barcelona - ICSJ Central Reservation Booking Centre*, Barcelona - Mare de Deu de Monserrat, Barcelona - ICSJ Youth Tourism, Booking Centre*. **SWEDEN** Gothenburg - Mölndal, Stockholm - af Chapman/Skeppsholmen. **SWITZERLAND** Basle, Böningen - Interlaken, Grindelwald, Lausanne, Lucerne, Montreaux - Territet, Pontresina, Sion, St Moritz, Zermatt, Zug, Zürich - Jugi Tours Booking Centre*, Zürich - Wollishofen. **TAIWAN** Taipei - KWCEF Booking Centre*. **USA** Boston - Travel Centre, Boston International, Chicago, Los Angeles - Santa Monica, Martha's Vineyard Island - Cape Cod, Miami Beach International, New York International, San Diego - Hostel on Broadway, San Francisco - Golden Gate Booking Centre*, San Francisco International, San Francisco - Union Square, Sausalito , Seattle International, Washington AYH National Office Booking Centre*, Washington International.

* Outward Booking Centre only.

Other YHAs In Britain & Ireland

YHA (England and Wales) is separate from the other YHA's in Britain and Ireland but your membership is valid at all of them.

Youth Hostel Association of Northern Ireland (YHANI)
22-32 Donegall Road
Belfast BT12 5JN
Tel: (01232) 324733
Fax: (01232) 439699
see also p.192.

Irish Youth Hostel Association (An Oige)
61 Mountjoy Street
Dublin 7
Tel: (0103531) 8304555
Fax: (0103531) 8305808

Scottish Youth Hostels Association (SYHA)
7 Glebe Crescent
Stirling FK8 2JA
Tel: (01786) 451181
Fax: (01786) 450198

Details about Youth Hostels worldwide and National Association addresses can be found in the two Hostelling International Guides — one detailing Europe and the Mediterranean and the second covering Africa, America, Asia and the Pacific. These essential reference guides cost £7.00 each (incl. p&p) and are available from YHA (address on p.1).

Full Hostel details for YHANI, An Oige and SYHA are given in their National Handbooks, which are available direct from the Association concerned or from YHA.

The map below indicates the tourist areas used in this Guide. As well as the Youth Hostels in England and Wales, we've included a section on the YHA Camping Barns (pages 186-190), plus details of the Youth Hostel network in Northern Ireland (YHANI) on pages 192-193.

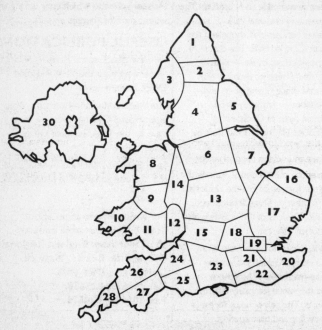

Please note that although we do our best to make sure that the Youth Hostel details in this Guide are accurate at the time of going to press, we reserve the right to change opening times and other Hostel details and prices if circumstances warrant. It's also a good idea to check details with the Youth Hostel before you arrive. **Triangle** magazine (mailed regularly to members) carries a special Guide Update to keep you informed.

Unspoilt and wild, this beautiful country captivates visitors with its open views of magnificent countryside and coastline. The Northumberland National Park encompasses heather-clad moorland and the majestic Cheviot Hills. The charm of the Northumberland coast — with its sweeping, sandy beaches teeming with birdlife, picturesque fishing ports and fairy-tale castles — has justly been designated an Area of Outstanding Natural Beauty. Hadrian's Wall, built by legions of the Roman Army in the second century and now a World Heritage Site, lies in the south of the county. Among the many border fortresses are the castles at Alnwick, Bamburgh, Dunstanburgh and Warkworth. The city of Newcastle is also full of historical interest.

The terrain is ideal for mountain biking and horse riding. Kielder Water, the largest man-made lake in Northern Europe, is the venue for many different water sports. The surrounding forest is good for cycling and orienteering.

Acomb, Bellingham and Wooler Youth Hostels are available on YHA's **Rent-a-Hostel scheme** which runs during the winter months (details on p.7).

USEFUL PUBLICATIONS

Pennine Way Central Booking Service — send s.a.e. to the YHA Regional Office listed below.

Northumberland and Hadrian's Wall: Inter-Hostel Cycling Route — send s.a.e. to the YHA Regional Office listed below.

Steel Bonnets Bike Ride — send s.a.e. to the YHA Regional Office listed below.

For more information about hostelling in this area contact: YHA Northern England Regional Office, P.O. Box 11, Matlock, Derbyshire, DE4 2XA. Tel: (01629) 825850. Fax: (01629) 824571.

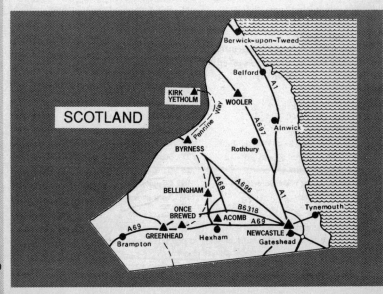

Acomb

Youth Hostel, Main Street, Acomb, Hexham, Northumberland NE46 4PL ☎ 01434 602864

Overnight Charges: Under 18 £3.60 Adult £5.35

R-a-H ☎ 01629 825850 2 GSC ✕ S ⊜ P On street

Jan 1 - Feb 27	Open Fr/Sat
Feb 28 - Jul 17	Open X:Mon
Jul 18 - Sep 3	Open
Sep 4 - Oct 29	Open X:Mon
Oct 30 - Dec 16	Open Fr/Sat
Dec 17 - Jan 4	Rent-a-Hostel

Open Apr 17 & May 29 Bank Hol Mon.
Rent-a-Hostel in Nov - Feb weekdays.

ACCOMMODATION

A simple Youth Hostel in a small village in the valley of the River Tyne. Converted from stable buildings, the Hostel offers basic self-catering facilities in an ideal location for visiting Hadrian's Wall and the Roman heritage sites.
Nearby is the bustling market town of Hexham, dominated by its fine church (Hexham Abbey). A network of winding lanes and pretty villages is ideal for exploring by bike or foot. Enjoy low level river walks, forest trails and the solitude of the high moorland of the North Pennines.

TRAVEL INFO

🚌 Tyne Valley 880-2 from Hexham (pass BR Hexham) (☎ 01434 602217); otherwise Northumbria 685, X85 Carlisle - Newcastle upon Tyne, alight Hexham, 2 ½miles (☎ 01434 602061). 🚉 Hexham 2m.
🛈 ☎ 01434 605225

NEXT HOSTELS

Once Brewed 15m, Bellingham 15m, Edmundbyers 16m

HOW TO GET THERE

A69 to 1m past Bridge End roundabout, turn right on A6079, then 1st right at Acomb Village sign and follow Main Street uphill to Hostel.
OS 87 GR 934666 Bart 39

Bellingham

Youth Hostel, Woodburn Road, Bellingham, Hexham, Northumberland NE48 2ED
☎ 01434 220313

Overnight Charges: Under 18 £4.00 Adult £5.95

R-a-H ☎ 01629 825850 1 GSC ✕ ⊜ ½m P

Jan 1 - Feb 28	Rent-a-Hostel
Mar 1 - Jul 16	Open X:Sun*
July 17 - Aug 31	Open
Sept 1 - Oct 31	Open X:Sun
Nov 1 - Feb 28	Rent-a-Hostel

* Open Bank Hol Sun Apr 16 & May 28.

ACCOMMODATION

A comfortable Hostel built of red cedarwood, situated on the Pennine Way high above the picturesque border town of Bellingham. Well-equipped self-catering facilities are provided here in a cosy, homely atmosphere enhanced by the cast-iron stove in the lounge.
Bellingham is the nearest town to Kielder Water, with its 27m of shoreline surrounded by the Northumberland hills and great Border Forest, as well as facilities for watersports like sailing and windsurfing. Hadrian's Wall is within easy reach and the quiet lanes offer excellent cycling routes.
1m

TRAVEL INFO

🚌 Tyne Valley 880 from Hexham (passes BR Hexham) (☎ 01434 602217). 🚉 Hexham 16m.
🛈 ☎ 01434 220616

NEXT HOSTELS

Acomb 15m, Byrness 15m (walking via Pennine Way), Once Brewed 18m

ADDITIONAL INFO

Credit cards are not accepted.

HOW TO GET THERE

OS 80 GR 843834 Bart 42

Byrness

Youth Hostel, 7 Otterburn Green, Byrness,
Newcastle upon Tyne, NE19 1TS
☎ 01830 520519

Overnight Charges: Under 18 £4.00 Adult £5.95

2 GSC 🏠 S 🏠 5m P

Mar 31 - Jul 18	Open X:Tu
Jul 19 - Aug 31	Open
Sep 1 - Sep 30	Open X:Tu

Open April 18 & May 30 following Bank Hols.

ACCOMMODATION   3   5-8 3

This simple self-catering Hostel, comprising two
adjoining houses in the peaceful village of Byrness,
is situated just 5m from the Scottish border in
the foothills of the Cheviot Hills. An ideal
stopping off point to and from Scotland and the
Borders.
Well located for exploring picturesque Jedburgh
and the Cheviots, Byrness is at the heart of the
Northumberland National Park. Explore the great
Border Forest on the Forest Drive from
Redesdale to Kielder Castle at the tip of Kielder
Water. Roe deer & red squirrels are among the
species of wildlife. 🚲12m 🅿12m ⛰12m
☂🍴16m

TRAVEL INFO

🚌National Express Edinburgh -
Newcastle-upon-Tyne (pass close BR Newcastle &
Edinburgh) (☎ 0191 261 6077). 🚉Morpeth 34m,
Newcastle 40m.

NEXT HOSTELS

Bellingham 15m, Kirk Yetholm 27m, Wooler 28m -
all by Pennine Way

ADDITIONAL INFO

Hostel keys available to families to give all day
access.

HOW TO GET THERE

OS 80 GR 764027 Bart 42

Greenhead

Youth Hostel, Greenhead, Carlisle, Cumbria
CA6 7HG ☎ 016977 47401
Fax: 016977 47401

Overnight Charges: Under 18 £4.45 Adult £6.55

R-a-H ☎ 01629 825850 2 IOI GSC 🍴 ⊕ P Limited.
BABA

Mar 1 - Apr 13	Open X:Wed/Th
Apr 14 - Jul 2	Open X:Sun
Jul 3 - Aug 31	Open
Sep 1 - Dec 19	Open X:Wed/Th

Open Bank Hol Sun Apr 16, May 7, May 28. The
Hostel may be available for groups when
otherwise closed - please contact Warden.

ACCOMMODATION   6

Stay in a former methodist chapel in the hamlet
of Greenhead on Hadrian's Wall. Complete with
high beamed roof, arched windows and thick
stone walls, this Hostel has a spacious yet cosy
feel to it. Situated on the Pennine Way, it is
popular with walkers.
On the edge of the Northumberland National
Park and the North Pennines Area of Outstanding
Natural Beauty, Greenhead offers many
opportunities for walking in wild, unspoilt
countryside. A network of quiet lanes, tracks and
forest trails are superb for cyclists. 🚲6m 🅿8m
⛰17m 🏊8m ☂8m 🍴4m

TRAVEL INFO

🚌Northumbria 685 Carlisle - Newcastle upon
Tyne, (passes BR Haltwhistle) (☎ 01434 602061).
🚉Haltwhistle 3m.
ℹ️ ☎01498 20351

NEXT HOSTELS

Once Brewed 7m, Alston 15m (by Pennine Way),
Ninebanks 16m

ADDITIONAL INFO

On the 'Steel Bonnets' Cycle Route (sae for
details).

HOW TO GET THERE

OS 86 GR 659655 Bart 38

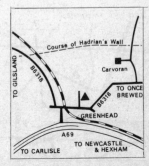

60 BEDS   Open: 17.00hrs

Newcastle upon Tyne

Youth Hostel, 107 Jesmond Road, Newcastle upon Tyne NE2 1NJ **0191 281 2570 Fax: 0191 281 8779**

Overnight Charges: Under 18 £4.45 Adult £6.55

1 |O| GSC Q S @ ½m P BABA

Feb 1 - Feb 28	Open X:Mon/Tu
Mar 1 - Oct 31	Open
Nov 1 - Nov 26	Open X:Mon/Tu

ACCOMMODATION   🛏 7 🛏 6

A large town house conveniently located for the centre of this vibrant city, the regional capital of the north east. Best viewed from one of the six bridges crossing the river Tyne, the city is a blend of ancient and modern — at the heart of which is the historic Quayside.

Explore the city's Roman heritage, maritime history, first-class museums, galleries and shops. Visit Europe's largest shopping centre (the Metro Centre) at nearby Gateshead, or the Theatre Royal. The wild countryside of the Northumberland National Park and superb stretches of coastline are nearby. 🚲2m 🅿3m
⚠ 🏊3m 🚃1m

TRAVEL INFO

🚌Frequent from surrounding areas (0191 232 5325). 🚇Jesmond (Tyne & Wear Metro) ¼ mile; Newcastle 1 ½m.

⛴ (to Hamburg/Esbjerg/Gothenburg/Bergen/Stavanger)
ℹ 0191 261 0691

NEXT HOSTELS

Acomb 20m, Edmundbyers 20m, Wooler 50m

ADDITIONAL INFO

On 'Steel Bonnets' cycle route (send sae for details). 'Wet 'n' Wild' water fun park.

HOW TO GET THERE

Excellent transport links by road, rail, air and ferry. To Jesmond Metro from city rail and bus stations and airport.

OS 88 GR 257656 Bart 39

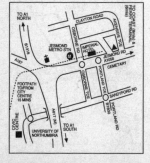

76 BEDS   Open: 13.00hrs

Once Brewed

Youth Hostel, Military Road, Bardon Mill, Hexham, Northumberland NE47 7AN
 01434 344360 Fax: 01434 344045

Overnight Charges: Under 18 £5.35 Adult £8.00

Family accommodation prices on p.11-13

4 |O| ▥ Q ☎ & S P BABA

Feb 1 - Mar 31	Open X:Sun
Apr 1 - Oct 31	Open
Nov 1 - Dec 2	Open X:Sun

ACCOMMODATION   🛏 13 🛏 5

A modern, comfortable Hostel just ½m from Hadrian's Wall. With plenty of accommodation for families and surrounded by a wealth of places to visit, this is an excellent base for exploring the beauty of the Northumberland National Park and North Pennines.

Close to some of the best preserved Roman heritage sites in the country including Roman forts and museums at Vindolanda, Housesteads, Carvoran, Chesters and Birdoswald. Further afield are lead mines, deer farms, forests, Kielder Water and the award-winning North of England Open Air Museum (Beamish). 🚲6m 🅿6m
⚠ ⚠25m 🚩½m 🏊 🚃4m

TRAVEL INFO

🚌From Hexham, Haltwhistle (passes BR Hexham & Haltwhistle), peak summer only (01434 600263); otherwise Northumbria 685 Carlisle - Newcastle upon Tyne, alight Henshaw, 2m (01434 602061). 🚇Bardon Mill 2 ½m.
ℹ 01434 344396

NEXT HOSTELS

Greenhead 7m, Bellingham 14m, Acomb 15m

ADDITIONAL INFO

Courses and special events can be arranged - call for details. Limited wheelchair access. Lunches and morning/afternoon teas are available for groups and coach parties if booked in advance.

HOW TO GET THERE

On B6318 above Bardon Mill. On corner of crossroads next to information centre.

OS 86 GR 752668 Bart 38

52 BEDS   **Open: 17.00hrs**

Wooler (Cheviot)

Youth Hostel, 30 Cheviot Street, Wooler,
Northumberland NE71 6LW
☏ 01668 281365

Overnight Charges: Under 18 £4.85 Adult £7.20

R-a-H ☏ 01629 825850

2 ⑩ GSC ⊞ ⬚ ⬚ S ⬚ ¼m P Cars and
mini-buses (coaches in village ⅓m)

Jan 1 - Feb 16	Rent-a-Hostel
Feb 17 - Feb 25	Open
Feb 26 - Mar 31	Open Fr/Sat
Apr 1 - Jul 9	Open X:Sun
Jul 10 - Aug 31	Open
Sep 1 - Nov 4	Open X:Sun
Nov 5 - Dec 16	Open Fr/Sat
Dec 17 - Dec 31	Rent-a-Hostel

Open Bank Hol Sun Apr 16, May 7 and 28.

ACCOMMODATION   🛏️2-4 10 🛏️5-8 3
The most northerly of English Youth Hostels
lying in the foothills of the Cheviot Hills. On the
edge of the Northumberland National Park and
close to the Scottish border, the Hostel is on the
outskirts of the market town of Wooler.
The area is steeped in history — with ancient hill
forts, Roman remains and splendid Border
castles. Explore the magnificent Northumbrian
coastline, including Holy Island, fairytale
Lindisfarne Castle, as well as castles at Alnwick
and Warkworth. 🚶8m ⓤ5m ⛰1m 🎣5m
🏊 ⬚

TRAVEL INFO
🚌Northumbria 464, 470/3, Border Villager/Swan
267, Goldleaf 710 from Berwick-upon-Tweed &
Alnwick, with connections from Newcastle (pass
close BR Newcastle) (☏ 01289 307283). Postbus
service. 🚉Berwick-upon-Tweed 16m.
ℹ️ ☏01668 81602

NEXT HOSTELS
Kirk Yetholm 14m, Byrness 28m by path,
Newcastle 50m

ADDITIONAL INFO
Facilities for disabled visitors.

HOW TO GET THERE
OS 75 GR 991278 Bart 41

---

35 BEDS   **Open: 17.00hrs**

Kirk Yetholm

Youth Hostel, Kelso, Roxburghshire TD5
8PG ☏ 01573 420631

GSC ⬚ ½m

Overnight Charges: Under 18 £4.30 Adult £5.25

Mar 17 - Sep 9	Open

ACCOMMODATION   🛏️3 🛏️9+ 2
This small modernised Hostel — ideally situated
at the end of the Pennine Way — is owned and
operated by the Scottish Youth Hostel
Association (7 Glebe Crescent, Stirling FK8 2JA.
☏ 01786 451181). Families are welcome.
This is an excellent centre for hill walking in the
Cheviots. Kirk Yetholm was the home for gypsies
and 'Gypsy Palace' cottage of the Faa family can
be seen from the road leading to the Halter Burn
Valley. In Kelso (8m) there is an abbey, Rennies
Bridge over the Tweed and Floors Castle.
🚶 ⓤ ⛰ 🎣

TRAVEL INFO
🚌Lowland Scottish 81 from Kelso (☏ 01573
24141) (Kelso is linked with BR
Berwick-upon-Tweed by Swan/Northumbria 23 -
☏ 01835 23301). 🚉Berwick-upon-Tweed 21m.

NEXT HOSTELS
Wooler 14m, Melrose 24m, Byrness 27m

HOW TO GET THERE
The Hostel is 50yds down the lane at the west
corner of the village green.
OS 74 GR 826282 Bart 41

The North Pennines, one of England's last areas of wilderness, has been designated an Area of Outstanding Natural Beauty. Its contrasting landscape ranges from high bleak moorlands to fertile valleys dotted with undisturbed stone-built villages. The beautiful riverside scenery includes the famous waterfalls of Low Force, High Force and Cauldron Snout.

Part of the North Pennines is now a National Nature Reserve and a Site of Special Scientific Interest — and the only area in Northern Europe where Spring Alpine Gentians are found. Traditional, unspoilt hay meadows are a welcome feature of the Northern Dales in early summer.

Beamish is a working example of the early 1900's in the North of England. Set in 300 acres of woodland, this unique open air museum authentically manages to take you back in time. For those interested in industrial history, old lead and fluorspar mine workings may be seen, and there is a living museum of lead mining at Killhope Wheel. Stay at Baldersdale Youth Hostel near Barnard Castle to visit the grand Bowes Museum, an enchanting art museum in a rural setting. With Raby, Witton and Appleby Castles, this area promises to be of both historic and architectural interest.

One of the most scenic and least used stretches of the Pennine Way passes through the area, linking up four Youth Hostels. As well as long and short distance walks, you can also enjoy a wide range of activities including weekend courses in cross country skiing at Dufton.

Alston, Dufton, Edmundbyers and Langdon Beck Youth Hostels are available on YHA's **Rent-a-Hostel scheme** which runs during the winter months (details on p.7).

USEFUL PUBLICATIONS

Pennine Way Central Booking Service — send large s.a.e. to the YHA Regional Office listed below.

Camping Barns in the North Pennines — send s.a.e to the YHA Regional Office listed below.

Group Visits to the North Pennines — send s.a.e. to the YHA Regional Office listed below.

**For more information about hostelling in this area contact: YHA Northern Regional Office, P.O. Box 11, Matlock, Derbyshire DE4 2XA.
Tel: (01629) 825850.
Fax: (01629) 824571.**

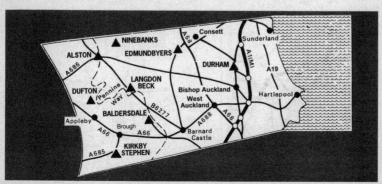

30 BEDS	**Open: 17.00hrs**

Alston

Youth Hostel, The Firs, Alston, Cumbria CA9 3RW ☎ 01434 381509
Fax: 01434 381509

Overnight Charges: Under 18 £4.85 Adult £7.20

R-a-H ☎ 01629 825850 2 ▥ ▤ ▦ S ◙ ½m
P Cars & minibuses only. Coaches 300yds behind Hendersons Garage. BABA

Jan 1 - Feb 2	Rent-a-Hostel
Feb 3 - Mar 30	Open Fr/Sat
Mar 31 - June 30	Open X:Sun
Jul 1 - Aug 31	Open
Sep 1 - Nov 4	Open X:Sun/Mon
Nov 5 - Nov 30	Open Fr/Sat
Dec 1 - Dec 31	Rent-a-Hostel

Open Sun Apr 16, May 7, May 28. Open for Rent-a-Hostel bookings in Feb/March/Nov when Hostel would otherwise be closed.

ACCOMMODATION ▨²⁻⁴ 2 ▨⁵⁻⁸ 3

Set on the edge of the highest market town in England, Alston Hostel overlooks the South Tyne River in an Area of Outstanding Natural Beauty. Here 'on top of the world' the steep cobbled streets and stone houses of the town are surrounded by wild, solitary moorland.
Walking and pony trekking are favourite activities on old drovers roads or the Pennine Way. Walk to the top of Cross Fell, the highest point of the Pennines (2930ft) or take a ride on the South Tynedale Railway, England's highest narrow-gauge line. ⛴4m ▲

TRAVEL INFO
🚌Wright Bros. 681 from BR Haltwhistle, 888 from BR Penrith (☎ 01434 381200).
🚉Haltwhistle 15m; Penrith 19m.
🛈 ☎01434 381696

NEXT HOSTELS
Ninebanks 8m, Langdon Beck 15m, Greenhead 15m (17m by Pennine Way)

HOW TO GET THERE
OS 86 GR 717461 Bart 38

---

46 BEDS	**Open: 17.00hrs**

Baldersdale

Youth Hostel, Blackton, Baldersdale, Barnard Castle, County Durham DL12 9UP ☎ 01833 650629 **Fax:** 01833 650629

Overnight Charges: Under 18 £4.45 Adult £6.55

2 ▥ GSC ▤ A ▦ ⊕ S ◙ 6m P Cars only - coaches 200 metres. BABA

Apr 1 - Aug 31	Open X:Sun*
Sep 1 - Oct 31	Open X:Sun/Mon

* Open Bank Hol Sun. The Hostel may be available for groups when otherwise closed - please contact Warden.

ACCOMMODATION ▨²2 ▨⁵5 ▨⁸⁺1

Baldersdale is a peaceful tributary valley of Teesdale, which leads up to the highest part of the Pennines. The Hostel is a stone-built farmhouse surrounded by open countryside, with views up the valley to Balderhead Reservoir. This wild landscape offers solitude and tranquility, but with many places to visit nearby. In the old market town of Barnard Castle is the magnificent Bowes Museum, built in the style of a French chateau and home to a European art collection.
🏛8m ⛴7m ▲½m ⛴½m

TRAVEL INFO
🚌United 75/A from BR Darlington, alight Cotherstone, 6m (☎ 01325 468771).
🚉Darlington 27m.
🛈 ☎01833 690000

NEXT HOSTELS
Langdon Beck 15m, Keld 15m, Kirkby Stephen 18m

ADDITIONAL INFO
Meals MUST be booked in advance. Half-way point on Pennine Way. Fishing at five reservoirs nearby.

HOW TO GET THERE
Use road from Romaldkirk (not Cotherstone) - no access by road via Clove Lodge.
OS 91 GR 931179 Bart 35

Dufton

Youth Hostel, 'Redstones', Dufton, Appleby, Cumbria CA16 6DB ☏ **017683 51236**
Fax: 017683 51236

Overnight Charges: Under 18 £4.85 Adult £7.20

R-a-H ☏ 01629 825850
1 ⓘⓞⓛ ⒼⓈⒸ ▥ ⊕ S ▤ 50yds BABA

Jan 1 - Jan 12	Rent-a-Hostel
Jan 13 - Mar 31	Open X:Tu/Wed
Apr 1 - Jun 30	Open X:Tu*
Jul 1 - Aug 31	Open
Sep 1 - Nov 4	Open X:Tu/Wed
Nov 5 - Jan 18	Rent-a-Hostel

* Open Bank Hol Tu Apr 11, 18 and May 30.

ACCOMMODATION 🛏²⁻⁴ 2 🛏⁵⁻⁸ 4
A large stone-built house (with a welcoming log fire) on the green of a quiet, pretty village. Extensive gardens are available for croquet, badminton, games and campfires. The Hostel is popular with cyclists and walkers; both the Pennine Way and the Cumbria Cycle Way pass through the village.

Unspoilt and untamed, the wild moorland of the North Pennines rises above Dufton to Cross Fell (its highest point) and the famous High Cup Nick. The green valley of the River Eden can be explored — on foot, bike or from the historic Settle to Carlisle Railway. Historic Appleby is 3 ½m away. 🚴3 ½m ⓤ15m ▲ 🎣 🎿 🏊4m

TRAVEL INFO
🚌No service. Local taxi service to Appleby.
🚉Appleby (no Sun service Nov - Mar) 3 ½m; Penrith 13m.
🛈 ☏017683 51177

NEXT HOSTELS
Landon Beck 12m by Pennine Way, Kirkby Stephen 15m, Alston 22m by Pennine Way

ADDITIONAL INFO
CROSS COUNTRY SKIING courses for beginners in Feb. Ski hire also available.

HOW TO GET THERE
Leave A66 at Appleby, follow signs for Long Marton and Dufton 3 ½m.
OS 91 GR 688251 Bart 34

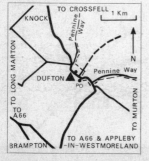

Durham

Youth Hostel, Durham Sixth Form Centre, The Sands, Providence Row, Durham City, Co. Durham DH1 1SG
☏ **0191 384 2217 (only when open)**

Advance bookings to: Mr D Hartley, 14 Auckland Street, Guisborough, Cleveland TS14 6HT
☏ 01287 635831

Overnight Charges: Under 18 £4.45 Adult £6.55

1 ▥ ⊕ S ▤ ½m P

Jul 21 - Aug 28	Open

ACCOMMODATION 🛏⁵⁻⁸ 2 🛏⁹⁺ 3
Open during the summer holiday only, the Youth Hostel offers self-catering accommodation in a school building close to the centre of this historic city.

Durham is dominated by its magnificent medieval Cathedral, standing on the peninsula in a twist of the River Wear high above the city. Flanked on one side by its protective Norman castle and on the other by monastic and collegiate buildings, it presents a skyline that is famous throughout the world. 🖼

TRAVEL INFO
🚌Frequent from surrounding areas (☏ 0191 384 3322). 🚉Durham ½m.
🛈 ☏0191 384 3720

NEXT HOSTELS
Newcastle 13m, Edmundbyers 21m, Acomb 30m

ADDITIONAL INFO
Camp bed accommodation only is offered at this Hostel. Credit card payments are not accepted.

HOW TO GET THERE
OS 88 GR 275429 Bart 39

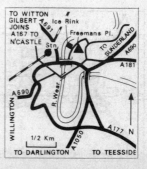

36 BEDS Open: 17.00hrs

Edmundbyers

Youth Hostel, Low House, Edmundbyers, Consett, County Durham DH8 9NL
01207 55651

Overnight Charges: Under 18 £4.00 Adult £5.95

R-a-H 01629 825850
1 GSC P Roadside.

Jan 1 - Mar 26	Rent-a-Hostel
Mar 27 - Oct 28	Open X:Sun
Oct 29 - Feb 28 '96	Rent-a-Hostel

Open Bank Hol Sun Apr 16, May 7, May 28 and Aug 27

ACCOMMODATION 2-4 1 5-8 2 9+ 2

This former inn dating from 1600 — situated in an attractive village surrounded by heather moorland — offers simple self-catering facilities, ideal for walkers and cyclists exploring the quiet lanes and countryside of this Area of Outstanding Natural Beauty.

Only ½m away is Derwent Reservoir, popular with anglers and yachtsmen and a pleasant spot for a picnic or to explore Pow Hill Country Park. Nearby is the pretty village of Blanchland, named after the white habits worn by the monks of the 12th century abbey. Durham is 20m and Beamish Museum 16m. 8m 25m 3m 1m 8m

TRAVEL INFO

Northumbria 773 Consett-Townfield, with connections on Go-Ahead Northern 719, 765 Durham Consett (pass close BR Durham) or X12, 745, 770/2 Newcastle-upon-Tyne - Consett (pass BR Newcastle); otherwise alight Consett 5m (0191 383 3337) Hexham 13m.
01207 591043

NEXT HOSTELS

Acomb 16m, Newcastle 20m, Durham 20m

HOW TO GET THERE

At the junction of trackways from the Tyne to Weardale and Allendale, 6m W of Shotley Bridge, ½m from Derwent Reservoir.
OS 87 GR 017500 Bart 39

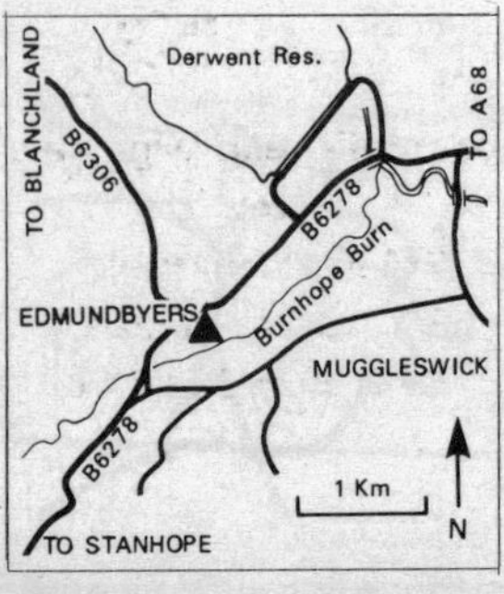

34 BEDS Open: 17.00hrs

Langdon Beck

Youth Hostel, Langdon Beck, Forest-in-Teesdale, Barnard Castle, County Durham DL12 OXN 01833 22228
Fax: 01833 22228

Overnight Charges: Under 18 £5.35 Adult £8.00

R-a-H 01629 825850
1 GSC S P On roadside. BABA

Jan 1 - Jan 31	Rent-a-Hostel
Feb 1 - Feb 28	Open Fr/Sat only
Mar 1 - Apr 30	Open X:Sun/Mon*
May 1 - Jul 31	Open X:Sun*
Aug 1 - Aug 31	Open
Sep 1 - Oct 31	Open X:Sun/Mon
Nov 1 - Nov 30	Open Fr/Sat only
Dec 1 - Jan 31	Rent-a-Hostel

* Open Bank Hol Sun. Out of season the Hostel may be available for individuals on a self-catering basis - please contact Warden in advance.

ACCOMMODATION 2-4 2 5-8 4

Set high amid the wild moorland of Upper Teesdale, just off the road from Middleton to Alston, this is a stone-built Hostel with all modern comforts. On the Pennine Way, it is popular with walkers seeking the solitude of the remote northern fells.

This is an area rich in plants and wildlife, of special interest to botanists, geologists and industrial archaeologists. 17m 9m 7m 7m 17m

TRAVEL INFO

United 75/A from BR Darlington alight High Force (01325 468711). Darlington 33m.
01833 690909

NEXT HOSTELS

Dufton 35m (12 by pathway), Baldersdale 16m

ADDITIONAL INFO

With effect from 1995 the telephone number will change to 01833 62 2228

HOW TO GET THERE

Sited on B6277 7m N of Middleton-in-Teesdale.
OS 91 GR 860304 Bart 35

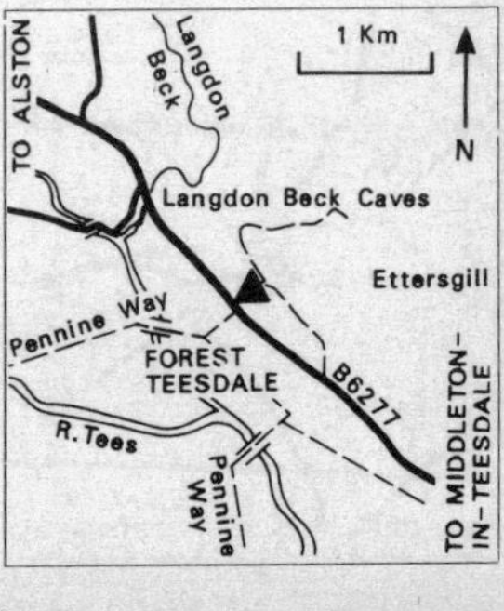

26 BEDS   **Open: 17.00hrs**

Ninebanks

Youth Hostel, Orchard House, Mohope, Ninebanks, Hexham, Northumberland NE47 8DO 📞 01434 345288

Overnight Charges: Under 18 £3.60 Adult £5.35

2 GSC S P

| Jan 3 - Dec 23 | Open |
| Dec 24 - Jan 1 | Open for groups |

The Hostel may be available for groups when otherwise closed - please contact Warden.

ACCOMMODATION 1 5-8 1 9+ 2

A stone built lead miners cottage in the valley of the Mohope burn in the North Pennines Area of Outstanding Natural Beauty. Situated above the village of Ninebanks at Mohope, this Hostel offers simple self-catering accommodation and lovely views of West Allendale.

Visit Killhope Lead Mining Centre to discover the history of lead mining in the area. Or explore the secluded valleys and wild moorland of this undiscovered area — rich in wildlife, industrial archaeology, flora and fauna. Allen Banks (NT) and suspension bridges are 8m. 🚴15m 🅿5m
🏞 🚲 🚂 8m

TRAVEL INFO

🚌 Wright Bros 888 Newcastle - Hexham - Alston - Penrith - Keswick alight Ouston 1m (📞 01434 381200). Wright Bros 688 Hexham - Allenheads. Alight Allendale. 🚂 Haydon Bridge 11m. Hexham 15m.
ℹ 📞01434 605225

NEXT HOSTELS

Alston 7m, Greenhead 16m, Once Brewed 16m (12m by path)

ADDITIONAL INFO

Credit cards are not accepted.

HOW TO GET THERE

Signposted from A686 2 ½m S of Whitfield. Hostel at Mohope signposted from Ninebanks hamlet.
OS 86 GR 771514 Bart 39

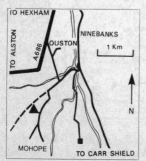

The Lake District — England's largest National Park with awe-inspiring mountains and lakes, picturesque towns and villages — is visited by thousands of people every year. Lake Windermere combines breathtaking scenery with a wide range of watersports. The recently refurbished Youth Hostels at Ambleside and Windermere, complete with family rooms, overlook the lake. There are also many forest and wildlife centres, as well as the museums of Lake District industries.

Derwentwater Youth Hostel offers excellent activity breaks throughout the year — ranging from canoeing to classic mountain scrambles and winter hill walking to wild flower drawing.

The museums of Wordsworth, Ruskin and Beatrix Potter, as well as the Keswick Pencil Museum, are all well worth a visit. For those interested in castles and ruins, visit the Hardknott Roman Fort and the castles at Sizergh, Kendal and Egremont.

Carrock Fell, Cockermouth and Ennerdale Youth Hostels are available on the YHA's **Rent-a-Hostel scheme,** which runs during the winter months (details on p.7).

USEFUL PUBLICATIONS

Inter-Hostel walks in the Lake District — send £2.00 (cheques payable to YHA) or s.a.e. for order form for individual routes to the YHA Regional Office listed below.

Coast to Coast Central Booking Service — send a large s.a.e. to the YHA Regional Office listed below.

**For more information about hostelling in this area contact:
YHA Northern Regional Office,
P.O. Box 11, Matlock, Derbyshire
DE4 2XA.
Tel: (01629) 825850.
Fax: (01629) 824571.**

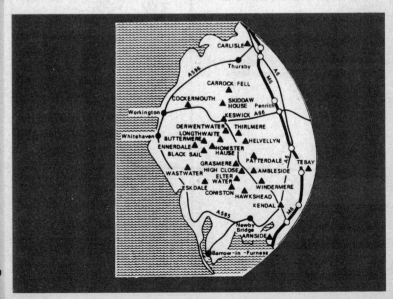

226 BEDS	Open: All Day		72 BEDS	Open: 17.00hrs

Ambleside

Youth Hostel, Waterhead, Ambleside, Cumbria LA22 0EU ☎ **015394 32304 Fax: 015394 34408**

Overnight Charges: Under 18 £5.95 Adult £8.80

Family accommodation prices on p.11-13

4 |◎| 👤 |GSC| ▥ |🔍| 🖉 |S| 🖃 1m P Cars and mini-buses only. Coach park ¼m towards Ambleside.

BABA IBN

Mar 24 - Jan 1   Open

ACCOMMODATION   31 21

On the shores of Lake Windermere, the Hostel enjoys an unrivalled location in the Lake District. Informal gardens slope down to the Hostel's own waterfront and jetty. Relax over a meal in the dining room with panoramic views across England's largest lake to the Coniston and Langdale fells.

Rowing boats, windsurfing, canoeing, sailing... watersports of every kind are available at Windermere. Steamboats stop within yards of the Hostel, calling at Brockhole (National Park Visitor Centre) 2m. All around is superb country for walking, climbing and exploring. 🚲 Ⓤ2m

▲ 🏕 🚲 🏊 🖃

TRAVEL INFO

🚌 Stagecoach Cumberland services from surrounding areas (many pass close BR Windermere) (☎ 01946 63222) 🚆 Windermere 3m.

🛈 ☎015394 32602

NEXT HOSTELS

Windermere 3m, Elterwater 3 ½m, Grasmere 5 ½m

ADDITIONAL INFO

Hostel open until 11.30pm. The Hostel has a jetty and slipway, launching facilities are available for sailing dinghies, canoes, windsurfers and rescue craft. Contact the Hostel for launching fees.

HOW TO GET THERE

1m S of Ambleside Village at Waterhead on the A591 Windermere Road, next to Steamer Pier.

OS 90 GR 377031 Bart 34

Arnside

Youth Hostel, Oakfield Lodge, Redhills Road, Arnside, Carnforth, Lancashire LA5 0AT ☎ **01524 761781 Fax: 01524 761781**

Overnight Charges: Under 18 £5.35 Adult £8.00

2 |◎| |GSC| ▥ |🔍| |S| 🖃 ¼m 🖉 1x20, 1x25 P Cars & Coaches. BABA

Jan 1 - Mar 31	Open X:Sun
Apr 1 - Sept 30	Open
Oct 1 - Dec 21	Open X:Sun
Dec 22 - Dec 27	Open

ACCOMMODATION   8 3 3

Arnside Youth Hostel is a lovely old stone house situated on the edge of the village, high above the Kent estuary. With views across the sands to the Lakeland fells, the Hostel is a perfect base for exploring Morecambe Bay, the Yorkshire Dales and the quieter parts of South Lakeland.

The area abounds in interest for the naturalist, with its limestone landscape and flowers, nature trails and the nearby RSPB reserve at Leighton Moss. It is also popular with cyclists, close to both the Lancashire and Cumbria cycleways, as well as offering cycle tours and bike hire from the Hostel. 🚲 Ⓤ3m ▲¼m 🏕¼m 🖉3m 🚲3m 🖃12m

TRAVEL INFO

🚌 Stagecoach Cumberland 552 from Kendal (☎ 01946 63222) 🚆 Arnside 1m. ⛴15m (Heysham-Isle of Man)

🛈 ☎01524 32878

NEXT HOSTELS

Kendal 12m, Ingleton 19m, Hawkshead 18m

HOW TO GET THERE

From Milnthorpe on A6 take B5282 to Arnside. Turn right at T-junction, follow main road through village to YHA sign on right (Redhills Road)

OS 97 GR 452783 Bart 34

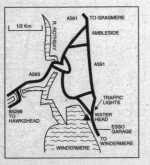

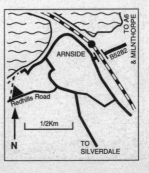

LAKE DISTRICT

3

17 BEDS   Open: 17.00hrs

Black Sail

Youth Hostel, Black Sail Hut, Ennerdale, Cleator, Cumbria CA23 3AY

During winter closed period contact: Alston Youth Hostel, The Firs, Alston, Cumbria CA9 3RW
☎ 01434 381509

Overnight Charges: Under 18 £4.00 Adult £5.95

1️⃣ 🍴 68C 🔆 Ⓢ 🔲 3m

Mar 31 - May 24	Open X:Sun/Mon*
May 25 - Aug 31	Open X:Mon
Sep 1 - Oct 28	Open X:Sun/Mon

* Open Sun Apr 16 & May 7

ACCOMMODATION

A unique Hostel, remote and isolated, in a spectacular part of the Lake District. The Hostel is a former shepherd's bothy at the head of Ennerdale and accessible only by footpath. With simple facilities, it is cosy and welcoming — a true 'away from it all' retreat in the mountains.
The names of the surrounding peaks capture the spirit of the Lake District — Great Gable, Pillar, Red Pike, Steeple... Long distance walkers on Wainwright's Coast-to-Coast route enjoy the solitude of Black Sail before reaching the more popular parts of the Lake District to the east.
🏔️ 🌲 🚲 🛶

TRAVEL INFO
🚌 Stagecoach Cumberland 79 Keswick-Seatoller, thence 3 ½m (☎ 010946 63222) (For BR connections see Keswick) 🚉 Whitehaven 19m.

NEXT HOSTELS
Honister 3m, Buttermere 3 ½m, Ennerdale 4m

ADDITIONAL INFO
Poor postal service - bookings should be sent well in advance. Groups restricted to 5 males and 5 females. No access for cars.

HOW TO GET THERE
OS 89 GR 194124 Bart 34

---

95 BEDS   Open: 13.00hrs

Borrowdale (Longthwaite)

Youth Hostel, Longthwaite, Borrowdale, Keswick, Cumbria CA12 5XE
☎ 017687 77257 Fax: 017687 77393

Overnight Charges: Under 18 £4.85 Adult £7.20

4️⃣ 🍴 🛏️ 🔆 Ⓢ 🔲 1m Ⓟ Cars & minibuses. Coaches in Seatoller 1m. BABA

Feb 10 - Mar 31	Open X:Mon/Tu
Apr 1 - Oct 28	Open
Oct 29 - Dec 17	Open X:Mon/Tu
Dec 28 - Jan 6 '96	Open

The Hostel may be available for groups when otherwise closed - please contact Warden.

ACCOMMODATION

This Youth Hostel with its own special character — purpose-built mainly of cedar wood to blend into its secluded riverside setting among oak woodlands and majestic mountains — combines all the facilities and comfort of a large traditional Lakeland Hostel with a relaxed, informal atmosphere.
Borrowdale is regarded by many as the loveliest part of the Lake District. Mountains rise steeply from a green valley floor, where tiny hamlets offer an unchanging picture of Lakeland life. Keswick, the Whinlatter Forest Centre and many northern Lake District attractions are nearby.
🚲 7m Ⓤ 10m 🏔️ 5m 🌲 3m 🛶 7m

TRAVEL INFO
🚌 Stagecoach Cumberland 79 from Keswick (☎ 01946 63222) (For BR connections see Keswick) 🚉 Workington 25m; Penrith 26m.
ℹ️ ☎ 017687 72645

NEXT HOSTELS
Honister 2m, Derwentwater 5m, Buttermere 7m

ADDITIONAL INFO
Resident members ☎ 017687 77618

HOW TO GET THERE
Follow 'Borrowdale' signs from Keswick, turn second right after Rosthwaite village to lane end.
OS 89 GR 254142 Bart 34

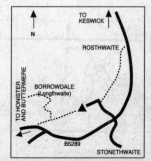

Buttermere

Youth Hostel, King George VI Memorial Hostel, Buttermere, Cockermouth, Cumbria CA13 9XA ☎ 017687 70245

Overnight Charges: Under 18 £5.35 Adult £8.00

2 🍴 GSC 📶 ⊕ S P Limited.

Jan 1 - Jan 3	Open
Jan 4 - Mar 31	Open X:Sun/Mon/Tu
Apr 1 - Sep 2	Open
Sep 3 - Nov 4	Open X:Mon
Dec 22 - Jan 2 '96	Open

ACCOMMODATION 🛏️2-4 6 🛏️5-8 9

Overlooking tranquil Buttermere and Crummock Water, the Youth Hostel is a traditional Lakeland slate building set in its own grounds. Relax here after a day on the fells, enjoying the views from the lounge across to High Stile Ridge and the waterfalls of Sour Milk Ghyll.

Low level walks along the lake shores and challenging routes over high ridges make this an ideal base for walkers of all abilities. Popular with families, rowing boats can be hired on the two lakes. There are many attractions to visit at nearby Keswick, Cockermouth and along the Cumbrian coastline. 🚶8m ⛵8m ⛰️ 🏊1m 🎣1m 🏊10m

TRAVEL INFO

🚌 From Keswick (May-Oct only) (☎ 01228 812812) (For BR connections see Keswick). 🚉Workington 18m.
ℹ️ ☎017687 72803

NEXT HOSTELS

Black Sail by mountain path 3 ½m, Honister 4m, Borrowdale 7m

ADDITIONAL INFO

Residents ☎ 017687 70254

HOW TO GET THERE

¼m S of Buttermere village on road to Honister Pass and Borrowdale on B5289
OS 89 GR 178168 Bart 34

Carlisle

Youth Hostel, Etterby House, Etterby, Carlisle, Cumbria CA3 9QS ☎ 01228 23934

Overnight Charges: Under 18 £4.00 Adult £5.95

1 🍴 GSC 🔲 S 🔲 ¼m P

Feb 17 - June 30	Open X:Mon/Tu*
Jul 1 - Aug 31	Open
Sep 1 - Oct 29	Open X:Mon/Tu

* Open Mon, Tu April 10, 11, April 17, 18 and May 29, 30.

ACCOMMODATION 🛏️1-4 1 🛏️5-8 2 🛏️4+ 2

Standing in its own grounds on the banks of the River Eden, the Hostel is a Victorian house in a quiet suburb. From the historic city of Carlisle go south into Lakeland, north up to Scotland or explore the wilds of unspoilt Northumbria.
The sandstone castle, city walls and sturdy cathedral bear witness to Carlisle's turbulent past as an important Border City. Learn more about it at the Tullie House Museum, take a ride on the famous Settle-Carlisle railway or explore Hadrian's Wall. 🚌 🏊2m

TRAVEL INFO

🚌Stagecoach Cumberland 62 Town Hall-St Ann's Hill, thence ¼m (☎ 01946 63222) 🚉Carlisle 2m.
ℹ️ ☎01228 512444

NEXT HOSTELS

Carrock Fell 17m, Greenhead 19m, Cockermouth 25m

HOW TO GET THERE

Cross Eden Bridge on A7, turn left at Etterby Street which becomes Etterby Scaur, left after ¾m by Redfern Pub onto Etterby Road. Hostel ¼m on left.
OS 85 GR 386569 Bart 38

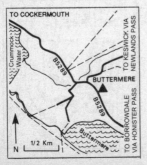

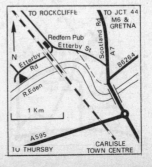

20 BEDS	Open: 17.00hrs

Carrock Fell

Youth Hostel, High Row Cottage, Haltcliffe, Hesket Newmarket, Wigton, Cumbria CA7 8JT ☎ 016974 78325

Overnight Charges: Under 18 £4.45 Adult £6.55

R-a-H ☎ 01629 825850 ☐ 68C S ☐ 2 ¼m P Cars and mini-buses only.

Jan 1 - Mar 30	Rent-a-Hostel
Mar 31 - Jun 30	Open X:Mon/Tu*
Jul 1 - Aug 31	Open X:Mon
Sep 1 - Oct 28	Open X:Mon/Tu
Oct 29 - Dec 31	Rent-a-Hostel

* Open Mon Apr 17, May 29

ACCOMMODATION

This old farmhouse retains its original character with stone flagged floors, beams and an open fire. Nestling in a peaceful hamlet on the edge of the Caldbeck Fells, the Hostel offers a traditional warm welcome in a quiet corner of the Lake District.

The northern fells offer excellent walking and cycling in an area of great geological interest. Caldbeck has a fascinating little mining museum and Carrock Fell boasts a Bronze Age hill fort. Walk from the Hostel up onto the Cumbria Way, across to Skiddaw and down into Keswick. ▲ ⊠

TRAVEL INFO
🚌 Contact Warden for info. 🚉 Penrith 15m.

NEXT HOSTELS
Skiddaw House 8m, Keswick 12m, Thirlmere 12m

HOW TO GET THERE
3m N of Mungrisdale at High Row. Turn right off Mungrisdale to Caldbeck Road. Hostel first house up track on left.
OS 90 GR 358355 Bart 38

---

28 BEDS	Open: 17.00hrs

Cockermouth

Youth Hostel, Double Mills, Cockermouth, Cumbria CA13 0DS ☎ 01900 822561

Overnight Charges: Under 18 £4.45 Adult £6.55

R-a-H ☎ 01629 825850 1 ☐ ▦ 🔍 ⚽ S ☐ ½m P Cars and mini-buses only.

Jan 1 - Mar 30	Rent-a-Hostel
Mar 31 - Jun 30	Open X:Tu/Wed
Jul 1 - Aug 31	Open X:Wed
Sep 1 - Oct 28	Open X:Tu/Wed
Oct 29 - Dec 31	Rent-a-Hostel

Open Tu Apr 18, May 30.

ACCOMMODATION

Stay in a restored 17th century watermill, complete with waterwheels, internal workings and mill race. Set in a secluded position on the banks of the River Cocker, the Youth Hostel is just 10 minutes walk from the town centre. Cockermouth is a charming, bustling market town close to the northern and western Lakeland fells and Cumbrian coastline. Visit William Wordsworth's birthplace, the Cumberland Toy and Model Museum, Jennings Brewery or the mining museum. Crummock Water, Loweswater and Buttermere are within easy reach. 🚶 ½m
🛒 4m ⛰ 8m 🏔 6m 🎣 10m 🚲 8m ⊠

TRAVEL INFO
🚌 Stagecoach Cumberland X5 BR Penrith-Workington-Whithaven (passes close BR Workington) (☎ 01946 63222) 🚉 Workington 8m.
ℹ ☎ 01900 822634

NEXT HOSTELS
Buttermere 10m, Keswick 12m, Derwentwater 15m

HOW TO GET THERE
From Main Street follow Station Street, left into Fern Bank, take track at end of Fern bank. From A66 take A5086 to Cockermouth then 2nd right into Fern Bank.
OS 89 GR 118298 Bart 34

Coniston (Holly How)

Youth Hostel, Holly How, Far End, Coniston, Cumbria LA21 8DD ☎ 015394 41323

Overnight Charges: Under 18 £4.85 Adult £7.20

3 ▢ ▥ ⊞ S ▣ ½m P Cars and mini-buses only (coaches ¼m).

Jan 13 - Mar 30	Open Fr/Sat/Sun*
Mar 31 - May 7	Open
May 8 - Jul 6	Open Fr/Sat/Sun*
Jul 7 - Sep 23	Open
Sep 24 - Dec 2	Open Fr/Sat/Sun*

* Also open for half-term holiday weeks Feb 17-26, May 26-Jun 4, Oct 20-29. May also be open Mon-Thurs after Sep 24 (please check with Warden).

ACCOMMODATION ⊨²⁻⁴2 ⊨⁵⁻⁸4 ⊨⁹⁺2

Nestling at the foot of the fells, Coniston Holly How is a traditional Lakeland slate building in its own attractive gardens. Only a few minutes walk from the centre of Coniston village and the lake, it is surrounded by magnificent scenery — dominated by the 'Old Man of Coniston'. Cruise Coniston Water aboard the restored steam yacht Gondola, or try windsurfing or sailing. Visit Ruskin's former home at Brantwood, or picnic at lovely Tarn Hows. Mountain bikes can be hired to follow the numerous forest trails, including fascinating sculpture trails through Grizedale Forest. 🚶½m Ⓤ1m 🏔 🏞½m ⚑½m 🚲🚠¼m

TRAVEL INFO

🚌Stagecoach Cumberland 505/6 from Ambleside (with connections from BR Windermere) (☎ 01946 63222) 🚉Windermere 13m.
ℹ ☎015394 41533

NEXT HOSTELS

Coniston Coppermines 1 ¼m, Hawkshead 5m, Elterwater 5m

ADDITIONAL INFO

Ground floor of Hostel open all day.

HOW TO GET THERE

OS 96 GR 302980 Bart 34

Coniston Coppermines

Youth Hostel, Coppermines House, Coniston, Cumbria LA21 8HP ☎ 015394 41261

Overnight Charges: Under 18 £4.45 Adult £6.55

3 ▢ S ▣ 1 ½m P Cars and mini-buses. Coaches in Coniston village 1 ½m.

Apr 1 - Jul 14	Open X:Wed/Th
Jul 15 - Aug 31	Open X:Wed
Sep 1 - Nov 5	Open X:Wed/Th

ACCOMMODATION 1 2

Surrounded by the Coniston fells, this little Hostel — originally home to the manager of the old coppermines — enjoys a spectacular mountain setting in the heart of classic Lake District scenery. Although it seems quite isolated, the Hostel is only 1m from the village of Coniston. Walk from the front door of the Hostel onto Wetherlam and along the ridge to Coniston Old Man and Dow Crag. Or drop down into Little Langdale, returning on a lower level route through Tilberthwaite Woods. The choice of walks is endless and views unsurpassed. Enjoy watersports, climbing and cycling. 🚶1 ½m Ⓤ2m 🏔🏞1 ½m ⚑½m 🚲

TRAVEL INFO

🚌Stagecoach Cumberland 505/6 from Ambleside (with connections from BR Windermere), thence 1m (☎ 01946 63222) 🚉Ulverston 14m.
ℹ ☎015394 41533

NEXT HOSTELS

Coniston 1 ¼m, Hawkshead 6m, Elterwater 6m

ADDITIONAL INFO

Wet weather shelter available during daytime. The track is rough but cars can reach the Hostel.

HOW TO GET THERE

From village, take road between the Black Bull and the Co-op. The road soon becomes a track, climbing steadily then levelling, overall distance 1 ¼m
OS 96 GR 289986 Bart 34

Derwentwater

Youth Hostel, Barrow House, Borrowdale, Keswick, Cumbria CA12 5UR
☎ 017687 77246 Fax: 017687 77396

Overnight Charges: Under 18 £5.95 Adult £8.80

4 ⊠ ♿ 6SC ▦ 🔍 ⊕ S ⊜ 2m ⚲ 1x30, 1x15, 1x95 P BABA

Jan 1 - Jan 3	Open
Jan 4 - Jan 31	Open X:Wed
Feb 1 - Sep 2	Open
Sep 3 - Nov 4	Open X:Sun
Dec 28 - Jan 5	Open
'96	

ACCOMMODATION 🛏️²⁴ 1 🛏️⁵⁸ 7 🛏️⁹⁺ 3

This magnificent 200-year old mansion overlooks Derwentwater in lovely Borrowdale. The Hostel's 15 acres of grounds, complete with 108ft waterfall, slope down to the lake shore. Nearby is a jetty landing point for the Keswick to Derwentwater Launch — a novel way to arrive at the Hostel.
Skiddaw, Scafell, Catbells and other well known names bring walkers and climbers to this area. Nearby Whinlatter Forest Centre runs orienteering and forest trails suitable for all ages. The Hostel offers a variety of activity and special interest breaks throughout the year. 🚲 2m
U 3m ⛰️ ♨️ 🎣 1m ⛵ 🏊

TRAVEL INFO
🚌 Stagecoach Cumberland 79 Keswick-Seatoller (☎ 01946 63222) (For BR connections see Keswick) 🚉 Penrith 20m; Windermere 24m.
ℹ️ ☎ 017687 72645

NEXT HOSTELS
Keswick 2m, Longthwaite 5m, Thirlmere 5m

HOW TO GET THERE
2m S. of Keswick on Borrowdale Road - 100metres past turn off to Ashness Bridge/Watendlath (concealed entrance)
OS 89 GR 268200 Bart 34

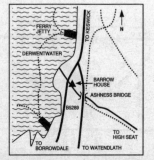

Elterwater (Langdale)

Youth Hostel, Elterwater, Ambleside, Cumbria LA22 9HX ☎ 015394 37245

Overnight Charges: Under 18 £4.85 Adult £7.20

1 ⊠ ▦ S ⊜ ¼m P Limited.

Feb 17 - Mar 31	Open Fr/Sat only*
Apr 1 - Sep 30	Open
Oct 1 - Nov 4	Open X:Mon
Nov 5 - Dec 17	Open Fr/Sat only*
Dec 28 - Jan 2	Open
'96	

* Midweek bookings may be accepted - enquiries welcome.

ACCOMMODATION 🛏️²⁴ 8 🛏️⁵⁸ 3 🛏️⁹⁺ 1

On the edge of the tiny hamlet of Elterwater, this Hostel is at the heart of classic Lakeland scenery. Originally converted from farm buildings, its closeness to the fells at the head of Langdale makes it a favourite with walkers and climbers. The two lovely Langdale valleys — with Crinkle Crags, Bowfell and the famous Langdale Pikes towering above — offer excellent walks with fine views. Close to Ambleside and Grasmere, and within easy reach of the western lakes and coast, this is a good base for exploring the whole of the Lake District. 🚲 4m U 4m ⛰️ ¼m 🏔️ 4m 🎣 2m ⛵ 🏊 1m

TRAVEL INFO
🚌 Stagecoach Cumberland 516 from Ambleside (connections from BR Windermere) (☎ 01946 63222) 🚉 Windermere 9m.
ℹ️ ☎ 015394 32602

NEXT HOSTELS
High Close 1m, Grasmere 4m, Coniston 6m

HOW TO GET THERE
OS 90 GR 327046 Bart 34

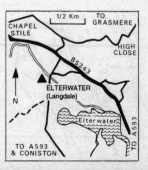

24 BEDS	Open: 17.00hrs

Ennerdale (Gillerthwaite)

Youth Hostel, Cat Crag, Ennerdale, Cleator, Cumbria CA23 3AX ✆ 01946 861237

Overnight Charges: Under 18 £4.45 Adult £6.55

R-a-H ✆ 01629 825850 3 5m

P Limited access for cars and mini-buses.

Jan 1 - Mar 30	Rent-a-Hostel
Mar 31 - Jun 30	Open X:Wed/Th
July 1 - Aug 31	Open X:Th
Sep 1 - Oct 28	Open X:Wed/Th
Oct 29 - Dec 31	Rent-a-Hostel

Open Wed Apr 19, May 31.

ACCOMMODATION 2-4: 3 5-8: 2

Converted from two former forest cottages in the quiet Ennerdale valley, this is a traditional Hostel with the added charm of gaslight. The cosy dining room/lounge has a log fire — a welcome sight after the first long day walk on the Coast-to-Coast route.

Peaceful Ennerdale is surrounded by majestic fells and stunning ridges such as Red Pike, High Stile and Haycock. Forest trails offer more sheltered walking among conifers and ancient oak woodlands. In summer enjoy a bathe in clear pools, or explore the sculpture trail on the Whitehaven cyclepath. 5m 1m

TRAVEL INFO

From Keswick (May-Oct only), alight Buttermere, 3m by path (✆ 01228 812812); otherwise CMS 17 from Whitehaven, alight Kirkland, 7m or CMS 79 from Keswick, alight Seatoller, 7m by path (✆ 01946 63222) (For BR connections see Keswick). Whitehaven 15m.

i ✆ 01946 695678

NEXT HOSTELS

Buttermere 3m (mountain path), Black Sail 4m (along valley), Honister 7m

HOW TO GET THERE

2 ½m from Bowness Knott car park along Forest Road, 5m from Ennerdale Bridge.

OS 89 GR 142141 Bart 34

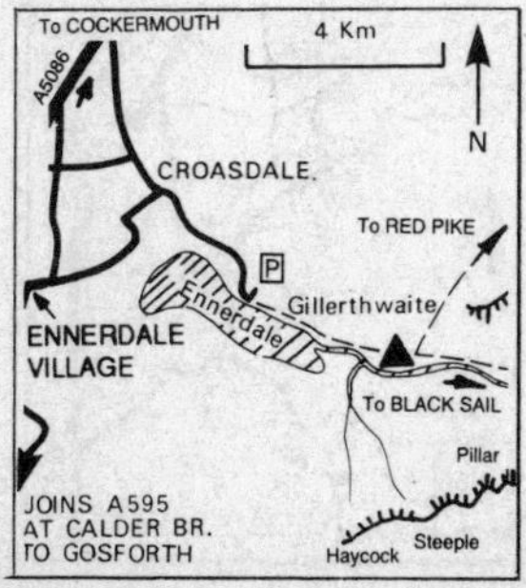

54 BEDS	Open: 17.00hrs

Eskdale

Youth Hostel, Boot, Holmrook, Cumbria CA19 1TH ✆ 019467 23219

Overnight Charges: Under 18 £5.35 Adult £8.00

Family accommodation prices on p.11-13

2 4m 1x30 P Cars and minibuses only. Coaches at Woolpack Inn (400yds)

Feb 17 - Mar 31	Open X:Sun/Mon
Apr 1 - Jun 30	Open X:Sun
Jul 1 - Sep 2	Open
Sep 3 - Dec 16	Open X:Sun/Mon
Dec 28 - Jan 2 '96	Open

Open Bank Hol Sun Apr 16, May 7, May 28.

ACCOMMODATION 2-4: 3 5-8: 5 9+: 1

This purpose-built Hostel with extensive grounds is set amidst the fells in the quiet south-west corner of the Lake District. Approach by car over the spectacular Hardknott Pass, by foot descending from Scafell or Harter Fell, or even by train on the delightful Ravenglass & Eskdale Steam Railway.

Peaceful riverside walks and exhilarating ridge walking make Eskdale a good base for walkers of all abilities. Close to the long coastline of Cumbria, family days out include Muncaster Castle and Gardens and Sellafield Visitor Centre. River bathing in crystal clear pools is popular in summer. 1 ½m 10m

TRAVEL INFO

Eskdale (Ravenglass & Eskdale Rly) 1 ½m; Ravenglass (not Sun) 10m; Drigg (not Sun) 10m.

i ✆ 015394 32582

NEXT HOSTELS

Wastwater 7m, Coniston 10m, Elterwater 9m (all by mountain path)

HOW TO GET THERE

Hardknott Pass suitable for cars and some mini-buses only. Mini-buses approach from Broughton-in-Furness. Coaches should approach from A595 Holmrook/Gosforth.

OS 89 GR 195010 Bart 34

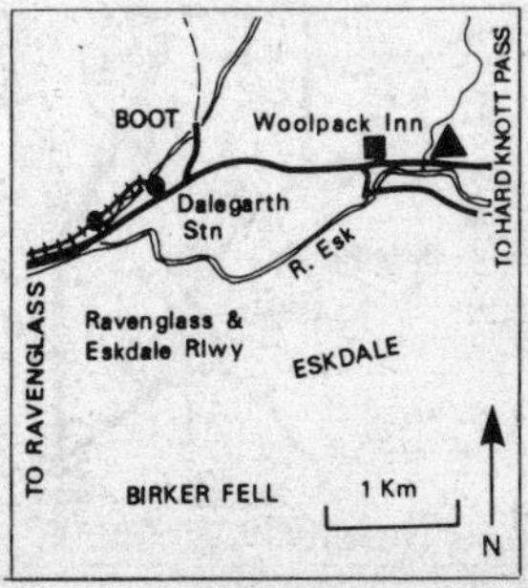

96 BEDS	**Open: 13.00hrs**

Grasmere (Butterlip How)

Youth Hostel, Butterlip How, Grasmere, Ambleside, Cumbria LA22 9QG
📞 015394 35316 Fax: 015394 35798

Overnight Charges: Under 18 £5.35 Adult £8.00

Family accommodation prices on p.11-13

4 🍴 📺 🔒 🚰 ♿ S 🔲 ¼m 🚿 1x24 P For cars only - coaches in village ¼m. BABA

Jan 5 - Mar 31	Open X:Mon
Apr 1 - Sep 30	Open
Oct 1 - Nov 4	Open X:Mon
Dec 28 - Jan 2	Open

ACCOMMODATION 🛏️²⁻⁴ 8 🛏️⁵⁻⁸ 4 🛏️⁹⁺ 3

A large Victorian house built in traditional Lakeland style in lovely grounds on the edge of Grasmere village. Relax in front of a log fire in the lounge, with impressive views of the surrounding fells. Good family accommodation is available.

A picturesque old-world village and home of the Wordsworth Museum (Dove Cottage), Grasmere is deep in the heart of the Lake District. Walk up to Easedale Tarn or Helm Crag, or tackle a more strenuous route such as Helvellyn or the classic round of the Fairfield Horseshoe. 🚴5m Ⓤ4m
🖼️1m 🏔️½m 🛶 🖼️6m

TRAVEL INFO
🚌 Stagecoach Cumberland 555
Lancaster-Keswick, alight Grasmere ¼m (all pass BR Windermere) 🚃 Windermere 8 ½m.
🅸 📞019665 245

NEXT HOSTELS
Thorney How ¾m, High Close 2m, Ambleside 5m

ADDITIONAL INFO
Special catering service available for functions/conferences etc. Resident members 📞 015394 35633

HOW TO GET THERE
Leave the village via Easedale Road. The Hostel Drive is on your right about 400yds.
OS 90 GR 336077 Bart 34

---

48 BEDS	**Open: 17.00hrs**

Grasmere (Thorney How)

Youth Hostel, Thorney How, Grasmere, Ambleside, Cumbria LA22 9QW
📞 015394 35591 Fax: 015394 35591

Overnight Charges: Under 18 £5.35 Adult £8.00

1 🍴 🔒 📺 📦 ♿ S 🔲 ¾m P Cars & mini-buses only. Coaches in village (¾m) BABA

Jan 1 - Jan 3	Open
Feb 17 - Mar 31	Open X:Tu
Apr 1 - Aug 30	Open
Sep 1 - Dec 21	Open X:Tu/Wed
Dec 22 - Jan 2	Open
Feb 16 - Feb 29 '96	Open X:Tu

ACCOMMODATION 🛏️²⁻⁴ 3 🛏️⁵⁻⁸ 3 🛏️⁹⁺ 2

This old Lakeland farmhouse dates from the 17th century, with a friendly atmosphere and lots of character. Situated just outside Grasmere towards Easedale, a little further on than Butterlip How.

Stop here on Wainwright's Coast-to-Coast walk, climb Helvellyn or explore the trails by mountain bike. Stroll into the village to buy some delicious gingerbread — made to a secret recipe and sold only at the tiny shop in Grasmere. Visit the Wordsworth Museum or hire a rowing boat on Grasmere. 🚴½m Ⓤ4m 🖼️¼m 🏔️¼m 🛶¼m 🖼️4m

TRAVEL INFO
🚌 Stagecoach Cumberland 555
Lancaster-Keswick, alight Grasmere ¾m (all pass BR Windermere) (📞 01946 63222). National Express Coaches ¾m. 🚃 Windermere 9m.
🅸 📞015394 35245

NEXT HOSTELS
Grasmere (Butterlip How) ¾m, Langdale (High Close) 2 ½m, Ambleside 5 ½m

ADDITIONAL INFO
Residents 📞 015394 35616

HOW TO GET THERE
Take Easedale Road from village for ½m. Turn right at sign. Hostel on left after ¼m
OS 90 GR 332084 Bart 34

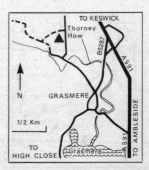

Hawkshead

Youth Hostel, Esthwaite Lodge, Hawkshead, Ambleside, Cumbria LA22 0QD
📞 015394 36293 Fax: 015394 36720

Overnight Charges: Under 18 £5.95 Adult £8.80

Family accommodation prices on p.11-13

4 ▢ 🛏 🖵 🔍 🚿 ⊕ S ▢ 1m 🅿 BABA

Jan 1 - Jan 4	Open
Feb 17 - Mar 31	Open X:Sun/Mon
Apr 1 - Oct 31	Open
Nov 1 - Dec 21	Open X:Sun/Mon
Dec 22 - Dec 28	Open

ACCOMMODATION 🛏²⁻⁴ 12 🛏⁵⁻⁸ 5 🛏⁹⁺ 2

This handsome Regency mansion — set in lovely wooded grounds overlooking Esthwaite Water — retains many of the elegant features that characterised it as the home of novelist Francis Brett Young. The courtyard has been converted into excellent family accommodation in an award-winning design.

Hawkshead, with its squares, courtyards and cobbled alleys, is an attractive old-world village. Nearby Sawrey is the 'birthplace' of Beatrix Potter's much loved characters. Visit Grizedale Forest with its sculpture park, theatre and orienteering and cycle trails. Trout fishing permits available. 🚶 1m 🔵 1m 🏔 🏕 5m 🎣 5m
🚲 🏊 7m

TRAVEL INFO

🚌 Stagecoach Cumberland 505/6 from Ambleside (connections from BR Windermere) alight Hawkshead 1m (📞 01946 63222) 🚂 Windermere 7m (by vehicle ferry)
ℹ️ 📞 015394 36525

NEXT HOSTELS

Coniston 5 ½m, Ambleside 6m, Windermere 9m (via ferry)

ADDITIONAL INFO

Residents 📞 015394 36588

HOW TO GET THERE

OS 96 GR 354966 Bart 34

Helvellyn

Youth Hostel, Greenside, Glenridding, Penrith, Cumbria CA11 0QR
📞 017684 82269

Overnight Charges: Under 18 £4.85 Adult £7.20

2 ▢ 🔒 S ▢ 1 ½m 🅿 Cars & mini-buses only.
Coaches in Glenridding 1 ½m.

Jan 1 - Jan 3	Open
Jan 4 - Mar 31	Open Fr/Sat only
Apr 1 - Jun 30	Open X:Sun
Jul 1 - Aug 31	Open
Sep 1 - Nov 4	Open X:Mon/Tu
Dec 28 - Jan 6	Open
'96	

Open Sun Apr 16, May 7, May 28.

ACCOMMODATION 🛏²⁻⁴ 16 🛏⁵⁻⁸ 2

Dramatically set at 900ft above sea level, this Hostel is isolated and peaceful, yet only 1 ½m from the village of Glenridding. Nestling beneath the towering mass of the Helvellyn range it is an ideal centre for walking and climbing the high level ridges.

For less strenuous walks try Place Fell or Glenridding Dodd. Or take a steamer ride on stately Ullswater and stroll back along the lake shore path. 🚶 1 ½m 🔵 1 ¾m 🏔 🏕 1 ½m
🎣 ¼m 🚲 🏊 15m

TRAVEL INFO

🚌 From Keswick, Windermere, alight Glenridding, 1 ½m (📞 01228 812812). 🚂 Penrith 14m, Windermere 15m.
ℹ️ 📞 017684 82414

NEXT HOSTELS

Patterdale 2 ½m, Thirlmere 4m, Grasmere 8m (all by mountain path)

ADDITIONAL INFO

Resident 📞 017684 82488.

HOW TO GET THERE

Hostel is due W of Glenridding Village on sign posted route. The lane up to the Hostel is untarmaced for the last ¾m.
OS 90 GR 366173 Bart 34

Honister Hause

Youth Hostel, Honister Hause, Seatoller, Keswick, Cumbria CA12 5XN
☎ 017687 77267

Overnight Charges: Under 18 £4.45 Adult £6.55

1 🍴 🏧 S 🔒 2 ½m P Cars & mini-buses adjacent to Hostel.

Mar 31 - Jun 30	Open X:Wed/Th
July 1 - Aug 31	Open X:Th
Sep 1 - Nov 11	Open X:Wed/Th

Open Wed Apr 19, May 31.

ACCOMMODATION   🛏️ 4   🛏️ 1

The Hostel sits at the summit of Honister Pass, a high level route (1200ft) connecting lovely Borrowdale with tranquil Buttermere to the west. A true mountain Hostel in a spectacular location, it is naturally popular with walkers and climbers seeking ease of access to the highest peaks.
Nearby are the most famous names of central Lakeland — Scafell, Great Gable, Pillar, Red Pike, Steeple... and many more. Dramatic descents into the neighbouring valleys are rewarded by breathtaking views. All around is a skyline of fells and ridges. 🚶 10m 🏔️ 10m 🏞️ 10m 🎣 ½m 🚲 🍴 10m

TRAVEL INFO
🚌 Stagecoach Cumberland 79 Keswick-Seatoller, thence 1 ½m (☎ 01946 632220) (For BR connections see Keswick) 🚉 Workington 23m.
🛈 ☎ 0159684 294

NEXT HOSTELS
Longthwaite 2m, Buttermere 4m, Black Sail 3m by mountain path.

HOW TO GET THERE
OS 89 GR 224135 Bart 34

Kendal

Youth Hostel, 118 Highgate, Kendal, Cumbria LA9 4HE *☎ 01539 724066*
Fax: 01539 724906

Overnight Charges: Under 18 £5.35 Adult £8.00

1 🍴 🏧 🍴 S 🔒 P Turn left just before Hostel for car park. Pay and display (free overnight). BABA

Feb 17 - Mar 31	Open X:Sun/Mon
Apr 1 - Sep 30	Open
Oct 1 - Dec 16	Open X:Sun/Mon
Dec 28 - Jan 2 '96	Open

ACCOMMODATION   🛏️ 7   🛏️ 4   🛏️ 1

Occupying a prime position in the centre of Kendal, the Hostel is a Georgian town house furnished to a high standard. At hand are all the amenities of a busy market town; on the fringe of England's largest National Park.
Easy to reach from the M6 motorway, Kendal lies between the Lake District and the Yorkshire Dales. Nearby are the secluded valleys of Kentmere and Long Sleddale. Adjacent to the Hostel is the Brewery Arts Centre — a popular venue for theatre, music and art. 🎭 🍴 1m 🏔️ 1m 🏞️ 12m 🚲 2m 🍴 1m

TRAVEL INFO
🚌 Frequent from surrounding areas (☎ 01228 812812). 🚉 Kendal ¾m; Oxenholme 1 ¾m.
🛈 ☎ 01539 725758

NEXT HOSTELS
Windermere 12m, Arnside 12m, Tebay 11m

ADDITIONAL INFO
For details of events at Brewery Arts Centre, send sae to Warden.

HOW TO GET THERE
OS 97 GR 515924 Bart 31

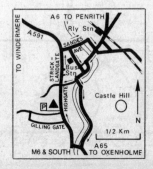

91 BEDS	**Open: 13.00hrs**

Keswick

Youth Hostel, Station Road, Keswick, Cumbria CA12 5LH ☎ 017687 72484
Fax: 017687 74129

Overnight Charges: Under 18 £5.95 Adult £8.80

4 40 🍴 🛏 🔍 🖥 🔳 S 🔲 P Cars & coaches in town.
BABA

Jan 1 - Jan 7	Open
Feb 17 - Mar 31	Open X:Wed
Apr 1 - Oct 31	Open
Nov 1 - Dec 18	Open X:Wed
Dec 19 - Dec 28	Open

ACCOMMODATION 🛏️²⁻⁴ 17 🛏️⁵⁻⁸ 1 🛏️⁹⁺ 2

Standing above the River Greta, the verandah at Keswick Youth Hostel is a fine place to relax on a summer's evening. Close to the centre of this popular Lakeland town, the Hostel looks out across the park to Skiddaw and the North Western fells.

Keswick is the northern hub of the Lake District — close to Derwentwater, Bassenthwaite and Thirlmere. Browse around interesting shops, visit museums or relax at the indoor leisure pool. Spectacular scenery, walks in every direction, cycle hire and watersports — you'll be spoilt for choice! 🚲 ⅛m ⓤ 5m ⛰ ¼m 🏛 1m 🎣 2m
🛒 ¼m 🛤 ⅛m

TRAVEL INFO

🚌 Stagecoach Cumberland X5, Wrights 888 from BR Penrith; 555 from Lancaster (pass BR Windermere) (☎ 01228 812812) 🚉 Penrith 17m, Windermere 22m
ℹ️ ☎ 017687 72645

NEXT HOSTELS

Derwentwater 2m, Skiddaw House 6m, Thirlmere 5m

ADDITIONAL INFO

Resident ☎ 017687 72485

HOW TO GET THERE

Follow Leisure Pool signs to Station Road. Turn left onto walkway by river.
OS 89 GR 267235 Bart 34

96 BEDS	**Open: 17.00hrs**

Langdale (High Close)

Youth Hostel, High Close, Loughrigg, Ambleside, Cumbria LA22 9HJ
☎ 015394 37313 Fax: 015394 37313

Overnight Charges: Under 18 £5.35 Adult £8.00

2 40 🍴 🛏 🔍 🖥 🔳 S 🔲 1m 🏃 1x30, 1x40 P Cars and minibuses only. BABA

Jan 1	Open
Jan 11 - Feb 16	Open Fr/Sat only*
Feb 17 - Mar 31	Open X:Sun
Apr 1 - Sep 30	Open
Oct 1 - Oct 31	Open X:Sun
Dec 28 - Jan 1	Open

* Midweek bookings may be accepted.

ACCOMMODATION 🛏️²⁻⁴ 2 🛏️⁵⁻⁸ 3 🛏️⁹⁺ 6

An impressive rambling Victorian mansion set in lovely gardens and woodland owned by the National Trust. The Youth Hostel is situated high on Red Bank between Elterwater and Grasmere with panoramic views of Windermere and the Langdale Valley.

This is an excellent walking base, close to the high Langdale Pikes and lower level lakeshore paths. From here stroll down into Grasmere, admire tiny Rydal Water from Loughrigg Terrace or tackle one of the classic Lakeland ridge walks. 🚲 4m ⓤ 2m ⛰ 🎣 6m 🎣 1m 🛒 🛤 7m

TRAVEL INFO

🚌 CMS 516 from Ambleside (connections from BR Windermere), alight ¾m SE at Elterwater, thence ¾m; otherwise any of the services to Grasmere Hostels, alight Grasmere, thence 1 ½m. (☎ 01539 733221). 🚉 Windermere 10m.
ℹ️ ☎ 015394 32729

NEXT HOSTELS

Elterwater 1m, Grasmere (BH) 2m, Ambleside 4m

ADDITIONAL INFO

Resident members ☎ 015394 37212

HOW TO GET THERE

From Ambleside take the A593 (Coniston and Langdale). After 2 ½km turn right and follow minor road uphill for 2.8km. At summit of Red Bank turn left and High Close is 0.4km on the left.
OS 90 GR 338052 Bart 34

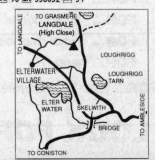

82 BEDS **Open: All Day**

Patterdale

Youth Hostel, Goldrill House, Patterdale, Penrith, Cumbria CA11 0NW
📞 017684 82394 Fax: 017684 82034

Overnight Charges: Under 18 £5.95 Adult £8.80

3 🍴 6sc ⛺ ⭐ 🚲 🏪 P Cars & minibuses only. Coaches ¼m. BABA

Feb 17 - Mar 31	Open X:Wed/Th
Apr 1 - Sep 2	Open
Sep 3 - Oct 30	Open X:Th
Oct 31 - Dec 18	Open X:Wed/Th
Dec 19 - Dec 28	Open

ACCOMMODATION 3 8 2

A unique Scandinavian-style building designed to blend with the fine scenery just south of Ullswater. Inside a warm welcome awaits, an atmosphere enhanced by the pine woodwork and spacious modern accommodation.
Take in the splendour of Ullswater on a steamer trip, sail, swim or fish in its deep, clear waters. Classic walks — such as the ascent of Helvellyn via Striding Edge — are on the doorstep, complemented by gentler low level routes along the lake shores. 🚶 1m 🚲 ½m ⛰ 🏔 1m 🎣 ½m 🏊 🛶 10m

TRAVEL INFO
🚌 From Penrith to Patterdale (📞 01228 812812). Not Sundays. 🚉 Penrith 15m.
🛈 📞 017684 82414

NEXT HOSTELS
Helvellyn 2 ½m, Grasmere 9m (by path), Ambleside 10m

ADDITIONAL INFO
Resident 📞 017684 82441

HOW TO GET THERE
¼m S of Patterdale Village, just off A592 leading to Kirkstone Pass.
OS 90 GR 399156 Bart 34

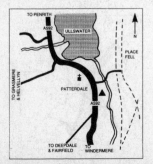

---

15 BEDS **Open: 17.00hrs**

Skiddaw House

Youth Hostel, Bassenthwaite, Keswick, Cumbria CA12 4QX

Postal bookings direct to Hostel. For information and telephone enquiries, contact: Carrock Fell Youth Hostel 📞 016974 78325

Overnight Charges: Under 18 £3.60 Adult £5.35

1 6sc 🔍 ⭐ S 🏪 6m P Cars can be left at end of Blease Road via Threlkeld at Fell car park, or at Lattrigg behind Keswick.

Mar 31 - Oct 28	Open

ACCOMMODATION 1 3

At 1550ft this is one of the highest, most remote and isolated buildings in the UK — with no sign of civilization in any direction. A former shooting lodge situated beneath the summit of Skiddaw with panoramic views all around.
Simple, self-catering accommodation is available for walkers and cyclists (NO ACCESS BY CAR). Surrounded by high fells and directly on the Cumbria Way, Skiddaw House is approached by a choice of footpaths from Keswick, Carrock Fell, Bassenthwaite or Threlkeld. 🚶 5m 🚲 4m ⛰ 🏔 5m 🏊 🛶 5m

TRAVEL INFO
🚌 Stagecoach Cumberland X5, Wright 888 from BR Penrith, alight Threlkeld thence 4 ½m
(📞 01228 812812)
🛈 📞 017687 72645

NEXT HOSTELS
Keswick 6m, Carrock Fell 8m, Thirlmere 9m

ADDITIONAL INFO
No showers. Hot water on tap. 24 volt lighting only. No access by car - nearest tarmac road 3 ½m. Very basic foodstore. Poor postal service - book well in advance. Due to remote location, no-one will be turned away. Credit cards are not accepted.

HOW TO GET THERE
From Keswick via Lattrigg and Lonscale Fell. From Carrock via Caldew Valley. From Threlkeld via Glenderaterra Valley. Bassenthwaite via Dash.
OS 89 GR 288291 Bart 34

| **46 BEDS** | **Open: 17.00hrs** |

Tebay

Youth Hostel, The Old School, Tebay, Penrith, Cumbria CA10 3TP
☎ 015396 24286

Overnight Charges: Under 18 £4.85 Adult £7.20

Feb 10 - Dec 2   Open X:Th

ACCOMMODATION   ⛺²⁻⁴ 3 ⛺⁵⁻⁸ 2 ⛺⁹⁺ 2

A converted stone-built school in the village of Tebay, close to junction 38 of the M6 motorway. This is a privately-owned Hostel adopted by the YHA. There are no self-catering facilities; home cooked meals are available if booked in advance. Tebay is in the Lune Valley on the edge of the Howgill Fells. Sandwiched between the Lake District and the Pennines, it is surrounded by walking and cycling country to suit all abilities. The many attractions of the lovely Eden Valley are nearby. 🚲12m 🛶12m 🏔 🏛 🎣 🌲 🏊 11m

TRAVEL INFO
🚍From Kendal, Penrith, Kirkby Stephen (pass close BR Kendal & Penrith) (☎ 01228 812812). 🚋Kendal 11m; Kirkby Stephen (not Sun, except Apr - Oct) 11m; Oxenholme 13m.

NEXT HOSTELS
Kirkby Stephen 10m, Kendal 11m, Dufton 14m

ADDITIONAL INFO
No credit card. No self-catering kitchen, but kettle and evening drinks available.

HOW TO GET THERE
OS 91 **GR** 618045 **Bart** 34

| **33 BEDS** | **Open: 17.00hrs** |

Thirlmere

Youth Hostel, The Old School, Stanah Cross, Keswick, Cumbria CA12 4TQ
☎ 017687 73224

Overnight Charges: Under 18 £3.60 Adult £5.35

 Very limited (check with Warden for alternatives).

Mar 31 - Jun 10	Open X:Mon/Tu
Jun 11 - Sep 16	Open X:Mon
Sep 17 - Nov 11	Open X:Mon/Tu

Open Mon Apr 17, May 29

ACCOMMODATION   ⛺²⁻⁴ 1 ⛺⁹⁺ 2

A cosy little building with a friendly atmosphere, complete wtih wood burning stove and welcoming pot of tea. The simple nature of the Hostel means limited facilities (no fitted carpets, showers or TV) but lots of character. Formerly the village school in the tiny hamlet of Legburthwaite.
The best ascent of Helvellyn's west flank starts within yards of the door and classic Lakeland crags of Castle Rock and Raven Crag are within a few minutes walk. Easy to reach from Keswick and Windermere (the bus stops here) Thirlmere offers a true 'away from it all' break. 🚲5m 🛶4m 🏔 🏛 6m 🎣 ¼m 🌲

TRAVEL INFO
🚍All services to the Grasmere Hostels, alight Stanah, 100yds. 🚋Penrith 18m.
ℹ ☎017687 74101

NEXT HOSTELS
Keswick 5m, Grasmere 6m, Helvellyn 4m

ADDITIONAL INFO
All meals MUST be booked in advance. Limited meals service with vegetarian/wholefood a speciality. Continental breakfast only. Teddy Bear convention every November.

HOW TO GET THERE
On B5322 100yds from A591 junction.
OS 90 **GR** 318190 **Bart** 34

50 BEDS	**Open: 17.00hrs**

Wastwater

Youth Hostel, Wasdale Hall, Wasdale, Seascale, Cumbria CA20 1ET
☏ 019467 26222

Overnight Charges: Under 18 £5.35 Adult £8.00

Family accommodation prices on p.11-13

 2 🔲 🔳 🔍 🖧 🅂 🔲 5m 🔲 1x32 🅿

Jan 1 - Jan 3	Open
Jan 4 - Mar 31	Open X:Tu/Wed
Apr 1 - Sep 2	Open
Sep 3 - Nov 4	Open X:Tu/Wed
Dec 24 - Dec 26	Open for Xmas package
Dec 28 - Jan 2	Open

ACCOMMODATION 🛏2-4 2 🛏5-8 2 🛏9+ 2

This lovely half-timbered house, dating from 1829, has been carefully refurbished in period style and retains many original features. Standing it its own grounds sloping down to the shores of Wastwater, it offers a high standard of accommodation in a breathtaking location. Wasdale is famous for the deepest lake, highest mountain and smallest church in England. Vast scree slopes descend into the deep dark waters, ringed by a skyline of challenging mountains. Visit the many family attractions of the Cumbria coastline, including the castle and owls at Muncaster. 🎿 🛶 13m ⛰ 🔺 🎣 🐎 🛳

TRAVEL INFO
🚌 CMS 12 Whitehaven - Seascale (passes close BR Seascale), alight Gosforth, 5m (☏ 01946 63222). 🚂 Seascale (not Sun) 9m; Irton Road (Ravenglass & Eskdale Rly) 5 ½m.
ℹ ☏ 01946 695678

NEXT HOSTELS
Black Sail 7m by mountain path, Eskdale 10m by road, Longthwaite 9m by mountain path.

ADDITIONAL INFO
Ideal for sole usage groups and conferences.

HOW TO GET THERE
From the south, come via A590, Greenodd, A595 Broughton-in-Furness, Ulpha, Eskdale Green, Santon Bridge to Nether Wasdale. From the north: A5086 to Egremont, Gosforth and Nether Wasdale.
OS 89 GR 145045 Bart 34

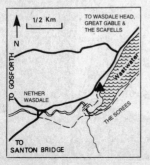

---

73 BEDS	**Open: 13.00hrs**

Windermere

Youth Hostel, High Cross, Bridge Lane, Troutbeck, Windermere, Cumbria LA23 1LA ☏ 015394 43543 Fax: 015394 47165

Overnight Charges: Under 18 £4.85 Adult £7.20

Family accommodation prices on p.11-13

4 🔲 🔳 🖳 🖧 🅂 🔲 1m 🅿 BABA

Jan 1 - Jan 5	Open
Jan 6 - Mar 31	Open X:Th
Apr 1 - Sep 30	Open
Oct 1 - Nov 4	Open X:Th*
Dec 23 - Dec 28	Open
Jan 5 - Feb 29	Open X:Th

* Open Th Oct 26.

ACCOMMODATION 🛏2-4 11 🛏5-8 2 🛏9+ 1

A large house enjoying an elevated position with panoramic views of Windermere lake and the mountains of South Lakeland. Situated in extensive wooded grounds 2m outside the busy town, the Hostel now has many small rooms ideal for families.

There is plenty to do in the area, with numerous walks and places to visit. The National Park Visitor Centre at Brockhole is nearby, an indoor swimming pool (1m), cruises and watersports on Windermere, the Windermere Steamboat Museum (2m) and the Beatrix Potter Exhibition (3m). 🎿 2m 🛶 1m ⛰ 🔺 3m 🎣 10m 🛳 1m

TRAVEL INFO
🚌 Frequent from surrounding areas (☏ 01946 63222). 🚂 Windermere 2m.
ℹ ☏ 015394 46490

NEXT HOSTELS
Ambleside 3m, Hawkshead 9m by ferry, Patterdale 11m

ADDITIONAL INFO
Resident members ☏ 015394 46147

HOW TO GET THERE
From Windermere follow the A591 N for 1m to Troutbeck Bridge. Take first turning right after filling station - Hostel is well sign-posted off the main road and is ¾m up lane, on left, just after Broad Oaks.
OS 90 GR 405013 Bart 34

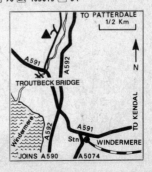

Heather-clad fells, lush green pastures and sparkling mountain streams cutting sheer-sided valleys are all set within the rural beauty of the Yorkshire Dales. Wild and unspoilt, the area includes the Yorkshire Dales National Park, the heart of which is Craven limestone. Spectacular features like Malham Cove, Kilnsey Crag, Gordage Scar and Gaping Ghyll can all be visited from here. The South Pennines Area of Outstanding Natural Beauty offers a different kind of rural scenery. The peat-clad moorlands are based on sand and gritstone which was used to build most of the towns and villages during the industrial revolution.

Inter-Hostel walking is particularly popular in this area — especially the "Herriot Way" through Wensleydale and Swaledale.

The Pennine Way crosses the area and the Calderdale Way offers an interesting circular tour of the South Pennines.

Earby, Ellingstring, Linton and Slaidburn Youth Hostels are available on YHA's **Rent-a-Hostel scheme** which runs during the winter months (details on p.7).

USEFUL PUBLICATIONS

Pennine Way Central Booking Service — send a large s.a.e. to the YHA Regional Office listed below.

Herriot Way — send £1 to the YHA Regional Office listed below.

Camping Barns in the Forest of Bowland — send s.a.e. to the YHA Regional Office listed below.

Camping Barns in North Yorkshire — send s.a.e. to the YHA Regional Office listed below.

Coast to Coast Central Booking Service — send a large s.a.e. to the YHA Regional Office listed below.

Yorkshire Dales Cycleway — Tel: National Park Information Centre at Malham on (01729) 830363 for information pack.

For more information about hostelling in this area contact: YHA Northern Regional Office, P.O. Box 11, Matlock, Derbyshire DE4 2XA. Tel: (01629) 825850. Fax: (01629) 824571.

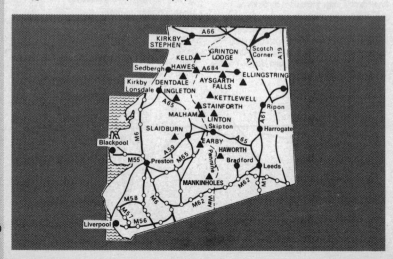

Aysgarth Falls

Youth Hostel, Aysgarth, Leyburn, North Yorkshire DL8 3SR ☎ **01969 663260**
Fax: 01969 663110

Overnight Charges: Under 18 £4.85 Adult £7.20

Family accommodation prices on p.11-13

1⃣ 🍴 GSC 🛏 🔍 ➕ 🚲 **S** **P** Cars and mini-buses only.
Coaches next door at Falls Country Club. BABA

Jan 13 - Mar 31	Open Fr/Sat
Apr 1 - Jun 30	Open X:Sun*
Jul 1 - Aug 31	Open
Sep 1 - Oct 31	Open X:Sun
Nov 1 - Nov 30	Open Fr/Sat

* Open Bank Hol Sun April 16, May 7, May 28.
This Hostel may be available for groups when otherwise closed - please contact Warden.

ACCOMMODATION   🛏²⁻⁴ 6   🛏⁵⁻⁸ 6

Built of mellow sandstone, the Hostel is just 1 mins walk from Aysgarth's famous falls. Here the foaming waters of the River Ure plunge over a series of broad rocky steps creating one of Yorkshire's most popular beauty spots. A good base for exploring Wensleydale.

An excellent choice of circular walks start from Aysgarth, including the 55 mile-long 'Herriot Way'. See Bolton Castle (where Mary Queen of Scots was imprisoned) or follow the Aysgarth Falls and Woodland Trail. 🚶1m 🅿4m 🏔🚶5m

TRAVEL INFO

🚌United 26 from Richmond (infrequent) (connections from BR Darlington) (☎ 01325 468771). Dales Bus (☎ 01423 566061). Also Postbus service from Northallerton (weekdays).
🚉Garsdale (not Sun, except Apr-Oct) 16m; Northallerton 24m; Darlington 34m.
ℹ ☎01969 663424

NEXT HOSTELS

Hawes 9m, Grinton Lodge 8m, Kettlewell 13m

HOW TO GET THERE

½m E of Aysgarth on the A684 to Leyburn at the junction with the road to Aysgarth Falls.
OS 98 GR 012884 Bart 35

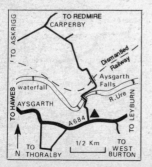

Dentdale

Youth Hostel, Cowgill, Dent, Sedbergh, Cumbria LA10 5RN ☎ **015396 25251**

Overnight Charges: Under 18 £4.85 Adult £7.20

1⃣ 🍴 GSC 🛏 ➕ **S** 🚲 5m **P**

Feb 10 - Mar 31	Open Fr/Sat
Apr 1 - Aug 31	Open X:Th
Sep 1 - Oct 31	Open X:Wed/Th
Nov 1 - Dec 16	Open Fr/Sat

The Hostel may be available for groups when otherwise closed - please contact Warden.

ACCOMMODATION   🛏 1   🛏 3

An attractive whitewashed building on the banks of the River Dee, the Youth Hostel is a former shooting lodge, now a Listed building. Situated in the upper reaches of lovely Dentdale, on the Dales Way path, the Hostel is popular with cavers and walkers alike.

The cobbled streets and tiny cottages of Dent evoke the days of the 17th century. Step back in time to enjoy the surrounding landscape of meadows and hedges; then walk to the top of Whernside (2424ft) for truly outstanding views. Or take a trip on the historic Settle to Carlisle Railway. 🅿5m 🏔 🚶5m 🚲5m 🚉 🅿5m

TRAVEL INFO

🚌As for Hawes, but alight Hawes, thence 8m.
🚉Dent 2m (not Sun except Apr-Oct)
ℹ ☎015396 20125

NEXT HOSTELS

Hawes 8m, Ingleton 11m, Stainforth 15m

HOW TO GET THERE

On Dentdale road N.E. of Whernside, about 2m from junction with Hawes - Ingleton road about 6m E. of Dent. 7'6" width restriction at Cowgill; large vehicles approach via Newby Head.
OS 98 GR 773850 Bart 34

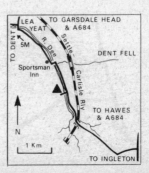

23 BEDS   Open: 17.00hrs

Earby

Katherine Bruce Glasier Memorial Hostel, Glen Cottage, Birch Hall Lane, Earby, Colne, Lancs BB8 6JX ✆ **01282 842349**

Overnight Charges: Under 18 £4.00 Adult £5.95

R-a-H ✆ 01629 825850 [2] ⊞ ⊞ ½m P Limited.

Jan 1 - Mar 30	Rent-a-Hostel
Mar 31 - Sep 30	Open X:Tu
Oct 1 - Dec 31	Rent-a-Hostel

ACCOMMODATION

A small cosy cottage on the outskirts of the town, the Youth Hostel offers simple self-catering accommodation just 1m from the Pennine Way. The pretty garden is adjacent to the local open park, providing plenty of space for outdoor recreation.

Look across from Earby to Pendle Hill, home of Lancashire's witches, and beyond to the edge of the Forest of Bowland. Explore the area's rich industrial heritage with a wealth of fascinating places to visit — museums, railways and historic houses. Or browse around the many mill shops and markets. ⛰ 🖼 ✉ 🖼

TRAVEL INFO

🚌 Various services from Burnley, Skipton (passing close BR Colne & Skipton), alight Earby, ½m (✆ 01257 241693). 🚉 Colne 5m; Skipton 8m.
ℹ ✆ 01756 792809

NEXT HOSTELS

Haworth 15m (via Pennine Way), Linton 15m, Malham 16m (via Pennine Way)

HOW TO GET THERE

The Hostel is 300yds beyond the Red Lion public house.
OS 103 GR 915468 Bart 31

20 BEDS   Open: 17.00hrs

Ellingstring

Youth Hostel, Lilac Cottage, Ellingstring, Masham, Nr Ripon, North Yorkshire HG4 4PW ✆ **01677 460216 (Warden's phone)**

Or book via: Mrs A C Wright, Hollybreen, Ellingstring, Ripon, North Yorks HG4 4PW.

Overnight Charges: Under 18 £3.60 Adult £5.35
R-a-H ✆ 01629 825850 [1] 68C ⊠ S ⊞ 3m P Cars and mini-buses.

Jan 1 - Mar 30	Rent-a-Hostel
Mar 31 - Jun 30	Open X:Wed/Th
Jul 1 - Aug 31	Open
Sep 1 - Oct 31	Open X:Wed/Th
Nov 1 - Dec 31	Rent-a-Hostel

ACCOMMODATION

The Hostel — a stone-built detached cottage surrounded by pretty gardens in the tiny hamlet of Ellingstring — offers simple self-catering accommodation just outside the Yorkshire Dales National Park.

The ancient town of Middleham is close by, famous for its castle and race horses. Follow the road and Yorkshire Dales Cycle Way down secret Coverdale, one of Wensleydale's many side-valleys, to Kettlewell in Wharfedale. Or visit the splendid monastic ruins of Fountains Abbey or Jervaulx Abbey. ⛰ 3m 🖼 14m

TRAVEL INFO

🚌 United 159 (infrequent) from Ripon to within 1m (✆ 01325 468771); otherwise postbus from Ripon (✆ 01325 447470) or Dales Bus (✆ 01423 566061). 🚉 Thirsk 16m; Northallerton 17m.
ℹ ✆ 01765 604625

NEXT HOSTELS

Grinton 12m, Aysgarth 14m, Osmotherley 25m

ADDITIONAL INFO

Credit card bookings are not accepted.

HOW TO GET THERE

OS 99 GR 176835 Bart 35

Grinton Lodge

Youth Hostel, Grinton, Richmond, North Yorkshire DL11 6HS 📞 01748 884206
Fax: 01748 884876

Overnight Charges: Under 18 £4.45 Adult £6.55

2 🍴 GSC 🚽 🔍 ⊕ S 📷 1m 🔦 1x20, 1x15
P BABA

Jan 1 - Jan 7	Open
Jan 8 - Mar 31	Open X:Sun/Mon
Apr 1 - Aug 31	Open
Sep 1 - Oct 31	Open X:Sun
Dec 22 - Dec 28	Open

The Hostel may be available when otherwise closed - please enquire.

ACCOMMODATION   🛏️2-4 4   🛏️5-8 6   🛏️9+ 1

Situated on the grouse moor overlooking Swaledale and Arkengarthdale, this former shooting lodge retains much of its original character. Complete with turret, log fires, courtyard and tiled game larder (now the cycle shed!), this is an excellent location for exploring 'Herriot Country'.

The swift-flowing river, green meadows and drystone walls of Swaledale give this dale a unique character. Further down the valley the market town of Richmond, with its narrow alleys steeped in history and dominated by the castle, is well worth a visit. 🚲 10m 🅿️ 25m 🏞️ 🎣 🔲

TRAVEL INFO

🚌 United 30 Richmond - Keld (infrequent) (connections from BR Darlington), alight Grinton, ¾m (📞 01325 468771); West Yorkshire Dales Bus (📞 01423 566061). 🚆 Kirkby Stephen (not Sun, except Apr - Oct) 24m; Darlington 25m.
ℹ️ 📞01748 825994

NEXT HOSTELS
Aysgarth 8m, Keld 13m, Ellingstring 13m

ADDITIONAL INFO
On the 'Herriot Way' coast-to-coast ¾m. Barbecue. Fishing in River Swale.

HOW TO GET THERE
¾m from Grinton due S on Reeth-Leyburn Road
OS 98 GR 048975 Bart 35

Hawes

Youth Hostel, Lancaster Terrace, Hawes, North Yorkshire DL8 3LQ 📞 01969 667368
Fax: 01969 667368

Overnight Charges: Under 18 £5.35 Adult £8.00

1 🍴 🚽 🔍 🚿 ↔️ S 📷 ¼m P Cars & coaches 300yds. BABA

Jan 6 - Mar 31	Open X:Wed/Th
Apr 1 - Jun 30	Open X:Su*
Jul 1 - Aug 31	Open
Sep 1 - Dec 21	Open X:Mon/Tu
Dec 22 - Dec 28	Open

* Open Bank Hol Sun Apr 16, May 7, May 28. The Hostel may be available for groups and parties when otherwise closed - please contact Warden.

ACCOMMODATION   🛏️2-4 7   🛏️5-8 5

This modern, comfortable Hostel overlooks the lovely village of Hawes and Wensleydale beyond. Its friendly atmosphere and small bedrooms make this a popular base for families, plus walkers on the Pennine Way and Herriot Way.

Hawes is at the heart of the Yorkshire Dales surrounded by heather-clad fells. Don't miss Hardraw Force waterfall (the highest single fall in England) or a glimpse of a steam train crossing the magnificent Ribblehead viaduct. Visit the factory where Wensleydale's famous cheese is made. 🚲 5m 🅿️ 12m 🏞️ 🎣

TRAVEL INFO

🚌 BR Harrington from BR Garsdale (📞 01969 50682); United 26 from Richmond (infrequent) (connections from BR Darlington) (📞 01325 468771); National Park bus from BR Garsdale in summer (📞 01423 566061). Also Postbus service.
🚆 Garsdale (not Sun, exc. Apr-Oct) 6m.
ℹ️ 📞01969 667450

NEXT HOSTELS
Dentdale 8m, Keld 9m, Aysgarth 10m

ADDITIONAL INFO
Gayle Institute 10mins walk from Hostel available for classroom/workshop.

HOW TO GET THERE
W of Hawes on the Ingleton Road.
OS 98 GR 867897 Bart 35

90 BEDS　　**Open: 17.00hrs**

Haworth

Youth Hostel, Longlands Hall, Longlands Drive, Lees Lane, Haworth, Keighley, West Yorkshire BD22 8RT ☎ 01535 642234 Fax: 01535 643023

Overnight Charges: Under 18 £5.35 Adult £8.00

③ ⊠ 🆚 ⬛ 🔍 ⬤ ⓢ ⬜ ¼m 🔌 1x50, 1x30
🅿 Cars & coaches. BABA

Feb 10 - Mar 31	Open X:Sun
Apr 1 - Sep 30	Open
Oct 1 - Dec 16	Open X:Sun
Dec 29 - Jan 2 '96	Open

The Hostel may be available for groups when otherwise closed - please contact Warden.

ACCOMMODATION 🛏️²⁻⁴ 1　🛏️⁵⁻⁸ 3　🛏️⁹⁺ 5

This impressive Victorian mansion in its own grounds overlooks the famous Bronte village of Haworth. Built in the grand style for a wealthy mill owner, with sweeping staircase and oak panelling, its character has been retained in a modern Hostel.
Explore the village and surrounding moors which provided inspiration for novels like 'Wuthering Heights'. Visit the Bronte Museum; Worth Valley Railway; the National Museum of Film, Photography & Television (at Bradford 8m); Saltaire Victorian village; or the Eureka children's museum at Halifax. ⓤ½m ▲1m 🚲¼m 🚈3m

TRAVEL INFO
🚌 Frequent from surrounding areas (☎ 01535 603284). 🚉 Keighley 4m; Haworth (Worth Valley Rly) ½m.
🛈 ☎ 01535 642329

NEXT HOSTELS
Mankinholes 12m, Earby 18m, York 45m

ADDITIONAL INFO
Ideal for conferences. Special menus available.

HOW TO GET THERE
🆗 104 🄶🅁 038378 Bart 32

---

66 BEDS　　**Open: 17.00hrs**

Ingleton

Youth Hostel, Greta Tower, Ingleton, Carnforth, Lancashire LA6 3EG ☎ 015242 41444 Fax: 015242 41854

Overnight Charges: Under 18 £4.45 Adult £6.55

① ⊠ ⬛ ⊛ ⓢ ⬜ 🅿 Community Centre in village
BABA

Feb 10 - Mar 31	Open X:Sun/Mon
Apr 1 - Jun 30	Open X:Sun*
Jul 1 - Aug 31	Open
Sep 1 - Sep 30	Open X:Sun
Oct 1 - Dec 2	Open X:Sun/Mon

* Open Bank Hol Sun Apr 16, May 7, May 28. The Hostel may be available for groups when otherwise closed - please contact Warden.

ACCOMMODATION 🛏️ 4　🛏️ 6　🛏️ 1

An enlarged stone-built cottage close to the centre of this popular village, overlooked by Ingleborough (2376ft) — one of the famous Three Peaks of the National Park. The Hostel sits in its own mature gardens, next to the village park. Enjoy the 4 ½m circular 'Waterfalls Walk' past Ingleton's famous waterfalls or a visit to the spectacular natural White Scar Caves. The area is a centre for caving and potholing, with miles of natural underground systems. The Yorkshire Dales Cycleway passes through Ingleton.
🚻 ⓤ ▲ 🚲 🔌 🚈

TRAVEL INFO
🚌 Stagecoach Ribble 200/1, 279-81 from Lancaster (passes close BR Lancaster & Bentham) (☎ 01257 241693) 🚉 Bentham 3m; Clapham 4m.
🛈 ☎ 0152 4241049

NEXT HOSTELS
Stainforth 10m, Dentdale 11m, Kendal 17m

HOW TO GET THERE
From market square take lane down hill opposite Nat West Bank (NB: leave vehicles at Community Centre car park)
🆗 98 🄶🅁 695733 Bart 31

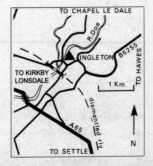

Keld

Youth Hostel, Keld Lodge, Upper Swaledale, Richmond, North Yorkshire DL11 6LL
☎ 01748 886259 Fax: 01748 886259

Overnight Charges: Under 18 £4.45 Adult £6.55

2 |O| |III| S P Roadside. BABA

Feb 3 - Mar 31	Open Fr/Sat
Apr 1 - Jun 30	Open X:Mo*
Jul 1 - Aug 31	Open
Sep 1 - Oct 31	Open X:Mon/Tu
Nov 1 - Dec 23	Open Fr/Sat
Dec 29 - Jan 2	Open
'96	

* Open Bank Hol Mon May 29. The Hostel may be available when otherwise closed.

ACCOMMODATION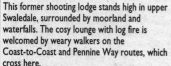

This former shooting lodge stands high in upper Swaledale, surrounded by moorland and waterfalls. The cosy lounge with log fire is welcomed by weary walkers on the Coast-to-Coast and Pennine Way routes, which cross here.

The tiny grey-stone villages of Keld and neighbouring Muker appear unchanged for centuries. Tan Hill Inn (5m) at 1732ft is the highest pub in England. Below Keld the valley widens into green pastures with drystone walls, summer wildflowers and Swaledale's distinctive field barns. ▣ ¼m ▣ ¼m ▣ ¼m

TRAVEL INFO

🚌 United 30 from Richmond (infrequent) (connections from BR Darlington) (☎ 01325 468771); Dales Bus (☎ 01423 566061). 🚉 Kirkby Stephen (not Sun, except Apr - Oct) 11m.
ℹ ☎ 01748 850252

NEXT HOSTELS
Hawes 8m, Kirkby Stephen 11m, Grinton 13m

ADDITIONAL INFO
Booking Bureau for Herriot Way walk - contact the Warden.

HOW TO GET THERE
Situated W of Keld village on B6270 Reeth to Kirkby Stephen Road.
OS 91 GR 891009 Bart 35

Kettlewell

Youth Hostel, Whernside House, Kettlewell, Skipton, North Yorkshire BD23 5QU
☎ 01756 760232 Fax: 01756 760402

Overnight Charges: Under 18 £4.85 Adult £7.20

Family accommodation prices on p.11-13

4 |O| |GSC| |III| S S O P Limited. In village. BABA

Feb 10 - Mar 31	Open X:Wed/Th
Apr 1 - Sep 30	Open
Oct 1 - Dec 19	Open X:Wed/Th

The Hostel may be available for groups when otherwise closed - please contact Warden.

ACCOMMODATION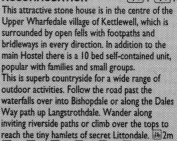

This attractive stone house is in the centre of the Upper Wharfedale village of Kettlewell, which is surrounded by open fells with footpaths and bridleways in every direction. In addition to the main Hostel there is a 10 bed self-contained unit, popular with families and small groups.

This is superb countryside for a wide range of outdoor activities. Follow the road past the waterfalls over into Bishopdale or along the Dales Way path up Langstrothdale. Wander along inviting riverside paths or climb over the tops to reach the tiny hamlets of secret Littondale. ▣ 2m
▣ 3m ▣ 2m ▣ 7m ▣ 2m ▣ 2m ▣ 3m

TRAVEL INFO

🚌 Pride of the Dales 72, Keighley & District 809 from BR Skipton, alight Grassington 6m (☎ 01756 753123); 🚉 Skipton 16m.
ℹ ☎ 01756 752774

NEXT HOSTELS
Linton 7m, Malham 14m, Aysgarth 16m

HOW TO GET THERE
OS 98 GR 970724 Bart 32

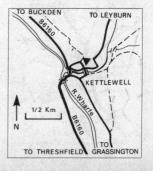

Kirkby Stephen

44 BEDS   Open: 17.00hrs

Youth Hostel, Fletcher Hill, Market Street, Kirkby Stephen, Cumbria CA17 4QQ
☎ 017683 71793 Fax: 017683 71793

Overnight Charges: Under 18 £4.85 Adult £7.20

Family accommodation prices on p.11-13

2 ⊙ 6SC ▦ ⚲ ⊙ ⊠ S ⬡ 5yds P Roadside or free car park 100yds. Coach park in road behind Hostel. BABA

Feb 17 - Mar 31	Open X:Mon/Tu
Apr 1 - Jun 30	Open X:Mon
Jul 1 - Aug 31	Open
Sep 1 - Nov 26	Open X:Mon/Tu
Nov 27 - Dec 17	Open Fr/Sat only

ACCOMMODATION   ▣²⁻⁴ 3   ▣⁵⁻⁸ 5

Experience the unique character of this former chapel in the historic market town of Kirkby Stephen. Sympathetically converted to retain the traditional wooden pews, oak beams and stained glass windows — combined with all the comforts of a modern Youth Hostel.

Interesting shops and places to visit make this the ideal place to linger on the Coast-to-Coast Walk or the Cumbria Cycle Way. Nearby the Settle to Carlisle Railway reaches its highest point below Wild Boar Fell at the head of the dale of Mallerstang, site of the romantic ruins of Pendragon Castle. ⌂⅛m U 2m ▲ 1m
🏵 2m ⊠ 2m ▱ ¼m

TRAVEL INFO

🚌 OK X74 Darlington - Carlisle; Primrose Coaches Newcastle-Upon-Tyne - Blackpool (passes BR Kirkby Stephen) (☎ 0191 413 2257). 🚉 Kirkby Stephen (not Sun, except Apr - Oct) 1 ½m.
🛈 ☎017683 71199

NEXT HOSTELS

Keld 10m, Dufton 10m, Hawes 15m

HOW TO GET THERE

Hostel in centre of town on main street A685. 12m from M6 junction 38 or 2m from A66 at Brough.
OS 91 GR 774085 Bart 34

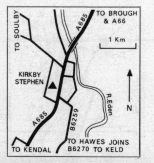

Linton (nr Grassington)

38 BEDS   Open: 17.00hrs

Youth Hostel, The Old Rectory, Linton-in-Craven, Skipton, North Yorkshire BD23 5HH ☎ 01756 752400

Overnight Charges: Under 18 £5.35 Adult £8.00

R-a-H ☎ 01629 825850 2 ⊙ ⊛ S ⬡ 1 ½m
P Cars & mini-buses only - coaches ½m.

Jan 1 - Mar 30	Rent-a-Hostel
Mar 31 - Sep 30	Open X:Sun*
Oct 1 - Oct 31	Open X:Sun/Mon
Nov 1 - Dec 31	Rent-a-Hostel

* Open Bank Hol Sun Apr 16, May 7, May 28, Aug 27.

ACCOMMODATION   ▣² 2   ▣³ 3   ▣ 1

A 17th century Rectory built of mellow stone in one of Wharfedale's prettiest villages. Looking out across the green, the Hostel's spacious lounge and large garden make it a popular base for exploring the Yorkshire Dales.

Wander around the village of Linton with its lovely old-world cottages, ancient clapper bridge and packhorse bridge by the ford. Or explore the many delights of Wharfedale — Bolton Abbey (8m), Linton Falls (½m) or the shops, cafes and Folk Museum at neighbouring Grassington. Kilnsey Crag (4m). ⌂ 1m U 3m ▲ ▲ 1m 🏵 2m
⊠ ▱ 2m

TRAVEL INFO

🚌 Pride of the Dales 72 (☎ 01756 753123) alight Linton; Keighley & District 72, 272, 809 & 76 (☎ 01535 603284) alight Linton or Grassington 1m. 🚉 Skipton 8m.
🛈 ☎01756 752774

NEXT HOSTELS

Kettlewell 8m, Malham 10m, Earby 15m

HOW TO GET THERE

Adjacent to village green (E side of Packhorse bridge over river).
OS 98 GR 998627 Bart 32

80 BEDS   Open: 17.00hrs

Malham

Youth Hostel, John Dower Memorial Hostel, Malham, Skipton, North Yorkshire BD23 4DE ☎ 01729 830321 Fax: 01729 830551

Overnight Charges: Under 18 £5.95 Adult £8.80

Family accommodation prices on p.11-13

🅿 Cars and mini-buses only, coaches 200metres BABA

Feb 10 - Feb 28	Open X:Sun/Mon
Mar 1 - Oct 31	Open
Nov 1 - Dec 21	Open X:Sun/Mon
Dec 29 - Jan 2 '96	Open

The Hostel may be available for groups when otherwise closed - please contact Warden.

ACCOMMODATION 🛏️²⁻⁴ 4 🛏️⁵⁻⁸ 12

A newly refurbished Hostel close to the centre of the popular village of Malham. With many small bedrooms, pretty furnishings and a pleasant garden, the Hostel is now a favourite with families — as well as walkers (on the Pennine Way) and cyclists (Yorkshire Dales Cycleway).

The huge natural amphitheatre of Malham Cove and the amazing limestone 'pavements' have created a unique landscape. Malham Tarn and its nature reserve are internationally important for nature conservation and the whole area is outstanding for cavers, geologists and birdwatchers. 🚶6m 🚲6m ⛰️¼m 🎣6m 🏊¼m 🏪8m

TRAVEL INFO

🚌Pennine 210 from Skipton (passes close BR Skipton) (☎ 01756 749215); West Yorkshire Dales Bus (☎ 01423 566061). 🚉Skipton 13m, or Gargrave 8m
ℹ️ ☎01729 830 363

NEXT HOSTELS

Stainforth 8m, Kettlewell 10m, Linton 10m

ADDITIONAL INFO

Travel cot and high chair available.

HOW TO GET THERE

OS 98 GR 901629 Bart 31

---

40 BEDS   Open: 17.00hrs

Mankinholes

Youth Hostel, Mankinholes, Todmorden, Lancashire OL14 6HR ☎ 01706 812340 Fax: 01706 812340

Overnight Charges: Under 18 £4.45 Adult £6.55

 1 ½m 🅿 Cars & minibuses only.
Coaches 150yds - approach via Walsden. BABA

Feb 10 - Mar 31	Open Fr/Sat
Apr 1 - Aug 31	Open X:Sun*
Sep 1 - Oct 28	Open X:Sun/Mon
Oct 29 - Nov 25	Open Fr/Sat

* Open Bank Hol Sun Apr 16, May 7, May 28, Aug 27. The Hostel may be available for groups when otherwise closed - please contact Warden.

ACCOMMODATION 🛏️⁵⁻⁸ 4 🛏️⁹⁺ 1

A stone-built house in the ancient hamlet of Mankinholes. Once the local manor house, the Hostel is now a Listed building, just ½m from the Pennine Way. This is an area of winding lanes and packhorse routes across wild moorland, yet still close to towns such as Hebden Bridge and Halifax.

The wealth of industrial heritage sites in the area are a legacy of the textile industry from the time of the Industrial Revolution. Walk the Calderdale Way or visit the magnificent Piece Hall at Halifax, the Clog Factory, Automobile Museum or Eureka children's museum. 🚶5m 🚲2m ⛰️ 🏪8m 🎣4m 🏊5m 🛶3m

TRAVEL INFO

🚌Yorkshire Rider T6 from Todmorden (passes close BR Todmorden) (☎ 01132 448133). 🚉Todmorden 2m (☎ 0161 8328353)
ℹ️ ☎01706 818181

NEXT HOSTELS

Haworth 12m (18m by Pennine Way), Earby 25m (by Pennine Way), Crowden 24m (by Pennine Way)

ADDITIONAL INFO

Paragliding school nearby. Bread and milk must be ordered in advance.

HOW TO GET THERE

Follow road to Lumbutts - Hostel ¼m W of Top Brink public house.
OS 103 GR 960235 Bart 31

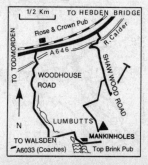

Slaidburn

Youth Hostel, King's House, Slaidburn, Clitheroe, Lancashire BB7 3ER
☎ 01200 446656

Overnight Charges: Under 18 £3.60 Adult £5.35

R-a-H ☎ 01629 825850 ⓵ GSC S P Coaches & mini-buses 200yds.

Jan 1 - Apr 13	Rent-a-Hostel
Apr 14 - Apr 22	Open
Apr 23 - May 26	Open Sat only*
May 27 - Jun 3	Open
Jun 4 - Jun 30	Open Sat only*
Jul 1 - Sep 3	Open
Sep 4 - Oct 31	Open Sat only*
Nov 1 - Feb 29	Rent-a-Hostel
'96	

* Available for advance group bookings mid-week. Open May 7.

ACCOMMODATION

Formerly a 17th century inn, the Youth Hostel is in the centre of the picturesque village of Slaidburn. It offers simple self-catering accommodation in the heart of the Forest of Bowland — a 300 sq mile Area of Outstanding Natural Beauty.

The Forest of Bowland is relatively undiscovered — despite being close to the towns of the north west and glimpsed from afar by motorists on the M6. Enjoy the hills and secret valleys on foot or by bike. From the south it is a convenient stepping stone for the Yorkshire Dales. 🚶 3m
U 2m ⛰ 1m 🚲 1m

TRAVEL INFO

🚌 Lakeland 110/1 from Clitheroe (connections from BR Blackburn) (☎ 01257 241693).
🚆 Clitheroe 8m
ℹ ☎ 01200 25566

NEXT HOSTELS

Stainforth 15m, Ingleton 15m, Earby 17m

HOW TO GET THERE

OS 103 GR 711523 Bart 31

Stainforth

Youth Hostel, 'Taitlands' Stainforth, Settle, North Yorkshire BD24 9PA
☎ 01729 823577 Fax: 01729 825404

Overnight Charges: Under 18 £4.85 Adult £7.20

⓵ 🍴 🎞 🌱 S 🔆 1x25 P Cars & mini-buses in grounds. Coaches - ask Warden. BABA

Feb 10 - Mar 31	Open Fr/Sat
Apr 1 - Aug 31	Open
Sep 1 - Oct 31	Open X:Sun
Nov 3 - Nov 25	Open Fr/Sat

ACCOMMODATION

A handsome stone-built Victorian house in its own grounds with an attractive walled garden. Now a Listed building, the Hostel retains its original character as a large country house, with a sweeping staircase and fine plasterwork.

From the graceful arch of the packhorse bridge at Stainforth, follow the River Ribble downstream to Stainforth Force. Or take the winding moorland road over to lovely Littondale, crossing the Pennine Way on its route down to Malham Tarn.
🚶 3m U 5m ⛰ 🚲 2m 🚲 🚂 2m

TRAVEL INFO

🚌 Ingfield Northern Rose, Settle - Horton (☎ 01729 822568). Good taxi service ☎ 01729 822219. 🚆 Settle (not Sun, except Apr - Oct) 2½m; Giggleswick 3m.
ℹ ☎ 01729 823617

NEXT HOSTELS

Malham 8m, Ingleton 10m, Kettlewell 12m

HOW TO GET THERE

2m N of Settle in the Yorkshire Dales National Park. ¼m S of village on main Settle - Horton-in-Ribblesdale Road. 3½m S of Pennine Way at Dale Head, and 4m S of Pennine Way at Horton.
OS 98 GR 821668 Bart 31

There are three main types of landscape in this area. First the North York Moors, the largest expanse of heather-clad moorland in the country. Second and further south are the Wolds, offering typical chalkland scenery with dry valleys and woods between rolling arable and grazing land. Finally, the varied coastline from Salturn to Spurn which ranges from steep mineral-rich cliffs in the north to the chalk headland of Flamborough and the dunes and the shingle of the south — all providing excellent opportunities for coastal studies.

The historic city of York is a major attraction, best known for its Minster and City Walls as well as many mediaeval buildings and the Jorvik Viking Centre.

Other attractions include the North York Moors Steam Railway, Rievaulx Abbey, Helmsley Castle and the Ryedale Folk Museum. The bustling harbour at Whitby and the traditional seaside resort of Scarborough ensure there is something for everyone to enjoy in this area.

Long distance walks include the Coast to Coast, Cleveland Way and Wolds Way which criss-cross the area using ancient tracks. Cyclists can enjoy many scenic by-roads and forest trails, as well as the challenge of steep hills in and out of valleys and down to the sea.

Helmsley and Lockton Youth Hostels are available on YHA's **Rent-a-Hostel scheme** which runs during the winter months (details on p.7). There is also a network of nine Camping Barns across North Yorkshire.

USEFUL PUBLICATIONS

Cleveland Way Long Distance Footpath — send s.a.e. to the YHA Regional Office listed below.

Camping Barns in North Yorkshire — send s.a.e. to the YHA Regional Office listed below.

Coast to Coast Central Booking Service — send a large s.a.e. to the YHA Regional Office listed below.

For more information about hostelling in this area contact: YHA Northern Regional Office, P.O. Box 11, Matlock, Derbyshire DE4 2XA. Tel: (01629) 825850. Fax: (01629) 824571.

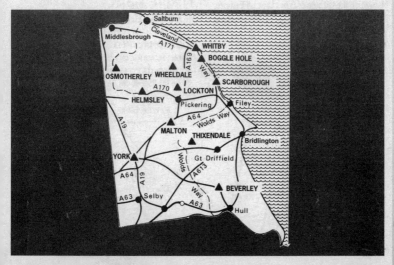

34 BEDS   **Open: 17.00hrs**

Beverley Friary

Youth Hostel, The Friary, Friar's Lane,
Beverley, East Yorkshire HU17 0DF
📞 01482 881751

Overnight Charges: Under 18 £4.45 Adult £6.55

1️⃣ 🍴 GSC ♿ 🅿️ S 🚿 ¼m 🅿️ Cars and mini-buses
only. Coaches - contact Warden.

Mar 31 - Oct 31	Open X:Sun*

* Open Bank Hol Sun Apr 16, May 7, May 28,
August 27. The Hostel may be available for groups
when otherwise closed - please contact Warden.

ACCOMMODATION   🛏️5-8 1 🛏️9+ 2

Stay in a mediaeval Dominican Friary, a restored
Listed building next to the magnificent Beverley
Minster. Containing wallpaintings from the 15th
century, the Friary is mentioned in "The
Canterbury Tales". Now comfortably furnished
with modern facilities, it retains much of its
original character.

Beverley has a wealth of historic buildings, over
400 in the town, including St Mary's Church and
the Guild Hall. An annual folk festival is held in
June. It is also an excellent base for birdwatchers,
with three RSPB reserves nearby — Hornsea,
Bempton Cliffs and Blacktoft Sands. 🚶 1 ½m
🏔️2m 🚲7m 🚉13m 🍴1m

TRAVEL INFO

🚌 Frequent from surrounding areas (📞 01482
881213). 🚉 Beverley ¼m. 🚢 12m
(Hull-Rotterdam/Zeebrugge)
🅱️ 📞 01482 867430

NEXT HOSTELS

Thixendale 18m, Scarborough 28m, Malton 30m

HOW TO GET THERE

¼m SE of the town centre and 100yds NE of the
Minster on the left side of Friars Lane off Eastgate.
OS 107 GR 038393 Bart 33

---

80 BEDS   **Open: 13.00hrs**

Boggle Hole

Youth Hostel, Boggle Hole, Mill Beck,
Fylingthorpe, Whitby, North Yorkshire
YO22 4UQ 📞 01947 880352
Fax: 01947 880987

Overnight Charges: Under 18 £5.35 Adult £8.00

Family accommodation prices on p.11-13

4️⃣ 🍴 GSC 🛏️ 🔍 🅿️ 🚿 S 🍴 2m 🔥 1x30, 1x50
🅿️ ¼m from Hostel. BABA

Dec 28 - Jan 1	Open
Mar 1 - Nov 3	Open
Nov 4 - Nov 26	Open X:Sat/Sun
Nov 27 - Dec 19	Open X:Wed/Th
Dec 30 - Jan 2 '96	Open

The Hostel may be available for groups when
otherwise closed - please contact Warden.

ACCOMMODATION   🛏️1-4 2 🛏️5-8 2 🛏️9+ 5

A Hostel almost on the beach with the tides of
Robin Hood's Bay reaching the doorstep, and the
North York Moors behind. Walk along the beach
or cliff path (or by car from the main
Whitby-Scarborough Road) to reach this secluded
former mill set in a wooded ravine.

This is part of the North Yorkshire and Cleveland
Heritage Coast — high cliffs, picturesque fishing
villages, sheltered bays and dramatic headlands.
Seabirds nest in the cliffs while marine life
abounds on the rocky shore below. Famous for
its geology, jet and ammonites can be found on
the beaches. 🚲7m 🚶2m 🍴7m

TRAVEL INFO

🚌 Tees & District 93A Scarborough - Whitby
(pass BR Whitby & Scarborough), alight Robin
Hood's Bay, 1m (📞 01947 602146). 🚉 Whitby
(not Sun, except Jun - Sep) 7m; Scarborough 15m.
🅱️ 📞 01947 602674

NEXT HOSTELS

Whitby 7m, Scarborough 13m, Wheeldale 15m

ADDITIONAL INFO

Nearest access for cars ¼m.

HOW TO GET THERE

OS 94 GR 954040 Bart 36

Helmsley

Youth Hostel, Carlton Lane, Helmsley, York YO6 5HB ☎ 01439 770433

Overnight Charges: Under 18 £4.85 Adult £7.20

R-a-H ☎ 01629 825850 [1] ◻ 6SC ▥ ⊕ S ◨ ¼m
P Outside Hostel on road.

Jan 1 - Jan 31	Rent-a-Hostel
Feb 1 - Mar 4	Open Fri/Sat only
Mar 5 - Apr 12	Open X:Tu/Wed
Apr 13 - July 16	Open X:Sun
Jul 17 - Sep 2	Open
Sep 3 - Oct 29	Open X:Sun
Oct 30 - Dec 4	Open X:Tu/Wed
Dec 5 - Dec 31	Rent-a-Hostel

Open Bank Hol Apr 16, May 7, May 28.

ACCOMMODATION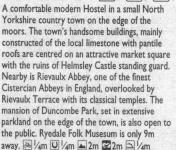

A comfortable modern Hostel in a small North Yorkshire country town on the edge of the moors. The town's handsome buildings, mainly constructed of the local limestone with pantile roofs are centred on an attractive market square with the ruins of Helmsley Castle standing guard. Nearby is Rievaulx Abbey, one of the finest Cistercian Abbeys in England, overlooked by Rievaulx Terrace with its classical temples. The mansion of Duncombe Park, set in extensive parkland on the edge of the town, is also open to the public. Ryedale Folk Museum is only 9m away. 🚶¼m U ¼m ▲ 2m ⊠ 2m ▭ ¼m

TRAVEL INFO

🚌 Scarborough & District 128 from Scarborough (passes close BR Scarborough) (☎ 01723 375463); Yorkshire Coastliner 94 from BR Malton (☎ 01653 692556). 🚉 Thirsk 15m; Malton 16m; York 24m.
ℹ ☎ 01439 770173

NEXT HOSTELS

Osmotherley 15m (20m by Cleveland Way), Malton 17m, Lockton 19m

HOW TO GET THERE

¼m E of Helmsley market place at junction of Carlton Road and Carlton Lane (just off A170)
OS 100 GR 616840 Bart 36

Lockton

Youth Hostel, The Old School, Lockton, Pickering, North Yorkshire YO18 7PY ☎ 01751 460376

Overnight Charges: Under 18 £3.60 Adult £5.35

R-a-H ☎ 01629 825850 [1] 6SC ▥ ⊠ ◨ 12yds P

Jan 1 - Apr 1	Rent-a-Hostel
Apr 2 - Sep 30	Open X:Sun
Oct 1 - Dec 31	Rent-a-Hostel

Open Bank Hol Sun Apr 16, May 7, May 28, Aug 27.

ACCOMMODATION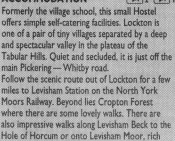

Formerly the village school, this small Hostel offers simple self-catering facilities. Lockton is one of a pair of tiny villages separated by a deep and spectacular valley in the plateau of the Tabular Hills. Quiet and secluded, it is just off the main Pickering — Whitby road.
Follow the scenic route out of Lockton for a few miles to Levisham Station on the North York Moors Railway. Beyond lies Cropton Forest where there are some lovely walks. There are also impressive walks along Levisham Beck to the Hole of Horcum or onto Levisham Moor, rich with tumuli and earthworks. 🚶4m
U ▲ ⊠ ▭ 5m

TRAVEL INFO

🚌 Yorkshire Coastliner 840 Whitby - Malton (passes close BR Whitby & Malton) (☎ 01653 692556). 🚉 Malton 14m; Levisham (North York Moors Rly & connecting with BR at Grosmont) 2m.
ℹ ☎ 01751 473791

NEXT HOSTELS

Wheeldale 11m (8m by path), Malton 14m, Scarborough 19m

ADDITIONAL INFO

No resident Warden.

HOW TO GET THERE

OS 94 GR 844900 Bart 36

60 BEDS	Open: 17.00hrs

Malton

Youth Hostel, Derwent Bank, 47 York Road, Malton, North Yorkshire YO17 0AX
☎ 01653 692077

Overnight Charges: Under 18 £4.45 Adult £6.55

 1 ½m P Cars and mini-buses only, coaches 1 ½m

Jan 2 - Jan 16	Open
Mar 31 - Sep 2	Open X:Sun/Mon*

Open Bank Hol Sun Apr 16, May 7, May 29 & Aug 28. The Hostel may be available for groups when otherwise closed - please contact Warden.

ACCOMMODATION 🛏️²⁻⁴ 3 🛏️⁵⁻⁸ 4 🛏️⁹⁺ 2

A large stone-built Victorian house on the banks of the River Derwent just outside Malton. Surrounded by rolling countryside, it is conveniently placed to visit the historic city of York, the North York Moors National Park and the Heritage coastline.
Flamingoland Zoo & Fun Park (5m) is ideal for a family day out. Visit the fascinating Beck Isle Folk Museum at Pickering or step back in time at Eden Camp Museum. Enjoy an 18m ride on a steam railway up to Grosmont near Whitby or admire the splendour of Castle Howard (of 'Brideshead Revisited'). 🚲🏊5m ▲ 🚉2m

TRAVEL INFO
🚌 From surrounding areas (☎ 01653 692556).
🚂 Malton ¾m.
ℹ️ ☎ 01653 600048

NEXT HOSTELS
Thixendale 10m, Lockton 13m, Helmsley 18m

HOW TO GET THERE
From traffic lights at centre of Malton follow signs for York. Hostel is last large house on left on York Road.
OS 100 GR 779711 Bart 33

80 BEDS	Open: 17.00hrs

Osmotherley

Youth Hostel, Cote Ghyll Osmotherley, Northallerton, North Yorkshire DL6 3AH
☎ 01609 883575 Fax: 01609 883715

Overnight Charges: Under 18 £4.85 Adult £7.20

Family accommodation prices on p.11-13

 2 ½m 🏊 1x20 P BABA

Feb 7 - Apr 3	Open X:Sun/Mon*
Apr 4 - Sep 2	Open
Sep 3 - Nov 4	Open X:Sun/Mon
Dec 24 - Dec 26	Open for Xmas package

* Open Feb 19 & 20 for spring half-term. The Hostel may be available for groups when otherwise closed - please contact Warden.

ACCOMMODATION 🛏️²⁻⁴ 2 🛏️⁵⁻⁸ 6 🛏️⁹⁺ 3

Stay in a former mill in a quiet secluded valley on the edge of the North York Moors. Modern and spacious, the Hostel has plenty of family accommodation and a safe area for playing outside. It is situated just outside the village of Osmotherley with its attractive mellow stone cottages.
The countryside is perfect for exploring by foot, bike or car. Winding lanes across open moorland, traditional farmland and villages all combine to create a unique landscape. Visit the Moors Centre at Danby and the market town of Thirsk. On the Coast-to-Coast route and the Cleveland Way. 🚶3m 🏊4m ▲ 🏕️1m 🎣3m 🚲🚉7m

TRAVEL INFO
🚌 Tees & District 90/A Middlesbrough - Northallerton (pass close BR Northallerton), alight Osmotherley ¾m (☎ 01642 210131).
🚂 Northallerton 8m.
ℹ️ ☎ 01609 776864

NEXT HOSTELS
Helmsley 15m, Ellingstring 23m, Grinton 31m

HOW TO GET THERE
OS 100 GR 461981 Bart 35

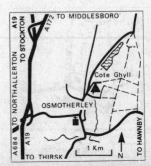

Scarborough

Youth Hostel, The White House, Burniston Road, Scarborough, North Yorkshire YO13 0DA ☎ 01723 361176 Fax: 01723 50054

Overnight Charges: Under 18 £4.45 Adult £6.55

1 🍴 ▥ S 🔒 ¼m P Cars and mini-buses. Coaches in nearby layby. BABA

Dec 31 - Jan 2	Open
Feb 1 - Mar 19	Open Fr/Sat
Mar 20 - Jul 22	Open X:Sun
Jul 23 - Sep 2	Open
Sep 3 - Dec 16	Open X:Sun/Mon

Open Bank Hol Sun Apr 16, May 7, May 28. The Hostel may be available for groups when otherwise closed - please contact Warden.

ACCOMMODATION 5 3

A former mill in a picturesque riverside setting just outside this popular seaside resort. Situated a 10 minute walk from the sea and on the fringe of the North York Moors, this Hostel is the ideal choice to enjoy many places to visit.
At the southern tip of the Heritage coastline, Scarborough is on the Cleveland Way and at the start of the 'Link Walk' through the Tabular Hills. Families can combine a traditional seaside holiday with walks in the National Park, a ride on a steam train or a visit to the Sea Life Centre. 🚴 1m
🅄 5m ⛰ 🅰 1m 🏊 ¼m 🛶 ½m

TRAVEL INFO
🚌 Frequent from surrounding areas (☎ 01723 375463). 🚉 Scarborough 2m.
ℹ ☎ 01723 373333

NEXT HOSTELS
Boggle Hole 13m, Lockton 19m (12m by path), Thixendale 25m

HOW TO GET THERE
Follow signs from roundabout at Peasholm Park.
OS 101 GR 026907 Bart 36

Thixendale

Youth Hostel, The Village Hall, Thixendale, Malton, North Yorkshire YO17 9TG
☎ 01377 288238

Overnight Charges: Under 18 £3.60 Adult £5.35

1 ▧ S 🔒 25yds P

Apr 13 - Apr 18	Open
Apr 21 - Apr 22	Open
Apr 28 - Apr 29	Open
May 5 - May 9	Open
May 10 - May 25	Open Fr/Sat
May 26 - Sep 30	Open X:Tu

ACCOMMODATION 1 1

Go 'back to school' at this tiny Hostel in a quiet village on the Wolds Way. The simple nature of the Hostel (a former school), cared for by the village postmistress, means that only limited facilities and self-catering are available.
The Yorkshire Wolds, a crescent of chalk hills from the Humber to the North Sea, offer gentle walking over beautiful rolling countryside. The green dales, arable-farmed hilltops and chalk banks give a variety of landscape, flora and fauna — and greatly contrast with other parts of Yorkshire. 🚴 10m 🅄 🅰 🆓 20m 🏊 20m 🛶 10m

TRAVEL INFO
🚌 E Yorks 135 from Driffield (infrequent) (passes close BR Driffield), alight Fridaythorpe, 3m (☎ 01377 252133). 🚉 Malton 10m (via Birdsall).
ℹ ☎ 01653 600048

NEXT HOSTELS
Malton 10m, York 17m, Beverley 18m

ADDITIONAL INFO
No showers.

HOW TO GET THERE
Take the Beverley Road left out of Malton, then right on mini roundabout signposted to Birdsall and Langton. Follow road through Birdsall up the hill, left at the cross roads, signed to Thixendale, ride down the prettiest valley in Thixendale.
OS 100 GR 843610 Bart 33

5

YORKSHIRE WOLDS, MOORS & COAST

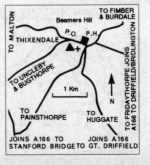

32 BEDS   **Open: 17.00hrs**

Wheeldale

Youth Hostel, Wheeldale Lodge, Goathland, Whitby, North Yorkshire YO22 5AP
☎ **01947 896350**

When the Hostel is closed, calls will automatically be diverted to another Hostel where the Warden can confirm your booking for Wheeldale.

Overnight Charges: Under 18 £3.60 Adult £5.35

1 ⦿ GSC ⊠ ⊛ S

Mar 31 - Jun 30	Open X:Wed/Th
Jul 1 - Aug 31	Open X:Wed
Sep 1 - Oct 3	Open X:Wed/Th

The Hostel may be available for parties of 15 or more in Oct - please book before end Sep.

ACCOMMODATION

A former shooting lodge surrounded by heather-clad moorland in the heart of the National Park. This Hostel offers basic accommodation in an area popular with walkers and cyclists.

Take a ride on a steam train from the 19th century railway station at nearby Goathland ('Aidensfield' in the TV series Heartbeat) down to Pickering with its medieval castle. ⛏ 12m
⛲ 12m ▲ ¼m ⚑ ¼m ⤢ 12m

TRAVEL INFO

🚌 Yorkshire Coastliner 840 Malton - Whitby, alight near Goathland, 2m (☎ 01653 692556).
🚂 Grosmont (not Sun, except Jun - Sep) 6m; Goathland (North York Moors Rly & connecting with BR at Grosmont) 3m.
ℹ ☎ 01287 60654

NEXT HOSTELS

Lockton 8m, Boggle Hole 13m, Whitby 11m

ADDITIONAL INFO

No showers. No access to door by car. No heating in bedrooms. Please bring torch.

HOW TO GET THERE

From village take Egton Bridge Road, take Hunt House road. Continue past the farm on dirt track ¼m. Cars park ¼m from Hostel in layby by turning circle above Hunt House; continue on foot. Access to Hostel for mini-buses only.
OS 94 GR 813984 Bart 36

---

66 BEDS   **Open: 17.00hrs**

Whitby

Youth Hostel, East Cliff, Whitby, North Yorkshire YO22 4JT ☎ **01947 602878**

Overnight Charges: Under 18 £4.45 Adult £6.55

1 ⦿ GSC ⊞ S ⬤ ½m P Pay & Display adjacent to Hostel (free overnight)

Feb 3 - Apr 1	Open Fr/Sat
Feb 17 - Feb 25	Open
Apr 2 - May 21	Open X:Sun
May 22 - Sep 9	Open
Sep 10 - Oct 31	Open X:Sun
Nov 1 - Dec 9	Open Fr/Sat

Open Bank Hol Sun Apr 16, May 7. The Hostel may be available for groups when otherwise closed - please contact Warden.

ACCOMMODATION

Perched on the headland above Whitby's bustling harbour, the Youth Hostel is at the top of the famous 199 steps leading to the Abbey. Converted from a stable range, it has lots of character — with beamed sloping ceilings, a log fire and panoramic views.

Cobbled streets, brightly painted boats, fishermen's cottages and a maze of old shops combine to give this ancient fishing town a lively atmosphere. Explore the Captain Cook heritage trail, take a ride on a steam train (from Grosmont 8m), enjoy a bracing clifftop walk or relax on the sandy beaches. ⛏ ½m ⛲ 8m ▲ 2m ⚑ ½m
⤢ ½m

TRAVEL INFO

🚌 Frequent from surrounding areas (☎ 01947 602146). 🚂 Whitby (not Sun, except Jun - Sep) ½m.
ℹ ☎ 01947 602674

NEXT HOSTELS

Boggle Hole 7m, Wheeldale 11m, Scarborough 20m

HOW TO GET THERE

Follow signs to abbey up Green Lane (by road) or up 199 steps (by foot)
OS 94 GR 902111 Bart 36

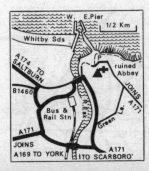

York

Youth Hostel, York International Youth Hostel, Water End, Clifton, York, North Yorkshire Y03 6LT 01904 653147
Fax: 01904 651230

Overnight Charges: Under 18 £9.70 Adult £13.10 Bed & Breakfast included.

Family accommodation prices on p.11-13

Jan 17 - Dec 10   Open

ACCOMMODATION   27   7

The Peter Rowntree Memorial Youth Hostel is a large Victorian house which was once the home of the Rowntree family, founders of the famous chocolate company. It has been extensively refurbished in recent years to offer a high standard of accommodation. Ideal for use by groups, families and individuals.

The ancient city of York is one of the main tourist attractions in Britain. There is an outstanding selection of museums and leisure attractions including the Jorvik Viking Centre, the National Railway Museum, York Minster, the City Walls, the Shambles and Castle Museum. 1m 5m 1m

TRAVEL INFO
Frequent from surrounding areas (01904 624161). York 1m (01904 642155)
01904 621756

NEXT HOSTELS
Thixendale 17m, Malton 19m, Helmsley 24m

ADDITIONAL INFO
Restaurant open all day until 22.00 hrs.

HOW TO GET THERE
Take the A19 N out of the city centre and turn left at Clifton Green or follow the riverside footpath.
OS 105 GR 589528 Bart 32

5

YORKSHIRE WOLDS, MOORS & COAST

Limestone valleys, gorges, soaring gritstone edges and wild, unspoilt moorland are just some of the attractions on offer to the thousands of people who visit the Peak District throughout the year.

Families are especially welcome and there are plenty of places to visit. The world famous Alton Towers Pleasure Park in Staffordshire and Gulliver's Kingdom at Matlock Bath are great favourites while the unique cable cars at The Heights of Abraham are popular with all ages. The show caves and caverns are also well worth a visit.

Edale YHA Activity Centre has a wide range of holidays and courses for groups and individuals.

Visit the vibrant city of Manchester and stay at YHA's brand new purpose-built Hostel which opens in Spring 1995. Situated in the Castlefield area, opposite the Museum of Science and Industry and around the corner from Granada Studios, the new Youth Hostel provides the ideal base for groups, individuals and families — with excellent facilities including small en-suite rooms and the building is fully accessible for people with disabilities.

Bretton, Crowden-in-Longdendale, Langsett, Meerbrook and Shining Cliff Youth Hostels are available on YHA's **Rent-a-Hostel scheme** which runs during the winter months (details on p.7).

USEFUL PUBLICATIONS

Peak District Inter-Hostel Walks — send s.a.e. to the YHA Regional Office listed below.

Pennine Way Central Booking Service — send a large s.a.e. to the YHA Regional Office listed below.

"Cycle and See" the Staffordshire Moorlands — send s.a.e. to the YHA Regional Office listed below.

Holidays and courses at Edale YHA Activity Centre — send large s.a.e. to the YHA Regional Office listed below or Tel: (01433) 670302.

For more information about hostelling in this area contact: YHA Northern Regional Office, P.O. Box 11, Matlock, Derbyshire DE4 2XA. Tel: (01629) 825850. Fax: (01629) 824571.

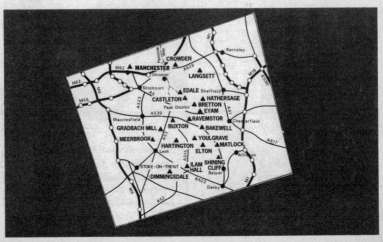

Bakewell

Youth Hostel, Fly Hill, Bakewell, Derbyshire DE45 IDN 📞 **01629 812313**
Fax: 01629 812313

Overnight Charges: Under 18 £4.45 Adult £6.55

 ¼m 🅿 Small car park - parking in town centre. BABA

Jan 2 - Apr 13	Open Fr/Sat
Apr 14 - Oct 28	Open X:Sun*
Oct 29 - Dec 23	Open Fr/Sat
Dec 24 - Dec 26	Open for Xmas party

* Open Bank Hol Sun, closed Bank Hol Mon. The Hostel may be available for families and groups when otherwise closed - please contact Warden.

ACCOMMODATION 🛏2 🛏2

Perched on a hill overlooking the lovely Wye valley, Bakewell Hostel is a modern building close to the town centre. Small and friendly, it is an ideal choice for exploring the Peak District while enjoying the atmosphere of a traditional market town.

Famous for its 'Bakewell Pudding' the town is centred around the River Wye and its medieval bridge. The surrounding countryside offers excellent walks in limestone dales and along gritstone edges. Nearby are two famous historic houses — Chatsworth House and Haddon Hall, open to the public in summer. 🚲6m 🅿7m
⛰1m 🏔18m 🦌8m 🏞9m

TRAVEL INFO
🚌 Frequent from surrounding areas (📞 01332 292200). 🚉 Matlock 8m.
ℹ 📞 01629 813227

NEXT HOSTELS
Youlgreave 3 ½, Matlock 8m, Buxton 12m

ADDITIONAL INFO
Bakewell offers guided walks, map and guidebook hire.

HOW TO GET THERE
From Rutland Square take Buxton Road turning. Turn left up North Church Street, then second turning on right after 450yds.
OS 119 GR 215685

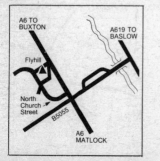

Bretton

Youth Hostel, near Eyam

Bookings c/o John and Elaine Whittington, 7 New Bailey, Crane Moor, Sheffield, S30 7AT. 📞 0114 2884541.

Overnight Charges: Under 18 £4.00 Adult £5.95

R-a-H 📞 01629 825850   2m 🅿 For cars and mini-buses only. Coaches nearby, ask booking secretary.

Jan 1 - Dec 31	Open Sat/Bank Hol Sun X:Xmas

Available for Rent-a-Hostel from Jan 1 - Feb 28 and Oct 29 - Dec 31 but not Sat when volunteer Wardened. Groups and families mid-week when booked in advance.

ACCOMMODATION 🛏1 🛏2

Bretton is a small, cosy Hostel perched high on Eyam Edge with breathtaking views over the moors and edges of the 'Dark Peak' area of the National Park. A secluded location in a tiny hamlet, close to several interesting Peak District villages.

The Hostel is less than 2m from the historic plague village of Eyam, with its fascinating church and monuments. Surrounded by unspoilt countryside, it offers a superb base for walking, cycling and exploring. Gliding available nearby (2m). 🚲7m 🅿4m 🦌 🚲½m 🏞4m

TRAVEL INFO
🚌 Various services from Sheffield, Buxton & Chesterfield (passing close BR Sheffield, Buxton Chesterfield), alight Foolow, 1m (📞 01298 23098). 🚉 Grindleford 4m; Hathersage 4m.

NEXT HOSTELS
Eyam 1 ½m, Hathersage 5m, Ravenstor 6m

ADDITIONAL INFO
Resident Warden on Sat and Bank Hol Sun only. No shop - all food must be brought. Credit card payments are not accepted at the Hostel.

HOW TO GET THERE
1 ¾m N W of Eyam
OS 119 GR 200780 Bart 29

55 BEDS	Open: 17.00hrs

Buxton

Youth Hostel, Sherbrook Lodge Harpur Hill Road, Buxton, Derbyshire SK17 9NB
☎ 01298 22287

Overnight Charges: Under 18 £4.45 Adult £6.55

🔟 🗖 ᴱˢᶜ 🗖 🔽 ⊕ S 🖐 ¼m P

Feb 10 - Mar 19	Open Fr/Sat
Mar 20 - Oct 28	Open X:Sun*
Oct 29 - Dec 23	Open Fr/Sat
Dec 24 - Dec 26	Open for Xmas package

* Open Bank Hol Sun, closed Bank Hol Mon. The Hostel may be available for groups when otherwise closed - please contact Warden.

ACCOMMODATION 2 4 2

A large house in its own wooded grounds on the outskirts of the town. Buxton is a gateway to the Peak National Park with the amenities of a busy market town — shops, indoor swimming pool, theatre, cinema etc. The Hostel is within easy walking distance of the railway station. Surrounded by the gritstone moorland with pretty limestone villages and dales to the south, Buxton is a spa town with many attractions. The town centre has some fine buildings, one of which houses the unique 'Micrarium'. Pooles Cavern is a fascinating show cave. 🏊 8m 🔟 3m 🏔 3m 🎿 3m 🚆 10m 🛶 1m

TRAVEL INFO

🚌 Frequent from surrounding areas. Many different operators. (☎ 01298 23098). 🚉 Buxton 1m.
ℹ ☎ 01298 25106

NEXT HOSTELS

Gradbach 7m, Ravenstor 7m, Castleton 12m

HOW TO GET THERE

½m S of Market Place on junction between A515 Ashbourne Road and Harpur Hill Road. Marked as 'Sherbrook Lodge' on OS.
OS 119 GR 062722 Bart 29

---

110 BEDS	Open: All Day

Castleton

Youth Hostel, Castleton Hall, Castleton, Sheffield, Derbyshire S30 2WG
☎ 01433 620235 Fax: 01433 621767

Overnight Charges: Under 18 £5.35 Adult £8.00

Seasonal Prices Jul 24 - Sep 7: Under 18 £4.85 Adult £7.20

Family accommodation prices on p.11-13

4️⃣ 🗖 🛏 🖵 🔍 🛇 S 🖐 10yds 🚲 P Nearby.
BABA

Feb 10 - Dec 23	Open

Available for Rent-a-Hostel, 32 bed annexe from Nov - Feb. The Hostel may be available for groups when otherwise closed - please contact Warden.

ACCOMMODATION 10 8 3

Situated in the heart of the village, Castleton Hall dates from the 15th century but offers all the comforts of a modern Youth Hostel. Nestling below the ruins of Peveril Castle, the village is popular with visitors, especially in the summer — with a wealth of craft shops and tea rooms. The spectacular 'Winnats Pass' and Mam Tor (the 'Shivering Mountain') overlook Castleton. Close by are several famous show caves and caverns — Treak Cliff, Blue John, Speedwell and Peak. A good centre for walking (start of the Limestone Way) and easily accessible from Sheffield and Manchester. 🏊 1m 🔟 3m 🏔 1m 🎿 5m 🚆 1m 🛶 1m 🛶 8m

TRAVEL INFO

🚌 Mainline/Hulleys/Chesterfield Transport 272/4, East Midland 280 from Sheffield (passes BR Hope) (☎ 01298 23098). 🚉 Hope 3m.
ℹ ☎ 01433 620679

NEXT HOSTELS

Edale 2m, Hathersage 6m, Eyam 7m

ADDITIONAL INFO

30-bed self-contained unit available for groups during Hostel closed period and quiet times.

HOW TO GET THERE

OS 110 GR 150828 Bart 29

Crowden-In-Longdendale

Youth Hostel, Peak National Park Hostel, Crowden, Hadfield, Hyde, Cheshire, SK14 7HZ ☎ **01457 852135 Fax: 01457 852135**

Overnight Charges: Under 18 £4.45 Adult £6.55

R-a-H ☎ 01629 825850 ① 🍴 GSC ▥ Ⓢ ◉ 4m Ⓟ Cars and coaches. BABA

Jan 1 - Mar 2	Rent-a-Hostel
Mar 3 - Apr 6	Open Fr/Sat
Apr 7 - Oct 29	Open X:Wed
Oct 30 - Nov 26	Open Fr/Sat
Nov 27 - Dec 30	Rent-a-Hostel
Dec 31 - Jan 1 '96	Open

The Hostel may be available for groups when otherwise closed - please contact Warden.

ACCOMMODATION 4 🏃²⁻⁸ 2 🏃⁹⁺ 2

Crowden-in-Longdendale is surrounded by the high moors of Bleaklow and Blackhill, the most remote and unspoilt areas of the Peak National Park. Overlooking the reservoirs of the Longdendale valley, the Hostel was converted from a row of railwaymen's cottages.

Situated on the Pennine Way and surrounded by varied walking country, the Hostel is particularly popular with walkers and climbers. It also offers a convenient rural base for visiting the many attractions of Manchester (Museum of Science and Industry, Castlefields, Granada Studios etc). 🚶6m Ⓤ7m ▲ ▲4m 🎿 🐎 🚲5m

TRAVEL INFO
🚌National Express Sheffield - Manchester (passes close BR Sheffield) 350. 🚉Hadfield (not Sun) 5m. 🛈 ☎01457 855920

NEXT HOSTELS
Edale 15m via Pennine Way, Mankinholes 24m via Pennine Way, Langsett 10m

ADDITIONAL INFO
Hostel also open to non-members.

HOW TO GET THERE
On N side of Manchester - Barnsley Road (A628) marked 'Crowden' on map.
OS 110 GR 073993 Bart 28

Dimmingsdale

Youth Hostel, Little Ranger, Dimmingsdale, Oakamoor, Stoke on Trent, Staffordshire ST10 3AS ☎ **01538 702304**

Overnight Charges: Under 18 £4.00 Adult £5.95

② GSC ▥ Ⓢ ◉ Ⓟ For cars and mini-buses (coaches at Oakamore 1m)

Jan 6 - Mar 5	Open Fr/Sat
Mar 6 - Oct 28	Open X:Sun*
Nov 1 - Jan 1	Rent-a-Hostel

* Open Bank Hol Sunday. The Hostel may be available for groups and parties when otherwise closed - please contact Warden.

ACCOMMODATION 2

A simple Hostel in secluded woods overlooking the Churnet Valley. Less than 2m from Alton Towers Leisure Park, the Hostel has basic facilities (self-catering only). It makes an ideal base for exploring this relatively undiscovered corner of the Staffordshire Moorlands.

Alton Towers is Britain's premier theme park, set in the grounds of a magnificent mansion with lovely gardens and woodland. Visit the restored canal and barge at Froghall (5m), Cheddleton Flint Mill and the pottery museums and visitor centres at Stoke-on-Trent. 🚶4m 🎣12m 🚲3m

TRAVEL INFO
🚌PMT 238 from Uttoxeter (passes close BR Uttoxeter), alight Oakamoor, ¾m (☎ 01785 223344). 🚉Blythe Bridge 6m.

NEXT HOSTELS
Ilam 12m, Meerbrook 14m, Gradbach 17m

ADDITIONAL INFO
No showers.

HOW TO GET THERE
From Oakamoor on B5417, take road S end of Bridge past Admiral Jervis. Take right fork to top of hill, turn left up farm track to Hostel.
OS 119 GR 052436 Bart 23

139 BEDS **Open: All Day**

Edale

Youth Hostel, Youth Hostel and Activity Centre, Rowland Cote, Nether Booth, Edale, Derbyshire S30 2ZH ☎ 01433 670302
Fax: 01433 670243

Overnight Charges: Under 18 £5.95 Adult £8.80

4 S 2m 1x12/18, 1x12/28 P Coaches - ring Hostel for best route into valley. Coach parking at bottom of drive. All other vehicles adjacent to centre. BABA

Jan 4 - Dec 3 Open*

* Open New Year for Activity Package.

ACCOMMODATION 2-4 10 5-8 13 9+ 2

A large country house in extensive grounds in the lovely Edale valley. Woodland, pasture and moorland extend up to the skyline — the edge of Kinder Scout plateau. A lively Hostel with holidays and courses in a wide range of outdoor activities available throughout the year (see adjacent advert).

Edale marks the start of the 'Pennine Way' and the wild moorland and heather that form the northern backbone of England. Explore gritstone edges, limestone caves, cycle trails and reservoirs. Splendid views from the Hostel tempt walkers to explore footpaths in every direction.

TRAVEL INFO

No Service. Edale 2m. On Friday evenings (16.00-20.00 hrs) all trains are met to take you to the Hostel.

i ☎ 01433 670207

NEXT HOSTELS

Castleton 4m, Hathersage 10m, Crowden 15m (Pennine Way over moors)

ADDITIONAL INFO

Ideal venue for conferences, seminars and group workshops. Activity holidays and courses for all levels of ability. Residents ☎ 01433 670225

HOW TO GET THERE

1m E of Edale village marked 'Rowland Cote' on OS. Good road and rail access.

OS 110 GR 139865 Bart 29

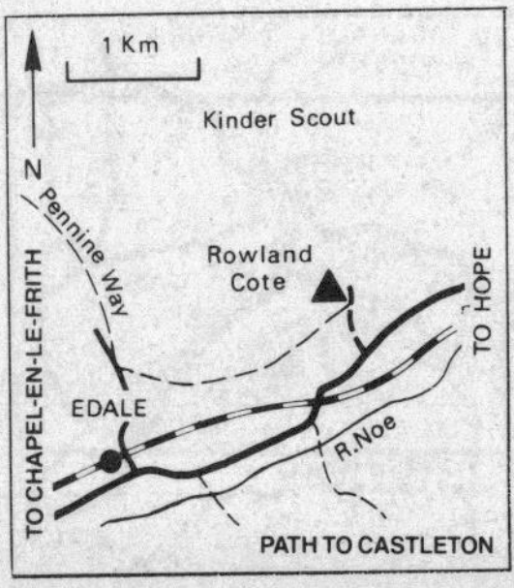

COME TO...

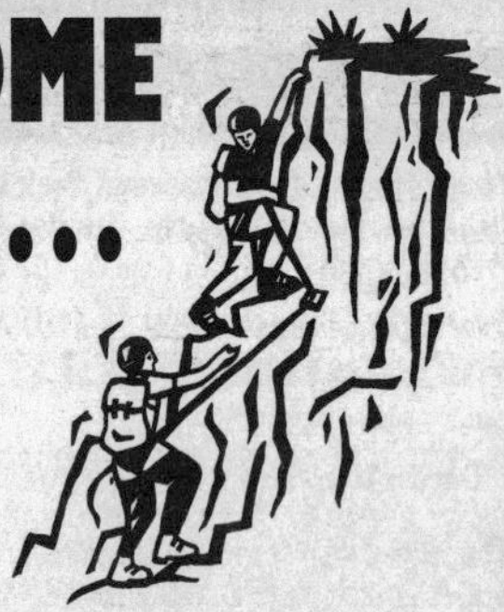

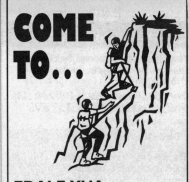

EDALE YHA ACTIVITY CENTRE for a weekend, mini-break or longer holiday. Try lots of different sports on our multi-activity breaks. Learn or improve new skills on our specialist courses.

Abseiling
Archery
Adventure Course
Caving
Climbing
Canoeing
Hang Gliding
Kayaking
Mountain Biking
Navigation
Orienteering
Pony Trekking
Walking

Qualified, experienced Instructors. All specialist equipment provided.

Approved by Mountain Leader Training Board, British Canoe Union, British Orienteering Federation. Member of British Activity Holiday Association. Affiliated to National Caving Association.

For details contact:
Edale YHA Activity Centre, Rowland Cote, Nether Booth, Edale, Derbyshire S30 2ZH

Tel (01433) 670302
Fax (01433) 670243

| **32 BEDS** | **Open: 17.00hrs** |

Elton

Youth Hostel, Elton Old Hall, Main Street, Elton, Matlock, Derbyshire DE4 2BW
☎ 01629 650394

Overnight Charges: Under 18 £4.00 Adult £5.95

2 6SC ⊞ ⊠ S ▣ 1m P Main Street

| Mar 4 - Oct 28 | Open |
| Dec 24 - Dec 26 | Open |

The Hostel may be available for groups when otherwise closed - please contact Warden.

ACCOMMODATION   2 2 1

The Old Hall is a 17th century listed building on the main street of the village. It is a simple Hostel, retaining its old-world character, cosy and friendly. A limited meals service is available (continental breakfasts, evening snacks and packed lunches).

Surrounded by a network of lanes and trails, Elton is popular with cyclists. Bicycles are available for hire at several centres. The nearby towns of Bakewell and Matlock offer many attractions for all the family and there is a wealth of industrial heritage sites to visit. 🚴 7m

▲ 🚃 7m

TRAVEL INFO
🚌 Hulleys 170 Matlock-Bakewell (passes close BR Matlock) (☎ 01298 23098). 🚉 Matlock (Not Sun, except Apr-Oct) 5m.
🛈 ☎ 01629 813227

NEXT HOSTELS
Youlgreave 2 ½m, Bakewell 7m, Matlock 7m

ADDITIONAL INFO
Snacks served up to 8pm.

HOW TO GET THERE
The Hostel is at the E end of Elton village on the main street.
OS 119 GR 224608 Bart 24

| **60 BEDS** | **Open: 17.00hrs** |

Eyam

Youth Hostel, Hawkhill Road, Eyam, Sheffield, Derbyshire S30 1QP
☎ 01433 630335

Overnight Charges: Under 18 £4.85 Adult £7.20

2 🍴 ⊞ 🔍 S ▣ ½m 🅿 1x25, 1x35 P

Feb 10 - Apr 13	Open X:Sun
Apr 14 - Sep 2	Open
Sep 3 - Oct 28	Open X:Sun
Oct 29 - Nov 25	Open Fr/Sat
Dec 27 - Jan 1 '96	Open for New Year party

The Hostel may be available for groups when otherwise closed - please contact Warden.

ACCOMMODATION   3 4 3

A large Victorian house perched on a wooded hillside overlooking the village. The Hostel — which enjoys extensive views across the countryside — is an ideal base for walking in both the limestone 'White Peak' and gritstone 'Dark Peak' areas of the National Park.

Famous as the plague village, Eyam has many historic reminders of 1665 when the Great Plague of London reached Derbyshire. Here and in the neighbouring villages, colourful well dressings are held throughout the summer. Eyam's annual carnival is at the end of August.

🚴 🍴 3m ▲ 🏛 20m 🎣 ½m 🚃 🚉 5m

TRAVEL INFO
🚌 As for Bretton, but alight Eyam. 🚉 Grindleford 3 ½m; Hathersage 4m.
🛈 ☎ 01629 813227

NEXT HOSTELS
Hathersage 6m, Bakewell 7m, Ravenstor 7m

HOW TO GET THERE
Follow signs to the public/coach park and continue up the hill - Hostel 600yds on the left past 'The Edge' and 'Windward House'.
OS 119 GR 219769 Bart 29

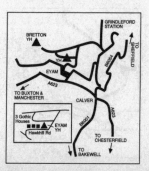

97 BEDS   Open: 17.00hrs

Gradbach Mill

Youth Hostel, Gradbach, Quarnford, Buxton, Derbyshire SK17 0SU ☎ **01260 227625**
Fax: 01260 227334

Overnight Charges: Under 18 £5.35 Adult £8.00

Family accommodation prices on p.11-13

| Feb 10 - Oct 28 | Open |
| Oct 29 - Dec 3 | Open X:Sun |

The Hostel may be available for groups and parties when otherwise closed - please contact Warden.

ACCOMMODATION 🛏 10 🛏 8 🛏 1

A former mill on the banks of the River Dane in a quiet, unspoilt corner of the Peak District. Set in its own secluded grounds with playing field, the Hostel is popular with families and walkers exploring this relatively unknown part of the Staffordshire Moorlands.

Nearby are the Roaches, gritstone crags offering superb climbing. Buxton (spa town with shops, indoor swimming pool, theatre etc) is 6m away, Manchester only 30m. Alton Towers theme park is 14m, Quarry Bank Mill at Styal (National Trust) 20m. 🚶 12m 🅿 2m 🚲 2m 🚩 7m

TRAVEL INFO

🚌 PMT X23 Sheffield - Hanley (passes close BR Sheffield & Buxton), alight Flash, 2 ½m (☎ 01298 23098). 🚉 Buxton 7m; Macclesfield 9m.
🛈 ☎ 01298 25106

NEXT HOSTELS

Buxton 7m, Hartington 12m, Ravenstor 12m

ADDITIONAL INFO

Ground floor accommodation suitable for people with disabilities.

HOW TO GET THERE

OS 118 GR 993661 Bart 29

---

120 BEDS   Open: 17.00hrs

Hartington Hall

Youth Hostel, Hartington, Buxton, Derbyshire SK17 0AT ☎ **01298 84223**
Fax: 01298 84415

Overnight Charges: Under 18 £5.35 Adult £8.00

Beds in courtyard barn with en-suite showers may also be booked: Under 18 £7.20 Adult £10.60

Family accommodation prices on p.11-13

P Limited with some roadside parking too. BABA

Feb 10 - Dec 23	Open
Dec 24 - Dec 26	Open for Xmas party
Dec 27 - Dec 30	Open

The Hostel may be available for groups and parties when otherwise closed - please contact Warden.

ACCOMMODATION 🛏 4 🛏 1 🛏 6

This magnificent 17th century manor house — complete with a room where Bonnie Prince Charlie once slept — retains many period features including oak panelling and open fires. A converted barn overlooking the courtyard offers good family accommodation with some en-suite facilities.

Surrounded by a patchwork of limestone walls, Hartington is one of Derbyshire's prettiest villages. Many walks centre on the Dove and Manifold valleys, and bikes can be hired to explore the Tissington and High Peak trails. Alton Towers and the American Adventure theme park are within easy reach. 🚶 3m 🅿 10m ⛰ 1m 🚲 10m 🚲 7m 🚩 10m 🚩 12m

TRAVEL INFO

🚌 Bowers 442 from BR Buxton; also from other areas on Sun & Bank Holidays only (☎ 01298 23098). 🚉 Buxton 12m, Matlock (Not Sun, except Apr - Oct) 13m

NEXT HOSTELS

Youlgreave 6m, Ilam 9m, Buxton 11m

ADDITIONAL INFO

Paddock for ponies available.

HOW TO GET THERE

OS 118 GR 131603 Bart 24

PEAK DISTRICT & MANCHESTER

42 BEDS — Open: 17.00hrs

Hathersage

Youth Hostel, Castleton Road, Hathersage, Sheffield S30 1AH ☎ 01433 650493
Fax: 01433 650493

Overnight Charges: Under 18 £4.85 Adult £7.20

  ⅛m P In village 300yds.

Jan 6 - Apr 11	Open Fr/Sat
Apr 12 - Oct 28	Open X:Sun*
Oct 29 - Nov 26	Open Fr/Sat
Dec 31 - Jan 1 '96	Open

* Open Bank Hol Sun, closed Bank Hol Mon. The Hostel may be available when otherwise closed - please contact Warden.

ACCOMMODATION 🛏3 🛏5

A Victorian house on the edge of this popular village, the Hostel is just a few minutes walk from the railway station (Manchester — Sheffield line) and a good starting point for exploring the Peak National Park or the 'White Peak Way' circular walk.

Overlooked by Stanage and Millstone Edge (two impressive gritstone edges) Hathersage attracts climbers of all abilities. The village has associations with Little John (buried here) and Charlotte Bronte who based 'Jane Eyre' on the area. Outdoor heated swimming pool open in summer. Sheffield is 10m. 🏊6m 🚲6m ▲1m 🎣1m 🛶¼m

TRAVEL INFO
🚌 Mainline/Hulleys 272, East Midland 280 from Sheffield (☎ 01298 23098). 🚉 Hathersage ½m.
ℹ️ ☎01433 620679

NEXT HOSTELS
Castleton 6m, Edale 12m, Eyam 4m

ADDITIONAL INFO
Booking bureau for 'White Peak Way' (sae for details).

HOW TO GET THERE
The Hostel is 100yds on right past the George Hotel on the road to Castleton.
OS 110 GR 226814 Bart 29

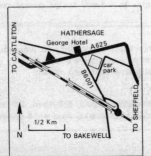

---

148 BEDS — Open: 13.00hrs

Ilam Hall

Youth Hostel, Ilam Hall, Ashbourne, Derbyshire, DE6 2AZ ☎ 01335 350212
Fax: 01335 350350

Overnight Charges: Under 18 £5.95 Adult £8.80

Beds in Brewhouse Wing with en-suite showers may also be booked: Under 18 £7.20 Adult £10.60

Family accommodation prices on p.11-13

  3m 1x40
P NT car park (NT charge). BABA

Jan 6 - Feb 9	Open Fr/Sat
Feb 10 - Nov 25	Open
Dec 27 - Jan 1	Open for New Year party

The Hostel may be available for groups and parties when otherwise closed.

ACCOMMODATION 🛏10 🛏12 🛏2

A magnificent National Trust mansion surrounded by a Country Park on the banks of the River Manifold near Dovedale. Beautifully decorated, it retains the atmosphere of a large country house while offering all modern comforts. Family rooms with en-suite showers are available in the 'Brewhouse Wing'.

Popular with walkers and hang gliders (course available), the area is one of the most beautiful in the National Park. Alton Towers is only 9m away.
🏊2m 🚲15m ▲🎿10m 🎣🛶5m

TRAVEL INFO
🚌 Infrequent from Ashbourne; otherwise from Derby, Manchester (passing close BR Derby & Macclesfield), alight Ilam Cross Roads, 2½m (☎ 01335 292200). 🚉 Matlock (Not Sun, except Apr-Oct) 14m; Uttoxeter 15m; Derby 18m.
ℹ️ ☎01335 43666

NEXT HOSTELS
Hartington 9m, Dimmingdale 12m, Matlock 14m

ADDITIONAL INFO
Facilities for people with disabilities. Residents call box ☎ 01335 350379. Ideal venue for conferences. Discounts for Alton Towers available for Hostel residents (tickets on sale at reception).

HOW TO GET THERE
OS 119 GR 131506 Bart 24

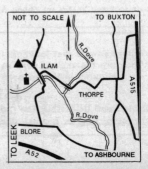

Langsett

Youth Hostel, Nr Penistone

Bookings to: c/o John and Elaine Whittington, 7 New Bailey, Crane Moor, Sheffield, S30 7AT. ☎ 0114 2884541.

Overnight Charges: Under 18 £4.00 Adult £5.95

 ☎ 01629 825850 ① 6SC ▥ ☒ ▣ P Cars and mini-buses (coaches contact Bookings Secretary)

Jan 1 - Jul 31	Open every Sat and Bank Hol Sun
Aug 1 - Aug 31	Open
Sep 1 - Dec 31	Open every Sat and Bank Hol Sun X:Xmas

Available for Rent-a-Hostel all year. Families and group bookings in advance. Voluntary Warden on Sat, Bank Hol Sun and during August.

ACCOMMODATION 🛏²⁻⁴ 4 🛏⁵⁻⁸ 1 🛏⁹⁺ 1

Overlooking Langsett village and reservoir and the superb heather moors beyond, this comfortable Hostel is in the north east of the Peak District. Popular with small self-catering groups, both the main Hostel (22 beds) and the annexe (14 beds but not Sat) are available for exclusive use all year.

The northern moorland of the National Park, Bleaklow, Margery Hill and the Derwent valleys are easily accessible from Langsett, as well as the gentler terrain to the north east. Holmfirth ('Summer Wine' country) is only 8m away. Sheffield with its superb leisure facilities, museums and shops is 12m. ▣ 🎬 5 ½m 🚇 3m

TRAVEL INFO

🚌 Globe/Barnsley & District/Yorkshire Traction 381 from BR Barnsley (pass close BR Penistone) (☎ 0742 768688). 🚉 Penistone 3m.

NEXT HOSTELS

Crowden 10m, Hathersage 18m, Edale 20m

ADDITIONAL INFO

No shop - all food must be brought. Credit card payments are not accepted at the Hostel.

HOW TO GET THERE

OS 110 GR 211005 Bart 29

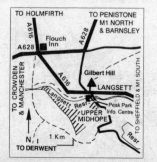

Manchester

Youth Hostel, Potato Wharf, Castlefield, Greater Manchester M3

For bookings and enquiries contact: Central Bookings, City of London YHA, 36 Carter Lane, London EC4V 5AD ☎ 0171 248 6547 Fax: 0171 236 7681

Overnight Charges: Under 18 £7.20 Adult £10.60

Family accommodation prices on p.11-13

  ¼m

⊞ P BABA IBN

Feb 1 - Dec 31	Open

ACCOMMODATION 🛏²⁻⁴ 32 🛏⁵⁻⁸ 4

Opening in Spring 1995, this brand new purpose-built Hostel on the canalside of the vibrant Castlefield area of Manchester offers accommodation in ultra modern rooms, mostly sleeping four — with en-suite facilities, TV, table and chairs. There are also facilities for people with disabilities.

Museums, galleries, historic houses, shops, restaurants and theatres are all on offer close to the Hostel — making it an ideal destination for an enjoyable city break for groups, individuals and families. ▣ 20m 🚇

NEXT HOSTELS

Crowden 20m, Mankinholes 50m, Edale 50m

ADDITIONAL INFO

Facilities for people with disabilities. Conference and meeting rooms facilities.

HOW TO GET THERE

From Picadilly and Victoria train stations and the bus station - take the metrolink and disembark at the G-Mex station. From the Airport - take the rail link to Picadilly station and then the metro to G-Mex. By Road - follow signs for Castlefied/Museum of Science and Industry. Hostel opposite the Museum and next door to the Castlefield Hotel.

49 BEDS   Open: 13.00hrs

Matlock

Youth Hostel, Youth Hostel & Training Centre, 40 Bank Road, Matlock, Derbyshire DE4 3NF ☎ 01629 582983
Fax: 01629 583484

Overnight Charges: Under 18 £5.95 Adult £8.80

Family accommodation prices on p.11-13

▢▢▢▢▢▢▢▢▢▢▢▢ 1x25, 2x8
▢ For cars only (coaches 300yds). BABA

Jan 1 - Oct 28	Open
Oct 29 - Dec 23	Open X:Sun
Dec 24 - Dec 26	Open for Xmas party

The Hostel may be available for groups when otherwise closed - please contact Warden.

ACCOMMODATION   12   1   1

This handsome Victorian building overlooks the town across to the hills beyond. Only 2 mins walk from the town centre, it is close to all amenities — shops, indoor swimming pool, bus and rail stations (with connections to London) and the M1.

The Derbyshire Dales offer many places to visit for all the family: the Heights of Abraham (cable cars), the Peak District Lead Mining Museum, the National Tramway Museum and the new watersports centre at Carsington Water. The American Adventure and Alton Towers theme parks are within easy reach. 7m

TRAVEL INFO

Frequent from surrounding areas (☎ 01332 292200). Matlock (not Sun, except Apr-Oct) ¼m.

ℹ ☎ 01629 55082

NEXT HOSTELS

Bakewell 8m, Youlgreave 10m, Hartington 13m

ADDITIONAL INFO

Excellent training and conference facilities available for all to use. Includes one conference room (25max) and two seminar rooms (8-10max)

HOW TO GET THERE

From Crown Square, the Hostel is 200yds up Bank Road on right.

OS 119 GR 300603 Bart 24

Meerbrook

Youth Hostel, Old School, Meerbrook, Leek, Staffordshire ST13 8SJ

Bookings c/o Mrs I Carlile, Elton Youth Hostel, Elton Old Hall, Main Street, Elton, Matlock, Derbyshire DE4 2BW. ☎ 01629 650394.

Overnight Charges: Under 18 £4.00 Adult £5.95

R-a-H ☎ 01629 825850 ② GtC ▥ ▦ S ▣ 3m
P For cars only - coaches on outskirts of village.

Jan 1 - Apr 13	Rent-a-Hostel
Apr 14 - Jun 30	Open Fr/Sat*
Jul 1 - Sep 9	Open
Sep 10 - Oct 28	Open Fr/Sat*
Oct 29 - Dec 23	Rent-a-Hostel

* Available for Rent-a-Hostel (Sun-Th). Open Bank Hol Sun.

ACCOMMODATION 🛏2 🛏1 🛏1

Popular with walkers exploring this quiet corner of the Staffordshire Moorlands, this simple self-catering Hostel — a former school house in the centre of Meerbrook village — has a cosy common/dining room which retains the original beamed roof.
The Roaches, a long ridge of millstone grit enjoyed by climbers, is within sight of the Hostel. For birdlife and fishing Tittesworth Reservoir is on the edge of the village. The museums, factory shops and potteries of Staffordshire are all within easy reach, as well as Alton Towers theme park (8m). 🚶2m ⛰ 🚲 🚆 🛏11m

TRAVEL INFO
🚌PMT X23 Shefield - Hanley (passes close BR Stoke-on-Trent & Buxton), alight Blackshaw Moor, 2m (☎ 01298 23098). 🚉Stoke-on-Trent 15m.

NEXT HOSTELS
Gradbach 5m, Buxton 11m, Hartington 12m

ADDITIONAL INFO
Credit cards can only be accepted for bookings made in advance.

HOW TO GET THERE
OS 119 GR 989608 Bart 29

Ravenstor

Youth Hostel, Millers Dale, Buxton, Derbyshire SK17 8SS ☎ 01298 871826
Fax: 01298 871275

Overnight Charges: Under 18 £5.95 Adult £8.80

① ▥ ⓕ ▦ ▨ ⊛ S ▣ 2m 🚲 1x30-40 P BABA

Feb 10 - Apr 7	Open X:Sun
Apr 8 - Oct 28	Open
Oct 29 - Dec 23	Open Fr/Sat

The Hostel may be available for groups when otherwise closed - please contact Warden.

ACCOMMODATION 🛏3 🛏2 🛏4

A large country house in extensive wooded grounds, Ravenstor stands high above the limestone dales of the River Wye. Owned by the National Trust, it offers modern comforts in a traditional atmosphere — with log fires, a grand staircase and stained glass windows.
The 'White Peak' around Ravenstor is a beautiful area of little fields bounded by limestone walls. Walkers enjoy the Monsal Trail with its famous viaduct and the picturesque villages with their summer well-dressings. The market towns of Bakewell and Buxton are both 7m. 🚶1 ½m ⛰4m 🚲 🚆 🛏9m

TRAVEL INFO
🚌From Sheffield, Buxton (passes close BR Sheffield & Buxton) (☎ 01298 23098). 🚉Buxton 8m.
🅱 ☎01298 25106

NEXT HOSTELS
Eyam 7m, Buxton 7m, Bakewell 7m

ADDITIONAL INFO
Special meals for groups and meetings. 'Sunship Earth' children's holidays. Residents ☎ 01298 871204

HOW TO GET THERE
From A6 between Bakewell and Buxton take the B6049 to Tideswell. The Hostel is 1m past Millers Dale.
OS 119 GR 152732

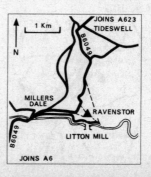

26 BEDS Open: 17.00hrs

Shining Cliff

Youth Hostel, Shining Cliff Woods, Nr Ambergate, Derbyshire

Bookings c/o Mrs I Carlile, Elton Youth Hostel, Main Street, Elton, Matlock, Derbyshire DE4 2BW. ☎ 01629 650394.

Overnight Charges: Under 18 £3.60 Adult £5.35

R-a-H ☎ 01629 825850 1 GSC 2m P Cars 10min walk from Hostel (coaches by arrangement).

Jan 1 - Apr 13	Rent-a-Hostel
Apr 14 - Jul 21	Open Sat*
Jul 22 - Sep 2	Open
Sep 3 - Oct 28	Open Sat*
Oct 29 - Dec 31	Rent-a-Hostel

* Available for Rent-a-Hostel (Sun-Fr). Open Bank Hol Sun.

ACCOMMODATION

2-4 2 5-8 3

This secluded Hostel in the middle of a wood offers simple accommodation ideal for self-catering small groups and families.

Shining Cliff Woods is a Site of Special Scientific Interest in the Derwent valley. Nearby is Matlock Bath with its attractions, Cromford with a former water mill open to the public and the varied scenery, villages and dales of the Peak National Park. 4m 8m

TRAVEL INFO

Trent 123, 124, R1 from Derby, alighting ½m NW of Ambergate on some, thence ¾m, or at Ambergate, 1m, on others (☎ 01332 292200). Ambergate (Not Sun, except Apr-Oct).

i ☎ 01629 55082

NEXT HOSTELS

Matlock 8m, Elton 10m, Youlgreave 12 ½m

ADDITIONAL INFO

No shop or resident Warden. Bring torch. Credit cards accepted for advance bookings only.

HOW TO GET THERE

From Ambergate cross river by church. Cyclists up hill, turn R into woods by 3rd farm. Walkers turn R by river, through works yard and up path through woods. From Wirksworth-Belper road, turn L at pack crossroad, L into woods and R at fork.

OS 119 GR 335522

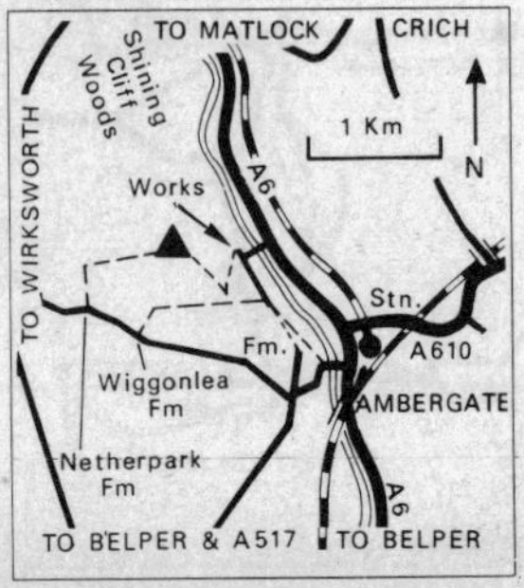

46 BEDS Open: 17.00hrs

Youlgreave

Youth Hostel, Fountain Square, Youlgreave, Nr Bakewell, Derbyshire DE4 1UR

☎ 01629 636518 Fax: 01629 636518

Overnight Charges: Under 18 £4.85 Adult £7.20

1 GSC S P For cars on street and in village car park (100yds). Coaches by arrangement. BABA

Feb 10 - Apr 13	Open Fr/Sat
Apr 14 - Oct 28	Open X:Sun
Oct 29 - Dec 23	Open Fr/Sat only

The Hostel may be available for groups when otherwise closed - please contact Warden.

ACCOMMODATION

2-4 1 5-8 1 9+ 2

Youlgreave Youth Hostel is a unique and impressive building — the former village Co-op. Externally it retains fascinating features from its days as the village store, internally it offers all the facilities of a traditional Youth Hostel.

The village is just 3m south of Bakewell, close to the limestone dales of the rivers Bradford and Lathkill with their numerous footpaths. Cycles can be hired at Parsley Hay (4m) with safe cycling along former railway lines. Chatsworth House and Haddon Hall are both close by. 2m 8m 10m 10m 9m

TRAVEL INFO

Hulleys 170/1 from Bakewell (with connections from BR Chesterfield & Matlock) (☎ 01298 23098). Matlock 11m.

i ☎ 01629 813227

NEXT HOSTELS

Bakewell 3m, Elton 3m, Matlock 8m

HOW TO GET THERE

Hostel in centre of village on main street opposite the Fountain Well.

OS 119 GR 210641 Bart 29

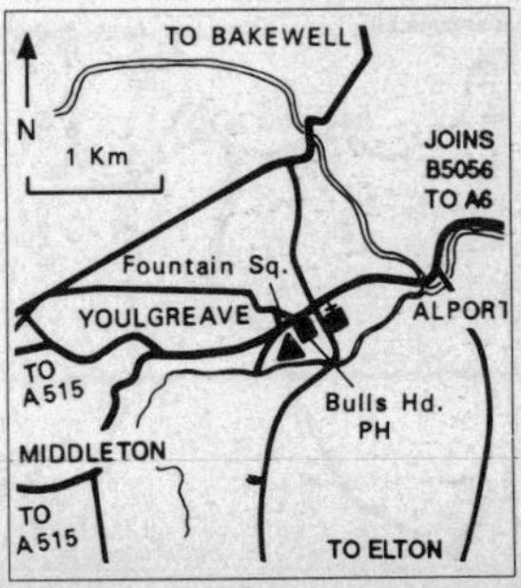

The contrast of rolling farmland, the high wolds of the North and the bulb fields around Spalding highlight the variety of landscapes in Lincolnshire. There are many fascinating houses and shops in the steep streets surrounding Lincoln's Castle and medieval cathedral. View the Magna Carta and enjoy discovering the market cafes and riverside pubs — not forgetting the famous Lincolnshire pork butchers.

The surrounding countryside has something to offer all year round — spring comes alive with spectacular blooms, summer is rich and green, and winter sees the arrival of wildfowl along the coast and upon the rivers to reserves such as Peakirk, near Thurlby. The whole area is also ideal cycling country with many quiet by-ways.

Woody's Top and Thurlby Youth Hostels are available on our **Rent-a-Hostel scheme** which runs during the winter months (details on p.7).

USEFUL PUBLICATIONS

Budget accommodation in Eastern England and individual Hostel Leaflets — send s.a.e. to the YHA Regional Office listed below or phone our Literature Line on (01426) 951683 (local call charge).

**For more information about hostelling in this area contact:
YHA South England Regional Office, 11B York Road, Salisbury, Wiltshire SP2 7AP.
Tel: (01722) 337494.
Fax: (01722) 414027.**

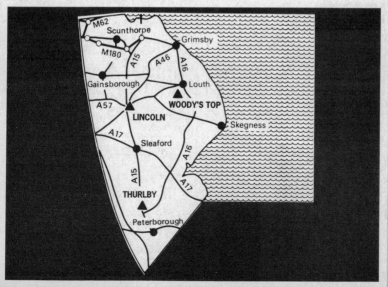

50 BEDS   Open: 17.00hrs

Lincoln

**Youth Hostel, 77 South Park, Lincoln,
Lincolnshire LN5 8ES** ✆ 01522 522076
Fax: 01522 567424

Overnight Charges: Under 18 £5.35 Adult £8.00

Family accommodation prices on p.11-13

1 🔲 🏧 🚿 ⊞ 🅿️ 1x35, 1x20 🅿 BABA

Mar 1 - Mar 31	Open X:Sun/Mon
Apr 1 - Jun 30	Open X:Sun*
Jul 1 - Aug 31	Open
Sep 1 - Oct 31	Open X:Sun/Mon
Nov 1 - Dec 16	Open Fr/Sat

* Open Bank Hol Sun.

ACCOMMODATION   🛏️2-4 3 🛏️5-8 4 🛏️9+ 2

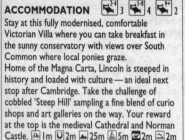

Stay at this fully modernised, comfortable
Victorian Villa where you can take breakfast in
the sunny conservatory with views over South
Common where local ponies graze.
Home of the Magna Carta, Lincoln is steeped in
history and loaded with culture — an ideal next
stop after Cambridge. Take the challenge of
cobbled 'Steep Hill' sampling a fine blend of curio
shops and art galleries on the way. Your reward
at the top is the medieval Cathedral and Norman
Castle. 🚲 1m ⛵ 2m 🏔️ 25m 🎿 5m ⛷️ 2m 🏊 2m

TRAVEL INFO
🚌 Frequent from surrounding areas (✆ 01522
532424). 🚉 Lincoln 1m.
ℹ️ ✆ 01522 529828

NEXT HOSTELS
Woody's Top 25m, Thurlby 35m, Cambridge 85m

ADDITIONAL INFO
Ideal venue for conferences and special out of
season/exclusive use.

HOW TO GET THERE
OS 121 GR 980700 Bart 30

---

34 BEDS   Open: 17.00hrs

Thurlby

**Youth Hostel, 16 High St, Thurlby, Bourne,
Lincolnshire PE10 0EE** ✆ 01778 425588

Overnight Charges: Under 18 £4.85 Adult £7.20

Family accommodation prices on p.11-13

R-a-H ✆ 01722 337494

2 🔲 🏧 🅰️ ⊠ 🚿 ⊞ 🔲 200yds 🅿 Cars and
mini-buses. Coaches by prior arrangement.

Jan 1 - Apr 6	Rent-a-Hostel
Apr 7 - Oct 31	Open X:Th
Nov 1 - Dec 31	Rent-a-Hostel

ACCOMMODATION   🛏️5-8 1 🛏️4+ 2

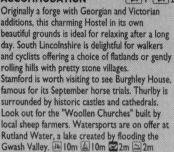

Originally a forge with Georgian and Victorian
additions, this charming Hostel in its own
beautiful grounds is ideal for relaxing after a long
day. South Lincolnshire is delightful for walkers
and cyclists offering a choice of flatlands or gently
rolling hills with pretty stone villages.
Stamford is worth visiting to see Burghley House,
famous for its September horse trials. Thurlby is
surrounded by historic castles and cathedrals.
Look out for the "Woollen Churches" built by
local sheep farmers. Watersports are on offer at
Rutland Water, a lake created by flooding the
Gwash Valley. 🚲 10m 🏔️ 10m ⛷️ 2m 🏊 2m

TRAVEL INFO
🚌 Delaine's service from Peterborough (passes
close BR Peterborough) (✆ 01778 422866).
🚉 Peterborough 15m; Grantham 18m.
ℹ️ ✆ 01780 55611

NEXT HOSTELS
Lincoln 35m, Kings Lynn 38m, Copt Oak 50m

HOW TO GET THERE
OS 130 GR 097168 Bart 25

Woody's Top

Youth Hostel, Ruckland, Nr Louth, Lincolnshire LN11 7RF 📞 **01507 533323**

For advance bookings, contact: Regional Booking Service, 11B York Road, Salisbury, Wilts. SP2 7AP 📞 01722 337494 Fax: 01722 414027. From Apr 14 - Aug 31, bookings for next night only direct to Hostel.

Overnight Charges: Under 18 £4.00 Adult £5.95

R-a-H 📞 01722 337494 1 GSC ▦ ⬚ ⊛ S ⬚ 3m
P Cars and mini-buses.

Jan 1 - Apr 13	Rent-a-Hostel
Apr 14 - Aug 31	Open
Sep 1 - Dec 31	Rent-a-Hostel

ACCOMMODATION   🛏️4   🛏️1

This small traditional Hostel is a converted barn in the rolling Lincolnshire Wolds. It has recently been carefully extended and improved to provide a good standard of accommodation — with small rooms and a cosy lounge with wood burning stove.

The tranquil Lincolnshire Wolds offer good opportunities for walking and cycling. There are small market towns to explore, as well as the famous coastal resorts of Skegness and Mablethorpe. You can also visit the National Fishing Heritage Centre and the Cadwell Park racing circuit. 🚶6m 🅿️6m ⛰️15m 🚲3m 🛒6m

TRAVEL INFO
🚌 Road Car/Stagecoach Grimsby/Cleethorpes/Appleby 25, 51, X21 Grimsby - Louth (all pass close BR Grimsby), thence 6m. Roadcar Lincoln - Louth (infrequent) (📞 01507 600800) 🚌 Thorp Culvert (not Sun, except Jun - Sep) 18m; Grimsby Town 22m; Lincoln Central 25m.
ℹ️ 📞01507 609289

NEXT HOSTELS
Lincoln 25m, Thurlby 55m, Beverley 50m

ADDITIONAL INFO
No credit cards accepted at Hostel.

HOW TO GET THERE
From A16 take minor road to Ruckland, turn left, Hostel 100yds from junction.
OS 122 GR 332786 Bart 30

7

LINCOLNSHIRE

Snowdonia National Park is home to some of the highest mountains in England and Wales as well as deep lakes, steep passes, valleys, waterfalls, beautiful beaches and a network of Youth Hostels.

Enthusiasts can enjoy exhilarating walks and climbs while valley and forest walks are ideal for the casual walker. Other recreational opportunities include abseiling, cycling, horse riding and a selection of watersports. The coastline of North Wales is a succession of sandy beaches and family resorts.

Attractions are as varied as the countryside — sea and mountain zoos, graceful abbeys, narrow gauge railways and the stately homes of Erddig Hall and Chirk Castle, as well as mighty castles like Conwy Caernarfon and the magnificent Harlech which were built by Edward I after conquering Wales. Experience the industrial heritage by visiting the slate caverns, copper mines, museums and other sites.

Historic Chester has been welcoming visitors since Roman times. Enjoy its complete circuit of city walls, medieval shopping galleries and other attractions.

In an area popular with cyclists, Bala Youth Hostel (Plas Rhiwaedog) lies close to Bala Lake (Llyn Tegid), a superb location for water sports and fishing. For long distance walkers, the Offa's Dyke Path starts on the north coast at Prestatyn and runs south passing close to Maeshafn and Llangollen Youth Hostels. The central Snowdonia Youth Hostels give climbers easy access to numerous crags providing some of the best routes in Europe. For walkers, the mountains and valleys offer many routes to suit all abilities.

Bryn Gwynant and Maeshafn Youth Hostels are available on YHA's **Rent-a-Hostel scheme** which runs during the winter months (details on p.7).

USEFUL PUBLICATIONS

Youth Hostel leaflets — send s.a.e. to the YHA Regional Office listed below.

Idwal Log — send 90p (incl. p&p, cheques payable to YHA) to the YHA Regional Office listed below.

For more information about hostelling in this area contact: YHA Wales Regional Office, 1 Cathedral Road, Cardiff, CF1 9HA. Tel: (01222) 396766 or 222122. Fax: (01222) 237817.

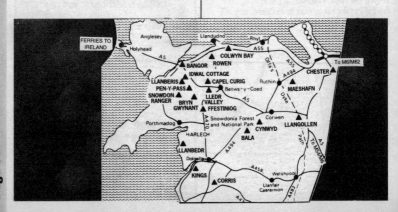

Bala

Youth Hostel, Plas Rhiwaedog,
Rhos-y-Gwaliau, Bala, Gwynedd, LL23 7EU
☎ 01678 520215

Overnight Charges: Under 18 £4.85 Adult £7.20

 1m **P** For cars and mini-buses.
Coaches - contact Warden.

Apr 4 - May 27	Open X:Sun/Mon*
May 28 - Sep 2	Open
Sep 5 - Sep 16	Open X:Sun/Mon
Oct 3 - Oct 28	Open X:Sun/Mon

* Open Bank Hol Mon May 8. The Hostel may be available for groups (max 30) when otherwise closed - please contact Warden.

ACCOMMODATION 🛏2 🛏3 🛏2

This 17th century manor house with walled garden provides traditional accommodation — including a cosy dining room. Located only 1m from Bala Lake on the eastern edge of Snowdonia National Park, it is a fantastic spot for undisturbed walking and a variety of watersports. Most of the beautiful Snowdonia National Park is within an hour's drive. The area is ideal for walks of all levels, winding through superb countryside. Cycling is popular in the quiet lanes or over four mountain passes, while watersports are well catered for at Bala Lake and the River Tryweryn.
🚶2m 🅿2m 🏞2m 🧗1½m 🎣2m 🛶1½m

TRAVEL INFO
🚌 Crossville Cymru 94 Wrexham-Barmouth (passes close BR Ruabon & Barmouth), alight Bala 2m (☎ 01286 679535). 🚃 Blaenau Ffestiniog 21m.
🛈 ☎01678 521021

NEXT HOSTELS
Cynwyd 12m, Kings 20m, Llangollen 22m

ADDITIONAL INFO
Barbecue in grounds. Wales Tourist Board approved.

HOW TO GET THERE
From Bala take road to hamlet of Rhos-y-Gwaliau over narrow bridge and left along farm road.
OS 125 **GR** 947348 **Bart** 22

Bangor

Youth Hostel, Tan-y-Bryn, Bangor, Gwynedd
LL57 1PZ ☎ 01248 353516
Fax: 01248 371176

Overnight Charges: Under 18 £5.35 Adult £8.00

 ½m **P** BABA

Feb 1 - Feb 28	Open X:Mon/Tu
Mar 1 - Oct 31	Open
Nov 1 - Nov 26	Open X:Mon/Tu
Dec 22 - Dec 31	Open

The Hostel may be available for groups in Feb and Nov when otherwise closed.

ACCOMMODATION 🛏3 🛏6 🛏3

This large Victorian house — with superb views of the Snowdonia mountains — offers comfortable accommodation, excellent facilities and a friendly atmosphere. Only 10mins walk from the city centre (and easily accessible by public transport), it is an ideal base for exploring Anglesey and Snowdonia.
Bangor is the gateway to Anglesey, Snowdonia and onwards to Ireland. The city boasts a Victorian Pier, cathedral, theatre and maritime centre. The popular Penrhyn, Beaumaris and Caernarfon castles are easily reached. A central location for North Wales coastline attractions and Snowdonia. 🏰1m 🏊5m 🚲3m 🛶½m

TRAVEL INFO
🚌 Frequent from surrounding areas (☎ 01286 679535). 🚃 Bangor 1¼m. ⛴17m (Holyhead-Dublin)
🛈 ☎01248 351915

NEXT HOSTELS
Idwal Cottage 9m, Llanberis 11m, Colwyn Bay 20m

ADDITIONAL INFO
Stay in the same room as Vivien Leigh or Lawrence Olivier who were regular visitors in the 40s when the building was a private home! Wales Tourist Board approved.

HOW TO GET THERE
On A5122 50yds before sharp bend into Bangor. From railway station, go along High Street onto A5122. Hostel on right.
OS 114 **GR** 590722 **Bart** 27

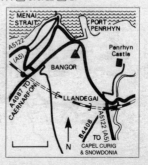

Bryn Gwynant

Youth Hostel, Bryn Gwynant, Nantgwynant, Caernarfon, Gwynedd LL55 4NP
☎ 01766 890251

Overnight Charges: Under 18 £5.35 Adult £8.00

Family accommodation prices on p.11-13

R-a-H ☎ 01222 396766

1 ⬛ GSC ▦ 🔍 ◪ 🌀 S ◩ 1m ⬛ 1x32 P Cars and mini-buses. Coaches - layby at end of drive.

Jan 3 - Mar 31	Open X:Sun/Mon
Apr 1 - Sep 3	Open
Sep 18 - Oct 31	Open
Dec 22 - Dec 31	Open

The Hostel may be available for sole group usage all year.

ACCOMMODATION   🛏2-4 8 🛏5-8 3 🛏9+ 2

This beautiful mansion with stunning views overlooking Llyn Gwynant lake has been recently refurbished to offer comfortable accommodation with wash-basins in every room. An ideal base for exploring Snowdonia. Popular with school groups mid-week in spring and summer terms.
The mountains appeal to walkers and climbers alike. Take the Watkin Path from the Hostel up to Snowdon summit or try mountain biking, orienteering, canoeing and pony trekking. 🚲5m
U 6m ▲ 🏕 🎿 ⛵ ¼m

TRAVEL INFO
🚌 Bws Gwynedd 11 Caernarfon-Llanberis; otherwise 11 or 97 to Beddgelert from Porthmadog (passes close BR and Ffestiniog Rly Porthmadog) or from Caernarfon, thence 4m (☎ 01286 679378) 🚃 Betws-y-Coed (not Sun, except Jul/Aug) 13m; Bangor 25m.
🛈 ☎01766 512981

NEXT HOSTELS
Pen-y-Pass 4m, Capel Curig 8m, Snowdon Ranger 9m (7m over Snowdon)

ADDITIONAL INFO
Wales Tourist Board approved.

HOW TO GET THERE
On the A498 with Capel Curig 8m to the E and Beddgelert 4m to the W.
OS 115 GR 641513 Bart 27

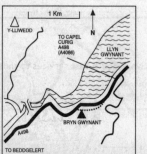

Capel Curig

Youth Hostel, Plas Curig, Capel Curig, Betws-y-Coed, Gwynedd LL24 0EL
☎ 016904 225

Overnight Charges: Under 18 £5.35 Adult £8.00

1 ⬛ ▦ S ◩ ¾m P For cars only. Coaches - contact Warden.

Mar 1 - Mar 31	Open X:Sun/Mon
Apr 1 - Aug 31	Open
Sep 1 - Sep 30	Open X:Sun/Mon
Oct 1 - Oct 31	Open
Nov 1 - Nov 30	Open X:Sun/Mon/Tu
Dec 1 - Dec 16	Open X:Sun/Mon

The Hostel may be available for groups in Nov and Dec when otherwise closed.

ACCOMMODATION   🛏2-4 8 🛏5-8 6

Conveniently situated in the heart of the Snowdonia National Park with good access by all modes of transport, the Hostel overlooks a river and forest with inspiring views of Moel Siabod. This is an ideal family base with many small dormitories, all with wash-basins.
Fine position for riverside walks, forest tracks and waterfalls leading to Betws-y-Coed. Nearby attractions are Swallow Falls (3m), Ugly House (2m), Gwydyr Forest and Penmachno Woollen Mill. 🚲5m ▲ 🏕 🎿¾m 🎿¾m ⛵5m

TRAVEL INFO
🚌 Bws Gwynedd 19 Llandudno - Llanberis (pass BR Betws-y-Coed & Llandudno Junction) (☎ 01286 679378). 🚃 Betws-y-Coed (not Sun, except Jul/Aug) 4m.
🛈 ☎01690 710426

NEXT HOSTELS
Lledr Valley 10m (5m by mountain), Pen-y-Pass 5m, Idwal Cottage 6m

ADDITIONAL INFO
As of May 1995 the telephone number will change to ☎ 01690 720225.

HOW TO GET THERE
Road access from Betws-y-Coed difficult. Proceed to junction with A4086, turn around and return to Hostel. Steep driveway.
OS 115 GR 726579 Bart 27

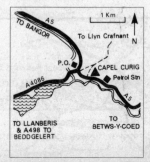

LOOKING FOR A BOOK OR MAP?

Then please send for a copy of our unique 24 page stocklist which contains over 3000 new books and maps for outdoor recreation/sport and travel, selected from publishers world-wide.

CORDEE

3a De Montfort Street
Leicester
LE1 7HD
Great Britain

Trade Also Supplied.

Rent-a-Hostel

Imagine having your own key to a Youth Hostel, with just you and your friends, family or group using the building as your own out-of-the-way retreat. A chance to escape everyday hassles, staying in a well kept property with good self-catering facilities, perhaps an open fire for chilly evenings and in a setting that takes your breath away.

Sounds good? Well, it's all possible with YHA's Rent-a-Hostel scheme where you do just that – 'rent' the whole building, on a short term basis of course. There are 52 Youth Hostels on the scheme which runs from September to March each year. Locations range from the beautiful Somerset Coast to the spectacular Lake District. Prices vary, but start at around £126 for a two night break. Details in the Rent-a-Hostel leaflet, available free fby filling in the coupon at the back of this guide.

yha

See Wiltshire by Public Transport

PUBLIC TRANSPORT INITIATIVES

✳ **DAY ROVER** valid on most bus services in the county (prices shown valid for 1995) £4.85 Adult, £3.60 Child (under 16)/OAP (over 60), £9.70 Family (2 adults, 2 children).

✳ **DAY ROVER** links to: Swidon, Salisbury, Bath, Cirencester, Oxford, YHA Hostels.

✳ TELEPHONE ENQUIRY SERVICE **0345 090899** ✳ Area Timetable Booklets

✳ *Wiltshire Bus* MAP & GUIDE ✳ Summer Sunday Bus Links

RAIL LINKS

✳ Fast Inter-City, Regional Railways and Network South East services to most parts of the country.

FURTHER INFORMATION

Director of Planning & Highways, Wiltshire County Council, County Hall, Trowbridge, BA14 8JD

Wiltshire
COUNTY COUNCIL
PLANNING & HIGHWAYS

Chester

Youth Hostel, Hough Green House, 40 Hough Green, Chester, Cheshire CH4 8JD
☎ 01244 680056 Fax: 01244 681204

Overnight Charges: Under 18 £5.95 Adult £8.80

3 ▢ ▦ ◉ ▦ S ▢ 1m ◈ 1x30 P Cars only - coaches ½m BABA

Jan 6 - Dec 2	Open

ACCOMMODATION ⬔²⁻⁴ 7 ⬔⁵⁻⁸ 8 ⬔⁹⁺ 5

This large Victorian house provides a very high standard of comfort and facilities, only 20mins walk from the historic city centre of Chester and close to a large park. All bedrooms have wash-basins and individual bed lights.
Chester is a fascinating city with a complete circuit of city walls, 'Rows' mediaeval shopping arcades, a beautiful 900 year old cathedral, Chester Zoo, Grosvenor museum and Deva Roman Experience. It is a convenient base for exploring Liverpool's attractions and a gateway to North Wales. ⬚ 1m ▢ 1m

TRAVEL INFO
🚌 Frequent from surrounding areas (☎ 01244 602666). 🚆 Chester 1 ½m.
Manchester airport 40m.
ℹ ☎ 01244 313126

NEXT HOSTELS
Llangollen 22m, Colwyn Bay 41m, Maeshafn 16m

ADDITIONAL INFO
Good venue for residential meetings, seminars and workshops.

HOW TO GET THERE
SW of city centre on A5104 (signposted to Saltney) 350yds from traffic lights on right-hand side.
OS 117 GR 397651 Bart 28

Colwyn Bay

Youth Hostel, Foxhill, Nant-y-Glyn, Colwyn Bay, Clwyd LL29 6AB ☎ 01492 530627

Overnight Charges: Under 18 £4.45 Adult £6.55

1 ▢ ⓢⓢⓒ ◉ ▦ S ▢ 1 ½m P Cars and mini-buses (coaches - contact Warden)

Feb 17 - Mar 31	Open Fr/Sat only
Apr 1 - Jun 30*	Open X:Sun
Jul 1 - Aug 31	Open
Sep 1 - Oct 28	Open X:Sun/Mon

* Open Bank Hol Sun Apr 16, May 7, May 28. The Hostel may be available for groups when otherwise closed - please contact Warden.

ACCOMMODATION ⬔⁵⁻⁸ 7 ⬔⁹⁺ 3

This large house — set in five acres of grounds in the peaceful and picturesque Nant-y-Glyn Valley — is surrounded by woodland yet only a mile inland from the popular seaside resort of Colwyn Bay.
This is an ideal base for visiting the north Wales coastline and seaside resorts of Llandudno, Rhyl and Colwyn Bay, while Bangor and Snowdonia are also within easy reach. Attractions in the area include the Welsh Mountain Zoo, Bodnant Gardens, Conwy Castle and Town Walls, and Rhyl Sun Centre. 🎡 ⓤ 4m ⬚ 1 ½m 🎣 4m
🏊 1m ▢ 1 ½m

TRAVEL INFO
🚌 Frequent from surrounding areas (☎ 01492 596969). 🚆 Colwyn Bay 2m. 🚢 35m (Holyhead-Dublin)
ℹ ☎ 01492 534432

NEXT HOSTELS
Rowen 12m, Bangor 20m, Chester 41m

ADDITIONAL INFO
Large grounds and annexe can be used for sole use by groups of max 24 people. Wales Tourist Board approved.

HOW TO GET THERE
Turn off A55 Old Colwyn exit to join A547 (Colwyn Bay). At Park Hotel turn left up Nant-y-Glyn road across crossroads. Hostel ½m on right.
OS 116 GR 847776 Bart 27

Corris

Youth Hostel, Canolfan Corris, Old School, Old Road, Corris, Machynlleth, Powys SY20 9QT ☎ **01654 761686**

Overnight Charges: Under 18 £4.85 Adult £7.20

Family accommodation prices on p.11-13

 1x35 P Small car park 30 metres. Coaches nearby.

Jan 1 - Feb 28	Open Fr/Sat only
Mar 1 - Apr 30*	Open X:Mon
May 1 - Aug 31	Open
Sep 1 - Oct 29	Open X:Mon
Nov 3 - Dec 16	Open Fr/Sat only
Dec 23 - Dec 31	Open

* Open Bank Hol Mon Apr 17. The Hostel may be available for groups when otherwise closed.

ACCOMMODATION 🛏2-4 2 🛏5-8 1 🛏9+ 2

This picturesque former village school with panoramic views of Corris was imaginatively renovated in 1992 to create an ambiance in keeping with its educational heritage. It has an energy efficiency and conservation theme. Attractions include: Centre for Alternative Technology 3m, Talyllyn Narrow Gauge Railway, Cader Idris 3m and King Arthur's Labyrinth. 🚲6m ⛰1m 🎣 🚌 6m

TRAVEL INFO
🚌 34 Machynlleth - Aberllefenni. Bws Gwynedd 94A Aberystwyth - Dolgellau (passes BR Machynlleth). Bws Gwynedd 30 Machynelleth - Tywyn (via Corris) (passes BR Machynlleth and Tywyn) Trawscambria 701 🚉 Machynlleth 6m. 🛈 ☎ 01654 702401

NEXT HOSTELS
Kings (Dolgellau) 15m, Borth 19m, Bala 19m

ADDITIONAL INFO
Cheques payable to 'Canolfan Corris'. Credit cards not accepted. Wales Tourist Board approved.

HOW TO GET THERE
Turn off A487 road at Briach Goch Hotel into village. At Slaters Arms Pub, turn left uphill. The Hostel is 150metres on the right.
OS 124 GR 753080 Bart 22

Cynwyd

Youth Hostel, The Old Mill, Cynwyd, Corwen, Clwyd. LL21 0LW ☎ **01490 412814**

Overnight Charges: Under 18 £3.60 Adult £5.35

Family accommodation prices on p.11-13

 ⅛m P

Apr 14 - Apr 22	Open
Apr 28 - Apr 30	Open
May 26 - Sep 30*	Open X:Sun

* Open Bank Hol Sun May 28, Aug 27. The Hostel may be available for groups when otherwise closed - please contact Warden.

ACCOMMODATION 🛏2 🛏1

This former water woollen mill on the banks of the River Trystion is now a basic, traditional Hostel in a tranquil village setting. Separate self-contained cottage sleeping five plus cot is available for advance bookings from April to October.
As well as fine walking in the Berwyn Mountains and good cycling country with 'Rough Stuff' routes, you'll also find Bala Lake nearby (12m) — excellent for sailing, canoeing and windsurfing. The Pistyll Rhaeadr Falls (the tallest in Wales) are also well worth a visit. 🚲10m 🛶3m ⛰1m 🏛10m 🚂2m

TRAVEL INFO
🚌 Bws Gwynedd 94 Wrexham - Barmouth (passes close BR Ruabon & Barmouth) (☎ 01286 679535). 🚉 Ruabon 18m. 🛈 ☎ 01978 860828

NEXT HOSTELS
Llangollen 12m, Bala 12m, Maeshafn 18m

ADDITIONAL INFO
Wales Tourist Board approved.

HOW TO GET THERE
On B4401 from Corwen, bear left before bridge and follow road for 100 metres. From Bala turn right before bridge then 2nd right.
OS 125 GR 057409 Bart 22

38 BEDS	**Open: 17.00hrs**

Ffestiniog

Youth Hostel, Caerblaidd, Llan Ffestiniog, Nr Blaenau Ffestiniog, Gwynedd LL41 4PH
☎ 01766 762765

Overnight Charges: Under 18 £4.45 Adult £6.55

1 ⓖ ⊕ Ⓢ ▣ ½m Ⓟ Cars and mini-buses only - coaches ¼m

Mar 31 - May 31	Open X:Wed
Jun 1 - Aug 31	Open
Sep 1 - Oct 31	Open X:Wed

ACCOMMODATION 2 1 3

This large house on the northern edge of the picturesque village of Llan Ffestiniog is ideally situated in the centre of the Snowdonia National Park — with magnificent views across the beautiful Vale of Ffestiniog. Two small dormitories good for families.

In an area of unsurpassed beauty, enjoy mountain walking on the Moelwyns or superb gentle walks to waterfalls and over moorlands — starting right from the Hostel's doorstep. Local sights include Ffestiniog Railway, Gloddfa Ganal slate mine and nature trails. 🚶12m Ⓤ5m ▲ 🚲1m ⊠

TRAVEL INFO
🚌 Bws Gwynedd 1, 2, 35 from BR & Ffestiniog Rly Blaenau Ffestiniog, Porthmadog and Machynlleth (☎ 01286 679378). 🚉Blaenau Ffestiniog (joint BR & Ffestiniog Rly) (no BR Sun service, except July - Aug) 3m.
ℹ️ ☎01766 830360

NEXT HOSTELS
Lledr Valley 10m, Bryn Gwynant 14m, Llanbedr 17m

ADDITIONAL INFO
Wales Tourist Board approved.

HOW TO GET THERE
From Blaenau Ffestiniog take A470 towards Llan Ffestiniog, turn right beside stone bus shelter, then ½m down road.
Ⓞ🅢 124 🅶🅡 704427 🄱🄰🄡🅃 22

---

56 BEDS	**Open: 17.00hrs**

Idwal Cottage

Youth Hostel, Nant Ffrancon, Bethesda, Bangor, Gwynedd LL57 3LZ
☎ 01248 600225

Overnight Charges: Under 18 £4.45 Adult £6.55

 2 🍴 ⓖ 🛏 ▲ ⊕ Ⓢ ▣ 5m Ⓟ

Jan 6 - Mar 31	Open X:Tu/Wed/Th
Apr 1 - Jun 30*	Open X:Sun
Jul 1 - Aug 31	Open
Sep 1 - Sep 30	Open X:Sun
Oct 3 - Oct 28	Open X:Sun/Mon

* Open Bank Hol Sun Apr 16, May 7, 28. The Hostel may be available for groups when otherwise closed - please contact Warden.

ACCOMMODATION 2 1 3

Originally a quarry manager's cottage, this Hostel stands in a small wood near Ogwen Lake below the impressive Glyder mountains and overlooks the Nant Ffrancon Pass. Log fire in winter. Idwal Cottage is an excellent base for fellwalking and climbing of all grades. The Cwm Idwal Nature Reserve just above the Hostel is good for birdwatching and a favourite spot for geology/geography field work. Easy access to North Wales beaches and other attractions. 🚶10m ▲ ▣12m 🚲½m ⊠ 🚽10m

TRAVEL INFO
🚌 Bws Gwynedd 95 Bangor - Llanrwst (passes BR Betws-y-Coed); otherwise Purple Motors 6/7 from Bangor (pass BR Bangor), alight Bethesda, 4m (☎ 01286 679535) 🚉Bangor 12m; Betws-y-Coed (not Sun, except July/Aug) 11m.
ℹ️ ☎01690 710426

NEXT HOSTELS
Pen-y-Pass 10m (5m by mountain), Capel Curig 6m, Llanberis 12m (7m by mountain)

ADDITIONAL INFO
Wales Tourist Board approved.

HOW TO GET THERE
On the A5, 5m S of Bethesda.
Ⓞ🅢 115 🅶🅡 648603 🄱🄰🄡🅃 27

Kings (Dolgellau)

Youth Hostel, Kings, Penmaenpool, Dolgellau, Gwynedd LL40 1TB
☎ 01341 422392

Overnight Charges: Under 18 £4.45 Adult £6.55

Family accommodation prices on p.11-13

1 ○ GSG ▦ ▲ S ● 4m P Cars and mini-buses. Coaches - contact Warden.

Feb 3 - Feb 25	Open Fr/Sat only
Mar 1 - Mar 31	Open X:Sun/Mon
Apr 1 - Jun 30*	Open X:Sun
Jul 1 - Sep 3	Open
Sep 19 - Oct 28	Open X:Sun/Mon
Nov 3 - Nov 25	Open Fr/Sat only
Dec 22 - Dec 31	Open

* Open Bank Hol Sun Apr 16, May 7, 28. The Hostel may be available for sole usage by groups Nov - Feb when otherwise closed.

ACCOMMODATION 7

This traditional Hostel is situated in a beautiful wooded valley with magnificent views up to Cader Idris and the Rhinog Mountain Ranges. Large grounds with a bonfire and barbecue site. As well as many high and low level walks and easy access to Cader Idris, the area is ideal for other outdoor activities. Attractions include: Welsh Gold, steam railways, beaches, RSPB & Forest Visitor Centres, Cymer Abbey and the Quaker Heritage Centre. 6m ▢ ▲ 5m 2m

TRAVEL INFO

Bws Gwynedd 28 Dolgellau - Tywyn (passes close BR Fairbourne), alight 1m W of Penmaenpool, thence 1m (☎ 01286 679535). Morfa Mawddach 5m.
☎ 01341 422888

NEXT HOSTELS
Corris 15m, Llanbedr 13m, Bala 20m

ADDITIONAL INFO
Wales Tourist Board approved.

HOW TO GET THERE
Follow A493 1m W Penmaenpool, turn uphill opposite Abergwynant Trekking Centre, then 1m along lane situated on right hand river bank
OS 124 GR 683161 Bart 22

Llanbedr (nr. Harlech)

Youth Hostel, Plas Newydd, Llanbedr, Barmouth, Gwynedd LL45 2LE
☎ 01341 241287

Overnight Charges: Under 18 £4.45 Adult £6.55

Family accommodation prices on p.11-13

1 ○ GSG ▦ 🔍 S ● P Cars and mini-buses, coaches ½m from Hostel

Mar 1 - Apr 30*	Open X:Sun/Mon
May 1 - Jun 30*	Open X:Mon
Jul 1 - Aug 31	Open
Sep 1 - Oct 28	Open X:Sun/Mon
Dec 22 - Dec 31	Open

* Open Bank Hol Sun/Mon Apr 16, 17, May 7, 8, 28, 29. The Hostel may be available for groups when otherwise closed - please contact Warden.

ACCOMMODATION 3 7

This homely former Victorian guest house in the centre of a picturesque village is well placed for both sandy seashores (1 ½m) and unspoilt mountain wilderness. It's also ideal for families with small dormitories and adjacent to a good public playground with safe access.
Excellent walking and climbing in the heart of the majestic Rhinog mountain range. Shell Island with its sand dunes is well known for its variety of shells and wildlife. Harlech Castle, narrow gauge railways and nature trails are also close by. 15m 3m 3m 10m 3m

TRAVEL INFO
Bws Gwynedd 38 Dolgellau-Blaenau Ffestiniog (☎ 01286 679535) Llanbedr ½m.
☎ 01766 780658

NEXT HOSTELS
Kings 13m, Ffestiniog 17m, Bryn Gwynant 20m

ADDITIONAL INFO
Excellent base for primary school visits. Wales Tourist Board approved.

HOW TO GET THERE
On A496 in centre of village.
OS 124 GR 585267 Bart 22

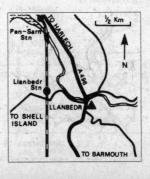

8

NORTH WALES

Llanberis

Youth Hostel, Llwyn Celyn, Llanberis,
Caernarfon, Gwynedd LL55 4SR
☎ 01286 870280

Overnight Charges: Under 18 £5.35 Adult £8.00

1 🍴 ☕ 🚿 🛍 🅿 Cars and mini-buses. Coaches, ask Warden.

Feb 12 - Feb 27	Open X:Tu/Wed
Mar 16 - Mar 31	Open X:Tu/Wed
Apr 1 - Aug 31	Open
Sep 1 - Oct 30	Open X:Tu/Wed
Nov 3 - Dec 18	Open X:Tu/Wed/Th

The Hostel may be available for groups in Feb, Mar, Nov and Dec when otherwise closed. Sole usage available Mon-Th for groups of 20 or more taking meals.

ACCOMMODATION 2 ⛺2-4 2 ⛺5-8 3 ⛺9+

This large comfortable Hostel, located on the hillside overlooking the lakes of Llyn Padarn and Llyn Peris only ½m from the town of Llanberis, is well placed for sightseeing in North Wales. Snowdon summit is visible from the Hostel. This is an excellent base for mountain walks providing contrasting scenery and pleasant low level rambling through Country Park. Tourist attractions include Snowdon Mountain Railway, Museum of the North, Welsh Slate Museum and Caernarfon Castle. ⛴2m ▲ 🏔1m 𝔽1m ▦

TRAVEL INFO
🚌 KMP 88 from Caernarfon; Williams 76/7 from Bangor (pass close BR Bangor), on both alight ½m NW of Llanberis, thence ½m (☎ 01286 679535) 🚉 Bangor 11m
🛈 ☎ 01286 870765

NEXT HOSTELS
Snowdon Ranger 11m (4m by mountain), Pen-y-Pass 5 ½m, Bangor 11m

ADDITIONAL INFO
Hostel is especially suitable for annual club re-unions. Wales Tourist Board approved.

HOW TO GET THERE
½m S W of Llanberis. From High Street take Capel Coch Road, keep left at fork in road.
OS 115 GR 574596 Bart 27

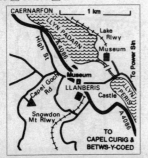

Lledr Valley (Betws-y-Coed)

Youth Hostel, Lledr House, Pont-y-Pant,
Dolwyddelan, Gwynedd LL25 0DQ
☎ 016906 202

Overnight Charges: Under 18 £4.85 Adult £7.20

2 🍴 ☕ 🅰 🅰 🚿 🛍 1m ✎ 1x35 🅿 Cars and one coach.

Mar 1 - Mar 31	Open X:Sun/Mon
Apr 1 - Apr 30*	Open X:Sun
May 1 - Aug 31	Open
Sep 1 - Oct 31	Open X:Sun
Nov 2 - Nov 30	Open X:Tu/Wed
Dec 1 - Dec 16	Open Th/Fr/Sat

* Open Bank Hol Sun Apr 16, May 7. The Hostel may be available for groups when otherwise closed - please contact Warden.

ACCOMMODATION 6 ⛺2-4 2 ⛺5-8 3 ⛺9+

This pleasant traditional Hostel — set in a beautiful steep sided wooded valley only 4 ½m from the popular town of Betws-y-Coed — offers comfortable accommodation, good home-cooked food and a friendly atmosphere. This is an excellent location for educational studies. The area offers good mountain, valley and forest walking. The rich industrial heritage can be seen at the slate quarries and caverns, copper mines and woollen mills. Visit the great Welsh castles at Caernarfon, Conwy and Dolwyddelan. 🚴5m ⛴4m ▲ 🏔2m 🐎 ▦

TRAVEL INFO
🚌 No Service. 🚉 Pont-y-Pant (not Sun, except July - Aug) ¾m.
🛈 ☎ 01690 710426

NEXT HOSTELS
Capel Curig 10m (5m by track), Ffestiniog 10m, Bryn Gwynant 18m (10m by path)

ADDITIONAL INFO
Large play area opposite Hostel. Wales Tourist Board approved.

HOW TO GET THERE
On A470 1m north west of Dolwyddelan. From Pont-y-Pant railway station turn left along road, then left across bridge and left along main road.
OS 115 GR 749534 Bart 27

Llangollen

Youth Hostel, YHA Study and Activity
Centre, Tyndwr Hall, Tyndwr Road,
Llangollen, Clwyd LL20 8AR

☎ 01978 860330 (Group bookings
☎ 01978 861750) Fax: 01978 861709

Overnight Charges: Under 18 £5.35 Adult £8.00

[4] [⌂] [♨] [📺] [🛁] [⊕] [S] [□] 1 ½m [✎] 3x40
[P] [BABA]

Mar 31 - Oct 31	Open

The Hostel may be available for group activity
holidays, conferences, management training,
school journey parties and other advance group
bookings when otherwise closed - contact
Warden.

ACCOMMODATION   2 🛏 7

This Victorian manor and coach house provides
good catering and comfortable accommodation
with a range of facilities for groups and
individuals. Set in the beautiful Vale of Llangollen,
the centre provides a superb base for exploring
north Wales and borders. Popular with school
groups mid-week in spring/summer terms.
Scenic area with walks in the Berwyn Mountains
and local canoe slalom course on the River Dee.
The area is ideal for studies in geography,
geology, history and industrial heritage. [⛷] [U] 6m
[▲] [⛺] [🎿] 4m [⛵] [🚣] 5m

TRAVEL INFO

🚌 Crosvillage Cymru 1/B. 94, Bryn Melyn X5
Wrexham-Llangollen (pass BR Ruabon), alight
Llangollen, thence 1 ½m (☎ 0353 704035)
🚂 Chirk 6m; Ruabon 6m.
🛈 ☎ 01978 860828

NEXT HOSTELS

Cynwyd 12m, Bala 22m, Maeshafn 16m

ADDITIONAL INFO

YHA Activity Centre offers a wide range of
adventure holidays for groups and individuals led by
our own qualified instructors. Wales Tourist Board
accredited activity centre. Good conference venue.

HOW TO GET THERE

From A5 E of Llangollen, follow Hostel signs.
[OS] 117 [GR] 232413 [Bart] 23

8

NORTH WALES

31 BEDS   **Open: 17.00hrs**

Maeshafn

Youth Hostel, Holt Hostel, Maeshafn, Mold, Clwyd CH7 5LR

All correspondence and enquiries to: YHA Wales Regional Office, 4th Floor, 1 Cathedral Road, Cardiff CF1 9HA ☏ 01222 222122
Fax: 01222 237817

Overnight Charges: Under 18 £4.45 Adult £6.55

R-a-H ☏ 01222 222122 ⅰ GSC ▦ ◭ ✚ S ◨ 2m
P

Apr 12 - Apr 18	Open
Apr 21 - Jun 29*	Open Fr/Sat
Jul 1 - Aug 31	Open
Sep 1 - Sep 30	Open Fr/Sat

* Open Bank Hol Sun May 7, 28. The Hostel is available during closed periods for Rent-a-Hostel.

ACCOMMODATION   🛏1-4 1 🛏5-8 1 🛏9+ 2
This purpose-built Swiss chalet-style Hostel on the slopes of Moel Findeg offers traditional accommodation in quiet, peaceful surroundings. Ideal walking in the Clwydian Range or on Offa's Dyke just 3m away. Ample opportunities to explore the beautiful countryside by bike. Attractions in the area include Loggerheads Country Park and nature trails, hill forts, Wrexham Geological and Industrial museums, and castles at Howarden and Flint. 🚲3m 🅿2m
▲2m ⛺15m ✈2m 🚂2m ⚓4m

TRAVEL INFO
🚌Crosville Cymru from Mold, with connections from BR Flint and Chester. Alight Maeshafn Road end, 1½ (☏ 01352 704035). 🚉Buckley 8m; Flint 10m; Chester 16m. 🛈 ☏01352 759331

NEXT HOSTELS
Llangollen 16m, Chester 16m, Cynwyd 18m

ADDITIONAL INFO
Good Hostel shop. Wales Tourist Board approved.

HOW TO GET THERE
From Mold take A494 to Ruthin, then follow Maeshafn sign. Bear left at village. Hostel ½m on left.
OS 117 GR 208606 Bart 28

Penmaenmawr

We regret that this Youth Hostel is now closed. The nearest Youth Hostels are Rowen 7m, Colwyn Bay 10m and Bangor 12m.

Pen-y-Pass

Youth Hostel, Pen-y-Pass, Nant Gwynant, Caernarfon, Gwynedd LL55 4NY
☎ 01286 870428 Fax: 01286 872434

Overnight Charges: Under 18 £5.95 Adult £8.80

Family accommodation prices on p.11-13

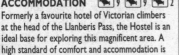

4 ⊠ 6SC ▤ ⚲ ⚲ S ⬛ 3 ½m ⚲ 1x30, 1x12

P Public car park opposite - permits from Warden.

Feb 1 - Mar 31	Open X:Sun/Mon
Apr 1 - Oct 31	Open
Nov 1 - Nov 30	Open X:Sun/Mon

The Hostel may be available for groups (Feb, Mar & Nov) when otherwise closed.

ACCOMMODATION ▦²⁻⁴9 ▦⁵⁻⁸9 ▦⁹⁺2

Formerly a favourite hotel of Victorian climbers at the head of the Llanberis Pass, the Hostel is an ideal base for exploring this magnificent area. A high standard of comfort and accommodation is provided with small dormitories, reception open at 13.00 hrs and plenty of information available. Ideal centre for groups.
Pen-y-Pass is central to a ring of Youth Hostels supplying a wide choice of walking routes from one to another. All of the natural wonders of the outstanding Snowdonia National Park can be easily reached, as well as many visitor attractions.
🚲 10m ⛰ 5m ▦ ▲ 5m ⚲ 1m ⛵ 11m

TRAVEL INFO
🚌 Bus Gwynedd 19 Llandudno-Llanberis; 11 Caernarfon-Llanberis, also 96 from Llanberis (pass BR Llandudno Junction & Betws-y-Coed) (☎ 01286 679535) 🚉 Bangor 18m; Betws-y-Coed (not Sun, except Jul/Aug) 12m.
ℹ ☎ 01286 870765

NEXT HOSTELS
Bryn Gwynant 4m, Capel Curig 5m, Llanberis 5m

ADDITIONAL INFO
Good drying room. Post collected at Hostel. Daily newspaper. Fax and photocopying service (charge). Wales Tourist Board approved. Walking, climbing and photography weekends run from Hostel.

HOW TO GET THERE
OS 115 GR 647556 Bart 27

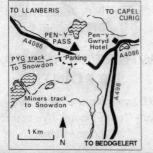

Rowen

Youth Hostel, Rhiw Farm, Rowen, Conwy, Gwynedd LL32 8YW

Bookings and enquiries: Colwyn Bay Youth Hostel, Foxhill, Nant-y-Glyn, Colwyn Bay, Clwyd LL29 6AB
☎ 01492 530627

Overnight Charges: Under 18 £3.60 Adult £5.35

6SC A ⊕ S ⬛ 2m P Cars and mini-buses - coaches 1 ½m.

| Apr 12 - Apr 18 | Open |
| Apr 29 - Sep 1 | Open |

The Hostel may be available to groups when otherwise closed - please contact Warden.

ACCOMMODATION ▦²⁻⁴2 ▦⁵⁻⁶1 ▦⁹⁺1

This simple, remote Welsh hill farmhouse — set high above Rowen village with panoramic views of Conwy Valley — provides very basic accommodation with open fires and no showers. Ideal for small, sole group use.
The area is good for cycling with many country lanes offering quietness and solitude. Located 5m south of the north Wales coastline and handy for Aber Falls and nature trail, Conwy Castle, Bodnant Gardens and Welsh Mountain Zoo.
🚲 2m ⛰ ⚲ 10m

TRAVEL INFO
🚌 Bws Gwynedd 19 Llandudno-Llanberis (pass close BR Llandudno Junction & Conwy) (☎ 01286 679535). 🚉 Tal-y-Cafn (not Sun, except Jul/Aug) 3m.
ℹ ☎ 01492 530478

NEXT HOSTELS
Colwyn Bay 12m, Bangor and Idwal Cottage both 12m by mountain

ADDITIONAL INFO
Access to Hostel up very steep hill, unsuitable for some vehicles. Advance booking recommended. Wales Tourist Board approved.

HOW TO GET THERE
Follow Roman road up to Tal-y-Fan and onto Aber village.
OS 115 GR 747721 Bart 27

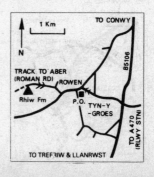

67 BEDS   **Open: 17.00hrs**

Snowdon Ranger

Youth Hostel, Rhyd Ddu, Caernarfon, Gwynedd LL54 7YS ☎ **01286 650391**

Overnight Charges: Under 18 £5.35 Adult £8.00

[i] [⌷] [GSC] [⊞] [🔍] [⌖] [S] [◨] | 1½m [P]

Jan 5 - Jan 29	Open X:Mon/Tu/Wed
Feb 2 - Feb 27	Open X:Tu/Wed
Mar 3 - Mar 31	Open Fr/Sat only
Apr 1 - Aug 31	Open
Sep 1 - Oct 30	Open X:Tu/Wed

The Hostel may be available for group and sole usage on any dates except Nov 1-Dec 31 1995 - please contact Warden.

ACCOMMODATION 6 6 1

This former Inn nestling at the foot of Snowdon provides comfortable, friendly accommodation — suitable for families, groups and individuals with many small rooms and a log fire. The Ranger Path up to Snowdon summit begins alongside the Hostel and pleasant riverside walks are close by. This area of the Snowdonia National Park is convenient for exploring the surrounding mountains, lakes, valleys and near to the lovely north Wales coastline. Close to the heartland of Welsh language, history and customs. Caernarfon Castle, one of the best preserved fortresses in Europe, is 8m away. 🚲4m ⛵4m ▲ 🏔10m
🎣15m ⌂

TRAVEL INFO
🚌Bws Gwynedd 11 Caernarfon-Beddgelert (connections from BR Bangor and BR Porthmadog) (☎ 01286 679535). Bus connections to Llanberis, Pen-y-Pass and Bryn Gwynant Youth Hostels.
🚂Bangor 16m, Porthmadog 13m
ℹ️ ☎01286 672232

NEXT HOSTELS
Llanberis 11m (4m by path), Bryn Gwynant 9m (7m by path), Pen-y-Pass 13m (10 by path)

ADDITIONAL INFO
Wales Tourist Board approved.

HOW TO GET THERE
On A4085 between Caernarfon and Beddgelert (8m from Caernarfon)
OS 115 GR 565550 Bart 27

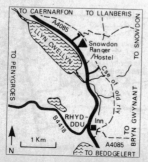

Unspoilt valleys, rushing streams and deserted farmhouses set the scene in mid Wales. The Elenith is an ideal area for those seeking peace and solitude as it is possible to walk for miles around this picturesque countryside without meeting a single person. In contrast, the Mid Wales Coast consists of several well known holiday resorts with sandy beaches and views of the nearby hills.

The 430ft climb of the Cliff Railway in Aberystwyth provides spectacular views of 26 peaks and hundreds of miles of coastline.

The Elenith Discount Package gives seven nights for the price of five at any one or more of these Youth Hostels: Blaencarnon, Bryn Poeth Uchaf, Dolgoch, Glascwm, Tyncornel and Ystumtuen. **Vouchers must be purchased in advance** and are available from the YHA Regional Office listed below. **The Mid Wales Booking System** covers the Youth Hostels listed above, plus Llanddeusant and Ystradfellte in the Brecon Beacons. Send details of booking requirements, payment and £2.00 per person fee to Wales Regional Office (address below). N.B. Bookings must arrive in the office at least 14 days prior to the first night of visit.

USEFUL PUBLICATIONS

Elenith: Walkers guide to Tywi and Elan Valley areas — send £1.50 (incl. p&p, cheques payable to YHA) to the YHA Regional Office listed below.

Offa's Dyke strip maps (set of 9) — send £3.50 (incl. p&p, cheques payable to YHA) to the YHA Regional Office listed below.

For more information about hostelling in this area contact: YHA Wales Regional Office, 1 Cathedral Road, Cardiff, CF1 9HA. Tel: (01222) 396766 or 222122. Fax: (01222) 237817.

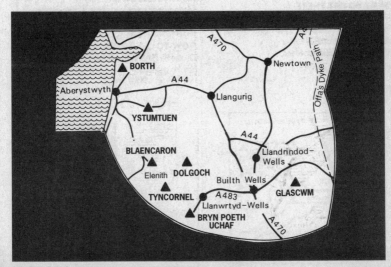

Blaencaron

Youth Hostel, Blaencaron, Tregaron, Dyfed SY25 6HL ☎ 01974 298441

Overnight Charges: Under 18 £3.60 Adult £5.35

[1] [SEC] [A] 3m [P] Cars and mini-buses nearby.
Coaches - Tregaron 3m.

Apr 1 - Oct 31	Open

The Hostel may be available for groups when otherwise closed - please contact Warden.

ACCOMMODATION 🛏²⁻⁴ 2 🛏⁵⁻⁸ 1

This traditional self-catering Hostel — formerly a small village school — is set in the unspoilt Afon Groes valley to the west of the Cambrian mountains.

As well as the Cambrian Way Footpath route and walks in unspoilt Elenith, there are also many attractions to enjoy — including Tregaron Bog/ National Nature Reserve (4m); Strata Florida Abbey (10m); Dolaucothi Gold Mines (20m); Devil's Bridge Narrow Guage Railway (17m); and even the local pub (3m)! [icons] 4m

TRAVEL INFO

🚌 Bws Dyfed 516, 589 BR Aberystwyth - Tregaron, alight Tregaron, thence 2m (Highway & Transport Dept ☎ 01267 231817).
🚉 Aberystwyth 20m; Devil's Bridge (Vale of Rheidol Rly - seasonal) 17m.
🛈 ☎ 01545 570602

NEXT HOSTELS

Dolgoch 12m (by mountains 9m), Tyncornel 14m (by mountains 8m), Ystumtuen 21m

ADDITIONAL INFO

Credit cards not accepted. Wales Tourist Board approved. Mid-Wales Booking Bureau. On Cambrian Way footpath route.

HOW TO GET THERE

From Red Lion Inn, Tregaron, on road N. Take 1st right for 2m to phone box. Turn right - Warden's farm 1st right, Hostel 1m.
[OS] 146 [GR] 713608 [Bart] 17

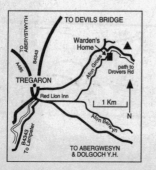

Borth

Youth Hostel, Morlais, Borth, Dyfed SY24 5JS ☎ 01970 871498

Overnight Charges: Under 18 £5.35 Adult £8.00

Family accommodation prices on p.11-13

[2] [icons] [SEC] [icons] [Q] [S] [icon] ½m [icon] 1x40, 1x30, 1x15 [P]

Mar 1 - Mar 28	Open X:Sun/Mon
Mar 29 - Aug 30	Open
Aug 31 - Sep 30	Open X:Sun
Oct 3 - Oct 28	Open X:Sun/Mon

The Hostel may be available for groups when otherwise closed - please contact Warden.

ACCOMMODATION 🛏 4 🛏 8

Close to the famous Borth & Ynylas Golf Course, this large Edwardian house on the seafront overlooks an award winning beach — with spectacular views of the Dyfi Estuary or the mountains behind from almost every room. This is a perfect location for families, with lots of family rooms available.

Squeezed between the nature-packed marshland of Cors Fochno and the sea, the friendly village of Borth extends over 2m of unbroken sands. Local attractions include the 'Animalarium', 'Fast Trax' and the Ynys Hir RSPB and Ynyslas Nature Reserve. Popular with field study groups.
[icons]

TRAVEL INFO

🚌 Crosville Cymru 511/512, 520/524 from Aberystwyth (☎ 01970 617951) 🚉 Borth ¾m.
🛈 ☎ 01970 612125

NEXT HOSTELS

Corris 19m, Ystumtuen 18m, Blaencaron 29m

ADDITIONAL INFO

Sand-yachting courses available all year. Wales Tourist Board approved. Safe, clean beach only 30 metres from Hostel.

HOW TO GET THERE

On the B4353 between Borth village and the Ynyslas golf links.
[OS] 135 [GR] 608907 [Bart] 22

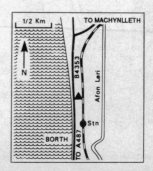

Bryn Poeth Uchaf

Youth Hostel, Hafod-y-Pant, Cynghordy, Llandovery, Dyfed SA20 0NB ☎ 015505 235

Overnight Charges: Under 18 £3.60 Adult £5.35

Family accommodation prices on p.11-13

2 | 65C | ◉ | 1m | P For cars and mini-buses only at farm (small charge). Coaches at Llandovery 8m.

Apr 1 - Oct 31	Open

The Hostel may be available for groups when otherwise closed - please contact Warden.

ACCOMMODATION   1   3

This former farmhouse and barn is in a beautiful isolated location in the south of the Cambrian mountains with extensive views of the Brecon Beacons National Park. The simple self-catering Hostel offers mountain hut-type accommodation, lit soley by gas and with a coal fire.

Local attractions include the Cambrian Way footpath (route runs alongside the Hostel), Twm Shon Catti's Cave 4m, RSPB Reserve 5m, old lead mines 1m, Llyn Brianne Reservoir 7m and Dolaucothi Gold Mines 11m. There's even a pub nearby 1m (by steep footpath)!

TRAVEL INFO
🚍 Postbus service. 🚂 Cynghordy (not Sun, except Jun - Sep) 2 ¼m.
ℹ ☎ 01550 20693 (seasonal)

NEXT HOSTELS
Dolgoch 15m, Llanddeusant 16m, Tyncornel 37m (10m by mountains)

ADDITIONAL INFO
A self-contained family annexe sleeping 4 is available for weekly hire. Wales Tourist Board approved. Mid-Wales Booking Bureau. No Hostel shop. Credit cards not accepted.

HOW TO GET THERE
Follow Tywi Valley Road N for 6m, turn right. From A483 turn left at N of village of Cynghordy, follow signs. Pass under Railway viaduct, climbing steep hill. Access to Hostel by foot only ¾m uphill from Warden's farm. Torch essential after dark.
OS 146 GR 796439 Bart 17

22 BEDS   Open: 17.00hrs

Dolgoch

Youth Hostel, Dolgoch, Tregaron, Dyfed SY25 6NR

All correspondence, bookings and enquiries to: Wales Regional Office, 4th floor, 1 Cathedral Road, Cardiff, CF1 9HA ☎ 01222 222122
Fax: 01222 237817

Overnight Charges: Under 18 £3.60 Adult £5.35

2 | 65C | ◉ | 9m | P Cars and mini-buses only.

Apr 1 - Oct 31	Open

For group usage when otherwise closed - please contact Wales Regional Office ☎ 01222 222122.

ACCOMMODATION   1   1   1

This remote farmhouse in the wild and lonely Tywi Valley is in the heart of the Cambrian mountains. Simple, spacious mountain-hut type accommodation lit solely by gas. Coal fire and self-catering only.

Walking and cycling are popular with many local attractions on offer: Twm Shon Catti's Cave 11m, Llyn Brianne Reservoir 2m, Drygarn Fawr 6m, RSPB Reserve 10m, Dolaucothi Gold Mines 18m, pub 9m.

TRAVEL INFO
🚍 Bws Dyfed 516, 589 BR Aberystwyth - Tregaron, alight Tregaron, 9m (Highways & Transport Dept ☎ 01267 231817). Post Bus.
🚂 Llanwrtyd Wells (not Sun, except May - Sep) 10m.
ℹ ☎ 01545 570602

NEXT HOSTELS
Tyncornel 19m (5m by mountains), Blaencaron 12m (9m by mountains), Bryn Poeth Uchaf 15m

ADDITIONAL INFO
Mid-Wales Booking Bureau. Pay telephone at the Hostel. Small Hostel shop.

HOW TO GET THERE
From Tregaron take Abergwesyn Mountain Road for 8m. From Beulah on A483 take road to Abergwesyn and then Tregaron Mountain Road 6m. Hostel ½m S of Bridge in Tywi Valley along very rough and uneven forestry track (not suitable for all vehicles).
OS 147 GR 806561 Bart 17

MID WALES

22 BEDS   Open: 17.00hrs

Glascwm

Youth Hostel, The School, Glascwm,
Llandrindod Wells, Powys LD1 5SE
☎ 01982 570415

Overnight Charges: Under 18 £3.60 Adult £5.35

2 GSC A ⬛ 4m P Nearby.

Apr 1 - Oct 31	Open

The Hostel may be available for groups when
otherwise closed - please contact Warden.

ACCOMMODATION   5-8 3

Formerly a small village school, this traditional
self-catering Hostel — in the centre of a quiet
hamlet of Glascwm in the Radnorship Hills —
provides basic accommodation, with two
dormitories in an annexe in the grounds and
outside toilets.
As well as beautiful walking country (with the
Offa's Dyke Long Distance footpath 4m and Wye
Valley walk 5m), the area has much to offer —
including Radnor Forest and Waterfalls 6m,
Giants Grave and Mawn Pool 1m, local pub 4m.
Hay-on-Wye only 10m away. 🅤5m
🖼 🖼 🖼 10m

TRAVEL INFO
🚌 Service to Builth Wells each Mon morning.
🚍 Builth Road (not Sun, except Jun - Sep) 11m.
ℹ ☎ 01982 553307 (seasonal)

NEXT HOSTELS
Capel-y-Ffin 20m, Ty'n-y-Caeau 25m, Clun 25m

ADDITIONAL INFO
Credit cards are not accepted. No showers.
Mid-Wales booking bureau. Wales Tourist Board
approved. Small Hostel shop.

HOW TO GET THERE
In centre of Glascwm village 10m from Kington and
4m from Hundred House.
OS 148 GR 158532 Bart 18

Tyncornel

Youth Hostel, Llanddewi - Brefi, Tregaron, Dyfed SY25 6PH

All correspondence, bookings and enquiries to Wales Regional Office, 4th Floor, 1 Cathedral Road, Cardiff. CF1 9HA ☎ 01222 222122 Fax: 01222 237817

Overnight Charges: Under 18 £3.60 Adult £5.35

2 GSC A ■ 7m P Limited. Coaches in layby 9m.

| Apr 1 - Oct 31 | Open |

The Hostel may be available for groups when otherwise closed - please contact Wales Regional Office ☎ 01222 222122.

ACCOMMODATION

This former farmhouse — in a very isolated, next-to-nature setting at the head of Doethie valley — offers simple mountain-hut type accommodation, self-catering only, lit soley by gas and with a cosy coal fire.
The area offers fine mountain walking on the Cambrian Way route, as well as local attractions like Soar-y-Mynydd Chapel 2 ½m, Llyn Brianne Reservoir 3m and pub 7m. U 20m ▲ ☒

TRAVEL INFO
🚌 Bws Dyfed 516, 589 BR Aberystwyth - Tregaron, some calling, some with connections on Bws Dyfed 588 to Llanddewi Brefi, thence 7m or alight Tregaron on others, thence 10m (☎ 01267 231817). 🚆 Aberystwyth 28m.
🛈 ☎ 01545 570602

NEXT HOSTELS
Blaencaron 14m (8m by mountains), Dolgoch 19m (5m by mountains), Bryn Poeth 37m (10m by mountains)

ADDITIONAL INFO
Mid-Wales Booking Bureau. No Hostel shop. Wales Tourist Board approved.

HOW TO GET THERE
From Llanddewi-Brefi follow road S E up Brefi valley (not S W to Farmers). Fork left at 4 ¾m. At signpost at 6 ¼m continue on rough track. Hostel 1m.
OS 146 GR 751534 Bart 17

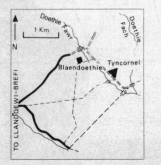

Ystumtuen

Youth Hostel, Glantuen, Ystumtuen, Aberystwyth, Dyfed SY23 3AE
☎ 01970 890693

Overnight Charges: Under 18 £3.60 Adult £5.35

2 GSC ■ 2m P Cars and mini-buses nearby. Coaches Ponterwyd 2m.

| Apr 1 - Oct 31 | Open |

The Hostel may be available for groups when otherwise closed - please contact Warden.

ACCOMMODATION

A former school, this traditional, self-catering Hostel is set in a quiet, old lead mining village at the north end of the Elenith and only 10m from Aberystwyth.
Local attractions include: Devil's Bridge (with spectacular waterfalls) 1 ½m, Narrow Guage Railway 3m, Plynlimon Fawr (2468ft), Nant-y-Moch Reservoir 5m, Llywernog silver and lead mines 2m, Rheidol Power Station 4m, Forestry Visitor Center 2m, pub 2m. You can even try your hand at trout fishing! ▲ 2m ☒

TRAVEL INFO
🚌 Crosville Cymru 501 from Aberystwyth (passes BR Aberystwyth), alight 1m W of Ponterwyd, thence 1 ½m (☎ 01970 617951). 🚆 Rhiwfron (Vale of Rheidol Rly - seasonal) 2m; Aberystwyth 12m.
🛈 ☎ 01970 612125

NEXT HOSTELS
Borth 18m, Blaencaron 21m, Tyncornel 28m

ADDITIONAL INFO
Wales Tourist Board approved. Cambrian Way footpath route. Mid-Wales booking bureau. Outside toilets. Small Hostel shop.

HOW TO GET THERE
From A44 turn S 1m W of Ponterwyd. Hostel 1 ½m. From A4120 Devil's Bridge via Parson's Bridge - unsuitable for cyclists and dangerous after dark.
OS 135 GR 735786 Bart 17

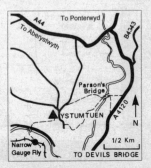

The Pembrokeshire Coast National Park combines breathtaking cliff scenery with sandy beaches, small coves and fishing harbours. In the spring and autumn, sea birds and seals are in abundance and beautiful wild flowers decorate the area. The National Nature Reserve on Skomer Island is well worth a visit.

The city of St David's will enchant you with its 12th century cathedral. The area's rich past is reflected in its fascinating castles, abbeys, museums and ancient sites — including burial chambers at Pentre Ifan Cromlech.

The Pembrokeshire Coast Path is popular with walkers and there are many opportunities for watersports.

The **West Wales Booking Bureau** can book your stays at Poppit Sands, Pwll Deri, Trevine, St. David's, Pencwym, Broad Haven, Marloes Sands, Manorbrier and Pentlepoir Youth Hostels. Send details of booking requirements, payment and £2.50 per person fee to YHA Llaethdy, St. David's, Haverfordwest, Dyfed SA62 6PR. Tel: (01437) 720345. N.B. Bookings must arrive in the office at least 14 days prior to first night of visit.

Manorbier Youth Hostel is available on YHA's **Rent-a-Hostel scheme** which runs during the winter months (details on p.7).

USEFUL PUBLICATIONS

Pembrokeshire Coast Path — send £3.50 (incl. p&p, cheques payable to YHA) to the YHA Regional Office listed below.

For more information about hostelling in this area contact: YHA Wales Regional Office, 1 Cathedral Road, Cardiff, CF1 9HA. Tel: (01222) 396766 or 222122. Fax: (01222) 237817.

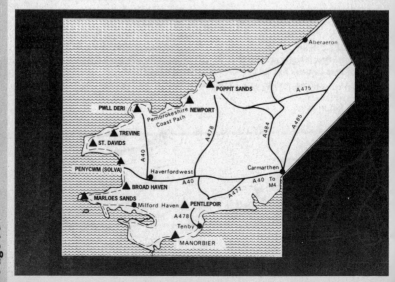

74 BEDS	Open: 17.00hrs

Broad Haven

Youth Hostel, Broad Haven, Haverfordwest, Dyfed SA62 3JH ☎ 01437 781688
Fax: 01437 781100

Overnight Charges: Under 18 £5.35 Adult £8.00

Seasonal Prices Jul 1 - Aug 31: Under 18 £5.95 Adult £8.80

Family accommodation prices on p.11-13

🚲 📺 🖥 🔍 🖼 ♿ ⊗ Ⓢ ◻ ½m 🚿 2x16, 1x24 🅿 BABA

Mar 1 - Mar 16	Open X:Fr/Sat/Sun
Mar 20 - Sept 23	Open
Sept 25 - Oct 31	Open X:Sun

The Hostel may be available for groups when otherwise closed - please check with Warden.

ACCOMMODATION 🛏2-4 9 🛏5-8 6

Situated in the only coastal National Park and adjacent to the Pembrokeshire Coast long distance footpath, this modern single storey Hostel provides comfortable accommodation in small rooms with en-suite facilities. Ideal family base with a sandy beach and many attractions. This area of beautiful beaches, flowers and birds offers many opportunities for watersports and walking — as well as visits to Skomer Island Bird & Marine Reserve and sites of historic interest.
🚴 ½m Ⓤ 2m 🏔 △ ½m 🎣 17m 🚲 🚐

TRAVEL INFO

🚌 Bws Dyfed 311 from Haverfordwest (passes close BR Haverfordwest) (☎ 01267 231817). 🚉 Haverfordwest 7m. ⛴ (Fishguard-Rosslare) 🛈 ☎ 01437 763110

NEXT HOSTELS

St David's 17m (25m by path), Marloes 10m (by path 13m), Penycwm (Solva) 8m

ADDITIONAL INFO

Fully accessible for people with disabilities. Conference facilities and field study laboratory available. Wales Tourist Board approved.

HOW TO GET THERE

From B4341 turn right into NP carpark, Hostel on left next to information centre.
OS 157 GR 863141 Bart 11

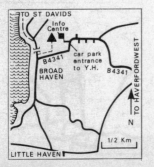

---

68 BEDS	Open: 17.00hrs

Manorbier

Youth Hostel, Manorbier, Nr Tenby, Dyfed SA70 7TT ☎ 01834 871803

Overnight Charges: Under 18 £5.35 Adult £8.00

Seasonal Prices Jul 1 - Aug 31: Under 18 £5.95 Adult £8.80

Family accommodation prices on p.11-13
R-a-H ☎ 01222 396766
🚲 📺 🖥 🔺 🔍 🖼 ♿ ⊗ Ⓢ ◻ 3m 🚿 1x35 🅿

Feb 17 - Feb 25	Open
Mar 3 - Apr 1	Open Fr/Sat
Apr 3 - Apr 22	Open
Apr 24 - Jul 1	Open X:Sun
Jul 3 - Sep 2	Open
Sep 11 - Oct 28	Open X:Sun

Open Bank Hol Sun May 7, 28, Aug 26, 27. The Hostel may be available for groups when otherwise closed - please contact Warden.

ACCOMMODATION 🛏5-8 6 🛏9+ 2

This modern Hostel is only 200yds from an award-winning beach in the Pembrokeshire Coast National Park. Fully accessible to people with disabilities. Superb family location with family rooms. Three self-contained appartments available for weekly hire.
Manorbier overlooks Skrinkle Beach, a safe beach with golden sands. Explore the magnificent coastline or take a boat trip to Caldey Island. Don't miss Manorbier, Pembroke & Carew Castles. Ⓤ 2m 🏔 △ 8m 🎣 ½m 🚲 🚐 6m

TRAVEL INFO

🚌 Bws Dyfed 358/9 Tenby - Haverfordwest, alight Manorbier 1m (☎ 01267 231817) 🚉 Manorbier 2 ½m. ⛴ 10m (Pembroke-Rosslare) 🛈 ☎ 01834 842402

NEXT HOSTELS

Pentlepoir 13m, Marloes 20m, Broad Haven 28m

ADDITIONAL INFO

Venue for meetings and seminars. Wales Tourist Board approved.

HOW TO GET THERE

Off the B4585 from Manorbier village.
OS 158 GR 081975 Bart 11

Marloes Sands

Youth Hostel, Runwayskiln, Marloes, Haverfordwest, Dyfed SA62 3BH
☎ 01646 636667

For bookings and enquiries, contact: Broad Haven Youth Hostel, Broad Haven, Haverfordwest Dyfed SA62 3JH ☎ 01646 781688

Overnight Charges: Under 18 £4.45 Adult £6.55

Seasonal Prices Jul 1 - Aug 31: Under 18 £4.85 Adult £7.20

1️⃣ 🄶🅂🄲 ⊠ 🅂 ▣ 1 ½m 🄿 Limited for cars ONLY.

Apr 11 - Apr 22	Open
Apr 25 - Jun 3	Open X:Sun/Mon
Jun 6 - Jul 15	Open X:Sun/Mon
Jul 17 - Sep 2	Open
Sep 5 - Oct 28	Open X:Sun/Mon

Open Bank Hol Sun/Mon May 7, 8, 28, 29. May be available for groups when otherwise closed.

ACCOMMODATION

These old farm buildings, alongside the Pembrokeshire Coastal footpath with spectacular views, offer traditional Hostel accommodation. Ideally situated for visits to Skomer Island, a famous bird sanctuary and marine reserve. The area has some of the most scenic coastal walks in the Pembrokeshire Coast National Park, as well as beautiful beaches and many watersports on offer. ⛰3m 🚲 🚤

TRAVEL INFO
🚌 From Haverfordwest or Milford Haven (not daily), thence 1m (☎ 01267 231817). 🚂 Milford Haven 11m; Haverfordwest 14m. 🚢 7m (Pembroke-Ireland)
ℹ️ ☎01437 763110

NEXT HOSTELS
Broad Haven 13m by path, Pentlepoir 24m, St Davids 22m

HOW TO GET THERE
B4327 from Haverfordwest 11m, turn right to Marloes, then at village church turn L to Marloes Sands car park. Hostel down private track on left approx 200yds (coaches not allowed).
🄾🅂 157 🄶🅁 778080 🄱🄰🅁🅃 11

Newport (Pembs)

Youth Hostel, Lower St Mary's Street, Newport, Pembrokeshire, Dyfed

Advance information and bookings, contact: YHA Regional Office, 1 Cathedral Road, Cardiff, S. Glamorgan CF1 9HA ☎ 01222 396766 Fax: 01222 237817

Overnight Charges: Under 18 £4.45 Adult £6.55

Seasonal Prices Jul 1 - Aug 31: Under 18 £4.85 Adult £7.20

🄶🅂🄲 🚻 🅗 ▣ ¼m 🄿 Cars and mini-buses.

> At time of going to press the opening date of this Youth Hostel is not known. ☎ YHA Regional Office for current info 01222 396766.

ACCOMMODATION

It is hoped that this small, self-catering Youth Hostel in the village of Newport will open in Spring 1995. With small dormitories, it will provide an excellent base for individuals, families and small groups.

As well as excellent walking country (including the Pembrokeshire Coastal Footpath), beaches, flora and fauna abound. Newport is on the main road to Fishguard/Goodwick for ferries to Ireland. 🏖1m ⛰1m 🚲1m 🚂½m 🚌½m

TRAVEL INFO
🚢 5m (Fishguard-Rosslare, Ireland)

NEXT HOSTELS
Pwll Deri 22m by coastal path (13 by road), Poppit Sands 11m by coastal path

HOW TO GET THERE
In the centre of the village of Newport. From A487 to Fishguard turn right on lower St Mary's Street. Hostel is on right.
🄾🅂 145 🄶🅁 058393

Pentlepoir

Youth Hostel, The Old School, Pentlepoir, Saundersfoot, Dyfed SA9 9BJ
☏ 01834 812333

Overnight Charges: Under 18 £4.45 Adult £6.55

🅾 🆂🆂🅲 🈁 ♿ Ⓢ 🍴 Ⓟ Cars ONLY. Coaches - Saundersfoot 1m.

Apr 3 - Apr 22	Open
Apr 28 - Jul 4	Open X:Wed/Th
Jul 7 - Sep 5	Open
Sep 8 - Oct 31	Open X:Wed/Th

The Hostel may be available for groups when otherwise closed - please contact Warden.

ACCOMMODATION

This small, relaxed and friendly Hostel was once a village school and now provides traditional accommodation including a large lounge/dining room with plenty of books and games, and a coal/wood burning stove.
The Hostel is convenient for visits to the seaside resorts of Tenby and Saundersfoot with their sandy beaches, attractive harbours and shops. As well as many opportunities for watersports, you can enjoy horse riding and boat trips to Caldey Island too. Oakwood Leisure Park is also within easy reach. 🚴3m Ⓤ4m 🏔5m 🎣12m 🚆5m 🚌5m

TRAVEL INFO

🚌 Bws Dyfed 350-2, 361 from Tenby (☏ 01267 231817). 🚉 Saundersfoot ¾m. ⛴11m (Pembroke-Rosslare)
ℹ️☏01834 811411

NEXT HOSTELS

Manorbier 13m, Broad Haven 21m, Marloes Sands 24m

ADDITIONAL INFO

Meals operated privately by Warden - separate payment appreciated. Wales Tourist Board approved.

HOW TO GET THERE

Take A478 to Tenby from Kilgetty roundabout. Stay on main road to Tenby, past garage on left and old school on the right.
Ⓞ🅢 158 🅖🅡 116060 Bart 11

Penycwm (Solva)

Youth Hostel, Hafod Lodge, Whitehouse, Penycwm, Nr Solva, Haverfordwest, Dyfed SA62 6LA ☏ 01437 720959
Fax: 01437 720959

Overnight Charges: Under 18 £4.85 Adult £7.20

Seasonal Prices Jul 1 - Aug 31: Under 18 £5.35 Adult £8.00

Family accommodation prices on p.11-13

2️⃣ 🅾 🆂🆂🅲 🏢 🈁 ♿ ⚽ Ⓢ 🍴 1 ½m Ⓟ BABA

Mar 1 - Oct 31	Open

The Hostel is available for advance bookings when otherwise closed.

ACCOMMODATION

This newly converted farm building set in two acres of grounds offers comfortable, modern accommodation (including en-suite facilities in every room) which is open all year — ideal for individuals, families and small groups. Excellent home-cooking too!
The Hostel enjoys a peaceful, rural location just 5m from the picturesque harbour of Solva. An ideal base for exploring St David's Peninsula with its beautiful coastline, wild flowers, sea birds, cliffs, headlands, harbours and beaches. 🚴8m Ⓤ6m 🏔1 ¾m 🏔2m 🎣2m 🚆2m 🚌2m

TRAVEL INFO

🚌 Bws Dyfed 340 from BR Haverfordwest or St David's. 411 Fishguard to St David's, then 340. Alight Penycwm. 🚉 Haverfordwest 11m. ⛴12m (Fishguard-Rosslare)
ℹ️☏01437 763110

NEXT HOSTELS

Broad Haven 8m, St David's 9m (17m by path), Trevine 8m

ADDITIONAL INFO

Credit cards not accepted. Wales Tourist Board approved.

HOW TO GET THERE

Access via A487 Newgale to Solva road. At Penycwm take minor road N towards Letterston/Mathry and follow signs to Hostel.
Ⓞ🅢 157 🅖🅡 857250

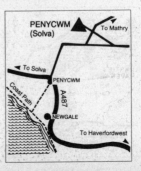

WEST WALES

10

Poppit Sands

Youth Hostel, Sea View, Poppit, Cardigan, Dyfed SA43 3LP ☎ 01239 612936

Overnight Charges: Under 18 £4.45 Adult £6.55

Seasonal Prices Jul 1 - Aug 31: Under 18 £4.85 Adult £7.20

1 GSC A S P Cars and mini-buses - coaches at bottom car park ½m below Hostel.

Mar 1 - Jul 2	Open X:Mon
Jul 4 - Sep 3	Open
Sep 5 - Oct 28	Open X:Mon

Open Bank Hol Apr 17, May 8, 29, Aug 28. The Hostel may be available for groups and individuals when otherwise closed - please contact Warden.

ACCOMMODATION

This simple, traditional Hostel overlooking Cardigan Island and Teifi Estuary is set in five acres of grounds reaching down to the sea. Relaxed atmosphere with magnificent views of the coastline.
Ideal for birdwatching with Teifi Nature Reserve nearby, the area is also convenient for visiting the 11th century abbey and watermill at St Dogmael's — with ancient burial chambers and an Iron Age village only 8m away. The Hostel is on the northern end of the Pembrokeshire Coastal foothpath. 3m

TRAVEL INFO
Bws Dyfed 407/9 from Cardigan to within ½m (Jul - Aug only), but to St. Dogmaels, 2m, at other times (☎ 01267 231817). Fishguard Harbour 20m; Carmarthen 26m; Aberystwyth 33m.
☎ 01239 613230

NEXT HOSTELS
Pentlepoir 25m, Pwll Deri 25m, Llanddeusant 43m

ADDITIONAL INFO
Good Hostel shop. Wales Tourist Board approved.

HOW TO GET THERE
Turn right in village of St Dogmaels to Poppit Sands (1 ½m). Hostel sign posted from Lifeboat station - second set of buildings on right.
OS 145 GR 144487 Bart 11

Pwll Deri

Youth Hostel, Castell Mawr, Tref Asser, Goodwick, Dyfed SA64 0LR ☎ 013485 233

Overnight Charges: Under 18 £4.45 Adult £6.55

Seasonal Prices Jul 1 - Aug 31: Under 18 £4.85 Adult £7.20

1 GSC A S 2 ½m P Nearby.

Apr 3 - Apr 8	Open
Apr 10 - Apr 22	Open
Apr 24 - May 31	Open X:Sat/Sun
Jun 1 - Jul 15	Open X:Sun
Jul 17 - Sep 9	Open

Open Bank Hol Sun Apr May 7, 28. The Hostel may be available for groups when otherwise closed.

ACCOMMODATION

This former private house — perched on 400ft cliffs overlooking Pwll Deri Bay in the Pembrokeshire Coast National Park — is an excellent bird and seal watching location, with dramatic sunsets too. The Pembrokeshire Coast long distance footpath runs alongside the Hostel. This peaceful part of the Pembrokeshire Coast National Park offers the chance to relax and enjoy the scenery, walk part of the footpath or explore the Iron Age hill fort behind the Hostel. The Llangloffan cheese farm is 4m.

TRAVEL INFO
Bws Dyfed 410/11 Fishguard - Goodwick (connections from BR Haverfordwest), alight Goodwick, thence 4m (☎ 01267 231817). Fishguard Harbour 4 ½m. 4 ½m (Fishguard-Rosslare)
☎ 01348 873484

NEXT HOSTELS
Trevine 9m by path, St David's 21m, Poppit Sands 37m by path.

ADDITIONAL INFO
Wales Tourist Board approved.

HOW TO GET THERE
Take Strumble Head road out of Goodwick, follow signs for Strumble Head, then Pwll Deri. From St Davids-Fishguard road, approach via St Nicholas.
OS 157 GR 891387 Bart 11

St David's

Youth Hostel, Llaethdy, St David's, Haverfordwest, Dyfed SA62 6PR

☎ 01437 720345

Overnight Charges: Under 18 £4.00 Adult £5.95

Seasonal Prices Jul 1 - Aug 31: Under 18 £4.85 Adult £7.20

Family accommodation prices on p.11-13

 2 68C A ✪ S ▣ 2 ½m P Cars & minibuses ONLY. No access for coaches - check with Warden.

Apr 1 - Jul 5	Open X:Th
Jul 7 - Sep 6	Open
Sep 8 - Oct 18	Open X:Th
Oct 20 - Oct 28	Open

Open Th Apr 13, 20 & Jun 1. The Hostel may be available for groups when otherwise closed.

ACCOMMODATION   🛏️²⁻⁴ 1   🛏️⁹⁺ 3

A white farmhouse nestled at the foot of the rocky outcrop Carn Llidi. Separate self-contained unit sleeping 4 available for weekly hire.
Set in the centre of the Pembrokeshire Coast National Park, the Hostel is well placed for reaching many clean, sandy beaches, St David's Oceanarium, St David's Cathedral and Bishops Palace. There are boat trips to Ramsey Island.

🏠2 ½m 🍴2m 🛒2 ½m 🍳2 ½m 🚲 🚉½m

TRAVEL INFO

🚌 Bws Dyfed 340 from BR Haverfordwest or 411 from Fishguard, alight St David's on both, thence 2m (☎ 01267 231817). 🚢 Fishguard Harbour 15m; Haverfordwest 18m. 🛳️15m (Fishguard/Rosslare)

🛈 ☎ 01437 763110

NEXT HOSTELS

Trevine 11m by path, Pwll Deri 21m by path, Penycwm (Solva) 9m by road

ADDITIONAL INFO

Good Hostel shop. Wales Tourist Board approved.

HOW TO GET THERE

Leave Fishguard Road just outside St Davids, follow signs to White Sands Bay. Hostel signs from golf club.

OS 157 GR 739276 Bart 11

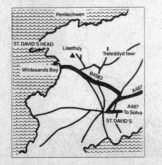

Trevine (Trefin)

Youth Hostel, 11 Ffordd-yr-Afon, Trefin, Haverfordwest, Dyfed SA62 5AU

☎ 01348 831414

Overnight Charges: Under 18 £4.45 Adult £6.55

Seasonal Prices Jul 1 - Aug 31: Under 18 £4.85 Adult £7.20

Family accommodation prices on p.11-13

 1 68C IIII ✈ ✪ S ▣ 🕮 1x40 P 30yds

Mar 3 - Jun 3	Open X:Sun/Mon
Jun 6 - Jul 1	Open X:Sun
Jul 3 - Sep 2	Open
Sep 4 - Oct 28	Open X:Sun/Mon

Open Bank Hol Sun/Mon Apr 16, 17, May 7, 8, 28, 29. The Hostel may be available for groups when otherwise closed - please contact Warden.

ACCOMMODATION   🛏️²⁻⁴ 5   🛏️⁵⁻⁸ 1

Completely refurbished to a high standard, this small Hostel is situated in the centre of a friendly village only ½m from the sea in the Pembrokeshire Coast National Park. A convenient base for walkers and families. A public children's playground, tennis court and bowls area are at the rear of Hostel.
The magnificent Pembrokeshire coastline comprises rugged cliffs, secluded bays and picturesque harbour villages — and an abundance of seabirds and wild flowers. 🏠3m 🍴6m 🛒12m 🥛1m 🍳1m 🚲 🚉6m

TRAVEL INFO

🚌 Bws Dyfed 411 from Fishguard or St David's (connections from BR Haverfordwest on 412 and 340 from Haverfordwest) (☎ 01267 233333). 🚢 Fishguard Harbour 12m; Haverfordwest 18m. 🛳️12m (Fishguard-Rosslare)

🛈 ☎ 01437 763110

NEXT HOSTELS

Pwll Deri 9m, St David's 11m, Penycwm (Solva) 8m

ADDITIONAL INFO

Nearest pub (serving food) is 200yds away. Wales Tourist Board approved.

HOW TO GET THERE

In centre of village near pub.

OS 157 GR 840324 Bart 11

10

WEST WALES

11

Brecon Beacons & South Wales

The Brecon Beacons National Park is 519 square miles of contrasting views including remarkable caves and waterfalls. Four main mountain blocks run right across the Park. Along the southern edge, narrow bands of Carboniferous Limestone and Millstone grit produce dramatically different scenery. The Park is home to a number of nature reserves while the Brecon Mountain Railway, Big Pit Mining Museum and Dan-Yr-Ogof Showcaves are favourite attractions.

The Gower Peninsula — an Area of Outstanding Natural Beauty — is renowned for its coastline, sheer limestone cliffs, crescent shaped bays and breezy Worm's Head.

Cardiff Castle is one of the many historic attractions in the capital city of Wales. The valleys to the north of Cardiff were main coal mining sites — now being returned to green hills, leaving industrial heritage sites of interest.

The Brecon Beacons offer good access and beautiful views to walkers and many opportunities for outdoor activities such as caving, climbing, abseiling, canoeing and horseriding.

Llanddeusant Youth Hostel is available on YHA's **Rent-a-Hostel scheme** which runs during the winter months (details on p.7).

USEFUL PUBLICATIONS

Offa's Dyke Strip Maps (set of 9) — send £3.50 (incl. p&p, cheques payable to YHA) to the YHA Regional Office listed below.

For more information about hostelling in this area contact: YHA Wales Regional Office, I Cathedral Road, Cardiff, CFI 9HA. Tel: (01222) 396766 or 222122. Fax: (01222) 237817.

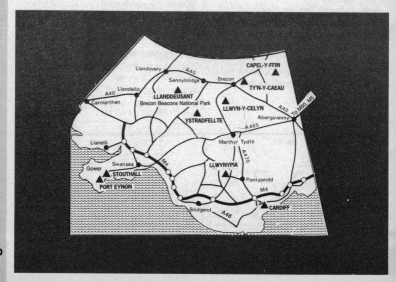

Capel-y-Ffin

Youth Hostel, Capel-y-Ffin, Abergavenny, Gwent. NP7 7NP ☎ 01873 890650

Overnight Charges: Under 18 £4.45 Adult £6.55

1 🍴 🔐 A 🌀 🚲 S P Limited space in layby 30m N of Hostel gate for cars and mini-buses only.

Feb	Open Fr/Sat only (SC)
Mar 2 - Apr 1	Open X:Wed
Apr 10 - Apr 25	Open
Apr 27 - Jun 30	Open X:Wed
Jul 1 - Sep 5	Open (SC Wed)
Sep 15 - Oct 31	Open X:Wed
Nov	Open Fr/Sat only (SC)

NB: SC = self-catering night. Also note that breakfast will not be served on the morning following the self-catering night.

ACCOMMODATION

This converted farmhouse in beautiful and peaceful Llanthony Valley offers traditional Hostel accommodation.

The Black Mountains area of the Brecon Beacons National Park is ideal for pony trekking and hill walking. The Hostel is on the Cambrian Way and near Offa's Dyke footpath. The small market town of Hay-on-Wye, famous for its second-hand bookshops, is only 7m away. 🚲 9m U ▲ ≋

TRAVEL INFO

🚌 Stagecoach Red & White 39, Yeomans Canyon 40 Hereford - Brecon (passes close BR Hereford), alight Hay-on-Wye, 8m (☎ 01905 766800). 🚉 Abergavenny 16m.
🛈 ☎ 01873 857588

NEXT HOSTELS

Ty'n-y-Caeau 23m (16m by mountain), Glascwm 20m, Monmouth 25m

ADDITIONAL INFO

The Hostel runs horse riding holidays for 2, 5 and 7 nights for anyone over 11yrs. Wales Tourist Board approved.

HOW TO GET THERE

Turn off the A465 at Llanfihangel Crucorney, follow signs to Llanthony and from there signs to Capel-y-Ffin.
OS 161 GR 250328 Bart 13

Cardiff

Youth Hostel, 2 Wedal Road, Roath Park, Cardiff, South Glamorgan CF2 5PG ☎ 01222 462303 Fax: 01222 464571

Overnight Charges: Under 18 £5.95 Adult £8.80

1 🍴 🛏 🏧 🍽 🌀 🚲 S 🛒 P Cars and mini-buses. Street parking for coaches. BABA IBN

Jan 2 - Feb 28	Open X:Sun
Mar 1 - Oct 31	Open
Nov 1 - Nov 31	Open X:Sun

The Hostel may be available for groups when otherwise closed - please contact Warden.

ACCOMMODATION

Conveniently located near the city centre and Roath Park Lake, the Hostel provides a good standard of accommodation with wash-basins in each room and a late entry system. Named "Ty Croeso" which is Welsh for "Welcome House", you can be sure of a warm welcome here. Cardiff is the exciting capital city of Wales offering a wide range of entertainment and attractions. Don't miss the Welsh Folk Museum, Cardiff Castle, National Museum of Wales and the Victorian & Edwardian shopping arcades. Activities include sailing, walking, cycling and a National Ice Rink. 🚲 3m U 4m ▲ 1m ≋ 2m ≋ 1m

TRAVEL INFO

🚌 Cardiff Bus 78/80/82 from BR Cardiff Central (☎ 01222 396521). 🚉 Cardiff Central Station 2 ½m
🛈 ☎ 01222 668750

NEXT HOSTELS

Llwynypia 18m, Llwyn-y-Celyn 42m, Port Eynon 56m

ADDITIONAL INFO

Wales Tourist Board approved. Laundry facilities.

HOW TO GET THERE

Follow signs from A470/A48 roundabout.
OS 171 GR 185788 Bart 12

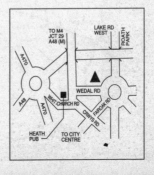

Llanddeusant

Youth Hostel, The Old Red Lion, Llanddeusant, Llangadog, Dyfed SA19 6UL ☎ 015504 634 and 619

Overnight Charges: Under 18 £4.00 Adult £5.95

R-a-H ☎ 01222 396766 [2] GSC ▦ △ ◫ 1m P Cars and mini-buses ONLY. Coaches Llangadog 7m.

Apr 1 - Sep 2	Open

The Hostel is available for Rent-a-Hostel bookings when otherwise closed.

ACCOMMODATION 🛏 2-4 1 🛏 5-8 2 🛏 9+ 1

This traditional Hostel is a former Inn adjacent to a 14th century church overlooking the magical Sawdde Valley. Situated in the western part of the Brecon Beacons National Park, it provides a good base for exploring the remote corners of this magnificent countryside. Beautiful sunsets.
As well as excellent high level walking (Bannau Brycheiniog 2632'), a selection of circular walks to lakes, Iron Age Forts, Roman Camps etc are available from the Hostel. Local attractions include: pre-historic Roman remains, Carreg Cennen Castle 9m, Dan-y-Ogof Caves 12m, pub 1m and pottery nearby. Ⓤ 1m ▲ 🎣 ✉

TRAVEL INFO
🚌 No Service. 🚆 Llangadog (not Sun, except Jun - Sep) 7m.
🛈 ☎ 01550 20693 (seasonal)

NEXT HOSTELS
Bryn Poeth Uchaf 16m, Ystradfellte 23m, Llwyn-y-Celyn 25m

ADDITIONAL INFO
As of May 95 Hostel telephone number will change to ☎ 01550 740634 and 740619. Llangadog Taxi ☎ 01550 777706. Mid-Wales booking bureau. No Hostel shop. Cambrian Way Footpath route. Wales Tourist Board approved.

HOW TO GET THERE
If approaching from E, turn off A40 at Castle Coaching Inn 9m. Approaching from W turn S off A40 at Llangadog 7m.
OS 160 GR 776245 Bart 12

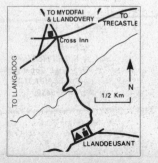

Llwyn-y-Celyn

Youth Hostel, Libanus, Brecon, Powys LD3 8NH ☎ 01874 624261

Overnight Charges: Under 18 £4.45 Adult £6.55

[1] ▣ GSC ▦ △ ⊕ S P Cars & mini-buses. Coaches in layby 200yds.

Feb 24 - Mar 6	Open
Mar 9 - Apr 10	Open X:Tu/Wed
Apr 13 - Apr 24	Open
Apr 27 - Jul 8	Open X:Sun
Jul 10 - Sep 30	Open X:Sun/Mon
Oct 2 - Oct 28	Open X:Sun

Open Bank Hol Sun May 7, May 28. The Hostel may be available for groups when closed.

ACCOMMODATION 🛏 1-8 1 🛏 9+ 2

A traditional Welsh farmhouse set in 15 acres of natural woodland in the heart of the Brecon Beacons National Park. The Hostel grounds include a nature trail, adventure playground and picnic area.
This area offers some of the best walking in Wales, from gentle strolls to spectacular ascents on the ridges and peaks of the National Park. Climbing, walking, abseiling and caving are popular. Places of interest: Dan-yr-Ogof Caves, Big Pit Mining Museum, Brecon Mountain Railway and nature reserves. ⚲ 7m Ⓤ 8m ▲ 1m ⚑ 12m 🎣 8m ✉ 🚲 7m

TRAVEL INFO
🚌 Silverline Rail-Link 43 BR Merthyr Tydfil - Brecon (☎ 01685 382406). National Express daily to Brecon, twice daily May - Aug. Trawscambria 702 to Brecon. 🚆 Merthyr Tydfil 11m; Abergavenny 28m.
🛈 ☎ 01874 625692

NEXT HOSTELS
Ty'n-y-Caeau 9m, Ystradfellte 12m, Llanddeusant 25m

ADDITIONAL INFO
Wales Tourist Board approved

HOW TO GET THERE
Hostel sign on main road A470 and 7m S of Brecon 12m N from Merthyr.
OS 160 GR 973225 Bart 12

Llwynypia

62 BEDS   Open: 17.00hrs

Youth Hostel, Glyncornel Centre, Llwynypia, Rhondda, Mid Glamorgan CF40 2JF
☎ 01443 430859

Overnight Charges: Under 18 £5.35 Adult £8.00

R-a-H ☎ 01222 396766

1 ⊙ GSC ⊞ ⚲ ⚧ S ⬛ 1m ⚲ 1x30, 2x20
P Large car park. BABA

Feb 17 - Feb 25	Open
Mar 3 - Oct 28	Open X:Sat/Sun
Dec 4 - Dec 22	Open X:Sun

Open Bank Hol Sat/Sun Apr 15, 16, May 6, 7, 27, 28, Aug 26, 27. The Hostel may be available for groups when otherwise closed - please contact Warden.

ACCOMMODATION

Set in 75 acres of natural woodland with a variety of plants and wildlife, the Youth Hostel shares the building with the Glyncornel Environmental Centre. There is a small museum with an interesting local history display.
The area is steeped in mining and industrial history. The Rhondda Heritage Park provides a real insight into the Rhondda Valleys. The heritage of Wales' rural life is displayed and interpreted at the popular Welsh Folk Museum and the attractions of Cardiff are within easy reach. ⚲8m ⓤ7m ▲ ⚲1m ⚲1m

TRAVEL INFO
🚃 Local ½m. 🚌 Llwynypia ½m.
ℹ ☎01443 402077

NEXT HOSTELS
Cardiff 18m, Ystradfellte 18m, Llwyn-y-Celyn 30m

ADDITIONAL INFO
This YHA centre is ideal for small conferences, seminars and workshops. Wales Tourist Board approved.

HOW TO GET THERE
From M4 turn off at junction 34, follow signs for Rhondda Valley and Glyncornel Centre.
OS 170 GR 993939 Bart 12

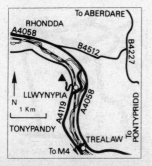

Port Eynon

Youth Hostel, The Old Lifeboat House, Port Eynon, Swansea, West Glamorgan SA3 1NN
☎ 01792 390706

Overnight Charges: Under 18 £4.85 Adult £7.20

1 | 6SC | S | ▢ | P Use seafront car park ¼m.

Feb 10 - Mar 25	Open Fr/Sat only
Mar 27 - Sep 30	Open X:Sun
Oct 16 - Oct 28	Open X:Sun
November	Open Fr/Sat only

Open Bank Hol Sun Apr 16, May 7, 28, Aug 27. The Hostel may be available for groups when otherwise closed - please contact Warden.

ACCOMMODATION

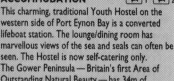

This charming, traditional Youth Hostel on the western side of Port Eynon Bay is a converted lifeboat station. The lounge/dining room has marvellous views of the sea and seals can often be seen. The Hostel is now self-catering only.
The Gower Peninsula — Britain's first Area of Outstanding Natural Beauty — has 34m of heritage coast with clean beaches, limestone cliffs, sea birds and rare flowers. Watersports abound. Culver Hole, Salthouse, Weobley Castle, Worms Head, Y Felin Ddwr and Three Cliffs Bay are also worth visiting. U 4m ▣ ▣ ▦ 1m ⌕ ▣

TRAVEL INFO

🚌 South Wales 18/A/C from Swansea (☎ 01792 475511), last bus 5.50 pm. 🚉 Swansea 16m (☎ 01792 467777)
🛈 ☎ 01792 468321

NEXT HOSTELS

Ystradfellte 39m, Llwynypia 44m, Llanddeusant 44m

ADDITIONAL INFO

Wales Tourist Board approved. Rooms for families and further dormitory accommodation also available 22 July to 9 September 1995 at nearby Stouthall. Bookings can be made there direct for this period throughout the year.

HOW TO GET THERE

Footpath from Port Eynon foreshore car park or across beach.
OS 159 GR 468848 Bart 12

Following a successful summer opening in 1994, arrangements have been made with Stouthall, 4m from Port Eynon, to take overflow bookings from families and individuals over the period Jul 22 - Sep 9 1995.

Stouthall

Reynoldston, Gower, West Glamorgan SA3 1AP ☎ 01792 391086

Overnight Charges: Under 18 £5.95 Adult £8.80

▢ | ▦ | 🔍 | ▨ | S | ▢ | ½m P Ample for cars & mini-buses.

| Jul 22 - Sep 9 | Open |

Only open for YHA members in summer but centre can be contacted for advance reservations.

ACCOMMODATION

A fine Georgian mansion standing in several acres of woodland and meadows. This spacious and well equipped building is available as a summer Youth Hostel. With many small dormitories, it provides an excellent base for families and individuals to explore the Gower.
The Gower is justly designated an Area of Outstanding Natural Beauty. Within a few miles are Oxwich Bay with fine beaches and a nature reserve. To the west are the impressive Rhossili Bay and Worms Head. Swansea offers leisure centres, a maritime museum, art galleries and shops. ▣ ▣ 4m ▦ 4m ⌕ ▣ 3m

NEXT HOSTELS

Port Eynon 4m

HOW TO GET THERE

OS 159 GR 473892

BRECON BEACONS & SOUTH WALES

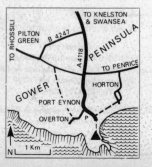

Ty'n-y-Caeau (Nr Brecon)

**Youth Hostel, Groesffordd, Brecon, Powys.
LD3 7SW** ☎ 01874 665270

Overnight Charges: Under 18 £4.45 Adult £6.55

[1] [◎] [GSC] [⅃] [❀] [S] [▣] 3m [P] Cars and mini-buses only.

Feb 17 - Feb 25	Open
Mar 3 - Apr 8	Open X:Sun/Mon
Apr 10 - Apr 22	Open
Apr 24 - Jul 8	Open X:Sun
Jul 10 - Sep 9	Open
Sep 26 - Oct 28	Open X:Sun/Mon

Open Bank Hol Sun/Mon May 7, 8, 28, 29. May be available for groups when otherwise closed.

ACCOMMODATION 🛏️1 🛏️3 🛏️2

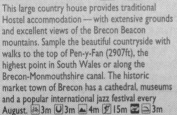

This large country house provides traditional Hostel accommodation — with extensive grounds and excellent views of the Brecon Beacon mountains. Sample the beautiful countryside with walks to the top of Pen-y-Fan (2907ft), the highest point in South Wales or along the Brecon-Monmouthshire canal. The historic market town of Brecon has a cathedral, museums and a popular international jazz festival every August. 🚶3m ⛽3m 🏔️4m 🚲15m 🚆3m

TRAVEL INFO

🚌Stagecoach Red & White 21 Newport - Brecon (passes close BR Abergavenny), alight Llanfrynach turn, 1m; 39 and Yeomans Canyon 40 from Hereford (passes close BR Hereford), alight Llanddew turn, ¾m (☎ 01633 266336 for Red & White, ☎ 01345 125436 Yeomans); Silverline Rail-Link 43 BR Merthyr Tydfil - Brecon, alight Brecon, thence 2 ½m by road (☎ 01685 382406). 🚉Merthyr Tydfil 20m; Abergavenny 19m. 🛈 ☎01874 623366

NEXT HOSTELS

Llwyn-y-Celyn 9m, Capel-y-Ffin 23m, Llanddeusant 21m

ADDITIONAL INFO

Wales Tourist Board approved.

HOW TO GET THERE

½m N of Groesffordd village.
[OS] 160 [GR] 074388 [Bart] 17

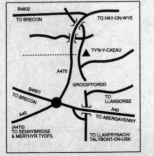

Ystradfellte

**Youth Hostel, Tai'r Heol, Ystradfellte,
Aberdare, Mid Glamorgan CF44 9JF**
☎ 01639 720301

Overnight Charges: Under 18 £4.00 Adult £5.95

[1] [GSC] [▣] 1 ¼m [P] Cars and mini-buses ONLY.

Apr 1 - Apr 19	Open X:Th
Apr 20 - May 10	Open
May 12 - May 31	Open X:Th
Jun 1 - Jun 7	Open
Jun 9 - Jul 19	Open X:Th
Jul 20 - Sep 6	Open
Sep 8 - Oct 31	Open X:Th

The Hostel may be available for groups when otherwise closed - please contact Warden.

ACCOMMODATION 🛏️3 🛏️1 🛏️1

This traditional, self-catering Hostel is a charming mixture of three 17th century cottages close to the Nedd and Mellte river systems in the Brecon Beacons National Park.
As well as offering good caving and climbing, this unique waterfall country is linked by an excellent network of footpaths. Dan-yr-Ogof Show Caves 12m, Penscynor Wildlife Park 14m. 🏔️4m ⛽4m 🚲4m 🚆¼m

TRAVEL INFO

🚌 From Aberdare (passes close BR Aberdare), alight Penderyn, 3 ½m (☎ 01443 409966). SWT X5, 160/1 Swansea-Glyn Neath (passes close BR Neath), thence 5m (☎ 01792 475511). 🚉Aberdare 10m. 🛈 ☎01639 721795

NEXT HOSTELS

Llwyn-y-Celyn 12m, Ty'n-y-Caeau 21m, Llanddeusant 23m

ADDITIONAL INFO

Credit cards not accepted. Wales Tourist Board approved. Mid-Wales Booking Bureau.

HOW TO GET THERE

From A4059 turn left 1m N of Penderyn. At fork go left and left again in Ystradfellte village. Hostel 1m. From Glyn Neath proceed to Pont Nedd Fechan, then left to Ystradfellte. Hostel 4m.
[OS] 160 [GR] 925127 [Bart] 12

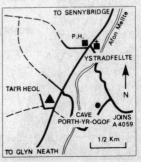

12

Wye Valley & Forest of Dean

The Wye Valley, south of Hereford, is a designated Area of Outstanding Natural Beauty. The River Wye winds its way through picturesque villages and past the magnificent ruins of Tintern Abbey. Other well-known points along the river include the Forest Nature Reserve of Wyndcliff and Symonds Yat Rock.

In the wild woodlands and forestry plantation of the Forest of Dean there are many marked trails for low level walking, while both the Wye Valley Walk and Offa's Dyke Trail provide a scenic way to see the countryside on foot. With its own river landing stage, Welsh Bicknor Youth Hostel makes an ideal base for canoeing.

Many castles, built between the 11th and 14th centuries to protect the Welsh/English borders, can be seen today at St. Briavel's Castle (once King John's hunting lodge), Chepstow, Raglan and Goodrich.

USEFUL PUBLICATIONS

Offa's Dyke Strip Maps (set of 9) — send £3.50 (incl. p&p) to the YHA Regional Office listed below.

Map 1: Beachley and Severn Bridge to St Briavels (2 routes) — send 70p (incl. p&p) to the YHA Regional Office listed below.

Map 2: St. Briavels and Monmouth to Symonds Yat, Forest of Dean, Welsh Bicknor — send 70p (incl. p&p) to the YHA Regional Office listed below.

Waymarked Path Leaflets: Highmeadow Woods - Symonds Yat — send 60p for one, 80p for both (incl. p&p) to the YHA Regional Office listed below.

Please make cheques payable to YHA.

For more information about hostelling in this area contact: YHA Wales Regional Office, 1 Cathedral Road, Cardiff, CF1 9HA. Tel: (01222) 396766 or 222122. Fax (01222) 237817.

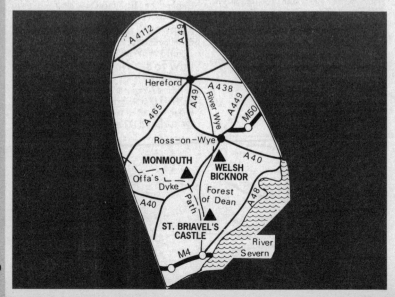

Monmouth

Youth Hostel, Priory Street School, Priory Street, Monmouth, Gwent. NP5 3NX
📞 **01600 715116**

Overnight Charges: Under 18 £4.45 Adult £6.55

[1] 68C ⬛ 🅿 Parking opposite Hostel for cars. Coaches ¼m - but can unload at Hostel first.

Mar 1 - Oct 31	Open

The Hostel may be available for groups when otherwise closed - please contact Warden.

ACCOMMODATION   1 2

Formerly a late 15th century priory and school, this simple Hostel — situated next to River Monnow and near the centre of an historic market town — offers traditional accommodation with wash-basins in all rooms and a coal fire. Monmouth is a small market town with several annual events (May — September), including a carnival, regatta and festival. The Hostel provides access to Offa's Dyke and the Wye Valley Walk as well as canoeing nearby. Places of interest include Raglan Castle, Forest of Dean and Tintern Abbey. 🚶 ⛰2m ⛰¼m 🎣4m 🚲½m 🍴½m

TRAVEL INFO
🚌Red & White 65/9 from Chepstow (pass close BR Chepstow); 60, X49 from Newport (pass close BR Newport) (📞 01633 265100). 🚉Hereford 16m; Chepstow 16m; Abergavenny 17m.
ℹ️📞01600 713899

NEXT HOSTELS
Welsh Bicknor 8m, St Briavels Castle 8m, Capel-y-Ffin 25m

ADDITIONAL INFO
Very small Hostel shop. Wales Tourist Board approved.

HOW TO GET THERE
Near the town centre adjacent to where the River Monnow runs along Priory Street.
OS 162 GR 508130 Bart 13

St. Briavels Castle

Youth Hostel, The Castle, St. Briavels, Lydney, Gloucestershire GL15 6RG
📞 **01594 530272 Fax: 01594 530849**

Overnight Charges: Under 18 £5.35 Adult £8.00

[2] 🍴 🛏 68C 🚿 🔲 S ⬛ 🅿 BABA

Feb 10 - Mar 4	Open
Mar 10 - Apr 4	Open X:Wed/Th
Apr 7 - Oct 28	Open
Nov 6 - Nov 30	Open X:Fr/Sat/Sun

During Nov (Fr/Sat/Sun), Christmas and New Year, special medieval banquets can be arranged.

ACCOMMODATION   5 4

This moated Norman castle was originally King John's hunting lodge. His bedchamber is now the lounge and you can sleep in a room that was once a cell — prisoners' graffiti can still be read on the walls. It has since been refurbished! Popular with school groups mid-week in spring/summer terms. The Hostel also features a 'hanging room', plus its own oubliette (a 30ft deep circular dungeon into which prisoners were thrown and forgotten). Medieval banquets are held at this atmospheric Hostel in the ancient Royal Forest of Dean — close to England's border with Wales. 🚶6m 🏙5m ⛰4m 🚲4m 🍴

TRAVEL INFO
🚌Red & White 69 from Chepstow (passes close BR Chepstow), alight Bigsweir Bridge, 2m (📞 01633 265100). Local services very infrequent - ask Warden. 🚉Chepstow 7m (connects with Red & White 69).
ℹ️📞01600 713899

NEXT HOSTELS
Monmouth 8m, Welsh Bicknor 12m, Slimbridge 30m

ADDITIONAL INFO
Medieval banquets every Sat in August. (Ordinary Hostel meals not available on these nights). Banquets cam also be arranged for groups.

HOW TO GET THERE
In centre of village follow signs from A466.
OS 162 GR 558045 Bart 13

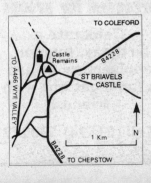

80 BEDS **Open: 17.00hrs**

Welsh Bicknor

Youth Hostel, Welsh Bicknor Rectory, Nr Goodrich, Ross-on-Wye, Herefordshire HR9 6JJ ☎ 01594 860300

Overnight Charges: Under 18 £5.35 Adult £8.00
Family accommodation prices on p.11-13

☐ ☐ ☐ ☐ ☐ ☐ ☐ ☐ S ☐ 2x36, 1x26
☐ Cars and mini-buses. Coaches - contact Warden. BABA

Feb 17 - Feb 25	Open
Feb 27 - Apr 1	Open Fr/Sat only
Apr 3 - Jul 1	Open X:Sun
Jul 3 - Sep 2	Open
Sep 15 - Oct 12	Open Fr/Sat only
Oct 13 - Oct 28	Open
Oct 30 - Nov 30	Open Fr/Sat only

Open Bank Hol Sun Apr 16, May 7, 28. May be available for groups when otherwise closed.

ACCOMMODATION ☐7 ☐7 ☐1

In an idyllic setting on the banks of the River Wye, this early Victorian Rectory is surrounded by meadows and wooded hillside with magnificent views across the Forest of Dean and Symonds Yat Rock. High standard of comfort and facilities. Popular with school groups mid-week in spring/summer terms.
The Wye Valley & Forest of Dean is a superb area for walking, canoeing, mountain biking and abseiling. ☐4m ☐ ☐ ☐3m ☐3m ☐6m

TRAVEL INFO
☐Stagecoach Red & White 34 Gloucester - Ross-on-Wye, alight Goodrich Village 1 ½m
(☎ 0345 125436) ☐Lydney 12m; Gloucester 19m.
☐ ☎01989 562768

NEXT HOSTELS
Monmouth 8m, St Briavel's Castle 12m

ADDITIONAL INFO
Separate self-contained cottage sleeps 14. Ideal for families and groups. Own river landing stage.

HOW TO GET THERE
Cars and mini-buses follow lane from Goodrich, second right after cattle grid. Coaches park in layby near SCA Packaging. Guests walk in via footbridge.
OS 162 GR 591177

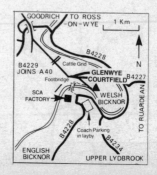

The Heart of England combines open countryside and picturesque, unspoilt villages with Shakespeare's Stratford and the new town of Milton Keynes.

The Edwardian spa town of Malvern leads onto the virtually unknown hills of Worcestershire which inspired Britain's finest composer, Sir Edward Elgar. Another undiscovered tourist attraction is Northamptonshire with its wide and sweeping countryside. Inland waterways pass near all Youth Hostels in the south of this area, with the Grand Union Canal — which offers walkers and cyclists an interesting route — joining the River Avon at Warwick, home to the castles of Warwick and Kenilworth. The many waterway museums are also well worth a visit.

Many Hostels are available for exclusive use by groups booked in advance; please enquire. Plus, Badby, Copt Oak and Bradwell Village Youth Hostels are on YHA's **Rent-a-Hostel scheme** which runs during the winter months (details on p.7).

USEFUL PUBLICATIONS

Educational Visits to Stratford-upon-Avon — send s.a.e to Stratford Youth Hostel, Hemmingford House, Alveston, Stratford-upon-Avon, Warks. CV37 7RG.

Budget Accommodation in the Heart of England and individual Hostel leaflets — send s.a.e. to the YHA Regional Office listed below or phone our Literature Line on (01426) 951683 (local call charge).

**For more information about hostelling in this area contact: YHA South England Regional Office, 11B York Road, Salisbury, Wiltshire SP2 7AP.
Tel: (01722) 337494.
Fax: (01722) 414027.**

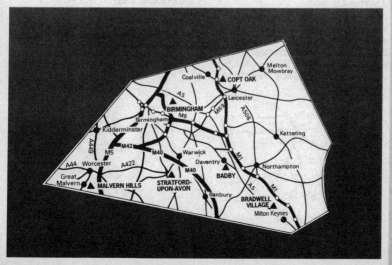

32 BEDS	**Open: 17.00hrs**

Badby

Youth Hostel, Church Green, Badby, Daventry, Northamptonshire NN11 3AS
📞 **01327 703883**

Out of season contact: Regional Booking Service, 11B York Road, Salisbury, Wiltshire SP2 7AP
📞 01722 337494 Fax: 01722 414027

Overnight Charges: Under 18 £4.45 Adult £6.55

R-a-H 📞 01722 337494 [i] [GSC] [⊠] [S] [◉] ⅓m

P Very limited.

Jan 1 - Apr 6	Rent-a-Hostel
Apr 7 - May 31	Open X:Sun/Mon
Jun 1 - Aug 31	Open X:Sun
Sep 1 - Oct 28	Open X:Sun/Mon
Oct 29 - Dec 31	Rent-a-Hostel

ACCOMMODATION

This 17th century country cottage — situated on the Church Green in Badby village — retains much of its original character with stone floors and wooden beams. This is a small traditional 'comfort improved' Hostel in one of the most picturesque villages in Northamptonshire.
As well as grand country houses, ancient churches and peaceful villages, the area offers sweeping landscapes and a network of quiet lanes and footpaths — ideal for walkers and cyclists.
⚅ ½m ▱ 3m

TRAVEL INFO

🚌 Stagecoach United Counties X64 Corby-Coventry; 41 from Northampton (both pass BR Northampton) (📞 01604 36681); Geoff Amos from BR Rugby (📞 01327 702181). On all, alight Daventry 2m. 🚉 Long Buckby 6m, Rugby 12m.
ℹ📞 01327 300277

NEXT HOSTELS

Bradwell 21m, Stratford 24m, Charlbury 29m

ADDITIONAL INFO

Due to nature of this building smaller bedrooms adjoin larger ones.

HOW TO GET THERE

Badby village is just off the A361, Daventry - Banbury Road. Follow Main Street past both Pubs, turn left into Vicarage Hill, up to Church Green and turn left.
OS 152 GR 561588

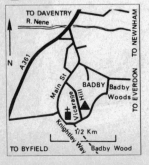

38 BEDS	**Open: 17.00hrs**

Bradwell Village (Milton Keynes)

Youth Hostel, Manor Farm, Vicarage Road, Bradwell Village, Milton Keynes, Bucks. MK13 9AJ 📞 **01908 310944**

Out of season contact: Regional Booking Service, 11B York Road, Salisbury, Wiltshire SP2 7AP
📞 01722 337494 Fax: 01722 414027

Overnight Charges: Under 18 £4.45 Adult £6.55

R-a-H 📞 01722 337494 [i] [GSC] [▥] [◉] 300meters

P At rear of Hostel. For coaches - contact Warden.

Jan 1 - Apr 6	Rent-a-Hostel
Apr 7 - Aug 31	Open X:Sun*
Sep 1 - Oct 28	Open X:Sun/Mon
Oct 29 - Dec 31	Rent-a-Hostel

* Open Bank Hol Sun.

ACCOMMODATION

A charming 18th century farmhouse in the village of Bradwell close to the city of Milton Keynes — for a unique blend of old and new, city and countryside, real cows and concrete!
Enjoy the extensive system of 'Redway' paths or look and learn with the town art trail. Enjoy a picnic in one of the city parks, discover the ruins dating back to Roman times or follow the Grand Union Canal out into the beautiful Buckinghamshire countryside. 🎣 ⛵ ⛰ ▱ ⚅

TRAVEL INFO

🚌 Frequent from surrounding areas (📞 01908 668366). 🚉 Milton Keynes Central 1m. 📞 01908 378883.
ℹ 📞 01908 232525

NEXT HOSTELS

Ivinghoe 19m, Badby 21m, Oxford 38m

ADDITIONAL INFO

We can cater for groups of 10 or more booked in advance.

HOW TO GET THERE

OS 152 GR 831395 Bart 14

80 BEDS   **Open: 17.00hrs**

Birmingham

Youth Hostel, Cambrian Halls, Brindley Drive, off Cambridge Street, Birmingham, West Midlands B1 2NB
📞 **0121 233 3044 (only when Hostel is open)**

Information and price details: Stratford-upon-Avon YHA, Hemmingford House, Alveston, Stratford-upon-Avon, Warwicks CV37 7RG
📞 01789 297093 Fax: 01789 205513

| Jul 10 - Sep 8 | Open |

ACCOMMODATION 🛏️²⁻⁴ 40

University Halls of Residence situated close to the city's many amenities. All rooms are singles with keys and private facilities. There is ample parking on-site.
As well as many shops, cinemas, theatres and restaurants, the International Convention Centre, Symphony Hall and National Indoor area are just 5 minutes walk from the Hostel. An ideal base for a city break.

TRAVEL INFO
🚌 Frequent from surrounding areas (📞 0121 200 2700). 🚉 Birmingham New Street ½m.
ℹ️ 📞 0121 643 2514

NEXT HOSTELS
Stratford-upon-Avon 20m, Ironbridge 25m, Malvern Hills 30m

ADDITIONAL INFO
This Hostel is only open during the summer from July - September.

HOW TO GET THERE
OS 139 GR 063870

---

20 BEDS   **Open: 17.00hrs**

Copt Oak

Youth Hostel, The Youth Hostel, Whitwick Rd, Copt Oak, Markfield, Leicestershire LE67 9QB 📞 **01530 242661**

Overnight Charges: Under 18 £4.00 Adult £5.95

 R-a-H 📞 01722 337494 [1] 6SC 🛏️ 🚿 🍽️ 🖼️ 2m P

Jan 6 - Mar 31	Open Fr/Sat
Apr 1 - Oct 31	Open X:Tu
Nov 1 - Dec 16	Open Fr/Sat
Dec 17 - Dec 31	Rent-a-Hostel

The Hostel may be available for groups when otherwise closed - please contact Warden.

ACCOMMODATION 🛏️⁵⁻⁸ 1 🛏️⁹⁺ 1

This converted school house in the hills of north west Leicestershire has recently been modernised to provide a good standard of accommodation — without losing any of its traditional appeal! It makes an ideal base for visiting the East Midlands. Nearby Charnwood Forest offers some superb countryside for walking and cycling, while the historic cities of Leicester and Nottingham are also well worth a visit. Other local attractions include Donington Race Circuit, the National Watersports Centre at Holme Pierpoint and Bosworth Battlefield. 🏛️12m 🚉4m

TRAVEL INFO
🚌 Midland Fox/Barton/Kinchbus 121 Leicester-Loughborough; otherwise Midland Fox 117-9, 217-8 Leicester-Coalville (pass close BR Leicester), alight Flying Horse roundabout 1m (📞 0116 2511411). 🚉 Loughborough 7m.
ℹ️ 📞 0116 2511300

NEXT HOSTELS
Badby 42m, Stratford 45m, Matlock 35m

HOW TO GET THERE
OS 129 GR 482129 Bart 24

59 BEDS	Open: 17.00hrs

Malvern Hills

Youth Hostel, 18 Peachfield Road, Malvern Wells, Malvern, Worcestershire WR14 4AP
☎ 01684 569131 Fax: 01684 565205

Overnight Charges: Under 18 £4.85 Adult £7.20

2 🍳 🛏 🔍 ⊞ ✉ ½m P Cars and mini-buses (coach parking 600yds). BABA

Feb 13 - Feb 28	Open
Mar 1 - Mar 31	Open X:Tu/Wed
Apr 1 - Oct 31	Open
Nov 1 - Dec 21	Open Fr/Sat
Dec 24 - Dec 26	Open for Xmas

The Hostel may be available for groups when otherwise closed - please contact Warden.

ACCOMMODATION 🛏2-4 4 🛏5-8 4 🛏9+ 2

Nestling on the slopes of the beautiful Malvern Hills, this homely Youth Hostel offers a very warm welcome and good food, as well as spectacular views of the hills and the Severn Valley. The large enclosed garden makes a great play area and is an ideal place to relax.
The majestic Malvern Hills and surrounding commons have been designated as an Area of Outstanding Natural Beauty. Great Malvern is a Victorian spa town. Inspiration for Elgar and home of the English String Orchestra, the Malverns have the unique atmosphere of an inland resort. 🚴3m U2m ✈½m 🏛13m ☎1m 🏠1m

TRAVEL INFO
🚌Frequent from surrounding areas (☎ 0345 212 555). 🚉 Great Malvern 1 ½m.
🛈 ☎01684 892289.

NEXT HOSTELS
Cleeve Hill 23m, Welsh Bicknor 28m, Ludlow 31m

HOW TO GET THERE
1 ½m S of Great Malvern on the Wells Road (A449). Turn opposite Railway Inn into Peachfield Road.
OS 150 GR 774440 Barl 13

156 BEDS	Open: 24hrs

Stratford-Upon-Avon

Youth Hostel, Hemmingford House, Alveston, Stratford-Upon-Avon, Warwickshire CV37 7RG ☎ 01789 297093
Fax: 01789 205513

Overnight Charges: Under 18 £9.05 Adult £12.20
Bed & Breakfast included.

4 🍳 🛏 🔍 ⊞ ✉ 🅂 ☎ 1m 🚿 P Large car park with space for mini-buses and coaches. BABA IBN

Jan 4 - Dec 16	Open

ACCOMMODATION 🛏2-4 6 🛏5-8 10 🛏9+ 7

This magnificent Georgian mansion — only 1 ½m from the historic town of Stratford-upon-Avon — is set in extensive grounds suitable for games and relaxation. Its modern cafeteria serves a wide range of excellent meals and snacks to suit all tastes and pockets.
Internationally famous as the birthplace of the world's greatest playwright and home of the Royal Shakespeare Company, Stratford-upon-Avon makes an ideal base for exploring Shakespeare's Country. Families, groups and travellers will also find plenty of scope for interesting 'days out'. 🚴2m 🏛1 ½m ☎🏠2m

TRAVEL INFO
🚌Stratford Blue 18 🚉Stratford-upon-Avon (not Sun, except May - Sep) 2 ½m.
🛈 ☎01789 293127

NEXT HOSTELS
Stow-on-the-Wold 20m, Badby 24m, Birmingham 20m (summer only)

ADDITIONAL INFO
IBN booking centre. Excellent conference location.

HOW TO GET THERE
OS 151 GR 231562

The beautiful hill country of Shropshire, designated an Area of Outstanding Natural Beauty, lies on the Welsh border. The old towns in the area house several exhibition centres on subjects which highlight the wide choice of attractions and activities — from historic costume to modern country life. The extensive Ironbridge complex is well worth a visit for a few days. There is a good mix of Hostels in this area including large full catering establishments and simple rural Hostels which are ideal for walkers and cyclists. Wenlock Edge and the Wrekin are two good viewpoints.

Many Hostels are available for exclusive use by groups booked in advance; please enquire. Plus, Clun Mill Youth Hostel is on YHA's **Rent-a-Hostel scheme** which runs during the winter months (details on p.7).

USEFUL PUBLICATIONS

Offa's Dyke information — contact: Offa's Dyke Centre, West Street, Knighton, Powys LD7 1EW.

"The Shropshire Way" by Robert Kirk (a 172-mile route through the Shropshire countryside) — available from the Rambler's Association, 1/5 Wandsworth Road, LONDON SW8 2XX. Tel: 0171 582 6878.

Budget Accommodation in the Heart of England and individual Hostel leaflets — send s.a.e. to the Regional Office listed below or phone our Literature Line on (01426) 951683 (local call charge).

For more information about hostelling in this area contact: YHA South England Regional Office, 11B York Road, Salisbury, Wiltshire SP2 7AP.
Tel: (01722) 337494.
Fax: (01722) 414027.

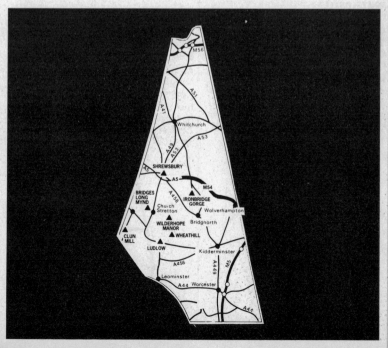

37 BEDS	Open: 17.00hrs

Bridges Long Mynd

Youth Hostel, Ratlinghope, Shrewsbury, Shropshire SY5 OSP ☎ 01588 650656
Fax: 01694 771296

Overnight Charges: Under 18 £4.45 Adult £6.55

2 ⭘ 6SC A ✳ ⊕ S ▣ 5m P For cars and coaches. BABA

Jan 1 - Feb 28	open for advance bookings only
Mar 1 - Nov 19	Open
Nov 20 - Dec 31	open for advance bookings only

ACCOMMODATION   🛏5-8 2 🛏9+ 2

This traditional Hostel — an old village school set in the beautiful countryside between the Long Mynd and Stiperstones in the Shropshire Hills — is an ideal base for walking, cycling, birdwatching and just getting away from it all! Good for families too.
As well as the Long Mynd and the Stiperstones, the Shropshire Way passes close to the Hostel and there are many quiet lanes for cycling. This interesting geological area has some of Britain's oldest rocks. Other attractions include the Acton Scott Farm Museum (8m) and Bishops Castle (8m). 🚲6m 🅤4m ⛰1m

TRAVEL INFO
🚌 Horrocks 551 from Shrewsbury (Tue only) (☎ 0345 056 785). 🚆 Church Stretton 5m.
🛈 ☎01743 350761

NEXT HOSTELS
Wilderhope 13m, Clun Mill 16m, Shrewsbury 14m.

ADDITIONAL INFO
Please make cheques payable to Bridges Youth Hostel. No credit cards accepted. Access from Church Stretton can be difficult in winter.

HOW TO GET THERE
From Church Stretton, take 'The Burway' and take right fork at top of Long Mynd. From Shrewsbury take road via Longden and Pulverbatch, then left by Horseshoe Inn.
OS 137 GR 395965 Bart 18

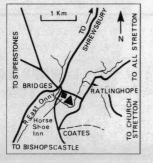

24 BEDS	Open: 17.00hrs

Clun Mill

Youth Hostel, The Mill, Clun, Near Craven Arms, Shropshire SY7 8NY ☎ 01588 640582

Out of season contact: Ironbridge Youth Hostel, Paradise, Coalbrookdale, Telford, Shropshire TF8 7NR ☎ 01952 433281 Fax: 01952 433166

Overnight Charges: Under 18 £4.45 Adult £6.55

R-a-H ☎ 01722 337494

1 6SC 🏃 A ✳ ⊕ S ▣ 1/3m P

Jan 1 - Apr 6	Rent-a-Hostel
Apr 7 - Aug 31	Open X:Wed
Sep 1 - Dec 31	Rent-a-Hostel

ACCOMMODATION   🛏5-8 2 🛏9+ 1

This charming Hostel, sympathetically upgraded and now very comfortable, was a former watermill (you can still see the workings). It is a haven of peace and tranquility set in a stone-built town unspoilt by modern development with its narrow 16th century humpbacked bridge and Norman castle.
Centuries past echo through this area with its picturesque ruins and magnificent restorations of castles and abbeys. From the sinuous ridge of Offa's Dyke on the Welsh border to the elegance of the fortified manor at Stokesay, the very earth and stones breath intrigue! 🚲 🅤 ⛰ 📷

TRAVEL INFO
🚌 Midland Red West 741-5 from Ludlow (pass close BR Ludlow and Bishop's Castle), alight Clun, 1/4m (☎ 0345 056 785). 🚆 Broome or Hopton (not Sun, except Jun-Sep) both 7m; Craven Arms 10m.
🛈 ☎01584 875053

NEXT HOSTELS
Bridges 16m, Ludlow 18m, Wilderhope 20m

ADDITIONAL INFO
No drying room.

HOW TO GET THERE
From Clun High Street (B4368) go to the end of Ford Street, turn right and immediately left. Hostel 250yds on right.
OS 137 GR 303812 Bart 18

Ironbridge Gorge

Youth Hostel, Paradise, Coalbrookdale, Telford, Shropshire TF8 7NR
☎ 01952 433281 Fax: 01952 433166

Overnight Charges: Under 18 £5.95 Adult £8.80

2 ▢ ▦ ▣ ▨ ▤ ½m ⚲ 2x30 P Small car park
(coaches contact Warden) BABA

Feb 1 - Nov 25	Open

The Hostel may be available for groups when otherwise closed - please contact Warden.

ACCOMMODATION 🛏️²⁻⁴ 13 🛏️⁵⁻⁸ 6 🛏️⁹⁺ 1

This imposing but friendly Hostel — built in the 19th century as the Literacy and Scientific Institute for workers at the nearby Ironworks — is ideal for groups and families, with lots of small rooms and speciality home-cooking. 'Heartbeat Award' winner for healthy menus. Popular with groups from April to June.
Set in the Severn Gorge close to the spectacular Iron bridge (the first in the world), the Hostel is at the centre of six square miles of World Heritage — including eight museums. There are also chocolate factories, the famous Severn Valley Steam Railway and beautiful walks in the area.
🏔️16m 🏛️3m 🚲 ⛲3m

TRAVEL INFO
🚌Frequent from Wellington & Telford (pass close BR Wellington Telford West & Telford Central) (☎ 0345 056 785). 🚉Telford Central 5m; Wellington Telford West 5m.
🛈☎01952 432166

NEXT HOSTELS
Shrewsbury 14m, Wilderhope 13m, Ludlow 26m

ADDITIONAL INFO
Holiday packages available all year round. Conference facilities available. Shropshire Hostel booking service.

HOW TO GET THERE
Take major motorways to Telford centre, then follow signs for Ironbridge - with bridge on left, turn right at roundabout into Coalbrookdale. Hostel ½m on right.
OS 127 GR 671043 Bart 18

Knighton

Temporary closure until further notice. Contact ☎ 01222 222122 for details of alternative Hostel accommodation in this area.

SHROPSHIRE & THE WELSH BORDERS

50 BEDS	Open: 17.00hrs

Ludlow

Youth Hostel, Ludford Lodge, Ludford, Ludlow, Shropshire SY8 1PJ
☎ 01584 872472 Fax: 01584 872095

Overnight Charges: Under 18 £4.45 Adult £6.55

Family accommodation prices on p.11-13

2 ⬛ 6SC ⬛ S ⬛ 50yds P Very limited. Free parking ¼m - ask Warden. BABA

Feb 1 - Feb 28	Open Fr/Sat
Mar 1 - Apr 6	Open X:Sun/Mon
Apr 7 - Aug 31	Open X:Sun*
Sep 1 - Oct 31	Open X:Sun/Mon
Nov 1 - Dec 23	Open Fr/Sat
Dec 24 - Dec 28	Open for Xmas

* Open Bank Hol Sun. The Hostel may be available for groups when otherwise closed - please contact Warden.

ACCOMMODATION 🛏²⁻⁴ 1 🛏⁵⁻⁸ 5 🛏⁹⁺ 2

Ideally placed for touring the Shropshire Hills and Welsh Marches, Ludford Lodge stands on the banks of the river Teme facing the town across the medieval Ludford Bridge.
Often praised as one of England's architectural gems, Ludlow is well worth visiting to view the blend of elegant Georgian town houses, the ruined castle and St Laurence's parish church.
�²⁴ U 1m 🏔️5m ⛰️ 🔄 🔲 ½m

TRAVEL INFO
🚌 Midland Red West 192, 292 Birmingham - Hereford to within ¼m (☎ 0345 212 555).
🚂 Ludlow ½m.
🅱 ☎ 01584 875053

NEXT HOSTELS
Wheathill 9m, Wilderhope Manor 15m, Clun Mill 18m

HOW TO GET THERE
OS 137 GR 513741

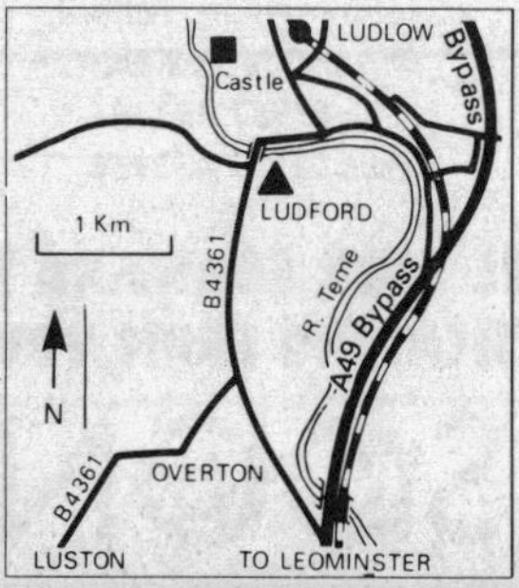

64 BEDS	Open: 17.00hrs

Shrewsbury

Youth Hostel, The Woodlands, Abbey Foregate, Shrewsbury, Shropshire SY2 6LZ
☎ 01743 360179 Fax: 01743 357423

Out of season contact: Ironbridge Gorge Youth Hostel ☎ 01952 433281

Overnight Charges: Under 18 £5.35 Adult £8.00

 ⬛ 6SC ⬛ S ⬛ ⅓m P BABA

Feb 10 - Feb 28	Open Fr/Sat
Mar 1 - Mar 31	Open X:Sun/Mon
Apr 1 - Jun 30	Open X:Sun*
Jul 1 - Aug 31	Open
Sep 1 - Oct 31	Open X:Sun
Nov 1 - Dec 10	Open Fr/Sat
Dec 28 - Dec 31	Open for New Year

* Open Bank Hol Sun. The Hostel may be available for groups when otherwise closed - please contact Warden.

ACCOMMODATION 🛏¹⁻⁴ 3 🛏⁵⁻⁸ 5 🛏⁹⁺ 2

A former Victorian Ironmasters house built in a distinct Red Sandstone, the Hostel is set in its own attractive grounds just on the outskirts of Shrewsbury. Comfortable accommodation, friendly service and great home-cooked meals. Shrewsbury, the county town of Shropshire, is built in a loop of the river Severn. As well as 500 listed buildings from all periods of history, this medieval market town is also the birthplace of Charles Darwin and home of Brother Cadfael. An ideal base to explore the Shropshire Hills. U 10m
🏔️10m ⛰️ 1m 🔲 10m 🔲 1 ½m

TRAVEL INFO
🚌 Frequent from surrounding areas (☎ 0345 056785). 🚂 Shrewsbury 1m.
🅱 ☎ 01743 350761

NEXT HOSTELS
Ironbridge 14m, Wilderhope 18m, Ludlow 28m

ADDITIONAL INFO
Good public transport links. Part of the Shropshire booking service.

HOW TO GET THERE
OS 126 GR 505120 Bart 23

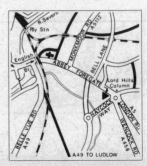

28 BEDS   **Open: 17.00hrs**

Wheathill

Youth Hostel, Malthouse Farm, Wheathill, Bridgnorth, Shropshire WV16 6QT
☎ **01746 787236**

Overnight Charges: Under 18 £3.60 Adult £5.35

2 6SC A ⌧ ⊙ S ▣ 3m P Cars only (coaches nearby).

Jan 1 - Mar 31	Open X:Mon
Apr 1 - Jun 4	Open
Jun 15 - Sep 10	Open
Sep 20 - Dec 21	Open X:Mon
Dec 29 - Dec 31	Open for New Year

ACCOMMODATION   🛏9+2

Part of a Malthouse Farm dating from the 17th century, this simple Youth Hostel is in a truly rural setting in the Clee Hills.

This is excellent walking country with easy access to the Shropshire Way, Shropshire Challenge Walk and Shropshire Ring Walk. The Hostel is also close to many pleasant cycling routes along quiet country lanes. 🚶9m 🅿12m ▲1m 🚲¼m 🛒9m

TRAVEL INFO

🚌Infrequent from Ludlow, alight Three Horseshoes 1m; otherwise Midland Red West 192, 292 Hereford - Birmingham (passes close BR Ludlow & Kidderminster), alight Hopton Bank, 5m (☎ 0345 056 785). 🚇Ludlow 9m.
🛈 ☎01584 875053

NEXT HOSTELS

Ludlow 9m, Wilderhope Manor 12m, Bridges 23m

ADDITIONAL INFO

No showers. No credit cards accepted. Snack meals available. Please make cheques payable to F. Powell.

HOW TO GET THERE

Leave Bridgnorth or Ludlow on B4364, look out for Three Horse Shoes pub in Wheathill. Turn off adjacent to pub car park. Hostel 1m on right.
OS 138 GR 613818 Bart 18

---

56 BEDS   **Open: 17.00hrs**

Wilderhope Manor

Youth Hostel, The John Cadbury Memorial Hostel, Easthope, Much Wenlock, Shropshire, TF13 6EG ☎ **01694 771363**
Fax: 01694 771520

Overnight Charges: Under 18 £5.35 Adult £8.00

1 ⋈ A ⌧ ⌧ ⊙ S ⌸ 1x25 P BABA

Jan 1 - Feb 28	Open for groups booking in advance
Mar 1 - Oct 31	Open X:Sun*
Nov 1 - Dec 31	Open for groups booking in advance

* Open Bank Hol Sun.

ACCOMMODATION   🛏2+1 🛏4+2 🛏9+3

Owned by the National Trust, this superb Elizabethan Manor House is idyllically situated on top of Wenlock Edge. Two spiral staircases, original plasterwork, the baronial banqueting room and timber-framed lounge are all evocative of a bygone era.

Shropshire's timeless beauty is unique. Its rich soils and varied landscapes have been farmed, fought over and hunted for centuries. This priceless heritage has awed visitors and inspired artists through the ages — a haven for country lovers. 🚶8m 🅿3m ▲ 🚲🛒13m

TRAVEL INFO

🚌Limited service. 🚇Church Stretton 8m.
🛈 ☎01743 350761

NEXT HOSTELS

Wheathill 12m, Bridges 13m, Ironbridge 13m

ADDITIONAL INFO

Banquets organised for groups.

HOW TO GET THERE

Coaches should come from Longville (B4371)
OS 137 GR 544928 Bart 18

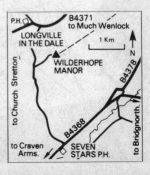

Cotswolds

Rolling hills and spreading valleys, orchards and market towns are all set in English countryside at its best. The Cotswold Area of Outstanding Natural Beauty, with its gently formed hills and rich upland pastures of the Cotswold Plateau, covers about 660 square miles from near Bath to the south of Evesham. Local yellow stone gives a mellow warmth to the buildings set in some of the most beautiful villages in Britain. 'Wool' churches and manor houses from days of prosperous sheep rearing can be visited, as well as viewpoints such as Bredon Hill, Salter's Hill and Haresfield Beacon. The university town of Oxford with its architectural splendour and meandering river can be explored easily by staying at Oxford Youth Hostel.

There are several long distance walks in the area, such as the Oxfordshire Way, the Ridgeway National Trail, Thames Footpath and the Cotswold Way (100 miles long).

USEFUL PUBLICATIONS

Ridgeway Information and Accommodation Guide — available from the Ridgeway Officer, Countryside Centre, Library Headquarters, Holton, Oxford, OX9 1QQ.

Walking routes around Stow-on-the-Wold — send s.a.e. and £1 to Youth Hostel.

Budget Accommodation in the Heart of England and individual Hostel leaflets — send s.a.e. to the YHA Regional Office listed below or phone our Literature Line on (01426) 951683 (local call charge).

For more information about hostelling in this area contact: YHA South England Regional Office, 11B York Road, Salisbury, Wiltshire SP2 7AP. Tel: (01722) 337494. Fax: (01722) 414027.

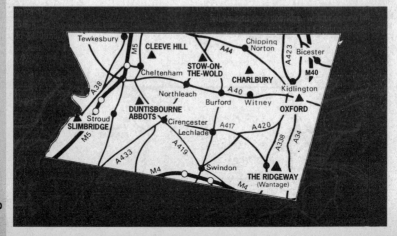

Charlbury

Youth Hostel, The Laurels, The Slade, Charlbury, Oxfordshire OX7 3SJ
☎ 01608 810202

Overnight Charges: Under 18 £4.45 Adult £6.55
[symbols] 1x30 P In layby 150yds and limited on site. NO PARKING IN DITCHLEY ROAD.

Jan 3 - Jan 31	Open Fr/Sat/Sun
Feb 1 - Mar 31	Open X:Mon/Tu
Apr 1 - Aug 31	Open X:Sun
Sep 1 - Oct 31	Open X:Mon/Tu
Dec 29 - Jan 2 '96	Open for New Year

The Hostel may be available for groups when otherwise closed - please contact Warden.

ACCOMMODATION 4 6

Situated in a quiet riverside village between Oxford and Stratford-upon-Avon, this attractive 19th century stone house —a former glove factory— has been recently refurbished to a good standard. Enjoy home cooking and a friendly atmosphere too.
You'll be ideally located for exploring the Cotswolds, with cycling and walking routes available at the Hostel. Or make the most of the good public transport or cycle hire at the Hostel to visit Blenheim Palace, the Cotswold Wildlife Park and North Leigh Roman Villa.

TRAVEL INFO
Worths from Oxford, Witney, Woodstock, Chipping Norton, ☎ 01608 677322. Charlbury 1m.
☎ 01993 811038

NEXT HOSTELS
Oxford 15m, Stow 12m, Stratford 30m

ADDITIONAL INFO
Please make cheques payable to Charlbury Youth Hostel.

HOW TO GET THERE
Turn off A44 Oxford - Stratford Road at Enstone. Follow B4022 into village, turn left at first crossroads. Hostel 75yds on left.
OS 164 GR 361198 Bart 14

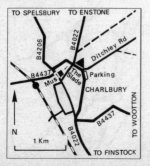

Cleeve Hill

Youth Hostel, Rock House, Cleeve Hill, Cheltenham, Gloucestershire GL52 3PR
☎ 01242 672065

Out of season contact: Duntisbourne Abbots Youth Hostel, Duntisbourne Abbots, Cirencester, Glos. GL7 7JN ☎ 01285 821682 Fax: 01285 821697

Overnight Charges: Under 18 £4.45 Adult £6.55
[symbols] P Layby on main road 200yds.

Apr 7 - Sep 30	Open X:Mon/Tu

The Hostel may be available for groups when otherwise closed - please contact Warden.

ACCOMMODATION 1 2

This traditional self-catering Hostel — once a Victorian golf clubhouse — is situated on the edge of Cleeve Common with magnificent views across the Seven valley and the spa town of Cheltenham. The common is ideal for walking holidays with its escarpment and rolling grassland. The spa town of Cheltenham has lots to offer — including parks, sports facilities, festivals and attractions — and historic Suderley Castle is just 5m away.
1 ½m 4m

TRAVEL INFO
Castleways from Cheltenham Spa (passes close BR Cheltenham Spa) (☎ 01242 602949).
Cheltenham Spa 5m.
☎ 01242 522878

NEXT HOSTELS
Duntisbourne Abbots 14m, Stow-on-the-Wold 16m, Malvern Hills 23m

ADDITIONAL INFO
Food provisions for self-catering groups can be provided if ordered in advance.

HOW TO GET THERE
B4632 passes Hostel.
OS 163 GR 983267 Bart 13

68 BEDS   **Open: 17.00hrs**

Duntisbourne Abbots

**Youth Hostel, Duntisbourne Abbots,
Cirencester, Gloucestershire GL7 7JN**
☎ 01285 821682 Fax: 01285 821697

Overnight Charges: Under 18 £4.85 Adult £7.20

Family accommodation prices on p.11-13

① ⊙ ⑤ⓢ⑥ 🗻 ▣ ⑨ ⑧ ⊕ ⊘ 1x36, 1x20 🅿 For cars, mini-buses and coaches. BABA

Jan 6 - Feb 28	Open Fr/Sat/Sun
Mar 1 - Nov 4	Open X:Sun*
Nov 5 - Dec 18	Open Sun/Mon

Open Bank Hol Sun. The Hostel may be available for groups when otherwise closed - please contact Warden.

ACCOMMODATION 🛏2-4 2 🛏5-8 3 🛏9+ 3

The Old Rectory — set in 2 acres of its own grounds — is in a quaint Cotswold village at the heart of this Area of Outstanding Natural Beauty. In an area steeped in history, visit nearby Cirencester, the second largest Roman city with its museum and leisure activities. Other attractions include Berkley Castle, Gloucester Cathedral and Crickley Hill Country Park, as well as picturesque Cotswolds villages and market towns. 🚲6m ⛴ △8m 🚂6m

TRAVEL INFO
🚌No Service. 🚉Kemble 10m; Gloucester 14 ½m; Cheltenham Spa 14 ½m; Swindon 22m. 🔰☎01285 654180

NEXT HOSTELS
Cleeve Hill 14m, Stow-on-the-Wold 20m, Slimbrige 23m

HOW TO GET THERE
OS 163 GR 970080 Bart 13

114 BEDS   **Open: 13.00hrs**

Oxford

**Youth Hostel, 32 Jack Straw's Lane, Oxford,
Oxfordshire. OX3 0DW** ☎ 01865 62997
Fax: 01865 69402

Overnight Charges: Under 18 £5.95 Adult £8.80

④ ⊙ ⑤ⓢ⑥ 🗻 ▣ ⑨ ⑧ ⊕ Ⓢ 🅢 ¼m 🅿 Cars and mini-buses. Coach parking available nearby.
BABA IBN

Jan 13 - 31 Dec	Open

ACCOMMODATION 🛏6 🛏5-8 6 🛏9+ 6

This large Victorian house — attractively converted to cater for groups and individuals — is situated in a conservation area only 1 ½m from the ancient university city. Superb copper beech trees and a fine redwood can be found in the Hostel's own grounds.
Oxford has a wealth of scenic attractions and places of interest, including 35 colleges that are open to the public. The Ashmolean University and Pitt Rivers Museums are among the finest in the country. Add Oxford's famous bookshops and not even bad weather could spoil your visit!
🚲¼m △2m 🚂2m

TRAVEL INFO
🚌Frequent from city centre (☎ 01865 711312). "Green Nipper" buses 72, 73, 74 from bus stop near to main Post Office in St Aldates. 🚉Oxford 2 ½m.
🔰☎01865 726871

NEXT HOSTELS
Charlbury 15m, Ridgeway 17m, Streatley 19m

HOW TO GET THERE
Hostel is located approx. 1 ¼m along Marston Road from foot of Headington Hill.
OS 164 GR 533074 Bart 14

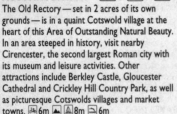

59 BEDS   Open: 17.00hrs

The Ridgeway

Youth Hostel, The Court Hill Ridgeway Centre, Court Hill, Wantage, Oxfordshire OX12 9NE ☏ 012357 60253
Fax: 012357 68865

Overnight Charges: Under 18 £4.85 Adult £7.20

Beds in small cabins with washing facilities may also be booked: Under 18 £5.95 Adult £8.80

Family accommodation prices on p.11-13

Feb 1 - Feb 28	Open Fr/Sat
Mar 1 - Mar 31	Open X:Sun*
Jun 1 - Aug 31	Open
Sep 1 - Dec 1	Open X:Sun
Dec 28 - Jan 2	Open for New Year

* Open Bank Hol Sun. The Hostel may be available for groups when otherwise closed.

ACCOMMODATION   7   9+ 2

This modern purpose-built Hostel on the Ridgeway has been beautifully reconstructed from five former barns around a traditional courtyard with stabling for horses, a Beech Wood, campsite, barbecue and picnic area. Close to many famous walks.
18m 2m ½m ½m 2m

TRAVEL INFO
Thames Transit 32/A, 35/A, 36/A from BR Didcot Parkway, alight Wantage, 2m. Didcot Parkway 10m.
☏ 01235 760176

NEXT HOSTELS
Streatley 14m, Oxford 17m, Charlbury 32m

ADDITIONAL INFO
Ideal venue for conferences and meetings.

HOW TO GET THERE
Turn at junction 14 on M4, follow signs to Wantage. From Oxford A420 turn on to A338. Well sign posted from A338 and market square. No direct route from Ridgeway. Access only from A338.
OS 174 GR 393851

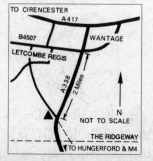

---

56 BEDS   Open: 17.00hrs

Slimbridge

Youth Hostel, Shepherd's Patch, Slimbridge, Gloucestershire GL2 7BP ☏ 01453 890275
Fax: 01453 890625

Overnight Charges: Under 18 £5.95 Adult £8.80

Family accommodation prices on p.11-13

Jan 1 - Feb 28	Open X:Sun
Mar 1 - Aug 31	Open
Sep 1 - Nov 30	Open X:Sun
Dec 22 - Dec 26	Open for Xmas

The Hostel may be available for groups when otherwise closed - please contact Warden.

ACCOMMODATION   7   5   1

This comfortable purpose-built Hostel has its own pond and wildfowl collection which can be enjoyed from an observation room. The Hostel has five 2-bedded rooms which can be booked by couples, as well as group leaders.
Sir Peter Scott's Wildfowl and Wetlands Trust is ½m away. Other local attractions include the National Waterways Museum, the historic Gloucester Docks, Gloucester Cathedral, Berkeley Castle, the Jenner Museum, the Severn Bore, the Cotswolds Way and Severn Way.
5m 10m 4 ½m 5m

TRAVEL INFO
Badgerline 308 Bristol - Gloucester; City of Gloucester 91 Gloucester - Dursley; Stroud Valleys 16 Stonehouse - Uley (☏ 01452 527516). On all alight Slimbridge Cross Roads, 1½m. Cam and Dursley 3m; Stonehouse 8½m
☏ 01452 421188

NEXT HOSTELS
Duntisbourne 23m, Cleeve Hill 22m, Bristol 25m

ADDITIONAL INFO
Ideal for conferences.

HOW TO GET THERE
By road turn off A38 at Slimbridge crossroads, go through main village and after 1½m turn right at Tudor Arms.
OS 162 GR 730043 Bart 13

60 BEDS | **Open: 17.00hrs**

Stow On The Wold

Youth Hostel, Stow On The Wold,
Cheltenham, Gloucestershire GL54 1AF
☎ 01451 830497 Fax: 01451 870102

Overnight Charges: Under 18 £4.45 Adult £6.55

[1] [⊙] [ESC] [⊞] [▣] [▣] [P] In square. [BABA]

Feb 1 - Feb 28	Open Fr/Sat /Sun
Mar 1 - Apr 30	Open X:Sun*
May 1 - Aug 31	Open
Sep 1 - Oct 28	Open X:Sun
Oct 29 - Dec 17	Open Fr/Sat/Sun
Dec 28 - Dec 31	Open for New Year

* Open Bank Hol Sun.

ACCOMMODATION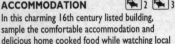

In this charming 16th century listed building,
sample the comfortable accommodation and
delicious home cooked food while watching local
life drift through the historic market square of
this beautiful Cotswold town.
Standing 800ft above sea level in an Area of
Outstanding Natural Beauty, the town is famous
for its honey coloured stone buildings and many
antique shops. As well as picturesque villages at
Bourton and the Slaughters, the Cotswold Farm
Park is well worth a visit to see the famous
Cotswold sheep. [▣]4m [U]3m [▲]20m
[▣][▣]20m

TRAVEL INFO
[▣]Pulhams Cheltenham Spa - Moreton-in-Marsh
(passes close BR Cheltenham Spa &
Moreton-in-Marsh) (☎ 01451 820369).
[▣]Kingham 4m; Moreton-in-Marsh 4m.
[ℹ]☎01451 831082

NEXT HOSTELS
Cleeve Hill 16m, Duntisbourne Abbots 20m,
Charlbury 12m

ADDITIONAL INFO
Special meals available for celebrations.

HOW TO GET THERE
[OS] 163 [GR] 191258 [Bart] 14

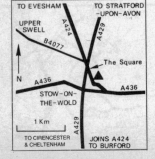

The glorious Norfolk coastline with its seaside attractions is home to good beaches and fun resorts including Sheringham and Hunstanton where the Youth Hostels offer excellent facilities for families.

For all those interested in nature, the sand dunes and cliffs house a number of Bird and Nature Reserves. North east of the cathedral city of Norwich are the famous Norfolk Broads, a series of connecting lakes and waterways which attract thousands of people throughout the year. The Peddars Way National Trail is a fine stretch of Roman Road which also forms a good cycling route across the country.

Sheringham Youth Hostel has specially adapted facilities for people with disabilities. Many of the Youth Hostels are available for exclusive use by groups who book in advance; please enquire. Great Yarmouth and Kings Lynn Youth Hostels are on YHA's **Rent-a-Hostel scheme** which runs during the winter months (details on p.7).

USEFUL PUBLICATIONS

The Norfolk Cycleway — available from the Department of Planning and Property, Norfolk C.C., County Hall, Martineau Lane, Norwich NR1 2DH.

Cycling in Norfolk and Suffolk (leaflet detailing routes, cycle hire and Hostels) — available from Norwich and Saffron Walden Youth Hostels.

Budget Accommodation in Eastern England and individual Hostel leaflets — send s.a.e. to the YHA Regional Office listed below or phone our Literature Line on (01426) 951683 (local call charge).

For more infomation about hostelling in this area contact: YHA South England Regional Office, 11B York Road, Salisbury, Wiltshire SP2 7AP. Tel: (01722) 337494. Fax: (01722) 414027.

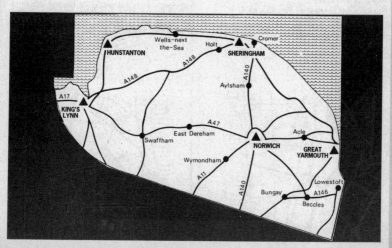

40 BEDS   **Open: 17.00hrs**

Great Yarmouth

Youth Hostel, 2 Sandown Road, Great Yarmouth, Norfolk NR30 1EY
☎ 01493 843991 Fax: 01493 843991

Out of season contact: Regional Booking Service, 11B York Road, Salisbury, Wilts. SP2 7AP
☎ 01722 337494 Fax: 01722 414027

Overnight Charges: Under 18 £5.35 Adult £8.00

Family accommodation prices on p.11-13

R-a-H ☎ 01722 337494 ① ⊙ⓄⓁ SSC Ⓢ ⓢ Ⓟ On roadside by Hostel. BABA

Jan 1 - Apr 6	Rent-a-Hostel
Apr 7 - Jun 30	Open X:Sun/Mon*
Jul 1 - Aug 31	Open
Sep 1 - Dec 31	Rent-a-Hostel

* Open Bank Hol Sun.

ACCOMMODATION 🛏²⁻⁴ 2 🛏⁵⁻⁸ 1 🛏⁹⁺ 1

This comfortable Victorian house is only minutes from the coast, as well as the beautiful Broads National Park. Not just a popular coastal resort, Great Yarmouth is also steeped in history — for instance, you can follow the medieval trail around town (route available from Warden).
Enjoy the modern and medieval, coastal and cultural setting of Yarmouth, one of Britain's favourite holiday towns with its sandy beaches and huge range of traditional seaside attractions and entertainment. This is ideal cycling country along quiet lanes and roads which link up the YHA network. 🚴½m Ⓤ½m ⚠½m 🎣½m 🛶½m

TRAVEL INFO
🚌 Frequent from surrounding areas, also local services (☎ 01603 613613) 🚂 Great Yarmouth ¾m
ℹ ☎ 01493 846345

NEXT HOSTELS
Norwich 21m, Sheringham 39m, Blaxhall 41

HOW TO GET THERE
OS 134 GR 529083 Bart 26

---

48 BEDS   **Open: 17.00hrs**

Hunstanton

Youth Hostel, 15 Avenue Road, Hunstanton, Norfolk PE36 5BW ☎ 01485 532061
Fax: 01485 532632

Overnight Charges: Under 18 £5.35 Adult £8.00

Seasonal Prices Jul 1 - Aug 31: Under 18 £5.95 Adult £8.80

Family accommodation prices on p.11-13

① ⊙ⓄⓁ SSC ⓢ Ⓢ ⓢ ½m Ⓖ 1x35 Ⓟ Road parking outside Hostel. BABA

Mar 1 - Apr 6	Open X:Sun/Mon
Apr 7 - Jun 30	Open X:Sun*
Jul 1 - Aug 31	Open
Sep 1 - Oct 31	Open X:Sun/Mon
Nov 1 - Dec 16	Open Fr/Sat

* Open Bank Hol Sun. The Hostel may be available for groups when otherwise closed - please contact Warden.

ACCOMMODATION 🛏²⁻⁴ 6 🛏⁵⁻⁸ 4

This Victorian town house in the heart of Hunstanton offers comfortable accommodation to suit groups, families and individuals. With its Blue Flag beach and magnificent cliffs, Hunstanton is an ideal holiday resort.
As well as good walking routes along Peddars Way and the Norfolk Coast path, there are many indoor activities on offer — visit Oasis, a large leisure complex, or the Sea Life Centre where you can view our coastal waters and what's lurking below. The Hostel runs canoeing and birdwatching courses. 🚴 Ⓤ ⚠ 🎣3m 🛶

TRAVEL INFO
🚌 Eastern Counties 410, 411 from Kings Lynn (passes close BR Kings Lynn) (☎ 01553 772343) 🚂 Kings Lynn 16m.
ℹ ☎ 01485 532610

NEXT HOSTELS
Kings Lynn 16m, Sheringham 38m, Norwich 40m

HOW TO GET THERE
OS 132 GR 674406 Bart 25

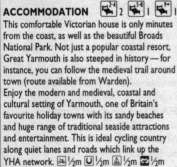

King's Lynn

Youth Hostel, Thoresby College, College Lane, Kings Lynn, Norfolk PE30 1JB
☎ 01553 772461 Fax: 01553 772461

Out of season contact: Regional Booking Service, 11B York Road, Salisbury, Wilts. SP2 7AP
☎ 01722 337494 Fax: 01722 414027

Overnight Charges: Under 18 £4.85 Adult £7.20

R-a-H ☎ 01722 337494 GSC ⬛ ⬛ P South quay 50yds from Hostel. BABA

Jan 1 - Apr 6	Rent-a-Hostel
Apr 7 - Jun 30	Open X:Tu/Wed
Jul 1 - Aug 31	Open
Sep 1 - Dec 31	Rent-a-Hostel

ACCOMMODATION  2 · 2 · 2

This charming traditional Hostel — located in a wing of the old Chantry college — is perfectly sited on the quayside for exploring the historic town of King's Lynn.

Step straight out of the Hostel into the medieval streets of King's Lynn. Hunt for the treasure trove lost when King John's baggage train miscalculated the tide and disappeared into the Wash. Or visit the Town Hall which houses the Tales of the Gaol House — a new crime and punishment attraction. 🚲 10m ⛴ 1m

TRAVEL INFO
🚌 Frequent from surrounding areas (☎ 01553 772343). 🚉 King's Lynn ½m.
ℹ ☎ 01553 763044

NEXT HOSTELS
Hunstanton 16m, Ely 24m, Brandon 25m

ADDITIONAL INFO
We can cater for groups of 10 or more booked in advance.

HOW TO GET THERE
OS 132 GR 616199 Bart 25

Norwich

Youth Hostel, 112 Turner Road, Norwich, Norfolk NR2 4HB ☎ 01603 627647
Fax: 01603 629075

Overnight Charges: Under 18 £5.35 Adult £8.00

Family accommodation prices on p.11-13

2 ⬛ GSC ⬛ 🔍 ⬛ ⬛ ¼m ⬛ 1x40 P BABA

Feb 1 - Apr 6	Open Fr/Sat
Apr 7 - Jun 30	Open X:Sun*
Jul 1 - Aug 31	Open
Sep 1 - Oct 31	Open X:Sun/Mon
Nov 1 - Dec 16	Open Fr/Sat

* Open Bank Hol Sun. The Hostel may be available for groups when otherwise closed - please contact Warden.

ACCOMMODATION 9 · 6

This large attractive Hostel — recently refubished to offer comfortable facilities — is perfectly sited in a quiet street with easy access to this ancient city.

Renowned for its Norman Castle, awe-inspiring Cathedral, 33 medieval churches and fascinating specialist shops, Norwich is also an ideal base for exploring East Anglia with the unique broads and varied coastline. 🚲 1m ⬛ 5m 🏔 1m ⬛ ⛴ 1m

TRAVEL INFO
🚌 Frequent from surrounding areas (☎ 01603 613613). 🚉 Norwich 2m.
ℹ ☎ 01603 666071

NEXT HOSTELS
Great Yarmouth 21m, Sheringham 25m, Brandon 36m

HOW TO GET THERE
From outer ring road take A1074 heading to City Centre, take second left hand turn onto Turner Road.
OS 134 GR 213095 Bart 26

Sheringham

Youth Hostel, 1 Cremer's Drift, Sheringham, Norfolk NR26 8HX ☎ 01263 823215
Fax: 01263 823215

Overnight Charges: Under 18 £5.35 Adult £8.00

Seasonal Prices Jul 1 - Aug 31: Under 18 £5.95 Adult £8.80

Family accommodation prices on p.11-13

4 🅿️ 🛏 GSC 🕮 🔍 🛒 🐶 🍴 ¼m 🚲 2x40, 1x10

🅿️ Cars, mini-buses and small coaches. Alternative coach park (public) ¼m. BABA

Mar 1 - Apr 6	Open X:Sun
Apr 7 - Aug 31	Open
Sep 1 - Oct 31	Open X:Sun
Nov 1 - Dec 17	Open Fr/Sat
Dec 29 - Dec 31	Open for New Year

The Hostel may be available for groups when otherwise closed - please contact Warden.

ACCOMMODATION 🛏2-4 24 🛏5-8 8

Set in its own tree-shaded flower gardens, this Hostel offers spacious, comfortable accommodation for families and individuals — with its own licensed restaurant serving freshly cooked food. The Hostel is a centre for group field study in spring and early summer.
Enjoy the spectacular scenery with gently rolling hills, sandy beaches and superb sunsets. 🚲¼m

🚇3m 🏔½m 🚌9m 🚉½m

TRAVEL INFO
🚌 Eastern Counties 758/9, 761, Sanders Coaches from Norwich (☎ 01603 613613). 🚉 Sheringham ¼m.
🅸 ☎01263 824329

NEXT HOSTELS
Hunstanton 38m, Norwich 25m, Gt Yarm'th 39m

ADDITIONAL INFO
Conference and seminar facilities. Ask for leaflets on our special activity packages.

HOW TO GET THERE
Hostel is off the main A149 behind St Joseph's R.C. Church only 5mins on foot from railway and bus station.
OS 133 GR 159428 Bart 26

Peaceful villages, idyllic surroundings and small seaside resorts all contribute to this Area of Outstanding Natural Beauty — the Suffolk coast and heaths.

The pastoral scenery of the area around Colchester has many rural views, some made famous by the artist John Constable. To the north is Thetford Forest and the vast sandy heaths and warrens of the Breckland on the Suffolk and Norfolk border.

The rolling farmland of Suffolk, with its ancient timbered buildings and flint-built 'wool' churches, is easily visited by staying at Castle Hedingham Youth Hostel. To the south in Essex you'll find attractive seaside resorts and the busier towns.

Historic Cambridge can be explored from Cambridge Youth Hostel, situated in the centre of this university town famous for its colleges, bicycles and the meandering river 'Cam'. Some college chapels were built during three or four monarchs' lives, making the often conflicting architectural styles fascinating.

The varied landscapes make this a popular cycling area. Other activities include watersports, fishing, horse riding, visits to the zoo and many museums.

Many Youth Hostels are available for exclusive use by groups booked in advance; please enquire. Plus, Blaxhall Youth Hostel is on YHA's **Rent-a-Hostel scheme** which runs during the winter months (details on p.7)

USEFUL PUBLICATIONS

Budget Accommodation in Eastern England and individual Hostel leaflets — send s.a.e. to the YHA Regional Office listed below or phone our Literature Line on (01426) 951683 (local call charge).

For more information about hostelling in this area contact: YHA South England Regional Office, 11B York Road, Salisbury, Wiltshire SP2 7AP. Tel: (01722) 337494. Fax: (01722) 414027.

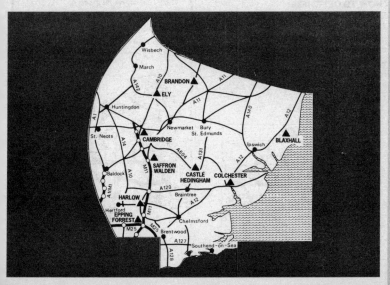

40 BEDS   Open: 17.00hrs

Blaxhall

Youth Hostel, Heath Walk, Blaxhall, Woodbridge, Suffolk IP12 2EA
☎ 01728 688206

Overnight Charges: Under 18 £4.45 Adult £6.55
R-a-H ☎ 01722 337494 [2] 🍴 📺 🏚 🕭 S 2m
🕭 1x35 P For cars and coaches.

Jan 1 - Feb 28	Rent-a-Hostel
Mar 1 - Apr 6	Open Fr/Sat only
Apr 7 - Jun 30	Open X:Sun*
Jul 1 - Sep 2	Open
Sep 18 - Oct 31	Open X:Sun/Mon
Nov 1 - Dec 31	Rent-a-Hostel

* Open Bank Hol Sun.

ACCOMMODATION 🛏️2 🛏️3 🛏️1

This comfortable Hostel — once a village school — is situated in a quiet village in the midst of the Suffolk sandlings heathland. Freshly cooked food using seasonal home-grown vegetables is a speciality — and not to be missed!

As well as great cycling and walking country, you'll find estuaries, coastline, forestry and reedbeds all close by. Visit the RSPB reserves of Minsmere and Havergate. Culture vultures should head for Snape Maltings concert hall only 2m away. 🚶10m 🅿️2m 🚲 🚃8m

TRAVEL INFO
🚌 Eastern Counties 80/1, 99 Ipswich - Aldeburgh (pass close BR Saxmundham), alight ½m SW of Stratford St Andrew, 2m (☎ 01473 265676). 🚉 Wickham Market 3m; Saxmundham 5m.
🛈 ☎ 01394 282126

NEXT HOSTELS
Colchester 32m, Norwich 39m, Brandon 50m

HOW TO GET THERE
From A12 turn off at Wickham Market to Campsea Ashe, then follow signs to Tunstall and then to Hostel following signs.
OS 156 GR 369570 Bart 21

38 BEDS   Open: 17.00hrs

Brandon

Youth Hostel, Heath House, Off Warren Close, Bury Road, Brandon, Suffolk IP27 0BU ☎ 01842 812075

Overnight Charges: Under 18 £5.35 Adult £8.00
Family accommodation prices on p.11-13
🍴 ssc 📺 🏚 🕭 ¼m 🕭 1x25 P in grounds.

Feb 9 - Feb 24	Open X:Sun/Mon
Mar 1 - Apr 6	Open X:Sun/Mon
Jul 1 - Aug 31	Open
Sep 17 - Oct 31	Open X:Sun/Mon
Nov 1 - Dec 16	Open Fr/Sat

* Open Bank Hol Sun. The Hostel may be available for groups when otherwise closed - please contact Warden.

ACCOMMODATION 🛏️2 🛏️1 🛏️2

A charming Edwardian house with a homely atmosphere provides a comfortable stay at Brandon — well situated for exploring Thetford Chase, the largest forested area in England. There are a wealth of activities close by — take a gentle forest walk, hire a bike and explore further afield or go aircraft spotting at Mildenhall. 🚶 🅿️½m 🚲 🚃6m

TRAVEL INFO
🚌 National Express Eastern Counties. 🚉 Brandon ¾m.
🛈 ☎ 01842 814955

NEXT HOSTELS
Ely 21m, King's Lynn 25m, Cambridge 34m

HOW TO GET THERE
OS 144 GR 786864 Bart 21

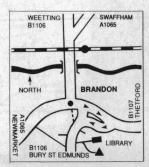

| **118 BEDS** | **Open: 24hrs** |

Cambridge

Youth Hostel, 97 Tenison Road, Cambridge, Cambridgeshire CB1 2DN ☎ 01223 354601
Fax: 01223 312780

Overnight Charges: Under 18 £6.55 Adult £9.70

Family accommodation prices on p.11-13

4 ⬛ 🔒 GSC 🍴 🔍 💬 S ▣ ½m 🚲 1x20

🅿 Coach park 4m. Free parking for cars roadside from 1700 - 0900hrs (metered at other times). BABA **IBN**

Open every day of the year.

ACCOMMODATION 🛏️²⁻⁴ 8 🛏️⁵⁻⁸ 13 🛏️⁹⁺ 1

This busy international Hostel offers a high standard of comfort and facilities — including relaxing lounges, small rooms, an excellent cafeteria and a courtyard garden.
Cambridge is a typically English city with a lazy river, green fields and cows grazing alongside the ancient colleges, museums and art galleries. The best way to get around is Cambridge-style — by bike! 🚲 ⅛m

TRAVEL INFO
🚌 Frequent from surrounding areas (☎ 01223 423554). 🚃 Cambridge ¼m.
🛈 ☎ 01223 322640

NEXT HOSTELS
Saffron Walden 15m, Ely 17m, Castle Hedingham 29m

ADDITIONAL INFO
Single/twin rooms available for group leaders. All customers are provided with room keys.

HOW TO GET THERE
OS 154 GR 460575 Bart 20

| **50 BEDS** | **Open: 17.00hrs** |

Castle Hedingham

Youth Hostel, 7 Falcon Square, Castle Hedingham, Halstead, Essex CO9 3BU ☎ 01787 460799

Overnight Charges: Under 18 £5.35 Adult £8.00

Family accommodation prices on p.11-13

1 ⬛ GSC 🍴 ♿ S ▣ 1m 🚲 1x35/40 🅿 Nearby.

Mar 1 - Mar 31	Open X:Fr/Sat/Sun
Apr 1 - Jun 30	Open X:Sun*
Jul 1 - Aug 31	Open
Sep 1 - Oct 31	Open X:Sun/Mon

* Open Bank Hol Sun. The Hostel may be available for groups when otherwise closed - please contact Warden.

ACCOMMODATION 🛏️²⁻⁴ 2 🛏️⁵⁻⁸ 3 🛏️⁹⁺ 2

As well as a 16th century building with fine exposed oak timbers, there is also a modern annexe on the site of an old maltings which offers wheelchair access. There is a large lawned garden with mature fruit trees, picnic tables and a BBQ. Home-cooked food and vegetarian meals a speciality! Popular with groups from April to June. One of the best kept secrets in East Anglia, the Hostel is set in a small attractive village square, overlooked by a well preserved Norman Castle. Within easy reach of many places of interest, this is an ideal base for holidays or more educational visits. 🚲 1m 🏊 6m ⛰️ 4m 🚂 18m 🛒 7m

TRAVEL INFO
🚌 Hedingham Omnibuses 6, 89/A from Braintree (pass close BR Braintree) (☎ 0345 000333).
🚃 Sudbury (Not Sun, except Jun-Sep) 7m; Braintree 8m
🛈 ☎ 01376 550066

NEXT HOSTELS
Colchester 18m, Saffron Walden 20m, Cambridge 29m

HOW TO GET THERE
Follow signs for Hedingham Castle. Opposite Castle entrance turn down Castle Lane. Hostel on left at bottom of hill. (Not suitable for coaches).
OS 155 GR 786355 Bart 16

Colchester

Youth Hostel, East Bay House, 18 East Bay, Colchester, Essex. CO1 2UE
☎ 01206 867982 Fax: 01206 868628

Overnight Charges: Under 18 £4.85 Adult £7.20

[i] [O] [ESC] [O] ¼m [P] [BABA]

Mar 1 - Mar 31	Open X:Sun/Mon
Apr 1 - Aug 31	Open
Sep 1 - Oct 31	Open X:Sun/Mon
Nov 1 - Dec 16	Open Fr/Sat

The Hostel may be available for groups when otherwise closed - please contact Warden.

ACCOMMODATION 3 3 2

This large Georgian house — reflecting the prosperity of Colchester's mercantile past — stands by the river Colne close to the centre of England's oldest recorded Roman town and the first port of call from Harwich. Cyclists will find many quiet lanes and roads, ideal for exploring Constable country.

A Norman Keep, Saxon Church and Roman Wall are among the many historic attractions to be found in Colchester. It's also the origins of Humpty Dumpty and Old King Cole of nursery rhyme fame. Nearby attractions include Colchester Zoo, Fingrinhoe Nature Reserve and Clacton seaside resort. 🚲 1m ⛺ 5m 🚤 5m 🏊 1m

TRAVEL INFO
🚌 Frequent local services (☎ 01206 571451) 🚉 Colchester North 2m (☎ 01206 564777). 🛈 ☎ 01206 712920

NEXT HOSTELS
Castle Hedingham 18m, Blaxhall 32m, Saffron Walden 39m

HOW TO GET THERE
Opposite Periquito Hotel. ½m E of bus station and castle. 2m from train station (77 bus).
[OS] 168 [GR] 006252 [Bart] 16

Ely

Youth Hostel, Sixth Form Centre, St. Audreys, Downham Road, Ely, Cambridgeshire CB6 1BD ☎ 01353 667423

Out of season contact: Regional Booking Service, 11B York Road, Salisbury, Wiltshire SP2 7AP
☎ 01722 337494 Fax: 01722 414027

Overnight Charges: Under 18 £4.45 Adult £6.55

[i] [▥] [🔍] [🍴] [🖵] [🝙] ¼m [P]

May 26 - Aug 28	Open

ACCOMMODATION 4 1

This summer-only Hostel within the Downham Road College Campus is a good base for exploring Cambridge and the surrounding fens. There are also many activities on offer in Ely — for instance, you can try your hand at brass rubbing, take a stroll along the river banks or visit the weekly market.

Ely is a pleasant riverside town with one of England's most magnificent cathedrals. The surrounding medieval buildings have been fully restored, as well as Bishops Palace and Oliver Cromwell's house — now a heritage attraction. Welney Wetlands Reserve, the Farmland Museum and Wicken Fen are nearby. 🏞 3m ⛺ 1m 🝙 ¼m

TRAVEL INFO
🚌 Frequent from surrounding areas (☎ 01223 423554) 🚉 Ely ¾m.
🛈 ☎ 01353 662062

NEXT HOSTELS
Cambridge 17m, Brandon 21m, Kings Lynn 24m

ADDITIONAL INFO
Limited cooking facilities but spacious dining area. The total number of beds increses from 24 to 42 in mid-July.

HOW TO GET THERE
Follow signs to TIC, then cross road and down Downham Road.
[OS] 143 [GR] 538908 [Bart] 20

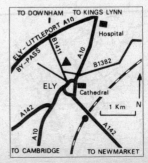

Epping Forest

Youth Hostel, Wellington Hall, High Beach, Loughton, Essex IG10 4AG

☎ 0181 508 5161 Fax: 0181 508 5161

Overnight Charges: Under 18 £4.45 Adult £6.55

1 6SC ⚠ ✠ ▣ 2m P Cars at Hostel. Coaches by arrangement. BABA

Feb 1 - Dec 23	Open

ACCOMMODATION 6 2

For fresh air, birdsong and forest walks all just 15km from central London, why not try this single storey traditional Hostel in a truly rural location. Walk freely and relax in 6000 acres of woodland, formerly a Royal hunting forest. As well as easy access to London, this area has lots to offer with Waltham Abbey, Conaught Water, Loughton Iron Age Camp and Queen Elizabeth Hunting Lodge all close by. 🚲4m

⛺ ⚠ �' �〜 2m

TRAVEL INFO

🚌 Townlink 250 BR Waltham Cross - Loughton Tube Station, alight Volunteer Inn, ¾m (☎ 01279 426349). 🚇 Loughton (Underground) 2m; Chingford (BR) 3 ½m.

🚲 ☎01992 652295

NEXT HOSTELS

Hampstead Heath 13m, City of London 13m, Saffron Walden 29m

ADDITIONAL INFO

Small shop at Hostel - milk must be ordered in advance.

HOW TO GET THERE

From junction 26 M25 take Epping/Loughton road. After ¼m turn right at Volunteer Inn. Right at next junction, left up Wellington Hill. Hostel on right after Duke of Wellington pub.

OS 167 GR 408983 Bart 15

Harlow

Youth Hostel, Corner House, Netteswell Cross, Harlow, Essex CM20 2QD

☎ 01279 421702

Overnight Charges: Under 18 £4.45 Adult £6.55

1 6SC 🏠 ⚠ 🔍 �〜 ▣ ¼m P Public car park (free) opposite.

ACCOMMODATION

This Hostel may not be open during 1995. Please check availability with YHA South England Regional Office ☎ 01722 337494 Fax: 01722 414027.

NEXT HOSTELS

Epping Forest 11m, Saffron Walden 17m, City of London 24m

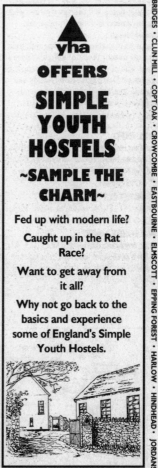

Saffron Walden

Youth Hostel, 1 Myddylton Place, Saffron Walden, Essex CB10 1BB ☎ 01799 523117

Overnight Charges: Under 18 £4.85 Adult £7.20

1 🍴 BBC ♿ 🅿 🍽 ¼m 🅿 800yds to free car park.

Mar 1 - Apr 6	Open Fr/Sat
Apr 7 - Jun 30	Open X:Sun/Mon*
Jul 1 - Aug 31	Open
Sep 1 - Oct 31	Open X:Sun/Mon
Nov 1 - Dec 16	Open Fr/Sat

* Open Bank Hol. The Hostel may be available for groups when otherwise closed - please contact Warden.

ACCOMMODATION 🛏1-4 1 🛏5-8 2 🛏9+ 2

A former maltings, this 500-year old building retains many original features including an oak-wheeled sack hoist in one of the high roofed dormitories. Children will love the contoured floors, huge beams and courtyard garden while adults can unwind in the comfortable oak pannelled lounge.

Continue your journey back in time with trails around the historic towns of Saffron Walden and Thaxted. You can even walk in the footsteps of TV's Lovejoy. Don't miss nearby Audley End House and Stansted Castle, while the gently rolling countryside makes cycling and easy rambling a pleasure. 🚶15m 🚲10m 🛒½m

TRAVEL INFO
🚌From surrounding areas, incl. link with BR Audley End by Hedingham/Viceroy 59 (☎ 0345 000333) 🚉 Audley End 2 ½m.
ℹ ☎01799 510444

NEXT HOSTELS
Cambridge 15m, Castle Hedingham 20m, Harlow 17m

HOW TO GET THERE
From the northbound M11 take junction 9, A11 and B184; from southbound M11 take junction 10, A505, A1301 and B184.
OS 154 GR 535386 Bart 15

This area of great contrasts, famous for its hills and river, exudes the lifeblood of England with thatched cottages, resplendent dwellings, sleepy villages, churches and awesome mediaeval cathedrals. The River Thames flows under the walls of Windsor Castle and runs through much of the area, offering stunning riverside scenery. The Chiltern Area of Outstanding Natural Beauty is covered in lovely beechwoods, particularly breathtaking in the autumn, and easily explored from Bradenham or Jordans Youth Hostel.

This is a favourite area for walkers and cyclists with many well marked footpaths and bridleways to choose from. The Ridgeway National Trail starts at Ivinghoe Beacon and follows through the Chilterns south west to the Thames at Streatley. Many Youth Hostels are available for exclusive use by groups booked in advance; please enquire.

USEFUL PUBLICATIONS

Ridgeway Information and Accomodation Guide — available from the Ridgeway Officer, Countryside Section, Library Headquarters, Holton, Oxford OX9 1QQ.

Budget Accommodation in the Thames and Chilterns and individual Hostel leaflets — send s.a.e. to the YHA Regional Office listed below or phone our Literature Line on (01426) 951683 (local call charge).

For more information about hostelling in this area contact: YHA South England Regional Office, 11B York Road, Salisbury, Wiltshire SP2 7AP. Tel: (01722) 337494. Fax: (01722) 414027.

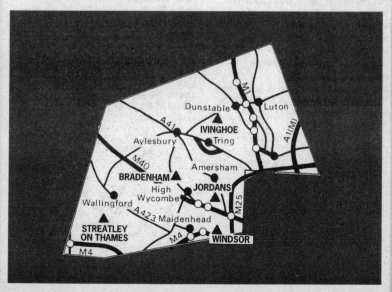

Bradenham

Youth Hostel, The Village Hall Bradenham, High Wycombe, Buckinghamshire HP14 4HF
☎ 01494 56 2929

Bookings to G. Lee, 54a Brixham Crescent, Ruislip Manor, Middlesex HA4 8TX ☎ 01895 673188
Fax: 01895 673188

Overnight Charges: Under 18 £4.00 Adult £5.95

[1] [GSC] [ ] [ ] [ ] [ ] 2m [P] On roadside layby.

Jan 6 - Apr 7	Open Fr/Sat*
Apr 8 - Apr 22	Open
Apr 23 - May 27	Open Fr/Sat* (also open Sun May 7)
May 28 - Jun 3	Open
Jun 4 - Jul 7	Open Fr/Sat*
Jul 8 - Sep 2	Open
Sep 3 - Dec 16	Open Fr/Sat*

* Opens at 19.30hrs on Fr. Available on all other nights for pre-booked groups/families/schools.

ACCOMMODATION

Known as the 'friendly Hostel with the simple appeal', this former village school is situated in a beautifully kept National Trust village tucked away in the folds of the Chiltern Hills.
This is a spectacular area for walking and cycling, with some 3,300 way marked footpaths, as well as many local attractions. [ ] [ ] 4m

TRAVEL INFO

🚌 Wycombe Bus/Aylesbury Bus X14/15, 321/5, 332, Yellow Bus M15 High Wycombe - Princes Risborough (pass close BR High Wycombe & Princes Risborough), alight Bradenham ¼m or Walter's Ash 1m (☎ 01296 382000). X80 bus from Heathrow to High Wycombe bus station.
🚉 Saunderton (not Sun) 1 ¼m; High Wycombe 4 ½m.
ℹ ☎ 01494 421892

NEXT HOSTELS

Jordans 12m, Ivinghoe 17, Windsor 18m

HOW TO GET THERE

At E end of village opposite church. Turn off West Wycombe - Princes Risborough Road (A4010) at Red Lion.
[OS] 165 [GR] 828972 [Bart] 14

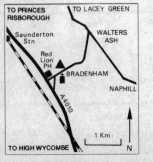

Ivinghoe

Youth Hostel, The Old Brewery House, Ivinghoe, Near Leighton Buzzard, Bedfordshire LU7 9EP ☎ 01296 668251
Fax: 01296 662903

Overnight Charges: Under 18 £4.85 Adult £7.20

[1] [ ] [GSC] [ ] [A] [ ] [ ] [P] [BABA]

Feb 1 - Feb 28	Open Fr/Sat
Mar 1 - Mar 31	Open X:Sun/Mon
Apr 1 - Aug 31	Open X:Sun*
Sep 1 - Oct 31	Open X:Sun/Mon
Nov 1 - Dec 16	Open Fr/Sat
Dec 29 - Jan 2	Open for New Year

* Open Bank Hol Sun. The Hostel may be available for groups when otherwise closed - please contact Warden.

ACCOMMODATION

Former home of the local brewer, this attractive Georgian mansion — situated in the heart of the picturesque village of Ivinghoe — offers traditional accommodation with spacious public rooms.
Ivinghoe village lies close to many places of interest. For instance, enjoy the dramatic scenery of Incombe Hole, discover the remains of an Iron Age Fort at Beacon Hill or explore the National Trust estate of Ashbridge. Nearby Whipsnade Zoo and Woburn Abbey are also well worth a visit. [ ] 4m [ ] 1m [ ] 1m [ ] 3m

TRAVEL INFO

🚌 Luton & District 61 Aylesbury - Luton (passes close BR Aylesbury & Luton) (☎ 01296 84919).
🚉 Cheddington 2; Tring 3m.
ℹ ☎ 01582 471012

NEXT HOSTELS

Jordans 19m, Bradwell Village 19m, Windsor 28m

ADDITIONAL INFO

Buckinghamshire Environmental Education centre available to visiting schools with full teaching service. Info pack available.

HOW TO GET THERE

In the centre of the village next to the church and opposite the village green on B489.
[OS] 165 [GR] 945161 [Bart] 15

Jordans

Youth Hostel, Welders Lane, Jordans, Beaconsfield, Buckinghamshire HP9 2SN
☎ 01494 873135 Fax: 01494 873135

Overnight Charges: Under 18 £4.45 Adult £6.55

k-a-H ☎ 01722 337494 i esc ▦ ⛺ ☒ ☺ ● ½m
P Cars and mini-buses (coaches by arrangement).

Jan 1 - Jan 31	Rent-a-Hostel
Feb 1 - Mar 1	Open Fr/Sat
Mar 1 - Sep 6	Open X:Th
Sep 25 - Nov 25	Open Fr/Sat
Nov 26 - Dec 31	Rent-a-Hostel

ACCOMMODATION ⛺ 4

Set in two acres of woodlands, this small traditional Hostel is full of character — with comfortable bedrooms and a cheerful open fire. The village of Jordans is closely associated with early Quakerism.

View the 17th century meeting house, the Mayflower barn and Willam Penn's grave. There are also many way marked paths and country lanes providing varied routes for walkers and cyclists. Further afield are the attractions of Belconscot Model Village and Milton's cottage.

▲ ⛱ ◳ 1m

TRAVEL INFO

🚌 Chiltern Bus 305 High Wycombe - Uxbridge, alight Seer Green ¾m; 35 Slough - Berkhamsted, alight Chalfont Leisure Centre 1m (☎ 01494 464647). 🚃 Seer Green ¾m. Taxis available.
ℹ ☎ 01494 421892

NEXT HOSTELS

Bradenham 12m, Windsor 13m, Ivinghoe 19m

HOW TO GET THERE

OS 175 GR 975910 Bart 9

Streatley On Thames

Youth Hostel, Hill House, Reading Road, Streatley, Reading, Berkshire RG8 9JJ
☎ 01491 872278 Fax: 01491 873056

Overnight Charges: Under 18 £5.35 Adult £8.00

Family accommodation prices on p.11-13

i ▣ esc ▦ ☺ S ● ½m 🚲 1x30 P Limited.
Coaches by arrangement nearby. BABA

Feb 1 - Apr 8	Open Fr/Sat/Sun
Apr 9 - Jun 30	Open X:Mon
Jul 1 - Aug 31	Open
Sep 1 - Nov 27	Open X:Mon/Tu

The Hostel may be available for groups when otherwise closed - please contact Warden.

ACCOMMODATION 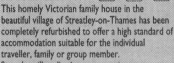 ⛺ 2 ⛺ 6 ⛺ 1

This homely Victorian family house in the beautiful village of Streatley-on-Thames has been completely refurbished to offer a high standard of accommodation suitable for the individual traveller, family or group member.

Streatley village lies in a conservation area nestling in the gap between the Chiltern Hills and Berkshire Downs on an extremely pretty stretch of the Thames. Watch the canal boats at Goring, tackle the Ridgeway path or visit the surrounding houses of historical interest. ▲ ⛰ ⛱

TRAVEL INFO

🚌 Oxford/Reading Buses 105 Reading-Oxford (☎ 01865 711312) 🚃 Goring & Streatley 1m.
ℹ ☎ 01734 566226

NEXT HOSTELS

Ridgeway 14m, Oxford 19m, Windsor 25m

ADDITIONAL INFO

Excellent facilities for meetings and (small) conferences - contact Warden for details.

HOW TO GET THERE

OS 174 GR 591806 Bart 8

Windsor

Youth Hostel, Edgeworth House, Mill Lane,
Windsor, Berkshire SL4 5JE
☎ 01753 861710 Fax: 01753 832100

Overnight Charges: Under 18 £5.95 Adult £8.80

4 ◎ GSC ▥ ▮ ▨ ⬚ S ▣ 1m P Cars only - it is
illegal for coaches to enter Mill lane (please use Windsor
Coach Park) BABA IBN

Jan 4 - Dec 23   Open

ACCOMMODATION   2-4 1   5-8 7   9+ 2

A Queen Anne residence in the secluded village
of Clewer only 15 minutes walk from Windsor,
this traditional Hostel offers good service and
food in a friendly atmosphere. There is also a
small car park and large garden.
The historic towns of Windsor and Eton have
plenty to offer visitors — from Windsor Castle
and Eton College to annual events like the Henley
Regatta and Royal Horse Show. The Thames Path
runs close to the Hostel. Dorney Court, Saville
Gardens and Virginia Water are nearby, with
London just 18m away. ⛴ 3m 300yds

TRAVEL INFO

🚌 Frequent from surrounding areas (☎ 01753
524144) 🚆 Windsor & Eton Central ¾m; Windsor
& Eton Riverside 1m.
🛈 ☎01753 852010

NEXT HOSTELS

Jordans 13m, Bradenham 18m, London 23m

ADDITIONAL INFO

Credit cards and eurocheques accepted. Foreign
exchange. IBN and BABA booking service.

HOW TO GET THERE

There is no through access for cars on Stovell Road.
OS 175 GR 955770 Bart 9

Steeped in history and loaded with culture London has all the ingredients for an exciting visit.

Museums, art galleries, theatres, historic buildings and the exciting nightlife are just some of the many attractions which go to make up the unique cosmopolitan atmosphere of this capital city.

London is also easy to get around — bus, tube, waterbus and ferry are all on offer, run regularly and are within easy reach of almost all locations.

From the rural settings of Highgate and Hampstead Heath to the spectacular purpose-built Rotherhithe in the heart of the Docklands, all London Youth Hostels provide an excellent base for exploring this vibrant city.

To make your stay really enjoyable, all seven London Youth Hostels provide a theatre and attraction booking service, *bureau de change* facility, bookings for National Express Coach tickets for travel throughout the country and sell one day travel cards entitling you to unlimited travel on the tubes and buses.

USEFUL PUBLICATIONS

Individual Hostel leaflets are available — send s.a.e. to the Central Bookings Office listed below.

Group Leaders Guide to London — send A4 s.a.e. to the Central Bookings Office listed below.

For information about hostelling in London (including advice and details about special discount rates available to groups and individuals) contact: Central Bookings Office, City of London YHA, 36 Carter Lane, London EC4V 5AD. Tel: 0171 248 6547. Fax: 0171 236 7681.

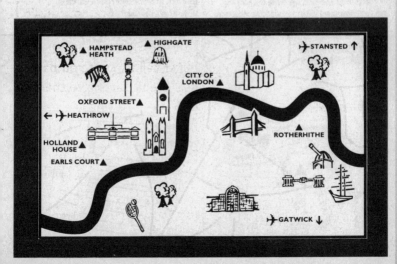

City Of London

Youth Hostel, 36 Carter Lane, London EC4V 5AD ☎ 0171 236 4965 Fax: 0171 236 7681

Overnight Charges: Under 18 £16.00 Adult £19.10

Bed & Breakfast included.

Family accommodation prices on p.11-13

④ 🍴 🛁 📺 🔲 🔒 🎱 🎾 2x30 **P** NCP Queen Victoria Street. Coaches park at St Pauls 150 metres. BABA IBN

Open every day of the year.

ACCOMMODATION 🛏²⁻⁴ 21 🛏⁵⁻⁸ 12 🛏⁹⁺ 2

Until 1968, this Victorian building situated beside St Paul's Cathedral was the school for St Paul's Choir Boys. It has recently been completely refurbished and provides modern surroundings, central heating and several single rooms, as well as new showers and washing facilities. Barbecues are a regular event in the summer, held on the roof-top area with spectacular views of the Cathedral. Due to its central location, the Hostel is within easy reach of London's many attractions — for instance, the West End with its theatres, restaurants and shopping is only 15mins walk away. 🚇½m 🅿1m 🚆½m

TRAVEL INFO
🚍Frequent LT services (☎ 0171 222 1234). Underground: St Pauls ¼m. 🚆 Blackfriars ¼m; City Thameslink ¼m; Liverpool Street 1m. 🛈 ☎0171 730 3488

NEXT HOSTELS
Rotherhithe 3m, Oxford Street 2m, Earl's Court 3m

ADDITIONAL INFO
The former oak-panelled chapel is available for hire for conferences and meetings while the roof-top area (with marquee) ideal for a wedding reception, disco or a barbecue. Theatre & attraction booking service, National Express ticket sales and IBN.

HOW TO GET THERE
OS 176 GR 319811 Bart 9

Earl's Court

Youth Hostel, 38 Bolton Gardens, London SW5 OAQ ☎ 0171 373 7083 Fax: 0171 835 2034

Overnight Charges: Under 18 £15.00 Adult £17.10

Bed & Breakfast included.

④ 🍴 📺 🔲 🔒 🎱 **P** Limited (1-2 spaces in private driveway). Warwick Road ¾m. BABA IBN

Open every day of the year.

ACCOMMODATION 🛏²⁻⁴ 8 🛏⁵⁻⁸ 5 🛏⁹⁺ 8

An old Victorian town house situated in the heart of a busy area full of shops and restaurants, the Hostel is particular popular with international visitors — and easily accessible from Heathrow and Gatwick airports, and Victoria Coach and Train station.
Ideally located next to Earl's Court and Olympia Exhibition Centres and within easy reach of all London's main attractions, the Hostel is an excellent base for exploring the city. 🚇½m 🚆

TRAVEL INFO
🚍Frequent LT services (☎ 0171 222 1234). Underground Earl's Court ¼m. Gloucester Rd ½m 🚆Kensington Olympia 1m. 🛈 ☎0171 730 3488

NEXT HOSTELS
Holland House 1m, City of London 5m, Oxford Street 5m

ADDITIONAL INFO
Theatre and attraction booking service, national Express ticket sales and IBN.

HOW TO GET THERE
Leave Earl's Court underground station by Earl's Court Road exit. Turn right outside station and take fifth street on left (Bolton Gardens).
OS 152 GR 258783 Bart 9

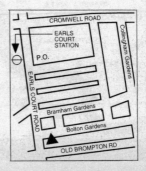

Hampstead Heath

Youth Hostel, 4 Wellgarth Road, London
NW11 7HR ☎ 0181 458 9054/7196
Fax: 0181 209 0546

Overnight Charges: Under 18 £11.90 Adult
£14.00

Family accommodation prices on p.11-13

4 🍴 🛏 ▥ ⊠ 🗄 📷 👤 ♿ **S** 🖨 **P** Off-street
parking for 8 cars (monitored by CCTV). Coaches free
½m. BABA IBN

Open every day of the year.

ACCOMMODATION 🛏²⁻⁴ 37 🛏⁵⁻⁸ 14 🛏⁹⁺ 1

Located in a quiet residential area of conserved
architectural and natural beauty, the Hostel —
formerly a training school for nursery nurses —
offers a high standard of accommodation in small
rooms overlooking beautiful gardens. The
licenced restaurant offers excellent value for
money.
The Hostel is a short walk from Golders Hill Park
& Children's Zoo, Hampstead Heath, Kenwood
House (setting for spectacular summer concerts
and firework displays), Freud's Museum and
Keat's House. Also handy for the RAF Museum,
Camden markets, Wembley and Leicester Square.
🖼 1m

TRAVEL INFO
🚌 Frequent LT services (☎ 0171 222 1234).
Underground: Golders Green ¼m. National
Express depot, Golders Green. 🚉 Hampstead
Heath 1 ½m.
🛈 ☎ 0171 730 3488

NEXT HOSTELS
Highgate 2m, Holland House 5m, Oxford Street 7m

ADDITIONAL INFO
Booking service for theatre, rock, pop and classical
music concerts, as well as sporting events. Ticket
sales for coach travel in Britain and Europe. Fax
service. Bureau de Change.

HOW TO GET THERE
OS 176 GR 258973 Bart 9

Highgate Village

Youth Hostel, 84 Highgate West Hill,
London N6 6LU ☎ 0181 340 1831
Fax: 0181 341 0376

Overnight Charges: Under 18 £7.90 Adult £11.85

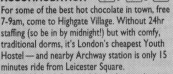 ¼m **P** Roadside parking for cars.
Coach parking difficult. BABA IBN

Feb 1 - Dec 17	Open

Reception may not be staffed until 5pm during
winter.

ACCOMMODATION 🛏²⁻⁴ 3 🛏⁵⁻⁸ 2 🛏⁹⁺ 4

For some of the best hot chocolate in town, free
7-9am, come to Highgate Village. Without 24hr
staffing (so be in by midnight!) but with comfy,
traditional dorms, it's London's cheapest Youth
Hostel — and nearby Archway station is only 15
minutes ride from Leicester Square.
George Michael, Sting and Annie Lennox live in
Highgate Village. Karl Marx doesn't but he's in
our cemetery. Eight great pubs have music, food
and decent prices. Relax in the Hostel garden or
take a stroll on the Heath with views of London.
🖼 1m

TRAVEL INFO
🚌 Frequent LT services (☎ 0171 222 1234).
Underground: Archway 1m. 214 from Kings Cross,
271 from Liverpool St Station, 210 from Golders
Green National Express depot, 210 from Finsbury
Park BR station.
🛈 ☎ 0171 730 3488

NEXT HOSTELS
Hampstead Heath 2m, City of London 5m, Holland
House 6m

HOW TO GET THERE
From Archway station walk or take bus (271, 210,
143) up to the Angel Pub. Turn left at South Grove,
walk five minutes.
OS 176 GR 281871 Bart 9

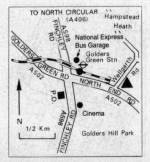

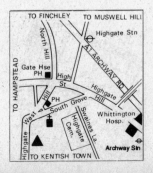

201 BEDS	**Open: 24hrs**

Holland House

Youth Hostel, Holland House, Holland Walk, Kensington, London W8 7QU
📞 **0171 937 0748 Fax: 0171 376 0667**

Overnight Charges: Under 18 £15.00 Adult £17.10

Bed & Breakfast included.

4 ⬛ ▦ ▣ S ▣ ¼m ⬛ 1x12 P Cars/coaches NCP 15 mins walk. Drop off/pick up corner of Duchess of Bedford Walk & Phillimore Gdns. No parking at Hostel. BABA IBN

Open every day of the year.

ACCOMMODATION 🛏 4 🛏 2 🛏 12
Formerly a Jacobean mansion built in 1607, the Hostel has since been extended and refurbished to offer comfortable accommodation in the middle of Holland Park with easy access by public transport to central London.
Holland Park is a delightful rural area — with woodlands, lawns, squash and tennis courts. Don't miss the open air theatre in July and August. You're also within easy reach of attractions like the Science & Natural History Museum, Royal Albert Hall, Victoria & Albert Museum and Kensington Palace.

TRAVEL INFO
🚇 Frequent LT services (📞 0171 222 1234). Underground: Holland Park ¼m; High Street Kensington ¼m. 🚉 Kensington Olympia ½m.
🚹 📞 0171 730 3488

NEXT HOSTELS
Earl's Court 1m, City of London 5m, Oxford Street 5m

ADDITIONAL INFO
Theatre and attraction booking service, IBN and National Express ticket sales.

HOW TO GET THERE
Turn left out of High Street Kensington Underground Station and walk down the High Street until you reach the entrance to Holland Park. The Hostel is located at the top of the walkway inside the park.
OS 176

89 BEDS	**Open: 24hrs**

Oxford Street

Youth Hostel, 14 Noel Street, London W1V 3PD 📞 **0171 734 1618 Fax: 0171 734 1657**

Overnight Charges: Under 18 £13.60 Adult £16.70

4 ▦ 🚿 S ▣ P NCP parking ¼m BABA IBN

Open every day of the year.

ACCOMMODATION 🛏 33
In the heart of Soho and Oxford Street, this Hostel is a perfect base for individual travellers. Sleeping accommodation is in small bedrooms with modern bunks and security lockers. There is a new self-catering kitchen and a relaxing TV lounge.
Just a two minute stroll from Oxford Street, Carnaby Street and central Soho with its top theatres and nightclubs, and within easy reach of London's other major attractions, the Hostel is an ideal base for sightseeing. 🚇 ½m

TRAVEL INFO
🚇 Frequent LT services (📞 0171 222 1234). Underground: Oxford Circus, Tottenham Ct Rd, both ¼m. 🚉 Charing Cross ¾m; Euston 1m.
🚹 📞 0171 730 3488

NEXT HOSTELS
City of London 2m, Holland House 5m, Earl's Court 5m

ADDITIONAL INFO
Theatre and attraction booking service, plus IBN. Advance booking recommended as the Hostel is very popular all-year round.

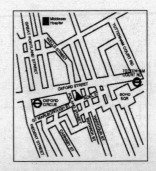

Rotherhithe

Youth Hostel, Salter Road, London SE16 1PP
☎ 0171 232 2114 Fax: 0171 237 2919

Overnight Charges: Under 18 £16.00 Adult £19.10

Bed & Breakfast included.

Family accommodation prices on p.11-13

4 | 回 | 占 | ⅢⅢ | 回 | 回 | 占 | S | 回 | ½m | 回 | 1x16, 1x30, 1x45 | P | BABA | IBN

Open every day of the year.

ACCOMMODATION 🛏️²⁻⁴ 34 🛏️⁵⁻⁸ 33 🛏️⁹⁺ 3

On the banks of the River Thames less than 1m from Tower Bridge, this purpose-built Hostel — with its ultra modern design in keeping with other Docklands architecture — provides the ultimate in luxury Hostelling. Accommodation is mostly in 2, 4 and 6 bedded rooms, all with en-suite facilities.
Centrally located, the Hostel is within easy reach of London's many attractions. You can explore the exciting Docklands area, visit Greenwich, see a top West End stage show, take a trip on the river, wander around London's many museums or just stoll through the parks.

TRAVEL INFO
🚌 LT 225, P11, N70 (☎ 0171 222 1234).
Underground: Rotherhithe 300 metres. 🚉 London Bridge 2m
ℹ️ ☎ 0171 730 3488

NEXT HOSTELS
City of London 3m, Holland House 8m, Hampstead Heath 10m

ADDITIONAL INFO
Well equipped meeting rooms for hire. The Hostel is fully accessible to people with disabilities with six specially adapted rooms suitable for wheelchair users. Theatre and attraction bookings service, National Express ticket sales and IBN.

HOW TO GET THERE
Exit Rotherhithe underground station, turn left and the Hostel is 300 metres on the same side of the road. Channel Tunnel service stops approx. 1m from Hostel (P11 bus runs door to door).

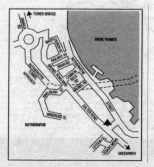

This area boasts more stately homes, gardens and castles than anywhere else in England — for instance, there are sixteen castles within touring distance!

The gently rolling downs and the High Weald provide magnificent viewpoints and a perfect backdrop to pretty villages, winding country lanes and farming land, while East Kent offers miles of varied coastline, sandy beaches, lively resorts with picturesque harbours and spectacular cliff-top walks.

Each part of Kent has its own atmosphere: Broadstairs retains a Victorian air, little changed since the days of Charles Dickens, whilst Dover in White Cliffs Country with its bustling modern port and Dover Castle (a giant among castles) successfully mixes the old with the new.

Canterbury is home to the famous Cathedral and the tombs of the archbishops (dating back to St. Augustine), of Henry VI and his Queen, and of the famous Black Prince. The shrine of St. Thomas a Beckett, murdered in 1170, has been visited for

centuries by pilgrims and can still be seen today. One such pilgrimage was the setting for Chaucer's Canterbury Tales. The Pilgrim's Way passes the doorstep of Kemsing Youth Hostel. Another literary connection, this time with Charles Dickens, can be found at Broadstairs Youth Hostel.

Broadstairs is available on YHA's **Rent-a-Hostel scheme** which runs during the winter months (details on p.7).

USEFUL PUBLICATIONS

Budget Accommodation in Surrey, Sussex and Kent and individual Hostel leaflets — send s.a.e. to the YHA Regional Office listed below or phone our Literature Line on (01426) 951683 (local call charge).

For more information about hostelling in this area contact: YHA South England Regional Office, 11B York Road, Salisbury, Wiltshire SP2 7AP. Tel: (01722) 337494. Fax: (01722) 414027.

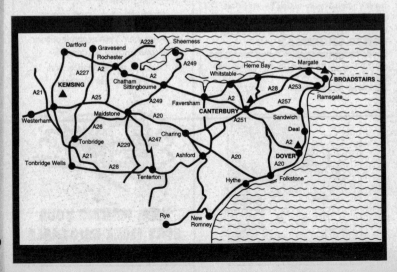

36 BEDS   Open: 17.00hrs

Broadstairs

Youth Hostel, Thistle Lodge, 3 Osborne Road, Broadstairs, Isle-of-Thanet, Kent CT10 2AE ☎ **01843 604121 Fax: 01843 604121**

Overnight Charges: Under 18 £5.35 Adult £8.00

Family accommodation prices on p.11-13

[R-a-H] ☎ 01722 337494 [2] [GSC] [📼] [🍴] [🏊] 50yds [BABA]

Jan 1 - Mar 17	Open for advance bookings only
Mar 18 - Nov 25	Open
Nov 26 - Dec 31	Rent-a-Hostel

The Hostel may be available for groups when otherwise closed - please contact Warden.

ACCOMMODATION

This Victorian villa, which has been imaginatively converted, offers small comfortable bunkrooms, a family atmosphere and pleasant garden with a barbecue for summer evenings. It's also easy to get to by train, coach, bus and from the Ferry Port.

Famous for its Dickensian connections, this traditional seaside resort has lots to offer — with museums, coastal walks and a sheltered sandy beach. You're also close to Ramsgate ferries for trips to Dunkerque and Ostend — ask for our group visit information pack. 🚶3m 🚇3m 🏛2m 🚢5m 🚆1m

TRAVEL INFO
🚌 From surrounding areas (☎ 0800 696996)
🚏 Broadstairs 100metres. 🚢 2½m
(Ramsgate-Dunkerque/Ostende)
🛈 ☎ 01843 862242

NEXT HOSTELS
Canterbury 18m, Dover 20m, Ostende 3m (via ferry)

ADDITIONAL INFO
Lunchpacks and breakfasts available. Discounts on ferry tickets purchased via the Hostel.

HOW TO GET THERE
From railway station go under bridge and turn left at traffic lights.
[OS] 179 [GR] 390679 [Bart] 10

81 BEDS   Open: 13.00hrs

Canterbury

Youth Hostel, 'Ellerslie', 54 New Dover Road, Canterbury, Kent CT1 3DT ☎ **01227 462911 Fax: 01227 470752**

Overnight Charges: Under 18 £5.95 Adult £8.80

[4] [🍴] [📼] [⚙] [✷] [🍴] ⅓m [P] [BABA] [IBN]

| Feb 1 - Dec 30 | Open |

The Hostel may be available for groups when otherwise closed - please contact Warden. The Hostel is open from 13.00 hrs each day. However, during winter months it may not be manned until 17.00 hrs.

ACCOMMODATION

This splendid Victorian villa is ideally placed close to the centre of the historic city. As well as all the facilities required by the city tourist, the friendly atmosphere and good home-cooking make it perfect for families too! Popular with groups from April to June.

Close to the Kent Downs, the Hostel is within easy reach of the North Downs Way and Pilgrims Way footpaths — while the city itself has the cathedral, St Augustines Abbey, various museums, guided tours and theatres. Further afield you'll find zoos, gardens and castles to explore. 🚶 🚆20m 🚢

TRAVEL INFO
🚌 Frequent from surrounding areas (☎ 0800 696996). 🚏 Canterbury East ¾m; Canterbury West 1¼m. 🚢 15m (Dover-Calais)
🛈 ☎ 01227 766567

NEXT HOSTELS
Dover 14m, Broadstairs 18m, Kemsing 42m

HOW TO GET THERE
[OS] 179 [GR] 157570 [Bart] 10

Dover

Youth Hostel, 306 London Road, Dover, Kent
CT17 0SY ☎ 01304 201314
Fax: 01304 202236

Overnight Charges: Under 18 £5.95 Adult £8.80
Family accommodation prices on p.11-13

4 🍴 🗄 🎱 🔍 🏐 🎱 🎱 1x30 🅿Nearby.
BABA IBN

| Jan 1 - Dec 31 | Open |

The Hostel is open from 1pm each day - however,
during the winter the reception may not be
manned until 5pm.

ACCOMMODATION 🛏6 🛏10 🛏5

This elegant listed Georgian town house — one
of two Hostel buildings in Dover, both recently
refurbished — has a large traditional walled
garden which includes a patio and barbecue.
As well as the North Downs Way, there are
spectacular cliff walks amid superb birdwatching
country. Historic Dover has many attractions on
offer, including Dover Castle and Hellfire Corner,
the White Cliffs Experience and even Dover
Gaol. France and the rest of Europe are only
30mins away! 🚲 ⛰2m 🚲2m 🏊2m

TRAVEL INFO

🚌Frequent from surrounding areas (☎ 01304
240024). 🚂Dover Priory 1m (☎ 01732 770111).
⛴(to Belgium/France)
🛈 ☎01304 205108

NEXT HOSTELS

Canterbury 14m, Broadstairs 20m, Kemsing 50m

HOW TO GET THERE

From BR Dover Priory turn left to roundabout, 1st
exit, ½m on left. M20/A20 4th roundabout 1st exit,
roundabout 2nd exit ½m on left (directions to
London Road only).
OS 179 GR 311421 Bart 10

Kemsing

Youth Hostel, Church Lane, Kemsing,
Sevenoaks, Kent TN15 6LU
☎ 01732 761341 Fax: 01732 763044

Overnight Charges: Under 18 £5.35 Adult £8.00

2 🍴 🗄 A 🗄 S 🎱 ¼m 🎱 1x30 🅿10 cars
max. Coaches in public car park by 'Wheatsheaf' Pub. No
access to Hostel for coaches. BABA

Jan 1 - Jan 2	Open for New Year
Feb 1 - Feb 28	Open Fr/Sat
Mar 1 - Apr 6	Open X:Sun/Mon
Apr 7 - May 31	Open X:Sun*
Jun 1 - Aug 31	Open
Sep 1 - Oct 30	Open X:Sun/Mon
Nov 1 - Dec 16	Open Fr/Sat
Dec 22 - Dec 27	Open for Xmas

* Open Bank Hol Sun. The Hostel may be
available for groups when otherwise closed -
please contact Warden.

ACCOMMODATION 🛏1 🛏5 🛏2

At the foot of the North Downs in a
conservation area, this imposing Victorian
vicarage (built largely of Kent ragstone) in its own
mature grounds commands fine views over the
valley towards Knole Park in Sevenoaks. London
is just 25m away.
From Romans at Lullingstone to Tudors and
Stuarts at Knole and Ightham moat, this is an area
steeped in history. Enjoy rural studies at
Whitbread Hop Farm, Paddock Wood and the
Museum of Kent Life, Maidstone. Or visit nearby
Rochester with its own castle, cathedral, museum
and historic dockyard. 🚲6m ⛰ 🚲 🏊

TRAVEL INFO

🚌Kentish Bus 425, 436 from Sevenoaks (pass
close BR Sevenoaks), alight Kemsing PO, 250yds
(☎ 0800 696996). East Surrey 321 from Sevenoaks
alight Kemsing (Sun only). 🚂Kemsing (not Sun)
1 ½m; Otford 1 ¾m.
🛈 ☎01732 450305

NEXT HOSTELS

Canterbury 42m, London 26m, Dover 50m

HOW TO GET THERE

OS 188 GR 555588 Bart 9

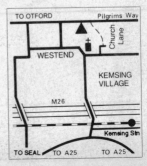

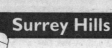
The Surrey Hills Area of Outstanding Natural Beauty is always popular — whatever your interests. Close to London, this accessible and attractive area has some of the most beautiful and varied countryside in England, enriched by heritage towns, villages and an impressive variety of tourist attractions. Many parts are owned by the National Trust including landmarks like Box Hill, Leith Hill and the deep wooded combe of the Devil's Punchbowl at Hindhead. Stay at Holmbury St. Mary, Tanners Hatch or Kemsing Youth Hostel to walk the North Downs Way which passes through the area.

Several Youth Hostels are available for exclusive use by groups booked in advance; please enquire. Plus, Hindhead Youth Hostel is on YHA's **Rent-a-Hostel scheme** which runs during the winter months (details on p.7).

USEFUL PUBLICATIONS

About the Hurtwood — available from Holmbury St. Mary Youth Hostel.

Budget Accommodation in Surrey, Sussex and Kent and individual Hostel leaflets — send s.a.e. to the YHA Regional Office listed below or phone our Literature Line on (01426) 951683 (local call charge).

For more information about hostelling in this area contact: YHA South England Regional Office, 11B York Road, Salisbury, Wiltshire SP2 7AP. Tel: (01722) 337494. Fax: (01722) 414027.

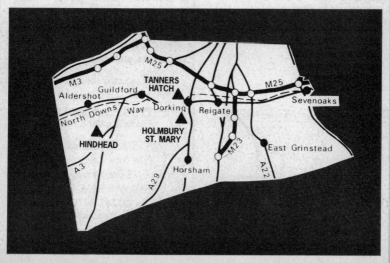

Hindhead

Youth Hostel, Highcoombe Bottom, Bowlhead Green, Godalming, Surrey GU7 6NS 📞 0142 8604285

Out of season contact: Regional Booking Service, 11B York Road, Salisbury, Wilts. SP2 7AP 📞 01722 337494 Fax: 01722 414027

Overnight Charges: Under 18 £3.60 Adult £5.35

ka-h 📞 01722 337494 [1] GSC ▭ ⊠ ⊛ ◉ 2m
P NT car park ¾m.

Jan 1 - Apr 6	Rent-a-Hostel
Apr 7 - Aug 31	Open X:Mon/Tu
Sep 1 - Dec 31	Rent-a-Hostel

ACCOMMODATION 2 5-8 1

This superb simple Hostel, set in the peaceful haven of the Devils Punchbowl, has been converted from three National Trust Cottages and sympathetically refurbished to a good standard, with a large open fire in the lounge adding to the cosy atmosphere.

This Area of Outstanding Natural Beauty can be easily reached with good road links from London and the South East. An abundance of flora and fauna can be found here, with the Pilgrims Way and an old fashioned steam fairground close by.

U ⚠ 4m ⊠ ▭ 10m

TRAVEL INFO

🚌 Stagecoach Hants & Surrey 18/9, 518/9 Aldershot-Haslemere (pass close BR Haslemere); 271, 292, 571 from Guildford (pass close BR Godalming & Farnham). Alight in Hindhead area; ½m to 1m according to stops (📞 01428 605757) 🚉 Haslemere 2½m by path, 4½m by road.
ℹ️ 📞 01483 444007

NEXT HOSTELS

Holmbury St Mary 20m, Portsmouth 29m, Winchester 30m

HOW TO GET THERE

OS 186 GR 892368 Bart 5

Holmbury St Mary

Youth Hostel, Radnor Lane, Holmbury St Mary, Dorking, Surrey RH5 6NW
☎ 01306 730777 Fax: 01306 730933
Overnight Charges: Under 18 £5.35 Adult £8.00
Family accommodation prices on p.11-13
1️⃣ 🍴 6️⃣5️⃣C A 🔄 S 🔲 1m P Cars and minibuses. Coaches - contact Warden. BABA

Feb 1 - Mar 31	Open Fr/Sat
Apr 1 - Jun 30	Open X:Sun*
Jul 1 - Aug 31	Open
Sep 1 - Nov 30	Open X:Sun/Mon
Dec 28 - Jan 2	Open for New Year
'96	

* Open Bank Hol Sun. The Hostel may be available for groups when otherwise closed.

ACCOMMODATION
 14

Get away from it all at this purpose-built Hostel set in its own grounds in the Surrey hills. Surrounded by 4000 acres of woodland in an Area of Outstanding Natural Beauty, you're still only 30m from London with its many attractions. Small rooms offer ideal accommodation for groups and families. Particularly popular with groups from April to June.
The Hostel offers excellent board games, an orienteering course and treasure hunt. Mountain bike hire and guided weekend breaks can be arranged locally. Archery, abseiling and wildlife talks available for groups. Local attractions include National Trust properties and Downs Link path. 🦌 🔄 4m 🏔️ 🔄 9m

TRAVEL INFO
🚌 Tillingbourne 21 Guildford - Dorking (Ask for Woodhouse Farm) (☎ 01483 276880).
🚉 Gomshall 3m; Dorking 6m.
ℹ️ ☎ 01483 444007

NEXT HOSTELS
Tanners Hatch 6m, Hindhead 20m, Windsor 27m

HOW TO GET THERE
2m south of Abinger Hammer on A25 (between Guildford and Dorking). Follow signs to Holmbury St Mary on B2126, Hostel 1m north of village.
OS 187 GR 104450 Bart 6

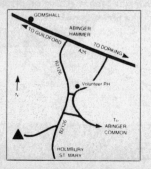

Tanners Hatch

Youth Hostel, Polesden Lacey, Dorking, Surrey RH5 6BE ☎ 01372 452528
Overnight Charges: Under 18 £4.00 Adult £5.95
2️⃣ 6️⃣5️⃣C A 🔄 S P National Trust car park ¾m (small charge).

Jan 1 - Jan 4	Open
Jan 5 - Feb 28	Open X:Tu/Wed
Mar 1 - Sep 30	Open X:Tu
Oct 1 - Dec 20	Open X:Tu/Wed
Dec 28 - Jan 4	Open for New Year
'96	

The Hostel may be available for groups when otherwise closed - please contact Warden.

ACCOMMODATION
 2

This National Trust cottage offers very simple accommodation in a truly next-to-nature setting in the Surrey Hills Area of Outstanding Natural Beauty. Boots, compass and torch essential! Discover the abundance of flora and fauna while walking through acres of Surrey Hills — with the scenic route of the North Downs Way proving popular with walkers, cyclists and horse riders.
🚲 2m 🔄 2m 🔄 🔄 3m

TRAVEL INFO
🚌 London & Country 465 Kingston - Horsham, alight West Humble, 2 ¼m (☎ 0181 668 7261).
🚉 Box Hill & Westhumble 1 ¾m; Dorking Town 2 ½m (by paths); Bookham 3 ½m.
ℹ️ ☎ 01483 444007

NEXT HOSTELS
Holmbury St Mary 6m, Hindhead 25m, London 23m

HOW TO GET THERE
OS 187 GR 140515 Bart 6

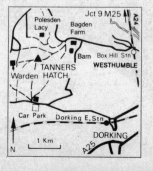

The sunny seaside resorts of the South Coast attract both weekend visitors and those on a longer holiday. Lively and vibrant Brighton with its Prince of Wales Royal Pavillion is popular with people of all ages. Stay at Brighton Youth Hostel, the 16th century Patcham Place, to explore the town. Other interesting seaside resorts are Eastbourne and Hastings. Travelling west towards Brighton, the coastline is backed by the dramatic hills of the South Downs, culminating in Beachy Head which offers spectacular views of chalk cliffs. Sussex is dotted with picturesque villages such as Alfriston and Telscombe.

Many Youth Hostels are available for exclusive use by groups booked in advance; please enquire. Plus, Blackboys, Eastbourne, Truleigh Hill and Telscombe Youth Hostels are on YHA's **Rent-a-Hostel scheme** which runs during the winter months (details on p.7).

USEFUL PUBLICATIONS

Budget Accommodation in Surrey, Sussex and Kent and individual Hostel leaflets — send s.a.e. to the YHA Regional Office listed below or phone our Literature Line on (01426) 951683 (local call charge).

The South Downs Way — send £1.25 (incl. p&p, cheques payable to YHA (England & Wales) Ltd.) to the YHA Regional Office listed below.

For more information about hostelling in this area contact: YHA South England Regional Office, 11B York Road, Salisbury, Wiltshire SP2 7AP. Tel: (01722) 337494. Fax: (01722) 414027.

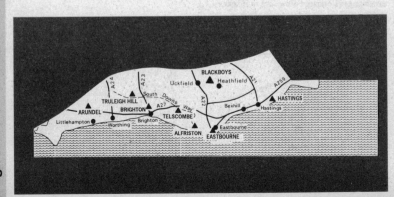

Alfriston

Youth Hostel, Frog Firle, Alfriston, Polegate, East Sussex BN26 5TT ☎ **01323 870423 Fax: 01323 870615**

Overnight Charges: Under 18 £5.35 Adult £8.00

Seasonal Prices Jul 1 - Aug 31: Under 18 £5.95 Adult £8.80

2 ⬚ ⬚ ⬚ S ⬚ 1m ⬚ 1x20, 1x40 P Ample space for cars and minibuses - coaches by arrangement. BABA

Feb 1 - Jun 30	Open X:Sun*
Jul 1 - Aug 31	Open
Sep 1 - Oct 31	Open X:Sun
Nov 1 - Dec 16	Open Fr/Sat only
Dec 22 - Dec 27	Open for Xmas

* Open Bank Hol Sun. The Hostel may be available for groups when otherwise closed - please contact Warden.

ACCOMMODATION ⬚ 4 ⬚ 4 ⬚ 3

This traditional Sussex flint house — set in the Cuckmere valley with views over the river and close to the picturesque village of Alfriston — offers comfortable accommodation with two lounges, including a cosy Tudor-beamed room. Popular with groups from April to June.
There are many local attractions ranging from the South Downs Way with superb walks and some of the most spectacular downland views in England to Druisillas Zoo with its own railway, craft centre and gardens. ⬚ 2m ⬚ 1m ⬚ ⬚ 3m ⬚ 25m ⬚ ⬚ 6m

TRAVEL INFO
⬚ Stagecoach South Coast 713
Eastbourne-Alfriston-Brighton (passes close BR Seaford & Polegate) (☎ 0345 581457) ⬚ Seaford 3m; Berwick 3m. ⬚ 6m (Newhaven-Dieppe)
⬚ ☎ 01323 442667

NEXT HOSTELS
Eastbourne 8m, Telscombe 11m, Blackboys 17m

HOW TO GET THERE
On foot, follow river bank to Litlington footbridge, take bridle path west for 400yds. By road, ¾m south of Alfriston on east side where road narrows.
OS 199 GR 518019 Bart 6

Arundel

Youth Hostel, Warningcamp, Arundel, West Sussex BN18 9QY ☎ **01903 882204**

Out of season contact: Regional Booking Service, 11B York Road, Salisbury, Wilts SP2 7AP
☎ 01722 337494 Fax: 01722 414027

Overnight Charges: Under 18 £4.85 Adult £7.20

Family accommodation prices on p.11-13

2 ⬚ ⬚ ⬚ ⬚ ⬚ S ⬚ 1½m P For cars and minibuses only. Coaches park in Arundel (closest access 400yds). BABA

Apr 7 - Jun 30	Open X:Sun*
Jul 1 - Aug 31	Open
Sep 1 - Oct 31	Open X:Sun/Mon

* Open Bank Hol Sun.

ACCOMMODATION ⬚ 4 ⬚ 4 ⬚ 2

This large impressive Georgian house — in its own peaceful grounds at the edge of the South Downs Way — makes an ideal base, especially for touring holidays. You'll find a magnificent castle, antiquities, heritage centre and safe sandy beaches (good for watersports) close by.
The area, known as the Pride of West Sussex, offers a wealth of things to do — for instance, if you've always wondered what goes on behind the scenes at the Body shop, join their tour in Littlehampton and all will be revealed! ⬚ 2m ⬚ 4m ⬚ 2m ⬚ 4m

TRAVEL INFO
⬚ Stagecoach Coastline 31 Brighton-Arundel, alight Arundel Station, then 1m (☎ 01903 237661). ⬚ Arundel 1m.
⬚ ☎ 01903 882268

NEXT HOSTELS
Truleigh Hill 16m, Brighton 20m, Portsmouth 26m.

HOW TO GET THERE
OS 197 GR 032076 Bart 6

Blackboys

Youth Hostel, Blackboys, Uckfield, East Sussex TN22 5HU ☎ 01825 890607

When Hostel is open, bookings and enquiries to: Brighton Youth Hostel, Patcham Place, London Rd, Brighton, BN1 8YD. ☎ 01273 556196 Fax: 01273 509366. Bookings for same and next night only, contact Blackboys YH direct. Out of season contact: Regional Booking Service, 11B York Road, Salisbury, Wiltshire SP2 7AP ☎ 01722 337494 Fax: 01722 414027

Overnight Charges: Under 18 £4.45 Adult £6.55

[R-a-H] ☎ 01722 337494 [1] [GSC] [A] [⚙] [◉] ³⁄₄m
[P] Cars and mini-buses

Jan 1 - Apr 6	Rent-a-Hostel
Apr 7 - Aug 31	Open X:Sun/Mon*
Sep 1 - Dec 31	Rent-a-Hostel

* Open Bank Hol.

ACCOMMODATION 4 ⁵⁻⁸ 3

This rustic wooden cabin in a deciduous sylvan setting offers good basic accommodation with a cosy open fire, spacious lounge/dining room and newly fitted self-catering kitchen.
Walk the Wealdon Way long distance path or take a scenic drive to Batemans at Burwash (once the home of Rudyard Kipling). [U]2m [⚑] [◫]4m

TRAVEL INFO
🚌Stagecoach South Coast/RDH 218, 728 Eastbourne-Uckfield (pass close BR Uckfield and close BR Eastbourne), alight Blackboys ½m
(☎ 01273 478007) 🚂Buxted 2 ½m; Lewes 11m. 🛈☎01273 483448

NEXT HOSTELS
Alfriston 17m, Telscombe 17m, Brighton 17m

ADDITIONAL INFO
Credit cards not accepted at Blackboys; bookings via Brighton.

HOW TO GET THERE
From Cross-in-Hand take right fork at Crown Inn, then second right. From Uckfield take Heathfield Road, 4m, then turn left into Gunn Road. Hostel on right after ½m.
[OS] 199 [GR] 521215 [Bart] 10

Brighton

Youth Hostel, Patcham Place, London Road, Brighton BN1 8YD ☎ 01273 556196
Fax: 01273 509366

Overnight Charges: Under 18 £5.95 Adult £8.80

[4] [◫] [🔍] [🔒] [🛏] [⚙] [◉] ¼m [P] [BABA]

| Feb 1 - Dec 31 | Open |

The Hostel will open at 17.00 hrs during the winter period. The Hostel may be available for groups when otherwise closed - please contact Warden.

ACCOMMODATION 4 4

This magnificent mansion — originally built in the 16th century (but with 18th century additions) and ideally located on the outskirts of this famous seaside resort — offers traditional dormitory accommodation and excellent home cooking. Brighton offers all the attractions of a traditional but stylish seaside resort: the beach and watersports; the pier and amusements; theatres and restaurants; even history too — with museums, galleries and the famous Brighton Pavillion. The ancient South Downs Way passes close by. [🏊]3m [⛰]4m [◫]3m

TRAVEL INFO
🚌Stagecoach Coastline 107, 137 Brighton-Horsham; 770 Brighton-Haywards Heath (pass close BR Preston park & BR Haywards Heath) (☎ 01903 237661). Bus from Town 5/5A to Patcham. National Express Coach from London stops outside Hostel. 🚂Preston Park 2m; Brighton 3 ½m. 🚢10m (Newhaven-Dieppe) 🛈☎01273 23755

NEXT HOSTELS
Truleigh Hill 6m, Telscombe 10m, Alfriston 18m

HOW TO GET THERE
On W. side of main London Road (A23), opp. Black Lion Hotel 4m N. of Brighton close to junction with A27.
[OS] 198 [GR] 300088 [Bart] 6

32 BEDS   Open: 17.00hrs

Eastbourne

Youth Hostel, East Dean Road, Eastbourne, East Sussex BN20 8ES ☎ **01323 721081 Fax: 01323 721081**

Out of season contact: Regional Booking Service, 11B York Road, Salisbury, Wiltshire SP2 7AP ☎ 01722 337494 Fax: 01722 414027

Overnight Charges: Under 18 £4.85 Adult £7.20

R-a-H ☎ 01722 337494 ② SSC Ⓐ 🌐 🏠 1m Ⓟ Limited. BABA

Jan 1 - Apr 6	Rent-a-Hostel
Apr 7 - Jun 30	Open X:Tu/Wed
Jul 1 - Aug 31	Open
Sep 1 - Dec 31	Rent-a-Hostel

ACCOMMODATION   🛏️⁹⁺3

This simple Hostel — a former golf clubhouse — offers engaging views across Eastbourne and Pevensay Bay. Observe the awesome beauty of Beachy Head, take a leisurely cruise, start or end your journey over the South Downs Way or explore the neighbouring peaceful woodland. The area offers many historical and contemporary attractions, including the Living World, Polegate Windmill, Pevensay Castle and Eastbourne Sovereign Castle — as well as many natural pleasures such as the local cliffs and gardens. 🚶 ⛰️ 🏚️ 🌳 🖼️

TRAVEL INFO

🚌 Brighton & Hove/Stagecoach South Coast 712 Eastbourne-Brighton (passes close BR Eastbourne & Newhaven Town) (☎ 0345 581457)
🚉 Eastbourne 1 ½m. ⛴️ 10m (Newhaven-Dieppe)
ℹ️ ☎ 01323 411400

NEXT HOSTELS
Alfriston 8m, Blackboys 19m, Hastings 25m

HOW TO GET THERE
OS 199 GR 588990 Bart 6

57 BEDS   Open: 17.00hrs

Hastings

Youth Hostel, Guestling Hall, Rye Road, Guestling, Hastings, East Sussex TN35 4LP ☎ **01424 812373 Fax: 01424 814273**

Out of season contact: Regional Booking Service, 11B York Road, Salisbury, Wiltshire SP2 7AP ☎ 01722 337494 Fax: 01722 414027

Overnight Charges: Under 18 £4.85 Adult £7.20

Seasonal Prices Jul 1 - Aug 31: Under 18 £5.35 Adult £8.00

Family accommodation prices on p.11-13

② 🍴 SSC Ⓐ 🌐 🏠 Ⓢ 📞 2 ½m Ⓟ Limited. BABA

Feb 11 - Apr 6	Open X:Sun/Mon
Apr 7 - Jun 30	Open X:Sun*
Jul 1 - Aug 31	Open
Sep 1 - Oct 31	Open X:Sun/Mon
Nov 1 - Nov 30	Open Fr/Sat

* Open Bank Hol Sun. The Hostel may be available for groups when otherwise closed.

ACCOMMODATION   🛏️²2 🛏️⁶6 🛏️⁹⁺3

This large Victorian manor house, set in four acres of beautiful grounds with its own small lake and leafy woodland, is in an isolated setting only 4m from Hastings town centre. Trails lead from the Hostel to nearby beauty spots.
Steeped in history, the area has much to offer — including the Smugglers Adventure and the 1066 Story. ⛰️ 1m 🏚️ 🌳 🖼️ 4m

TRAVEL INFO

🚌 East Kent 11/12 Hastings - Rye (passes BR Hastings & Rye) (☎ 0800 696996). 🚉 Three Oaks 1 ½m by footpath, 2 ½m by road; Ore 2 ½m, Hastings 6m.
ℹ️ ☎ 01424 718888

NEXT HOSTELS
Eastbourne 25m, Blackboys 25m, Alfriston 33m

HOW TO GET THERE
From Hastings follow A259 Folkstone/Rye, 4m from Hastings Centre. The Hostel is 200yds past the White Hart Beefeater on left. From Rye approaching the Hostel on right 500yds after Guestling School.
OS 199 GR 848133 Bart 6

22

SOUTH COAST

Telscombe

Youth Hostel, Bank Cottages, Telscombe, Lewes, East Sussex BN7 3HZ
📞 01273 301357

When Hostel is open, bookings & enquiries to: Brighton Youth Hostel, Patcham Place, London Road, Brighton, BN1 8YD. 📞 01273 556196. Fax: 01273 509366. Bookings for same and next night only, contact Telscombe YH direct. Out of season contact: Regional Booking Service, 11B York Road, Salisbury, Wilts. SP2 7AP 📞 01722 337494 Fax: 01722 414027

Overnight Charges: Under 18 £4.85 Adult £7.20

R-a-H 📞 01722 337494 1 BBC ⊠ ⊕ 🖵 2 ½m
P By arrangement with Warden.

Jan 1 - Apr 6	Rent-a-Hostel
Apr 7 - Aug 31	Open X:Tu/Wed
Sep 1 - Dec 31	Rent-a-Hostel

ACCOMMODATION 🛏️²⁻⁴ 5

Sympathetically refurbished, this charming mixture of 200-year old cottages makes a superb simple Hostel. Nestled in the pastoral village of Telscombe in the Sussex Downs, this is an ideal base for country walking and enjoying the splendour of the Telscombe Cliffs.
Famous for its rolling hills and chalk downs, south east England is also steeped in ancient history and full of local colour. It makes an ideal stop-over from the South Down's Way.

🚶10m U ⛰️ ⛱️10m ⛵ 🏊6 ½m

TRAVEL INFO
🚌 Brighton & Hove 14/B from Brighton (passes close BR Brighton), alight Heathy Brow, ¾m (📞 01273 821111). 🚂 Southease 2 ½m; Lewes 6 ½m; Brighton 7m. 🚢 5m (Newhaven-Dieppe)
ℹ️ 📞 01273 23755

NEXT HOSTELS
Brighton 10m, Alfriston 11m, Blackboys 17m

ADDITIONAL INFO
Credit cards are not accepted. Advance booking via Brighton.

HOW TO GET THERE
OS 198 GR 405033 Bart 6

Truleigh Hill

Youth Hostel, Tottington Barn, Truleigh Hill, Shoreham-by-Sea, West Sussex BN43 5FB
📞 01903 813419 Fax: 01903 812016

Overnight Charges: Under 18 £5.35 Adult £8.00

Family accommodation prices on p.11-13

2 🍴 🛁 BBC ⊞ 🖵 S 🚰 4m P BABA

Jan 1 - Feb 28	Rent-a-Hostel
Mar 1 - Apr 6	Open Fr/Sat
Apr 7 - Jun 30	Open X:Sun*
Jul 1 - Aug 31	Open
Sep 1 - Oct 31	Open X:Sun/Mon
Nov 1 - Dec 31	Rent-a-Hostel

*Open Bank Hol Sun. The Hostel may be available for groups when otherwise closed.

ACCOMMODATION 🛏️²⁻⁴ 7 🛏️⁵⁻⁸ 6

This modern Hostel — which offers comfortable 4/6 bedded rooms — is situated on top of the beautiful South Downs with panoramic views over Downs town and the sea. There is a conservation area in the Hostel grounds with a Dew pond and climatological station.
Iron Age Hillforts, Domesday villages and town conservation areas are accessible on foot, plus circular walking routes. The area is ideal for mountain biking, walking and watersports, close to coastal resorts for entertainment and shopping. U 10m ⛰️ ⛱️4m 🚴4m 🏊4m

TRAVEL INFO
🚌 Brighton & Hove 20A from BR Shoreham-by-Sea, alight ½m S of Upper Beeding, then 1 ¾m by bridlepath (📞 01273 821111). 🚂 Shoreham-by-Sea 4m.
ℹ️ 📞 01273 23755

NEXT HOSTELS
Brighton 6m, Arundel 16m, Holmbury 35m

ADDITIONAL INFO
Ideal for family groups, house parties, seminars, small conferences and conservation projects.

HOW TO GET THERE
From Upper Shoreham Road (signposted Southlands Hospital), north via Erringham Road and Mill Hill.
OS 198 GR 220105 Bart 6

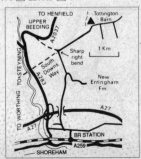

Lying between the River Avon and Southampton Water, the New Forest covers about 140 square miles of forest and heath which is particularly attractive in June when the famous wild ponies have had their foals.

Burley Youth Hostel is a good base for exploring the nature reserve where you'll see red, fallow and roe deer.

The Isle of Wight is known for its seaside resorts, chines and cliff paths. There are several historic sites open to the public such as Carisbrooke Castle and Osbourne House — Queen Victoria's favourite country retreat. The historic towns of Winchester, Portsmouth and Southampton can all be found in Hampshire.

Many Youth Hostels are available for exclusive use by groups booked in advance; please enquire. Burley and Winchester Youth Hostels are on YHA's **Rent-a-Hostel scheme** which runs through the winter months (details on p.7).

USEFUL PUBLICATIONS

Individual Hostel leaflets are available — send s.a.e to the YHA Regional Office listed below or phone our Literature Line on (01426) 951683 (local call charge).

For more information about hostelling in this area contact: YHA South England Regional Office, 11B York Road, Salisbury, Wiltshire SP2 7AP. Tel: (01722) 337494. Fax: (01722) 414027.

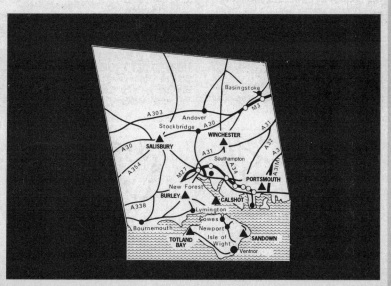

Burley

Calshot Activities Centre

Youth Hostel, Cottesmore House, Cott Lane, Burley, Ringwood, Hampshire BH24 4BB 📞 01425 403233

Overnight Charges: Under 18 £5.35 Adult £8.00

Seasonal Prices Jul 1 - Aug 31: Under 18 £5.95 Adult £8.80

Family accommodation prices on p.11-13

R-a-H 📞 01722 337494

  1 🍴 SSC A ⊕ 🖒 P Limited for cars and minibuses. Coaches at village end of Cott Lane.

Feb 11 - Apr 6	Open X:Sun/Mon
Apr 7 - Jun 30	Open X:Sun*
Jul 1 - Aug 31	Open
Sep 1 - Oct 28	Open X:Sun/Mon
Oct 29 - Nov 30	Open Fr/Sat only
Dec 1 - Dec 31	Rent-a-Hostel

* Open Bank Hol. The Hostel may be available for groups when otherwise closed.

ACCOMMODATION 🛏️2-4 1 🛏️5-8 3 🛏️9+ 1

A former family home, the Hostel is set in 1 ½ acres of grounds in the heart of the New Forest. Enjoy good food and a friendly atmosphere.
This is a perfect setting to relax in the peace and quiet of the countryside. Or why not make the most of the many tourist attractions on offer. For the more adventurous, cycling, ponytrekking and watersports are all within easy reach. 🚴 1m
🏊 2m ⛰️ 10m 🚤 🏊 10m

TRAVEL INFO

🚌 Wilts & Dorset/Solent Blue Line X1 Bournemouth - Southampton (passes BR Lyndhurst Road & Southampton), alight Durmast Corner, ¼m; 105, 116 from Christchurch, alight Burley, ½m (📞 01202 673555). 🚉 Sway 5 ½m; New Milton 6m, Brockenhurst 6m.
ℹ️ 📞 01703 282269

NEXT HOSTELS

Totland Bay 17m, Salisbury 21m, Winchester 23m

HOW TO GET THERE

From centre of Burley follow Lyndhurst Road past Burley School on left, then take left hand turn into Cott Lane and follow signs to Hostel.
OS 195 GR 220028 Bart 5

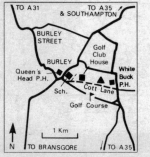

Youth Hostel, Calshot Spit, Fawley, Southampton, Hampshire SO41 1BR
📞 01703 892077 Fax: 01703 891267

Overnight Charges: Under 18 £5.95 Adult £8.80

 4 🍴 ⊞ 🔍 🏷️ ⊕ 🖒 1m P

Jan 9 - Jul 16	Open X:Sun
Jul 17 - Sep 3	Open
Sep 4 - Dec 16	Open X:Sun

All bookings should be made in advance. Reception open 17.00-19.30 hrs. In an emergency for arrivals after 19.30hrs please contact the duty instructor.

ACCOMMODATION 🛏️2-4 1 🛏️5-8 3

Uniquely situated on a shingle spit reaching out into the sea, this former RAF flying boat base includes a tudor castle, RNLI station, coastguard tower and nature reserve. Accommodation within the old HQ building is simple but benefits from panoramic views of the Solent.
This is an ideal base for touring — with the New Forest, Beaulieu, Bucklers Hard, Exbury Gardens, Lyndhurst, Longdown Butterfly and Dairy Farms, and Lymington (Sat market) all close by. We offer on-site tuition in most watersports (including powerboating), as well as skiing, climbing, archery, etc. ⛷️ 🏄 🚤 🏊 4m

TRAVEL INFO

🚌 Solent Blue Line X9, 39 BR Southampton-Calshot Beach, thence 1m (📞 01703 226235) 🚉 Southampton Central via Hythe ferry 9m; Totton 13m
ℹ️ 📞 01703 221106

NEXT HOSTELS

Winchester 27m, Burley 32m, Portsmouth 34m

ADDITIONAL INFO

All cheques to be made payable to 'Hampshire County Council'. Additional bed numbers to those listed above can be made available.

HOW TO GET THERE

Once on A326 to Fawley, follow brown tourist road signs to Calshot Castle.
OS 196 GR 488023

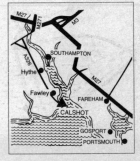

Portsmouth

Youth Hostel, Wymering Manor, Old Wymering Lane, Cosham, Portsmouth, Hampshire PO6 3NL ☎ **01705 375661 Fax: 01705 214177**

Overnight Charges: Under 18 £5.35 Adult £8.00

1 ⊙ 6SC ▢ ¼m P Cars and mini-buses (coaches contact Warden) BABA

Feb 1 - Apr 6	Open X:Sun/Mon
Apr 7 - Jun 30	Open X:Sun*
Jul 1 - Aug 31	Open
Sep 1 - Oct 31	Open X:Sun/Mon
Nov 1 - Dec 9	Open Fr/Sat
Dec 22 - Dec 27	Open for Xmas

* Open Bank Hol Sun. The Hostel may be available for groups when otherwise closed - please contact Warden.

ACCOMMODATION 1 5 2

This beautiful Tudor manor house with a magnificent entrance hall and two 350 year-old Jacobean staircases is one of the oldest known houses in Hampshire — and the ultimate place to stay to experience England's historic maritime heritage.
Home to the Mary Rose and Lord Nelson's HMS Victory, Portsmouth has much to offer — whether you want to explore historic flagships, discover the underwater world or visit a military museum. 🚶5m ⚓4m 🚲5m 🏊4m

TRAVEL INFO
🚌 Frequent from surrounding areas (☎ 01705 498894). 🚉 Cosham ½m. ⛴ (to Caen/St Malo/Le Havre/Santander)
ℹ ☎01705 826722

NEXT HOSTELS
Sandown 10m via ferry, Winchester 25m, Arundel 26m

HOW TO GET THERE
From Cosham police station, take Medina Road; seventh turning on right, Old Wymering Lane. Hostel opposite church entrance.
OS 196 GR 640955 Bart 5

Salisbury

Youth Hostel, Milford Hill House, Milford Hill, Salisbury, Wiltshire SP1 2QW ☎ **01722 327572 Fax: 01722 330446**

Overnight Charges: Under 18 £5.95 Adult £8.80

Family accommodation prices on p.11-13

4 ⊙ ▢ ⬚ A ⬚ ⊙ ⊙ ▢ ¼m P Cars and mini-buses. Space for one coach - arrange with Warden. BABA

| Jan 1 - Dec 31 | Open |

The Hostel is open from 13.00 hrs each day - however, during the winter the reception may not be manned until 17.00 hrs.

ACCOMMODATION 🛏6 🛏4 🛏2

This 200-year old listed building is set in its own secluded grounds only a few minutes walk from the centre of the lovely cathedral city of Salisbury. A fine old Cedar of Lebanon tree is the outstanding feature of the Hostel's well tended garden.
The bustling market town is a pleasing mix of old and new. Traditional open markets are held on Tuesdays and Saturdays. The area offers good off road cycling and Stonehenge is only 9m away.
🚶 ⛵ 🏊

TRAVEL INFO
🚌 Frequent from surrounding areas (☎ 01722 336855). 🚉 Salisbury 1m.
ℹ ☎01722 334956

NEXT HOSTELS
Burley 21m, Winchester 24m, Bath 39m

ADDITIONAL INFO
Foreign exchange. One single room. The Hostel reception may not open until 5pm in the winter.

HOW TO GET THERE
Motorists - avoid city centre. Hostel signposted from A36 (Southampton). Near Wrynams garage.
OS 184 GR 149299 Bart 5

Sandown

Youth Hostel, The Firs, Fitzroy Street, Sandown, Isle of Wight PO36 8JH
☎ 01983 402651 **Fax: 01983 403565**

Out of season contact: Regional Booking Service, 11B York Road, Salisbury, Wilts SP2 7AP
☎ 01722 337494 Fax: 01722 414027

Overnight Charges: Under 18 £4.85 Adult £7.20

Seasonal Prices Jul 1 - Aug 31: Under 18 £5.95 Adult £8.80

Family accommodation prices on p.11-13

1 🍴 🅶🆂🅲 📺 🚭 ½m 🅿 Small car park. BABA

Apr 7 - Jun 30	Open X:Mon*
Jul 1 - Aug 31	Open
Sep 1 - Sep 30	Open X:Tu/Wed

* Open Bank Hol Mon.

ACCOMMODATION   🛏3 🛏2 🛏2

The Firs — originally a 19th century house — became a Hostel in the 1930s. It has a small sun trap which is perfect for evening barbecues. Only minutes from the thriving seaside resort with its pier, beach and theatre, you're also close to the beautiful views and peace of the Bembridge Down.
Ideal for traditional seaside holidays, the island also offers a wealth of geographical and historical interest, as well as some spectacular scenery — from rolling downs to clean sandy beaches.

TRAVEL INFO
🚌 Frequent from surrounding areas (☎ 01983 862224). 🚉 Sandown ½m (No cycles permitted on island trains). Ferry Terminal: Ryde Pierhead (Wightlink) 8m (☎ 01705 827744); East Cowes (Red Funnel) 12m (☎ 01983 292101).
🛈 ☎ 01983 403886

NEXT HOSTELS
Portsmouth 10m, Totland Bay 24m

ADDITIONAL INFO
As an alternative to evening meals, barbecues can be provided for groups.

HOW TO GET THERE
OS 196 GR 597843 Bart 5

Southampton

We regret that this Youth Hostel is no longer open. The nearest Youth Hostels are Winchester 9m, Portsmouth 16m and Burley 16m.

VOLUNTARY WARDENS

**are needed
for small
self-catering Youth
Hostels throughout
South England.**

Can you spare a week or two?

Would you like to be considered for this challenging role?

**Then write to:
YHA Voluntary
Wardening Co-ordinator.
11B York Road,
Salisbury,
Wilts. SP2 7AP
with a 9"x 6" s.a.e.**

Totland Bay (West Wight)

Youth Hostel, Hurst Hill, Totland Bay, Isle of Wight PO39 0HD 01983 752165
Fax: 01983 756443

Overnight Charges: Under 18 £5.35 Adult £8.00

Seasonal Prices Jul 1 - Aug 31: Under 18 £5.95 Adult £8.80

Family accommodation prices on p.11-13

1 | 0 | GSC | ⊞ | A | ⊟ ½m P In grounds, coaches in road. BABA

Feb 1 - Apr 6	Open X:Sun/Mon
Apr 7 - Jun 30	Open X:Sun*
Jul 1 - Aug 31	Open
Sep 1 - Nov 25	Open X:Sun/Mon

* Open Bank Hol Sun. The Hostel may be available for groups when otherwise closed - please contact Warden.

ACCOMMODATION   🛏4 🛏2 🛏3

Formerly a private home and hotel, this charming Hostel is situated on the westernmost village of the island just a short walk from Alum Bay and the famous 'Wight' needles.
Surrounded by National Trust land, this Area of Outstanding Natural Beauty boasts downland, cliffs, beaches and beautiful, quiet country walks. Good ferry and public transport access make this an ideal base for exploring the island. 🚲3m
⛱2m 🏔1m ✉½m ⛵1m

TRAVEL INFO
🚌Southern Vectis 7/A, 17, 42 from Yarmouth; 1B/C from Ryde, alight Totland War Memorial, ¼m (01983 523831).
🛈 01983 867979

NEXT HOSTELS
Sandown 24m, Burley 17m

HOW TO GET THERE
From roundabout in centre of Totland, take left fork past garage up Weston Road. Take second left up Hurst Hill - Hostel at top of short hill on left.
OS 196 GR 324865 Bart 5

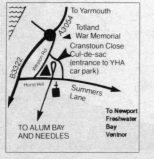

Winchester

Youth Hostel, The City Mill, 1 Water Lane, Winchester, Hampshire SO23 0ER
 01962 853723

Overnight Charges: Under 18 £4.85 Adult £7.20

Seasonal Prices Jul 1 - Aug 31: Under 18 £5.35 Adult £8.00

R-a-H 01722 337494 1 | 0 | ✉ | ⊟ ¼m P Chesil Street car park ¼m

Jan 1 - Mar 14	Rent-a-Hostel
Mar 15 - Jun 30	Open X:Sun/Mon*
Jul 1 - Aug 31	Open
Sep 1 - Oct 31	Open X:Sun/Mon
Nov 1 - Dec 31	Rent-a-Hostel

* Open Bank Hol.

ACCOMMODATION   🛏1 🛏2

This simple Hostel, owned by the National Trust, is a charming 18th century watermill which spans the River Itchen at the east end of King Alfred's capital. The interior is dominated by the magnificent beamed common room. A charming island garden lies within the mill-race.
Famous for its Cathedral, the city is rich in monuments and historic buildings — including the venerable College and the ancient almshouse of St Cross. Local attractions include Marwell Zoo (endangered species) and the Watercress Line Steam Railway. 🚂12m ✉½m

TRAVEL INFO
🚌Frequent from surrounding areas (01962 852352). 🚉Winchester 1m.
🛈 01962 867871

NEXT HOSTELS
Burley 23m, Salisbury 24m, Portsmouth 25m

ADDITIONAL INFO
The Hostel's charm lies in its simple character which means it lacks certain amenities common elsewhere. Families and group leaders should discuss facilities with the Warden in advance.

HOW TO GET THERE
From Guildhall, walk over Eastgate Bridge and turn first left into Water Lane (no vehicle entry). The Hostel is the third door on the left.
OS 185 GR 486293 Bart 5

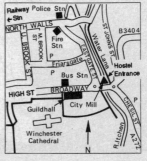

Spectacular cliffs, awesome caves, ancient settlements and historic architectural achievements can all be found in this Area of Outstanding Natural Beauty. The Cheddar Gorge has 450ft high cliffs and its caves, some open to the public, are famous for their stalactites and stalagmites. Another dazzling sight is the great cave at Wookey Hole with its deep underground river. Cheddar and Street Youth Hostels are excellent bases for taking in some of the most amazing sites in the country. Or use Bath Youth Hostel as a base to explore the Roman city with the only hot springs in Britain. Bristol with its two cathedrals, I.K. Brunel's Clifton Suspension Bridge and the S.S. Great Britain are also well worth a visit.

Street Youth Hostel is available on YHA's **Rent-a-Hostel scheme** which runs during the winter months (details on p.7).

USEFUL PUBLICATIONS

Individual Hostel leaflets are available — send s.a.e. to the YHA Regional Office listed below or phone our Literature Line on (01426) 951683 (local call charge).

For more information about hostelling in this area contact: YHA South England Regional Office, 11B York Road, Salisbury, Wiltshire SP2 7AP. Tel: (01722) 337494. Fax: (01722) 414027.

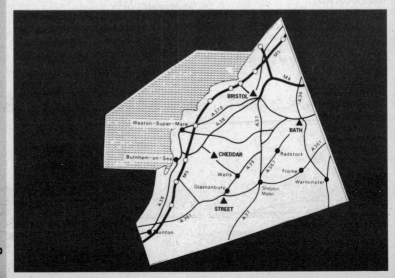

Bath

Youth Hostel, Bathwick Hill, Bath, Avon BA2 6JZ ☎ **01225 465674 Fax: 01225 482947**

Overnight Charges: Under 18 £5.35 Adult £8.00

Seasonal Prices Jul 1 - Aug 31: Under 18 £5.95 Adult £8.80

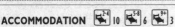 ½m P On Bathwick Hill.
BABA IBN

Open every day of the year.

ACCOMMODATION 🛏️²⁻⁴ 10 🛏️⁵⁻⁸ 6 🛏️⁹⁺ 3

A handsome Italianate mansion situated in a wooded conservation area with panoramic views of the city centre and surrounding countryside. The Hostel has recently undergone several improvements and now boasts a superb cafeteria, as well as additional shower and washing facilities. Bath is a World Heritage City famous for its Hot Spring, Roman Baths and Georgian architecture. Other attractions include Bath Abbey, Royal Crescent and the Theatre Royal. As well as boat hire and river cruises, enjoy the city's many shops, restaurants, pubs and entertainment.
🚶 1m U 4m 🏊 1m

TRAVEL INFO
🚌 Badgerline 18 from Bus Station adjacent BR Bath Spa (☎ 01225 464446). 🚉 Bath Spa 1 ¼m.
ℹ️ ☎ 01225 462831

NEXT HOSTELS
Bristol 14m, Cheddar 27m, Slimbridge 30m

HOW TO GET THERE
Follow signs to University and American Museum.
OS 172 GR 766644 Bart 7

Bristol

YHA International Centre, 14 Narrow Quay, Bristol, Avon BS1 4QA ☎ **0117 9221659 Fax: 0117 9273789**

Overnight Charges: Under 18 £7.20 Adult £10.60

Family accommodation prices on p.11-13

  1m 🅿️ 1x50, 2x25 P At NCP Prince St. Meter parking outside Hostel. Coach parking (10 mins walk). BABA IBN

Jan 4 - Dec 17	Open

ACCOMMODATION 🛏️²⁻⁴ 22 🛏️⁵⁻⁸ 6 🛏️⁹⁺ 1

Situated in an impressive refurbished warehouse on the quayside of the historic harbour, the Hostel has been purposely designed and equipped to a high standard. The location is superb with extensive views of the harbour and close to the city's many social, cultural and leisure facilities. Steeped in history and innovation, Bristol is one of the most fascinating cities in England. The magnificent Avon Gorge, Brunel's suspension bridge, the historic harbour and the surrounding countryside all combine to make Bristol an exciting place to stay. 🚶 2m 🏊 25m 🏊 2m

TRAVEL INFO
🚌 Frequent from surrounding areas (☎ 0117 9553231). Bus and coach station ¾m. 🚉 Bristol Temple Meads ¾m (☎ 0117 9294255).
ℹ️ ☎ 0117 9260767

NEXT HOSTELS
Bath 14m, Cheddar 20m, Slimbridge 25m

ADDITIONAL INFO
Three conference rooms (seating 1x50, 2x25) are available for hire, as well as resources such as OHP and slide projectors. IBN booking service.

HOW TO GET THERE
From London or Southwolds: M4 to Junction 19 then M32. From Birmingham or South West: M5 to Junction 18 then A4.
OS 172 GR 586725 Bart 7

To University & American Museum

NOT TO SCALE

NOT TO SCALE

Cheddar

Youth Hostel, Hillfield, Cheddar, Somerset BS27 3HN ☎ 01934 742494
Fax: 01934 744724

Overnight Charges: Under 18 £4.45 Adult £6.55

Family accommodation prices on p.11-13

2 ⊠ GSC ▣ ▣ P Cars & mini-buses only. Coaches nearby. BABA

Feb 1 - Apr 6	Open X:Sun/Mon
Apr 7 - Jun 30	Open X:Sun*
Jul 1 - Aug 31	Open
Sep 1 - Oct 31	Open X:Sun/Mon
Nov 1 - Dec 17	Open Fr/Sat

* Open Bank Hol Sun. The Hostel may be available for groups when otherwise closed - please contact Warden.

ACCOMMODATION   🛏2-4 4 🛏5-8 5 🛏9+ 1

At this Victorian stone-built house you'll find traditional accommodation and some wonderful home-cooking — all set in the centre of this world famous village, only 5 mins walk from the Cheddar Gorge and for extensive walks on the Mendip Hills (an Area of Outstanding Natural Beauty).
We can organise adventure courses for groups all year round. Local attractions include Wells (England's smallest Cathedral city), Glastonbury (with its famous abbey) and the Victorian seaside resort of Weston-super-Mare. 🚲4m U 1m
▲ 1m 🏔 1m 🎣 1m 🏊 1m 🛒 ½m

TRAVEL INFO
🚌Badgerline 126, 826 Weston-super-Mare - Wells (pass close BR Weston Milton & Weston-super-Mare) (☎ 01934 621201).
🚉Weston Milton 10m; Weston-super-Mare 11m.
ℹ️ ☎01934 744071

NEXT HOSTELS
Street 17m, Bristol 20m, Bath 27m

ADDITIONAL INFO
Daytime access available to groups.

HOW TO GET THERE
OS 182 GR 455534 Bart 7

Street

Youth Hostel, The Chalet, Ivythorn Hill, Street, Somerset BA16 0TZ
☎ 01458 442961

Out of season contact: Regional Booking Service, 11B York Road, Salisbury Wilts. SP2 7AP
☎ 01722 337494 Fax: 01722 414027

Overnight Charges: Under 18 £4.85 Adult £7.20

Family accommodation prices on p.11-13

 R-a-H ☎ 01722 337494 1 GSC A 🏠 ⊕ ● ½m P

Jan 1 - Apr 6	Rent-a-Hostel
Apr 7 - Jun 30	Open X:Tu
Jul 1 - Aug 31	Open
Sep 1 - Oct 31	Open X:Tu/Wed
Nov 1 - Dec 31	Rent-a-Hostel

ACCOMMODATION   🛏2-4 4 🛏5-8 1 🛏9+ 1

This attractive Swiss-style chalet, built by the Clarks family (of shoemaking fame) as a holiday home for their employees and now a cosy and comfortable Hostel, is set on a small hill overlooking Glastonbury Tor and the Mendip Hills in the heart of Somerset.
Famous for Clarks shoes, the town of Street has many amenities while nearby Glastonbury is a centre for mysticism and Arthurian legends (plus host to the famous music festival) and the city of Wells boasts a magnificent cathedral. The hills and levels of Somerset offer easy walking and cycling. 🚲3m 🏊 🚲2m

TRAVEL INFO
🚌Badgerline 376, Clapton 676/7, Southern National 29A Bristol - Yeovil (passes BR Bristol Temple Meads), alight Marshalls Elm then 500yds. (☎ 0117 9553231). 🚉Castle Cary 11m; Bridgwater 13m.
ℹ️ ☎01458 832954

NEXT HOSTELS
Cheddar 17m, Quantock Hills 28m, Bristol 33m

HOW TO GET THERE
From Street, take the Somerton road (B3151) S for 2m. Turn right at crossroads at Marshalls Elm, Hostel 500yds on right.
OS 182 GR 480345 Bart 4

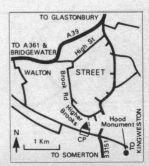

The distinctive coastline of Dorset, much of which is designated an Area of Outstanding Natural Beauty, offers unusual cliff formations and a vast variety of seaside resorts from Bournemouth to Lyme Regis. It's ideal for those interested in geology, fossil hunting, long sandy beaches and gentle coastal walks.

The unique Chesil Beach is a long line of shingle which shelters a swannery with hundreds of birds. Part of the South West Coastal Footpath runs from Poole Harbour around to Lyme Regis which was made famous by Meryl Streep's haunting portrayal of the French Lieutenant's Woman.

An area plentiful in natural and geological interest, the Dorset coast is popular all year round thanks to its mild climate.

Lulworth Cove Youth Hostel is available on YHA's **Rent-a-Hostel scheme** which runs during the winter months (details on p.7).

USEFUL PUBLICATIONS

Individual Hostel leaflets are available — send s.a.e to the YHA Regional Office listed below or phone our Literature Line on (01426) 951683 (local call charge).

The South West Way: a guide to the coast path — send £4.50 (inc. p&p) to the South West Way Association, 1 Orchard Drive, Kingskerwell, Newton Abbot, Devon TQ12 5DG.

For more information about hostelling in this area contact: YHA South England Regional Office, 11B York Road, Salisbury, Wiltshire SP2 7AP. Tel: (01722) 337494. Fax: (01722) 414027.

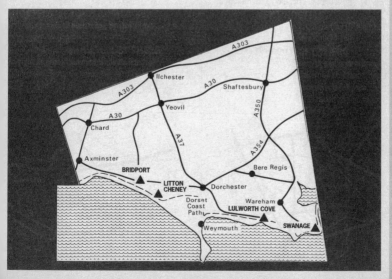

Bridport

Youth Hostel, West Rivers House, West Allington, Bridport, Dorset DT6 5BW
📞 01308 422655 Fax: 01308 425319

Out of season contact: Regional Booking Service, 11B York Road, Salisbury, Wilts. SP2 7AP
📞 01722 337494 Fax: 01722 414027

Overnight Charges: Under 18 £4.85 Adult £7.20

Family accommodation prices on p.11-13

 10 yds 🅿 Large car park suitable for coaches, cars and trailers. BABA

Feb 17 - Apr 6	Open X:Sun
Apr 7 - Aug 31	Open
Sep 1 - Oct 31	Open X:Wed/Th

The Hostel may be available for groups when otherwise closed - please contact Warden.

ACCOMMODATION 🛏6 🛏5 🛏1

This spacious detached building, formerly a rope and flaxmill, on the edge of a busy market town offers comfortable accommodation and good facilities with immediate access onto large playing fields.

Founded on rope and net making — still a local trade — Bridport is set in the heart of Hardy's Wessex with rolling hills and breathtaking coastal scenery all around. Hunt for fossils at Charmouth, enjoy the shingle beach at West Bay or visit the interesting towns of Dorchester and Weymouth. ⅓m 🅄4m 🏔🏔1½m 🎣🏠1m

TRAVEL INFO

🚌 Southern National 31/X31 Weymouth - Taunton (pass close BR Dorchester West & South and Taunton & pass BR Axminster) (📞 01823 272033). 🚉 Axminster 11m; Dorchester South or West, both 15m.
ℹ️ 📞 01308 424901

NEXT HOSTELS

Litton Cheney 7m, Lulworth Cove 30m, Beer 22m.

HOW TO GET THERE

OS 193 GR 461930 Bart 4

Litton Cheney

Youth Hostel, Litton Cheney, Dorchester, Dorset DT2 9AT 📞 01308 482340

Out of season contact: Regional Booking Service, 11B York Road, Salisbury, Wiltshire SP2 7AP
📞 01722 337494 Fax: 01722 414027

Overnight Charges: Under 18 £3.60 Adult £5.35

1 10 🚼 🍴 ¾m 🅿 Limited.

| Mar 31 - Aug 31 | Open X:Mon |

ACCOMMODATION 2

This Dutch Barn, once a cheese and milk factory, offers simple accommodation in an area of outstanding natural beauty in rural Dorset. A la carte menu service is often available — and not to be missed!

Close to Chesil Beach (3m) and the inland coastal path (2½m) with connecting paths to the Hostel. Many archaeological and geological sites within easy walking distance make it ideal for an extended visit. 🚲🏔1m 🏔13m 🎣18m 🏠14m 🏠3m

TRAVEL INFO

🚌 Southern National 31/X31 Weymouth - Taunton, alight Whiteway, 1½m. (📞 01823 272033) 🚉 Dorchester South or West, both 10m.
🚢 14m (Weymouth-Channel Isles)
ℹ️ 📞 01305 267992

NEXT HOSTELS

Bridport 7m, Lulworth Cove 25m, Beer 28m.

HOW TO GET THERE

From A35 into village follow International Youth Hostel signs. Next door to White Horse Pub.
OS 194 GR 548900 Bart 4

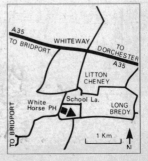

Lulworth Cove

Youth Hostel, School Lane, West Lulworth, Wareham, Dorset BH20 5SA
📞 **01929 400564 Fax: 01929 400640**

Overnight Charges: Under 18 £4.85 Adult £7.20

Seasonal Prices Jul 1 - Aug 31: Under 18 £5.35 Adult £8.00

Family accommodation prices on p.11-13

R-a-H 📞 01722 337494 ½m
P BABA

Jan 1 - Feb 28	Rent-a-Hostel
Mar 1 - Mar 31	Open X:Sun/Mon
Apr 1 - Jun 30	Open X:Sun*
Jul 1 - Aug 31	Open
Sep 1 - Oct 31	Open X:Sun/Mon
Nov 1 - Dec 31	Rent-a-Hostel

* Open Bank Hol Sun.

ACCOMMODATION   🛏1 🛏6
This purpose-built single storey Hostel has small comfortable rooms, a bright sunny lounge and dining room with wonderful views of the Dorset countryside. You'll also find excellent home cooking!
You'll be just off the South West Coastal path in an Area of Outstanding Natural Beauty with some spectacular coastal walks. The unusual oyster shape of Lulworth Cove is of great geological interest, ideal for school groups. The stone arch of the Durdle Door and rare fauna and flora are also nearby. 🚶14m 🏊2m 🏔¼m 🏕14m ✂1m 🚉1m

TRAVEL INFO
🚌 Garrison Cars 225 BR Wool - Lulworth Cove (📞 01929 462467); Dorset Queen 220 Dorchester - Lulworth (📞 01305 852829).
🚉 Wool 5m.
ℹ️ 📞01929 422885

NEXT HOSTELS
Swanage 17m, Litton Cheney 25m, Bridport 30m

HOW TO GET THERE
100yds east of B3070 turn opposite Castle Inn into School Lane.
OS 194 GR 832806 Bart 4

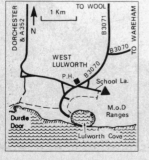

Swanage

Youth Hostel, Cluny, Cluny Crescent, Swanage, Dorset BH19 2BS
📞 **01929 422113 Fax: 01929 426327**

Overnight Charges: Under 18 £5.95 Adult £8.80

1 🍴📺🔍🖥️🏠 ¼m ♿ 1x40, 1x30, 2x20
P BABA

| Feb 1 - Mar 31 | Open X:Sun |
| Apr 1 - Oct 31 | Open |

The Hostel may be available for groups when otherwise closed - please contact Warden.

ACCOMMODATION   🛏6 🛏8 🛏4
This large Victorian house overlooking the town with fine views across the Bay to the Purbeck Hills has been refurbished to a high standard. There is a large well-equipped games room with its famous fantasy mural and giant compendium of games. The Hostel is popular with groups from April to June.
Swanage is a major unspoilt family resort on the 'Isle of Purbeck'. Spectacular coastal scenery, safe sandy beaches and high sunshine ratings combine to make it an ever popular holiday destination.
🚶10m 🏊4m 🏔🚲🚉

TRAVEL INFO
🚌 Wilts & Dorset 150 from Bournemouth (passes BR Branksome); 142-4 from Poole (pass BR Wareham). Alight Swanage Bus Station on all services, thence ¼m (📞 01202 673555).
🚉 Wareham 10m. ⛴15m (Cherbourg-Poole)
ℹ️ 📞01929 422885

NEXT HOSTELS
Lulworth Cove 17m, Burley 29m

ADDITIONAL INFO
Ideal venue for conferences.

HOW TO GET THERE
OS 195 GR 031785 Bart 4

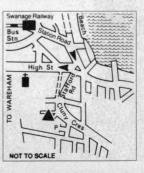

North Devon, Exmoor & the Quantocks

High cliffs and jutting headlands, long sandy beaches and waterfalls can all be found in the North Devon Area of Outstanding Natural Beauty. This magnificent coastline has several well known seaside resorts such as Minehead, Lynton and Ilfracombe. Much of atmospheric Exmoor, with its heather covered moors and deep wooded combes, is in Somerset as well as the Quantock Hills Area of Outstanding Natural Beauty — with Kilve Beach, best known for its fossils. This popular area combines breathtaking views and hill walking with all the attractions of a seaside holiday.

Many of the area's Youth Hostels are available for exclusive use by groups booked in advance; please enquire. Plus, Exford, Minehead and Quantock Hills Youth Hostels are available on YHA's **Rent-a-Hostel scheme** which runs during the winter months (details on p.7).

USEFUL PUBLICATIONS

Individual Hostel leaflets are available — send s.a.e. to the YHA Regional Office listed below or phone our Literature Line on (01426) 951683 (local call charge).

The South West Way: a guide to the coast path — send £4.50 (inc. p&p) to the South West Way Association, 1 Orchard Drive, Kingskerwell, Newton Abbot, Devon TQ12 5DG.

For more information about hostelling in this area contact: YHA South England Regional Office, 11B York Road, Salisbury, Wiltshire SP2 7AP. Tel: (01722) 337494. Fax: (01722) 414027.

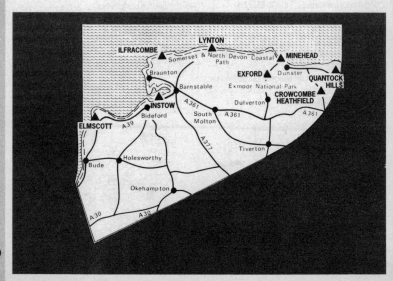

Crowcombe Heathfield

Youth Hostel, Denzel House, Crowcombe Heathfield, Taunton, Somerset TA4 4BT
☎ 01984 667249

Out of season contact: Regional Booking Service, 11B York Road, Salisbury, Wiltshire SP2 7AP
☎ 01722 337494 Fax: 01722 414027

Overnight Charges: Under 18 £4.45 Adult £6.55

R-a-H ☎ 01722 337494 [1] GSC A ⊕ ▣ 1m
P Plenty for cars and minibuses. Coaches 100yds.

Mar 1 - Apr 6	Rent-a-Hostel
Apr 7 - Apr 23	Open
Apr 28 - May 21	Open Fr/Sat/Sun*
May 26 - Jun 4	Open
Jun 5 - Jul 13	Open Fr/Sat/Sun*
Jul 14 - Sep 3	Open
Sep 8 - Oct 31	Rent-a-Hostel

* Mon - Th, open for exclusive use of groups booked in advance.

ACCOMMODATION   🛏️2-4 5 🛏️5-8 2 🛏️9+ 1

This delightful country house has been recently refurbished to enhance its rustic charm and offer greater comfort. Stroll in the beautiful extensive grounds and let the hiss and whistle of passing steam trains capture images of days gone by. Why not take a trip on the West Somerset Steam Railway, sample the rural attraction of Exmoor and the Quantock Hills or enjoy the nearby coastline with its many bays and beaches. 🚶 1m 🏔️16m 〰️4m 🌊14m

TRAVEL INFO
🚌 Southern National 28/C Taunton - Minehead (passes BR Taunton), alight Triscombe Cross, ¾m (☎ 01823 272033). 🚂 Taunton 10m; Crowcombe (West Somerset Rly) ½m.
ℹ️ ☎ 01823 274785

NEXT HOSTELS
Quantock Hills 10m by road (7m by foot), Minehead 16m, Exford 22m

HOW TO GET THERE
A385 from Taunton 10m. Turn left at Triscombe Cross signposted Crowcombe Station. Hostel ¾m on right after railway bridge.
OS 181 GR 138339 Bart 4

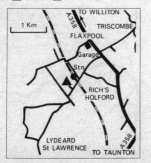

Elmscott (Hartland)

Youth Hostel, Elmscott, Hartland, Bideford, Devon EX39 6ES ☎ 01237 441367

Out of season contact, Regional Booking Service, 11B York Road, Salisbury, Wiltshire SP2 7AP
☎ 01722 337494 Fax: 01722 414027

Overnight Charges: Under 18 £3.60 Adult £5.35

Seasonal Prices Jul 1 - Aug 31: Under 18 £4.00 Adult £5.95

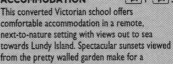

[2] GSC A ▣ 4m P For cars and minibuses. Coaches - ask Warden.

Mar 31 - Jun 30	Open X:Th
Jul 1 - Sep 16	Open
Sep 17 - Oct 31	Rent-a-Hostel

ACCOMMODATION   🛏️2-4 1 🛏️5-8 5

This converted Victorian school offers comfortable accommodation in a remote, next-to-nature setting with views out to sea towards Lundy Island. Spectacular sunsets viewed from the pretty walled garden make for a memorable stay!
Get away from it all in this glorious location — with unspoilt coastline, amazing rock formations, a profusion of wild flowers and many quiet lanes to explore. The surfing beaches of north Cornwall are within easy reach. 🚶5m 🏔️2m 〰️ 🌊

TRAVEL INFO
🚌 Filer's Travel from Barnstaple (passes close BR Barnstaple), alight Hartland, 3 ½m (☎ 01392 382800). 🚂 Barnstaple 25m.
ℹ️ ☎01237 477676

NEXT HOSTELS
Instow 19m, Boscastle 28m, Tintagel 32m

ADDITIONAL INFO
Fresh bread and milk available if ordered in advance.

HOW TO GET THERE
Hostel is signposted from A39 just N of West Country Inn. Ignore signs for Hartland.
OS 190 GR 231217 Bart 3

51 BEDS	**Open: 17.00hrs**

Exford (Exmoor)

Youth Hostel, Exe Mead, Exford, Minehead,
Somerset TA24 7PU ☎ 0164383 288
Fax: 0164383 650

Out of season contact: Regional Booking Service,
11B York Road, Salisbury, Wilts SP2 7AP
☎ 01722 337494 Fax: 01722 414027

Overnight Charges: Under 18 £5.35 Adult £8.00

Family accommodation prices on p.11-13

R-a-H ☎ 01722 337494

[i] [iO] [BSC] [iii] [A] [◉] [⊕] [S] [●] 1/8m [P] Cars,
mini-buses and coach. [BABA]

Jan 1 - Feb 28	Rent-a-Hostel
Mar 1 - Apr 6	Open X:Sun/Mon
Apr 7 - Jun 30	Open X:Sun*
Jul 1 - Aug 31	Open
Sep 1 - Oct 28	Open X:Sun/Mon
Oct 29 - Dec 31	Rent-a-Hostel

* Open Bank Hol Sun. The Hostel may be
available for groups when otherwise closed -
please contact Warden.

ACCOMMODATION   8 [5-8] 4

This attractive Victorian house is perfectly
situated for exploring atmospheric Exmoor. In an
idyllic village setting, the Hostel — which has
been refurbished to a high standard — is
surrounded by lovely grounds with the river Exe
flowing right through the garden.
Enjoy Exmoor National Park with its heather
covered heights and byways of the lowlands and
moors offering excellent walking and cycling.
Along the way catch a glimpse of red deer, stop
and admire the Exmoor ponies or watch the
buzzards soar in the land of Lorna Doone.
[🚴]15m [U]2m [▲] [△]8m [⚓]

TRAVEL INFO

[🚌]Scarlet Coaches from Minehead, alight Porlock,
7m (☎ 01643 704204). [🚂]Taunton 28m;
Minehead (West Somerset Rly) 13m.
[ℹ]☎01398 23665 / 01643 702624

NEXT HOSTELS

Minehead 13m, Lynton 15m, Crowcombe 22m

HOW TO GET THERE

[OS] 181 [GR] 853383 [Bart] 3

---

50 BEDS	**Open: 17.00hrs**

Ilfracombe

Youth Hostel, Ashmour House,
1 Hillsborough Terrace, Ilfracombe, Devon
EX34 9NR ☎ 01271 865337
Fax: 01271 862652

Overnight Charges: Under 18 £5.35 Adult £8.00

Family accommodation prices on p.11-13

[i] [iO] [BSC] [iii] [🔍] [●] 1/4m [P] Limited. [BABA]

Apr 10 - Jun 30	Open X:Sun*
Jul 1 - Aug 31	Open
Sep 1 - Sep 30	Open X:Sun

* Open Bank Hol Sun. The Hostel may be
available for groups when otherwise closed.

ACCOMMODATION   10 [5-8] 3

This well preserved Georgian building is perfectly
placed to observe activity in the picturesque
harbour below — with magnificent views across
the Bristol Channel from the splendid lounge. The
many small rooms provide comfort and privacy
for families, groups and individuals.
'Moor to Sea' at this Centre of Attraction! You'll
find Blue Flag sandy beaches and access to
Exmoor National Park close by, as well as farm
parks, theme parks, coastal and country walks,
historic houses... and that's not all! Send for our
brochure. [🚴]1/2m [U]1m [▲]4m [△]1/4m [🎣]10m
[⛵]15m [⛴]1/4m

TRAVEL INFO

[🚌] Red Bus 30, 62 & 300, B, Filer's 301 / 304 from
Barnstaple (passing close BR Barnstaple) (☎ 01271
45444). [🚂] Barnstaple 13m. [⛴] (to Lundy Island)
[ℹ]☎01271 863001

NEXT HOSTELS

Lynton 18m, Instow 18m, Exford 25m

ADDITIONAL INFO

Considerable experience in catering for orchestras,
theatre and dance groups - strong links with local
organisations which can provide practice, recording
and performance facilities.

HOW TO GET THERE

On main 'A' road. Follow Combe Martin road signs
out of Ilfracombe High St. Opposite Hydro Hotel.
[OS] 180 [GR] 524476 [Bart] 3

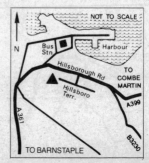

58 BEDS   Open: 17.00hrs

38 BEDS   Open: 17.00hrs

Instow

Lynton

Youth Hostel, Worlington House, New Road, Instow, Bideford, Devon EX39 4LW
☎ 01271 860394 Fax: 01271 860055

Overnight Charges: Under 18 £5.35 Adult £8.00

Family accommodation prices on p.11-13

2 🍴 📷 🚿 🅂 🔒 1m 🛏 1x20, 1x40 🅿 Cars and mini-buses only. Coaches in layby 150metres.

Mar 1 - Apr 30	Open X:Sun/Mon*
May 1 - Aug 31	Open
Sep 1 - Nov 11	Open X:Sun/Mon
Dec 22 - Dec 27	Open for Xmas

* Open Bank Hol Sun. The Hostel may be available for groups when otherwise closed.

ACCOMMODATION   🛏²⁻⁴ 4 🛏⁵⁻⁸ 2 🛏⁹⁺ 2

This Victorian house, set in two acres of garden with excellent views, has gained an excellent reputation for its food, friendly welcome and comfortable accommodation. Open most of the year with good transport links, it's an ideal location if you want to get off the beaten track. Instow, a charming village with a fine beach and views, is in the heart of 'Tarka Country'. Explore the whole of northern Devon — spectacular coast and moorland, lush green valleys, pretty villages and many attractions for families and schools alike. Travel the Tarka Trail on foot or by bike. 🚴2m 🅄5m ⛰5m ⚓1m ⛵1m 🚣4m

TRAVEL INFO
🚌 Red Bus 1, 2, B, Filers 301 from Barnstaple (passing BR Barnstaple), alight Instow, ¾m (☎ 01392 382800) 🚉 Barnstaple 6m.
ℹ ☎ 01271 388583/388584

NEXT HOSTELS
Ilfracombe 18m, Elmscott 19m, Lynton 25m

ADDITIONAL INFO
Ideal venue for youth training courses, seminars and conferences

HOW TO GET THERE
Turn off B3233 Barnstaple - Bideford Road at signpost, Hostel ¾m at top of hill
🆗 180 🅶🆁 842303 Bart 3

Youth Hostel, Lynbridge, Lynton, Devon
EX35 6AZ ☎ 01598 53237 Fax: 01598 53305

Out of season contact: Regional Booking Service, 11B York Road, Salisbury, Wilts. SP2 7AP
☎ 01722 337494 Fax: 01722 414027

Overnight Charges: Under 18 £4.85 Adult £7.20

Seasonal Prices Jul 1 - Aug 31: Under 18 £5.95 Adult £8.80

1 🍴 🅂🅂🄲 📷 🔒 1m 🅿 Limited for cars and mini-buses. Coaches 1m in Lynton town centre. BABA

Feb 1 - Feb 28	Open Fr/Sat
Mar 1 - Mar 31	Open X:Sun/Mon
Apr 1 - Jun 30	Open X:Sun*
Jul 1 - Aug 31	Open
Sep 1 - Oct 31	Open X:Sun/Mon
Nov 1 - Dec 21	Open Fr/Sat

* Open Bank Hol Sun. The Hostel may be available for groups when otherwise closed - please contact Warden.

ACCOMMODATION   🛏²⁻⁴ 4 🛏⁵⁻⁸ 4

This homely Victorian house is set in the tranquil wooded gorge of the West Lyn river where Exmoor meets the sea at Lynmouth. Fine views and fresh air guaranteed!
This is a perfect base for moorland, riverside and coast walks — with the Exmoor National Park and South West Coastal Path close by. Local attractions like the Cliff Railway, Valley of the Rocks and Watersmeet are within easy reach too. 🅄1m ⛰1m ⚓1m 🚣20m

TRAVEL INFO
🚌 Red Bus 310 from Barnstaple (passes close BR Barnstaple) (☎ 01271 45444) 🚉 Barnstaple 20m.
ℹ ☎ 01598 52225

NEXT HOSTELS
Exford 15m, Minehead 21m, Ilfracombe 18m

HOW TO GET THERE
🆗 180 🅶🆁 720487 Bart 3

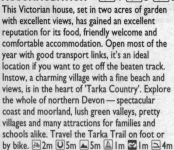

Minehead

Youth Hostel, Alcombe Combe, Minehead, Somerset TA24 6EW ☎ 01643 702595
Fax: 01643 703016

Out of season contact: Regional Booking Service, 11B York Road, Salisbury Wiltshire SP2 7AP
☎ 01722 337494 Fax: 01722 414027

Overnight Charges: Under 18 £4.85 Adult £7.20
Family accommodation prices on p.11-13

R-a-H ☎ 01722 337494 [1] 🍴 😊 🅂 🖭 1m 🅿 Cars and mini-buses ONLY. Free coach park 2m - ask Warden. BABA

Jan 1 - Apr 6	Rent-a-Hostel
Apr 7 - Jun 30	Open X:Mon
Jul 1 - Aug 31	Open
Sep 1 - Oct 31	Open X:Mon/Tu
Nov 1 - Dec 31	Rent-a-Hostel

ACCOMMODATION 2 4

This attractive country house, surrounded by woodland in a beautiful secluded combe, is only 2m from the sea. As well as good facilities (including small well-furnished bunkrooms), you'll find a friendly, homely atmosphere.
Set in the Exmoor National Park, the Hostel has direct access to the footpath network — with some lovely walks close by. The medieval town of Dunster is a short walk away and the family holiday resort of Minehead is nearby. The South West Coastal Path starts by the harbour in Minehead. 🚴2m 🅿3m ⛰ 🏞2m 🚲 🚃2m

TRAVEL INFO
🚌 As for Crowcombe Heathfield, but alight Alcombe, 1m. Southern National 28. 🚉 Taunton 25m; Minehead or Dunster (West Somerset Rly) both 2m.
🛈 ☎01643 702624

NEXT HOSTELS
Exford 13m (10m on foot), Quantock Hills 14m, Crowcombe Heathfield 16m

HOW TO GET THERE
Turn off A39 at Alcombe into Brook Street to Britannia Inn, then on to Manor Road which becomes a private road for ⅔m. Turn sharp left up to Hostel. NB: Difficult to find after dark.
OS 181 GR 973442 Bart 3

Quantock Hills (Holford)

Youth Hostel, Sevenacres, Holford, Bridgwater, Somerset TA5 1SQ
☎ 01278 741224

Out of season contact: Regional Booking Service, 11B York Road, Salisbury, Wilts. SP2 7AP
☎ 01722 337494 Fax: 01722 414027

Overnight Charges: Under 18 £4.45 Adult £6.55

R-a-H ☎ 01722 337494 [1] 😊 🅰 😊 🖭 1 ½m 🅿 No access for coaches. Limited for cars and mini-buses.

Jan 1 - Apr 10	Rent-a-Hostel
Apr 11 - Jun 30	Open X:Sun/Mon*
Jul 1 - Aug 31	Open
Sep 1 - Dec 31	Rent-a-Hostel

*Open Bank Hol Sun

ACCOMMODATION 2 3

Stay well off the beaten track at this characterful country retreat where you can enjoy views from the terrace across the Bristol Channel to Wales. Leave the car behind and walk straight out onto the open hills to appreciate the wildlife and beautiful scenery. Or venture down to Kilve beach to hunt for fossils. Watchet Harbour, Hinkley Point, the West Somerset Steam Railway and Minehead are also within easy reach. 🚴6m
🛶1m ⛰1m 🚲🚃14m

TRAVEL INFO
🚌 Southern National 15 from Bridgwater (passing close BR Bridgwater) (☎ 01823 272033)
🚉 Bridgwater 14m.
🛈 ☎01278 427652

NEXT HOSTELS
Crowcombe Heathfield 10m (7m by foot), Minehead 14m, Street 28m

ADDITIONAL INFO
Meals provided for groups booked in advance.

HOW TO GET THERE
WALKERS ONLY from Kilve, take Pardlestone Lane opposite Post Office (1m). Vehicular access from Holford, take road through the Alfoxton Park Hotel (1 ½m), cross 2nd cattle grid, uphill to sharp bend, take Hostel track on right.
OS 181 GR 145416 Bart 7

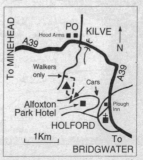

The combination of bustling resorts, remote bays, thatched cottages, cream teas and a mild climate makes South Devon a popular holiday area with plenty of attractions.

The many winding lanes of Devon are particularly beautiful in spring when the roads are lined with wild flowers. Here you can visit the seaside towns of Salcombe and Beer, as well as the historic cities of Exeter and Plymouth.

Dartmoor, the vast major wilderness in Southern England, is founded on solid granite. Surmounting many hilltops are the tors — thousands of years' exposure to the varying weather conditions claims responsibility for their curious shape. The easily accessible beauty spots around the area make ideal picnic grounds.

Bellever and Dartington Youth Hostels are available on YHA's **Rent-a-Hostel scheme** which runs during the winter months (details on p.7).

USEFUL PUBLICATIONS

Inter-Hostel Walking Routes (Exeter, Steps Bridge, Bellever, Dartington and Maypool) — 25p each, send s.a.e. to the YHA Regional Office listed below or phone our Literature Line on (01426) 951683 (local call charge).

Budget Accommodation in the South West and individual Hostel leaflets — send s.a.e. to the YHA Regional Office listed below or phone our Literature Line on (01426) 951683 (local call charge).

The South West Way: a guide to the coast path — send £4.50 (inc. p&p) to the South West Way Association, 1 Orchard Drive, Kingskerwell, Newton Abbot, Devon TQ12 5DG.

For more information about hostelling in this area contact: YHA South England Regional Office, 11B York Road, Salisbury, Wiltshire SP2 7AP. Tel: (01722) 337494. Fax: (01722) 414027.

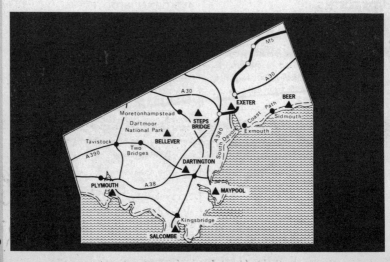

Beer

Youth Hostel, Bovey Combe, Townsend, Beer, Seaton, Devon EX12 3LL
☎ 01297 20296

Out of season contact: Regional Booking Service, 11B York Road, Salisbury, Wilts. SP2 7AP
☎ 01722 337494 Fax: 01722 414027

Overnight Charges: Under 18 £4.85 Adult £7.20

Seasonal Prices Jul 1 - Aug 31: Under 18 £5.35 Adult £8.00

Family accommodation prices on p.11-13

 ½m 🅿 Cars and minibuses in the grounds. Coaches in the village.

Apr 7 - Jun 30	Open X:Sun*
Jul 1 - Aug 31	Open
Sep 1 - Oct 31	Open X:Sun/Mon

* Open Bank Hol Sun.

ACCOMMODATION 3 2 2

This impressive stone-built country house has large lawned gardens — ideal for playing games or just relaxing and making the most of the lovely views. Only ½m from Beer village with its good pubs, quaint shops and pebble beach, this is the perfect destination for a weekend break or main holiday.

Why not stroll along a stretch of the South West Coastal Footpath or try one of the many watersports on offer — like swimming, sailing and fishing. Steam train enthusiasts should enjoy the excitement of a trip to Pecorama! 4m ½m 2 ½m ½m

TRAVEL INFO
Axe Valley from Seaton with connections from BR Axminster (☎ 01297 80338). Axminster 10m, Honiton 10m.
🛈 ☎ 01297 21689

NEXT HOSTELS
Bridport 22m, Exeter 24m, Litton Cheney 28m

HOW TO GET THERE
OS 192 GR 223896 Bart 4

Bellever (Dartmoor)

Youth Hostel, Bellever, Postbridge, Yelverton, Devon PL20 6TU ☎ 01822 88227

Out of season contact: Regional Booking Service, 11B York Road, Salisbury, Wilts. SP2 7AP
☎ 01722 337494 Fax: 01722 414027

Overnight Charges: Under 18 £5.35 Adult £8.00

Family accommodation prices on p.11-13
R-a-H ☎ 01722 337494 1m 🅿 Limited for cars.

Jan 1 - Mar 31	Rent-a-Hostel
Apr 1 - Jun 30	Open X:Sun*
Jul 1 - Aug 31	Open
Sep 1 - Nov 4	Open X:Sun/Mon
Nov 5 - Dec 31	Rent-a-Hostel

* Open Bank Hol Sun.

ACCOMMODATION 4 3

This recently refurbished converted barn, idyllically situated at the heart of the Dartmoor National Park, has a relaxing, friendly atmosphere with an open fire and small rooms.

Explore the varied landscape of wild open moors, exposed granite Tors, forests and reservoirs. Investigate the mythical land of Devon on horseback or bike visiting Bronze Age monuments, stone circles and medieval villages — a truly magical experience! Historic Exeter and Totnes are nearby.

TRAVEL INFO
Western National 98 from Tavistock (Fr only); 82 Exeter-Plymouth, May-Sep only, alight Postbridge 1m; otherwise Western National 98/A Tavistock-Princetown 6m, or Red Bus 359 from BR Exeter Central, alight Chagford 9m (☎ 01392 382800) Newton Abbott 19m.
🛈 ☎ 01822 88272

NEXT HOSTELS
Steps Bridge 18m, Dartington 19m, Plymouth 21m

HOW TO GET THERE
OS 191 GR 654773 Bart 2

30 BEDS	Open: 17.00hrs

Dartington

Youth Hostel, Lownard, Dartington, Totnes, Devon TQ9 6JJ ☏ 01803 862303
Fax: 01803 862303

Out of season contact: Regional Booking Service, 11B York Road, Salisbury, Wiltshire SP2 7AP
☏ 01722 337494 Fax: 01722 414027

Overnight Charges: Under 18 £4.85 Adult £7.20

Seasonal Prices Jul 1 - Aug 31: Under 18 £5.35 Adult £8.00

Family accommodation prices on p.11-13

R-a-H ☏ 01722 337494 2 🅑 🅐 🔲 ¼m

🅿 Cars and mini-buses only. Coaches - use public car park in Shinners Bridge ¼m. BABA

Jan 1 - Apr 3	Rent-a-Hostel
Apr 4 - Jun 30	Open X:Mon
Jul 1 - Aug 31	Open
Sep 1 - Oct 31	Open X:Mon/Tu
Nov 1 - Dec 31	Rent-a-Hostel

ACCOMMODATION 🛏 5-8 5

This 16th century cottage beside a babbling brook is set in the beautiful Dart Valley village of Dartington — a peaceful haven enjoyed by country lovers and urban escapees alike!
An ideal base for exploring the River Dart and South Hams countryside. The historic town of Totnes with its Norman Castle, medieval Guildhall and many interesting shops is only 2m away. 🚶 2m 🅤 5m 🚲 🚃 2m

TRAVEL INFO

🚌 Western National X80 Torquay - Plymouth (passes BR Paignton & Totnes), alight Shinner's Bridge, ¼m. 🚉 Totnes 2m.
🆔 ☏ 01803 863168

NEXT HOSTELS

Maypool 11m, Bellever 19m, Plymouth 22m

ADDITIONAL INFO

We can cater for groups of 10 or more booked in advance.

HOW TO GET THERE

Take the A385 from the Shinners bridge roundabout in the centre of Dartington. Turn right after ¼m into narrow lane. Hostel 200yds on right.
OS 202 GR 782622 Bart 2

94 BEDS	Open: 17.00hrs

Exeter

Youth Hostel, 47-49 Countess Wear Road, Exeter, Devon EX2 6LR ☏ 01392 873329
Fax: 01392 876939

Overnight Charges: Under 18 £5.35 Adult £8.00

Seasonal Prices Jul 1 - Aug 31: Under 18 £5.95 Adult £8.80

Family accommodation prices on p.11-13

2 🍴 🅑 🔲 🅐 🔲 ♿ ✚ 🔲 ¼m 🅿 For cars and minibuses. Coaches - ask Warden. BABA

Jan 6 - Dec 2	Open
Dec 28 - Jan 4 '96	Open for New Year

The Hostel may be available for groups when otherwise closed - please contact Warden.

ACCOMMODATION 🛏 4 🛏 3 🛏 3

The Hostel, which provides a high standard of accommodation, is set in its own grounds near the River Exe. You can walk to the city along the river or the historic Exeter Ship Canal to visit the beautiful Cathedral and Exeter Quay.
Exeter's historic past is best explored by strolling through its intriguing lanes and alleyways. Take time to visit the Royal Albert museum and the world renowned Maritime Museum. 🚶 2m 🅤 4m 🏛 2m 🚲 2m 🚃 2m

TRAVEL INFO

🚌 Exeter Bus K, T, Devon General 57 (pass close BR Exeter Central), alight Countess Wear PO, ¼m (☏ 01392 56231) 🚉 Topsham 2m; Exeter Central 3m; Exeter St David's 4m.
🆔 ☏ 01392 265700

NEXT HOSTELS

Steps Bridge 10m, Beer 24m, Dartington 27m

HOW TO GET THERE

From A30 or M5 jct 30 follow signs for Topsham: turn right at Countess Wear Roundabout, then left in to School Lane. From A379 follow signs for Topsham; turn left at Countess Wear Roundabout, then left into School Lane. From Exeter city centre follow signs to Exmouth and Topsham; turn right into School Lane at Countess Wear Post Office.
OS 192 GR 941897 Bart 2

Maypool

93 BEDS **Open: 17.00hrs**

Youth Hostel, Maypool House, Galmpton,
Brixham, Devon TQ5 0ET ☎ 01803 842444
Fax: 01803 845939

Overnight Charges: Under 18 £4.85 Adult £7.20

2 🍴 🔍 ✦ S ▣ 1m 🚲 1x20, 1x40, 1x60
P BABA

Mar 1 - Apr 6	Open X:Sun
Apr 7 - Aug 31	Open
Sep 1 - Nov 4	Open X:Sun/Mon

The Hostel may be available for groups when
otherwise closed - please contact Warden.

ACCOMMODATION 🛏️2-4 3 🛏️5-8 6 🛏️9+ 4

A large Victorian country house with
breathtaking views of the River Dart and
Dartmoor, this traditional Hostel was originally
built for the local boat builder — with timbers in
the beautiful minstrals gallery reputed to have
come from old sailing ships.
Set in the heart of the English Riviera, there are
many things to do and see. Hire boats or bring
your own — we have moorings. Travel on the
Dart Valley steam railway which runs across the
bottom of the Hostel grounds or simply relax in
this romantic idyll. 🚶4m 🛶5m ⛰️¼m 🎣5m
🚲2m

TRAVEL INFO

🚌 Bayline 100 Torquay BR Paignton-Brixham,
alight Churston Pottery 1 ⅓m (☎ 01803 613226).
🚉 Paignton 5m; Churston (Dart Valley Rly) 1 ⅓m.
Paignton and Dartmouth Steam Railway.
🛈 ☎ 01803 558383

NEXT HOSTELS

Dartington 11m, Exeter 32m, Salcombe 26m

HOW TO GET THERE

A38 - A380 - A3022 intersection A379 second
turning on right (Manor Vale Road). Follow signs to
Youth Hostel.
OS 202 GR 877546 Bart 2

Plymouth

68 BEDS **Open: 17.00hrs**

Youth Hostel, Belmont House, Belmont
Place, Stoke, Plymouth, Devon PL3 4DW
☎ 01752 562189 Fax: 01752 605360

Overnight Charges: Under 18 £5.35 Adult £8.00

Seasonal Prices Jul 1 - Aug 31: Under 18 £5.95
Adult £8.80

Family accommodation prices on p.11-13

1 🍴 🖥️ 🔍 ✦ ▣ ¼m 🚲 1x20 P BABA

Jan 3 - Feb 28	Open X:Tu/Wed
Mar 1 - Oct 31	Open
Nov 1 - Dec 27	Open X:Mon/Tu*

* Open for Christmas

ACCOMMODATION 🛏️2-4 7 🛏️5-8 2 🛏️9+ 3

Inspired by Greek architecture, the building is
one of the finest in Plymouth. Set in extensive
grounds, the Hostel has many original features
including an impressive entrance hall (with a
marble floor) and library. You can even dine in
the old ballroom with its beautiful lantern ceiling.
Soak up the historic atmosphere of the Barbican,
remember Sir Francis Drake, Captain Cook,
Darwin and the Pilgrim Fathers. Take a harbour
cruise, stroll along the wide green promenade
and spend the evening at the theatre or cinema.
Dartmoor and safe sandy beaches are only ½
hour away. 🚶3m ⛰️3m 🚲4m 🛶1m

TRAVEL INFO

🚌 Western National 14A, 15/A, 81, Plymouth
Citybus 33/A, 34/A from City Centre (some pass
BR Plymouth) (☎ 01752 222666 or 222221).
🚉 Devonport ¼m; Plymouth 1 ½m. ⛴️ (to
Roscoff/Santander)
🛈 ☎ 01752 264849

NEXT HOSTELS

Golant 38m, Bellever 21m, Salcombe 25m

ADDITIONAL INFO

Famous for sea and river fishing - trout, sea-trout
and salmon.

HOW TO GET THERE

From A38 follow A386 to Torpoint. Past a small
shopping centre the Hostel is signposted on the left.
OS 201 GR 461555 Bart 2

Salcombe

Steps Bridge

Youth Hostel, 'Overbecks', Sharpitor, Salcombe, Devon TQ8 8LW
☎ 0154884 2856

Youth Hostel, Steps Bridge, Dunsford, Exeter, Devon EX6 7EQ ☎ 01647 252435
Fax: 01647 252435

Out of season contact: Regional Booking Service, 11B York Road, Salisbury, Wiltshire SP2 7AP
☎ 01722 337494 Fax: 01722 414027

Out of season contact: Regional Booking Service, 11B York Road, Salisbury, Wilts. SP2 7AP
☎ 01722 337494 Fax: 01722 414027

Overnight Charges: Under 18 £4.85 Adult £7.20

Overnight Charges: Under 18 £4.00 Adult £5.95

Seasonal Prices Jul 1 - Aug 31: Under 18 £5.35 Adult £8.00

Seasonal Prices Jul 1 - Aug 31: Under 18 £4.45 Adult £6.55

1 ⓘⓞⓛ ⓖⓢⓒ Ⓟ National Trust Car Park. Coaches 2m (Salcombe).

1 ⓖⓢⓒ Ⓐ Ⓡ 1m Ⓟ Public car park opposite end of Hostel drive. ⒷⒶⒷⒶ

Apr 7 - May 31	Open X:Fr (open Good Friday)
Jun 1 - Aug 31	Open
Sep 1 - Oct 31	Open X:Th/Fr

| Apr 7 - Jun 30 | Open X:Wed/Th |
| Jul 1 - Sep 12 | Open |

ACCOMMODATION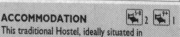

This traditional Hostel, ideally situated in secluded woodland overlooking the Teign Valley, has been a haven for generations of Hostellers seeking peace and tranquility.
Steps Bridge is perfectly placed for walking on the rugged Dartmoor Tors and delightful lower slopes. Look out for rare and interesting wild flowers, butterflies and birds. Horse riding is available locally and with so much on offer, the Hostel makes an ideal base for all country lovers.
Ⓤ ⒶⒶ 1m ⓢ

ACCOMMODATION

A truly stunning location overlooking the sea and estuary. Salcombe Youth Hostel is part of the National Trust's 'Overbecks' museum and is set in semi-tropical gardens on the cliffs just below Sharpitor rocks.
A haven for anyone interested in small boats, the busy market town of Salcombe has an excellent harbour providing sheltered moorings. For an excellent day's walking, head for the coastal footpath at the foot of the hills to Overbecks.
Ⓤ2m ⒶⒶ1m Ⓐ½m ⓢ1m ⓢ ⓢ

TRAVEL INFO
🚌 Red Bus 359 from Exeter departs Belgrave Road and passes BR Exeter Central (☎ 01392 382800). Transmoor Express 82 Exeter - Plymouth, May-Sep only, alight Steps Bridge. 🚉 Exeter Central 9m; Exeter St David's 9m.
ⓘ ☎ 01392 265297

NEXT HOSTELS
Exeter 10m, Bellever 18m, Dartington 25m

HOW TO GET THERE
ⓞⓢ 191 ⒼⓇ 802882 Ⓑⓐⓡⓣ 2

TRAVEL INFO
🚌 Tally Ho! from Kingsbridge (connects from Plymouth, Dartmouth and, for BR connections, from Totnes), alight Salcombe, 2m (Devon C.C Enquiry Line ☎ 01392-382800) 🚉 Totnes 20m. Plymouth 26m.
ⓘ ☎ 01548 853195

NEXT HOSTELS
Dartington 21m, Plymouth 25m, Maypool 26m via Dart Ferry or Totnes

HOW TO GET THERE
Follow signs for National Trust - Overbecks.
ⓞⓢ 202 ⒼⓇ 728374 Ⓑⓐⓡⓣ 2

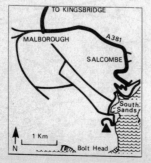

The granite cliffs, picturesque fishing harbours and sandy coves all go to make the Cornish coastline one of the most popular holiday areas in the country.

The inland countryside also has its charms and attractions with wooded valleys and high moors. Bodmin Moor at 1400ft is an Area of Outstanding Natural Beauty. A particular favourite with tourists is Land's End where you can have your photograph taken next to a road sign indicating how far you have travelled. Predominantly agricultural, this mild climate produces some of the richest farming land in Britain. However it is the sea that is most associated with the area — you are never more than 20 miles from the coast in any part of Cornwall.

Stay at Boscatle Youth Hostel to visit the National Trust fishing harbour and Pendennis Castle Youth Hostel (English Heritage property) for the seal sanctuary.

Boscastle Harbour, Boswinger, Perranporth and Treyarnon Bay Youth Hostels are on YHA's **Rent-a-Hostel scheme** which runs through the winter months (details on p.7).

USEFUL PUBLICATIONS

Budget Accommodation in the South West and individual Hostel leaflets — send s.a.e. to the YHA Regional Office listed below or phone our Literature Line on (01426) 951683 (local call charge).

The South West Way: a guide to the coast path — send £4.50 (inc. p&p) to the South West Way Association, 1 Orchard drive, Kingskerwell, Newton Abbot, Devon TQ12 5DG.

For more information about hostelling in this area contact: YHA South England Regional Office, 11B York Road, Salisbury, Wiltshire SP2 7AP. Tel: (01722) 337494. Fax: (01722) 414027.

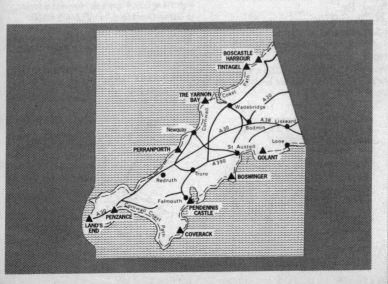

Boscastle Harbour

Youth Hostel, Palace Stables, Boscastle, Cornwall PL35 OHD ☎ 01840 250287

Out of season contact: Regional Booking Service: 11B York Road, Salisbury, Wiltshire SP2 7AP ☎ 01722 337494 Fax: 01722 414027

Overnight Charges: Under 18 £4.85 Adult £7.20

Seasonal Prices Jul 1 - Aug 31: Under 18 £5.35 Adult £8.00

R-a-H ☎ 01722 337494 [1] ⬚ GSC ⬚ ⬚ P Public car park for cars and coaches 250yds.

Jan 1 - Mar 12	Rent-a-Hostel
Mar 13 - Jun 30	Open X:Mon/Tu*
Jul 1 - Aug 31	Open
Sep 1 - Nov 4	Open X:Mon/Tu
Nov 5 - Dec 31	Rent-a-Hostel

* Open Bank Hol Mon except May 2.

ACCOMMODATION

This traditional stone Hostel overlooking the harbour was originally a stable for horses pulling cargo ashore. The tastefully converted hayloft with single beds retains the original beams with an open fire in the lounge/dining room.

Set at the high water line where the River Valency meets the sea, the Hostel is on the South West Coastal Path surrounded by superb coastal scenery and walks. There are interesting Thomas Hardy connections too. The fishing harbour with its blow-hole is preserved by the National Trust.

⬚4m ⬚2m ⬚6m

TRAVEL INFO

⬚Western National 52/B from BR Bodmin Parkway, X4 from Bude (☎ 01209 719988); Fry's from Plymouth (passes close BR Plymouth) (infrequent) (☎ 01840 770256) ⬚ Bodmin Parkway 24m.

ℹ☎01566 772321

NEXT HOSTELS

Tintagel 5m, Elmscott 28m, Golant 30m

HOW TO GET THERE

Walk from the bridge on the B3226 towards the harbour alongside the river. Last building on right, top of slip way.

OS 190 GR 096915 Bart 1

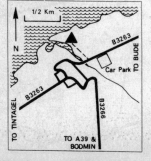

Boswinger

Youth Hostel, Boswinger, Gorran, St Austell, Cornwall PL26 6LL ☎ 01726 843234

Out of season contact: Regional Booking Service, 11B York Road, Salisbury, Wiltshire. SP2 7AP ☎ 01722 337494 Fax: 01722 414027

Overnight Charges: Under 18 £4.85 Adult £7.20

Seasonal Prices Jul 1 - Aug 31: Under 18 £5.35 Adult £8.00

Family accommodation prices on p.11-13

R-a-H ☎ 01722 337494

[1] ⬚ GSC ⬚ ⬚ ⬚ P Cars and mini-buses (coaches at B&B in Gorran)

Jan 1 - Apr 6	Rent-a-Hostel
Apr 7 - Jun 30	Open X:Tu/Wed
Jul 1 - Aug 31	Open
Sep 1 - Nov 4	Open X:Tu/Wed
Nov 5 - Dec 31	Rent-a-Hostel

ACCOMMODATION

This former old farmhouse and stone barns, converted into a cosy Hostel, offers small bunk rooms and a snug, easy atmosphere — ideal for families and small groups. Take your time and relax in the homely lounge, browse through the wealth of local information available and decide where to go next.

Amid wonderful Cornish countryside and near the South West Coastal Footpath, this Hostel is a rural retreat only 4m from the fishing village of Mevagissey and 10m from the town of St Austell. There are also many coastal activities in the area from sailing to fishing. ⬚4m ⬚2m ⬚6m

⬚ ⬚ ⬚⅓m

TRAVEL INFO

⬚Western National 26/A from BR St Austell, alight Mevagissey, 4 ½m, with infrequent extension to Gorran Churchtown, 1m (☎ 01872 40404). ⬚ St Austell 10m.

ℹ☎01872 74555

NEXT HOSTELS

Golant 17m, Pendennis 24m, Perranporth 25m

HOW TO GET THERE

Follow brown Boswinger YH signs.

OS 204 GR 991411 Bart 1

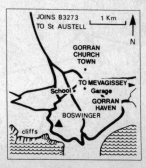

Coverack

Youth Hostel, Park Behan, School Hill, Coverack, Helston, Cornwall TR12 6SA
✆ 01326 280687

Out of season contact: Regional Booking Service, 11B York Road, Salisbury, Wilts. SP2 7AP.
✆ 01722 337494 Fax: 01722 414027

Overnight Charges: Under 18 £4.85 Adult £7.20

Seasonal Prices Jul 1 - Aug 31: Under 18 £5.35 Adult £8.00

Family accommodation prices on p.11-13

Apr 1 - Sep 30	Open	
Oct 1 - Oct 31	Open X:Sun/Mon	

The Hostel may be available for groups when otherwise closed - please contact Warden.

ACCOMMODATION ⛺2-4 1 ⛺5-8 4 ⛺9+ 1

This large country house is situated above an old fishing village, once a notorious smuggling haunt, with panoramic views of the coast. There is also an ancient orchard for camping, extensive lawns and a volleyball court. Good home-cooking and barbecues a speciality!

There is easy access to the South West Coastal Footpath, dramatic cliffs and deserted coves — ideal for sea bathing, fishing and boating trips. The RYA windsurfing school offers week or weekend courses, plus you can hire mountain bikes and surf-skis.

TRAVEL INFO
Truronian 326 from Helston with frequent connections from BR Penzance (✆ 01872 73453 or 01726 69469 for connections). Penryn or Penmere (not Sun, except May - Sep), both 18m.
✆ 01326 312300

NEXT HOSTELS
Pendennis 20m, Penzance 25m, Lands End 31m

ADDITIONAL INFO
Early morning music requests welcome.

HOW TO GET THERE
200yds W of village centre, take road opposite to harbour, drive entrance next to village school
OS 204 GR 782184 Bart 1

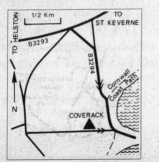

Golant

Youth Hostel, Penquite House Golant, Fowey, Cornwall PL23 1LA
✆ 01726 833507 Fax: 01726 832947

Overnight Charges: Under 18 £5.95 Adult £8.80

Family accommodation prices on p.11-13

  4m 1x50, 1x30

Feb 1 - Aug 31	Open	
Sep 1 - Nov 4	Open X:Fr	
Dec 28 - Jan 4	Open for New Year	

The Hostel may be available for groups when otherwise closed - please contact Warden.

ACCOMMODATION ⛺2-4 6 ⛺5-8 7 ⛺9+ 2

This imposing Georgian house — Grade II listed with superb decorative plasterwork — was recently refurbished to a high standard. As well as three acres of grounds and 14 acres of woodland to explore, there is no passing traffic which means the Hostel is ideal for families with young children.

Surrounded by farmland yet only four miles from the sea, the Hostel is an excellent base for discovering the rugged Cornish coastline and moorland. As well as many watersports on offer, there's a wide choice of local walks and cycle rides. Unspoilt Fowey and the South West Coastal Footpath are 4m. 4m 15m
1m 5m

TRAVEL INFO
Western National 24 St Austell-Fowey (passes BR Par), alight Castle Dore Crossroads, 1½m (✆ 01209 719988). Par (not Sun, except Jun - Sep) 3m; St Austell 7½m.
✆ 01726 833616

NEXT HOSTELS
Boswinger 17m, Tintagel 28m, Plymouth 38m

ADDITIONAL INFO
Conference facilities available.

HOW TO GET THERE
Take B3269 (Fowey) from A390 1½m west of Lostwithiel. Hostel is signposted from Castle Dore crossroads after 2m.
OS 200 GR 118556 Bart 1

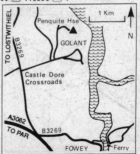

Land's End (St Just)

Newquay

Youth Hostel, Letcha Vean, St Just-in-Penwith, Penzance, Cornwall TR19 7NT ☎ 01736 788437 Fax: 01736 787337

Out of season contact: Regional Booking Service, 11B York Road, Salisbury, Wiltshire SP2 7AP ☎ 01722 337494 Fax: 01722 414027

Overnight Charges: Under 18 £4.85 Adult £7.20

Seasonal Prices Jul 1 - Aug 31: Under 18 £5.35 Adult £8.00

1 ⬚ A ⬚ S ⬚ 1 ½m P Cars and mini-buses only, no access for coaches (use coach park in St Just 1 ½m) BABA

Apr 1 - Nov 5	Open

The Hostel may be available for groups when otherwise closed - please contact Warden.

ACCOMMODATION

This friendly, traditional Hostel — set in three acres of grounds in the beautiful Cot Valley — has open log fires, good food and fine sea views, as well as lots of local books, maps and guides on walking routes. There is an excellent bus service from Penzance.

This is an area with spectacular coastline (seals and dolphins can often be seen), clean sandy beaches and wildflowers — as well as desolate moorland studded with stone circles, neolithic burial chambers and standing stones. Ideal for walking, cycling and birdwatching.

TRAVEL INFO

🚌 Western National 10/A/B, 11/A from Penzance (passes BR Penzance), alight St Just ¾m; 15 from St Ives (not Sat), Jun-Sep only, alight Kelynack, ½m (☎ 01209 719988) 🚉 Penzance 8m.
ℹ ☎ 01736 62207

NEXT HOSTELS

Penzance 8m, Pendennis 30m, Coverack 31m

HOW TO GET THERE

From St Just bus station walk past library, turn left, follow lane past chapel and farm to end, turn right down track to Hostel.
OS 203 GR 364305

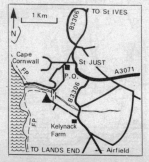

90 BEDS	Open: 17.00hrs

Pendennis Castle

Youth Hostel, Falmouth, Cornwall TR11 4LP
☎ 01326 311435 Fax: 01326 315473

Overnight Charges: Under 18 £5.35 Adult £8.00

Seasonal Prices Jul 1 - Aug 31: Under 18 £5.95 Adult £8.80

2 🍴 6sc 👤 🚿 S 🔵 ¾m 🚲 1x40 P 100yds
overnight only - outside castle gates. BABA

Mar 1 - Apr 6	Open X:Sun/Mon
Apr 7 - Aug 31	Open
Sep 1 - Nov 25	Open X:Sun/Mon

The Hostel may be available for groups when otherwise closed - please contact Warden.

ACCOMMODATION 🛏²⁻⁴ 14 🛏⁵⁻⁸ 4 🛏⁹⁺ 1

The Youth Hostel — once Victorian army barracks (and now much more comfortable!) — is perfectly sited inside a 16th century fortified castle. Floodlit at night, the castle faces out to sea on its own pointed peninsula with breathtaking views across the rugged Cornish coastline.
You'll find safe sandy beaches and the South West Coastal footpath nearby, as well as a host of attractions including a Seal Sanctuary, Maritime museum and historical re-enactments with the Sealed Knot Society. 🚶 1m 🚲 5m ⛰ 🏊 🏖

TRAVEL INFO

🚌 Frequent from surrounding areas (☎ 01209 719988). 🚉 Falmouth Docks (not Sun, except 10 Jul - 18 Sep) ¾m.
ℹ ☎ 01326 312300

NEXT HOSTELS

Boswinger 24m, Coverack 20m, Penzance 24m

HOW TO GET THERE

From roundabout outside Falmouth Docks, follow English Heritage signs up hill and across to sea front. Youth Hostel is within castle grounds.
OS 204 GR 823319 Bart 1

84 BEDS	Open: 17.00hrs

Penzance

Youth Hostel, Castle Horneck, Alverton, Penzance, Cornwall TR20 8TF
☎ 01736 62666 Fax: 01736 62663

Overnight Charges: Under 18 £5.95 Adult £8.80

2 🍴 6sc 👤 🚿 🔵 ½m P BABA

| Mar 1 - Dec 21 | Open |
| Dec 28 - Jan 1 '96 | Open for New Year |

The Hostel may be available for groups when otherwise closed - please contact Warden.

ACCOMMODATION 🛏²⁻⁴ 1 🛏⁵⁻⁸ 5 🛏⁹⁺ 4

This early 18th century Georgian mansion, built on the site of a 14th century medieval fort, is reputed to have a smugglers tunnel! There are superb views across Mounts Bay to the Lizard Peninsula and St Michael's Mount. Don't go home without trying the speciality ice cream!
You'll find easy access to the South West coastal footpath with miles of magnificent scenery and some of Britain's finest beaches. The area is steeped in celtic culture with ancient burial chambers and stone circles. The subtropical climate fosters a varied selection of fauna and flora. 🚶 1m 🚲 5m ⛰ 3m 🎣 6m 🏊 🏖 ¼m

TRAVEL INFO

🚌 Western National B, 5, 10B from BR Penzance to Pirate pub (☎ 01209 719988) 🚉 Penzance 2m.
ℹ ☎ 01736 62207

NEXT HOSTELS

Land's End 8m, Perranporth 29m, Pendennis Castle 24m

HOW TO GET THERE

All vehicles follow A30 and Penzance and turn at the 'Castle Horneck' signs. Do not go into Penzance Town Centre.
OS 203 GR 457302 Bart 1

Perranporth

22 BEDS   **Open: 17.00hrs**

Youth Hostel, Droskyn Point, Perranporth, Cornwall TR6 0DS ☎ 01872 573812

Out of season contact: Regional Booking Service, 11B York Road, Salisbury, Wilts. SP2 7AP
☎ 01722 337494 Fax: 01722 414027

Overnight Charges: Under 18 £4.45 Adult £6.55

Seasonal Prices Jul 1 - Aug 31: Under 18 £4.85 Adult £7.20

R-a-H ☎ 01722 337494 🄸 6SC ⌗ 🖭 ½m 🅿 Free parking 250yds.

Jan 1 - Apr 6	Rent-a-Hostel
Apr 7 - Jun 30	Open X:Tu/Wed
Jul 1 - Aug 31	Open
Sep 1 - Sep 30	Open X:Tu/Wed
Oct 1 - Dec 31	Rent-a-Hostel

ACCOMMODATION 🛏2 🛏5-8 🛏9+1

Teetering on the rugged west coast of Cornwall, this former coastguard station offers wonderful views over an exciting coastline with untamed seas and isolated bays. And with three miles of excellent surf beach, it's also a surfers' paradise. This traditional Hostel stands on the South West Coastal Foothpath with walks to St Agnes, Hollywell Bay and Newquay. Local attractions include the World in Miniature, St Agnes Leisure Park, Newquay Zoo and the historic city of Truro. 🍴1m 🅿️2m 🏧1m 🚮 🖳½m

TRAVEL INFO
🚌Western National 87/A/B/C, 88A Truro-Newquay (pass close BR Truro & Newquay) (☎ 01209 719988) 🚂Truro 10m; Newquay (not Sun, except Jun - Sep) 10m.
🄸 ☎01872 573368

NEXT HOSTELS
Pendennis Castle 19m, Treyarnon Bay 22m, Bowsinger 25m

HOW TO GET THERE
Along cliff to W of village, Hostel beyond locked gate on coastal footpath. No vehicular access.
OS 204 GR 752544 Bart 1

Tintagel

25 BEDS   **Open: 17.00hrs**

Youth Hostel, Dunderhole Point, Tintagel, Cornwall PL34 0DW ☎ 01840 770334

Out of season contact: Regional Booking Service, 11B York Road, Salisbury, Wilts. SP2 7AP
☎ 01722 337494 Fax: 01722 414027

Overnight Charges: Under 18 £4.85 Adult £7.20

Seasonal Prices Jul 1 - Aug 31: Under 18 £5.35 Adult £8.00

🄸 6SC ⌗ 🖭 🅿 Limited. Alternative parking at Tintagel Church 300yds.

| Apr 5 - Jun 30 | Open X:Wed |
| Jul 1 - Sep 30 | Open |

ACCOMMODATION 🛏1 🛏2

Owned by the National Trust, this small, traditional (self-catering) Hostel is perched on the Glebe Cliffs with stunning views of the coastline, sea and wonderful sunsets.
Enjoy the superb views along the South West Coastal footpath, visit Rocky Valley with its ancient rock carvings, or explore the 13th century remains of Tintagel Castle. At Tintagel, best known for its Arthurian legends, you can watch the waves break over the threshold of Merlin's Cave. 🍴 🖳 🏧 🚮

TRAVEL INFO
🚌Western National 52/B from BR Bodmin Parkway, X4 from Bude (☎ 01209 719988); Fry's from Plymouth (passes close BR Plymouth) (infrequent). On all, alight Tintagel, ¾m (☎ 01840 770256). 🚌Bodmin Parkway 20m.
🄸 ☎01840 212954

NEXT HOSTELS
Boscastle Harbour 5m, Treyarnon Bay 23m (18m by ferry), Golant 28m

HOW TO GET THERE
Vehicular access along rough track via Tregatta corner only.
OS 200 GR 047881 Bart 1

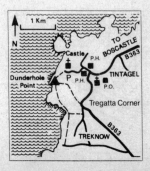

42 BEDS   **Open: 17.00hrs**

Treyarnon Bay

Youth Hostel, Tregonnan, Treyarnon, Padstow, Cornwall PL28 8JR
☎ 01841 520322

Out of season contact: Regional Booking Service, 11B York Road, Salisbury, Wilts. SP2 7AP
☎ 01722 337494 Fax: 01722 414027

Overnight Charges: Under 18 £4.85 Adult £7.20

Seasonal Prices Jul 1 - Aug 31: Under 18 £5.35 Adult £8.00

R-a-H ☎ 01722 337494 2️⃣ 🍴 63℃ 🔌 📷 P Cars and mini-buses (coaches 100 metres by arrangement)

Jan 1 - Mar 31	Rent-a-Hostel
Apr 1 - Jun 30	Open X:Fr*
Jul 1 - Aug 31	Open
Sep 1 - Nov 4	Open X:Fr
Nov 5 - Dec 31	Rent-a-Hostel

* Open Bank Hol Fr.

ACCOMMODATION 🛏1 🛏5-8 2 🛏9+ 2

This former seaside residence with stunning views is close to the beach. It makes an ideal base for exploring the North Cornish coast.
The nearby lighthouse on Trevose Head watches over many fine surfing beaches, lifeguard patrolled from May-September. The lively resort of Padstow is 4m. 🚲4m ⤵3m ⛰4m

---

TRAVEL INFO
🚌 Western National 55 BR Bodmin Parkway-Padstow, alight Padstow, 4 ½m, on most, but some extended to Constantine, ½m; 56 Newquay-Constantine Jun-Sep only. 🚉 Newquay (not Sun, except May - Sep) 10m; Bodmin Parkway 21m.
ℹ️ ☎ 01841 533449

NEXT HOSTELS
Perranporth 22m, Tintagel 23m, Boscastle 24m

HOW TO GET THERE
From A39 take A389 or B3274 to Padstow then B3276 to St Merryn (Farmers Arms PH), then 3rd right turn signposted Treyarnon. From Newquay take B3276 towards Padstow then left turn after Porthcothan (11m).
OS 200 GR 859741 Bart 1

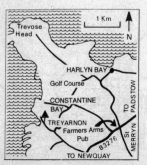

Camping Barns

Quernmore Barn

The YHA has four networks of Camping Barns — in the Forest of Bowland; North Yorkshire; North Pennines; and Exmoor, Dartmoor and Tarka country. They make excellent bases for exploring the countryside with good access to spectacular walking and cycling routes.

Holwick Barn

Sometimes known as stone tents, camping barns are farm buildings owned and operated by farmers which provide basic communal accommodation — with wooden sleeping platforms, tables and benches for preparing and eating food, a supply of cold water and a flush toilet. Barns are not usually heated so it's essential that you bring a good sleeping bag and warm clothing with you. Prices start from £2.75 per person per night.

Sinnington Barn

Brompton-On-Swale

Sleeps: 12 🏠 📷 P U ⚠ ✉ 📋

ACCOMMODATION

A former byre in a farmyard in the attractive village of Brompton-On-Swale. Sleeping accommodation is on the first floor, along with the toilet and shower. Drying facilities available. Electric light, a heater, a cooker and crockery are available. It makes an excellent stopping off point for the Coast to Coast Walk which is ½m away.

GR 216997
ℹ 📞 01748 822943

Farndale

Sleeps: 12 🏠 📷 10m 🚿 ✉

ACCOMMODATION

Within the North York Moors National Park, the barn is in High Farndale. Sleeping accommodation is in the barn loft with electric light, a heater and a cooker available. There is a small farm shop at the Farm. Activities include the Coast to Coast Walk ½m, Cleveland Way 3m, Lyke Wake Walk 2m and Rosedale Circuit 2½m.

OS 659986 **GR** 659986
ℹ 📞 01904 621756

Kildale

Sleeps: 12 🏠 📷 1m 🐟

ACCOMMODATION

Superbly located in the North York Moors National Park, the building was formerly a barn and wheelhouse. Sleeping accommodation is in the first floor loft. Electric light, heat and cooking facilities are available on a meter. Toilet in adjacent building. Attractions include the Esk Valley Railway. There are many good local walks including the Cleveland Way.

GR 602085

Leyburn

Sleeps: 12 🏠 📷 1m 🚿 U

ACCOMMODATION

A field byre with magnificent views of Wensleydale. The building contains bunks beds, a gas cooker, two toilets and washbasins. Metered electricity powers the light, heater, fridge and shower. Visit nearby Wensleydale or try one of several local walks including the Riverside footpath along the River Ure.

GR 216997
ℹ 📞 01969 22773

Lovesome Hill

Sleeps: 15 🏠 📷 4m 🚿 U ⚠ ✉

ACCOMMODATION

Ideally placed for exploring both the Yorkshire Dales and North York Moors National Park. There is electric light and a heater, plus a cooker and shower on meter. Sleeping accommodation is on the first floor and there are two toilets on the ground floor.
On Coast to Coast walk 16m E of Richmond. Popular cycling area. Working farm with plenty to see. 8m from Cleveland Way. Many waterways for fishing.

OS 99 **GR** 361998
ℹ 📞 01609 776864

Low Row

Sleeps: 15 🏠 📷 2m

ACCOMMODATION

Well located in Swaledale in the Yorkshire Dales National Park. Sleeping accommodation is on the first floor, with toilets and a shower on the ground floor. There is electric light and a calor gas heater and cooker available.
As well as the Coast to Coast Walk (1m), there are many local walks including the Corpse Road between Keld and Reeth.

GR 003983

Richmond

Sleeps: 12 🏠 📷 3m ✉

ACCOMMODATION

Consisting of three former byres, this camping barn is located on the edge of the Yorkshire Dales National Park and has sweeping views across Swaledale. Sleeping accommodation is in two rooms. There is electricity and a flush toilet. Heat and cooking facilities available on meter. There are several pleasant local walks as well as the Coast to Coast Walk.

GR 133016
ℹ 📞 0174882 2943

Free leaflet and booking details from: Camping Barn Booking Service, YHA Northern Region, PO Box 11, Matlock, Derbyshire DE4 2XA   Tel: 01629 825850

NORTH YORKSHIRE - CAMPING BARNS

Sinnington

Sleeps: 12 ⬚ 📷 3m Ⓟ Ⓤ

ACCOMMODATION

Converted granary on family farm, with selection of animals to see. Situated on edge of North York Moors. Sleeps nine on first floor, three on ground floor. Electric light, heat, cooking facilities available. Toilets, shower, washing facilities are in an adjacent building.

Attractions include the Pickering to North Yorks Steam Railway, Crofton Forest and Flamingo land. Many local walks including Sinnington — Cropton, Sinnington — Rosedale, Newtondale Trial (3m) and the Link (2m).

GR 752849
🏠 📞 01751 73791

Westerdale Bunk House Barn

Sleeps: 12

ACCOMMODATION

Set in the North York Moors National Park, the building has lovely views over Westerdale Moor and Castleton Rigg. Formerly a byre, it is now equipped with electric lights, heaters, showers and a calor gas cooker.

There are many local walks including the Coast to Coast Walk (3m), Lyke Wake Walk (3m) and the Rosedale Circuit.

OS 6605 **GR** 671049

Free leaflet and booking details from: Camping Barn Booking Service, YHA Northern Region, PO Box 11, Matlock, Derbyshire   DE4 2XA   Tel: 01629 825850

NORTH PENNINES - CAMPING BARNS

Holwick

Sleeps: 20 ⬚ 📷 3m ⛰

ACCOMMODATION

A field bunkhouse barn near the River Tees. Sleeping accommodation is in beds on the first floor. The ground floor has a cooking area, worktops, and hot and cold water supply. There are two flush toilets, a shower and a sitting area. There is gas heating and lighting downstairs.

A separate self-contained 8-bedded bunkhouse barn is also available to a similar standard with all accommodation on ground floor. Close to High Force and the Pennine Way with lots of good walks nearby.

GR 914270

Lartington

Sleeps: 15 ⬚ 📷 2m ⛰

ACCOMMODATION

Set in a farmyard, this former corn store is a listed building. The sleeping accommodation is on the first floor along with a toilet. On the ground floor there are two more flush toilets, two showers and an area for cooking and sitting. There is also electric light, drying facilities and heating.

An excellent base for exploring Teesdale, with Barnard Castle nearby.

GR 029177

Wearhead

Sleeps: 12 ⬚ 📷 1m ♨ Ⓤ 🍴

ACCOMMODATION

A listed building, formerly a farmhouse, this barn is next to a stream. On the ground floor there is an area for cooking food, sitting and eating where there is also a coal fire. The sleeping accommodation and flush toilet are on the first floor.

Weardale Way ½m.

GR 851397

Witton

Sleeps: 15 ⬚ 📷 Ⓟ ♨ Ⓤ 🍴

ACCOMMODATION

A former byre and dairy, this barn is on the Witton Castle Estate which offers a range of facilities including an outdoor swimming pool, public bars, games and TV rooms, a shop and cafeteria. The barn itself is a single storey building with sleeping platform, a cooking/eating area and two flush toilets.

There is electric light, a wood burning stove and a cooker. As well as Weardale Way only ½m away, Escombe Saxon Church and Hamsterly Forest are also well worth a visit.

GR 155298
🏠 📞 01833 690000

Free leaflet and booking details from: Camping Barn Booking Service, YHA Northern Region, PO Box 11, Matlock, Derbyshire   DE4 2XA   Tel: 01629 825850

Chipping

Sleeps: 15 P 🖭 🗊 🐾

ACCOMMODATION

A former stable, this barn has superb views of Wolf Fell and Parlick Pike, just ½m away. Sleeping accommodation is on the upper floor with shower, hand basin and toilet with two further toilets in a converted pig sty. Electric on a meter. Two hot place cookers and woodburner available.

GR 616435
ℹ️ ☎01200 25566

Downham

Sleeps: 12 🖼 📷 ½m P In former quarry opposite.

ACCOMMODATION

A field barn in an attractive setting near the foot of Pendle Hill. Downham Camping Barn is ideally situated for walkers and is just 4m from Clitheroe. Sleeping accommodation is provided on the first floor of the barn. Flush toilet on the ground floor. There is gas lighting, cooking rings and a wall mounted heater available on a meter. As well as attractions like Downham, Pendle Hill and Clitheroe, the Lancashire Cycle Way, Ribble Way and Pendle Way are all close by.

GR 795445
ℹ️ ☎01200 25566

Giggleswick

Sleeps: 12 🖼 📷 1 ½m P Rear of the barn. 🏔️

ACCOMMODATION

This camping barn, built in 1761, is situated in the farmyard opposite Grain House only 6m from Ingleborough. Sleeping accommodation is on the first floor. Electric light, cooking rings and shower are provided on a meter. There is also a wood burning stove and a drying area.
Local attractions include the town of Settle, the Settle to Carlisle Railway and the Three Peaks. Walkers will find the Ribble Way 1 ½m and North Bowland Traverse 2 ½m.

GR 795632
ℹ️ ☎01468 62252

Hurst Green

Sleeps: 12 🖼 📷 1 ½m P In the farmyard. 🖭 🐾

ACCOMMODATION

Henry VII is reputed to have stayed in the former hunting lodge adjacent to this converted byre. The barn is only a mile from Longridge Fell. Sleeping accommodation is on the upper floor and the toilet is in another building close by. Barbecue available. Electric light, cooking rings and a drying room are provided on a meter. There is a wood burning stove. Attractions include Stoneyhurst College, Ribchester and Clitheroe. Ribble Way 2m.

GR 674389
ℹ️ ☎01200 255666

Quernmore

Sleeps: 15 🖼 📷 1m P In the farmyard. 🖭 🐾

ACCOMMODATION

This field barn enjoys a superb remote location on an elevated hill top with magnificent open views over Morecambe Bay and the Lake District Fells. Sleeping accommodation is in two areas on the ground floor. There are two wood burning stoves. There is no electricity so bring a torch. Snacks available 1m, farm cafe.
There are two flush toilets. Cars can be parked in the farmyard 10-15 mins walk from the barns. There is no access for vehicles to the barn. Attractions include the Clougha Access Area and North Bowland Traverse (Tambrook Fell).

GR 528588
ℹ️ ☎01200 25566

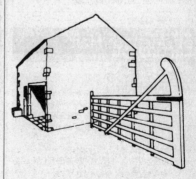

CHIPPING BARN

Free leaflet and booking details from: The Bowland Barns Reservations Office, 16 Shawbridge Street, Clitheroe, Lancashire BB7 1LY   Tel: 01200 28366

Great Houndtor

Sleeps: 14 ⊠ P ▣ 𝄢

ACCOMMODATION

A converted shippen sleeping 14 in two separate areas on the first floor. Ground floor has toilets, a shower and washroom and large cooking and recreation area. Electric light. Nearest pub 1 ½m. On the eastern edge of Dartmoor near Manaton, underneath the famous Houndtor. Bridleways to the open moor.

OS 191 GR 749795

Higher Cadham

Sleeps: 12 ⊠ ▣ 2m P ▣

ACCOMMODATION

A converted barn in peaceful farmyard setting. Accommodation all on one floor with toilets, shower, small cooking area, recreation area and sleeping for 12. Meals and small shop on farm. Electric light. Heater and drying facilities. Nearest Post Office and Pub 2m. On Tarka Trail and West Devon Cycle route in heart of Tarka Country with disabled access and other nearby walks.

OS 191 GR 585025

Runnage

Sleeps: 15 ⊠ ⚠ P ▣ ⚠

ACCOMMODATION

Sleeping upstairs with showers and toilets. Cooking and sitting area on ground floor. Big breakfast available! Electric light. Woodburner. Nearest pub ½m. In the middle of Dartmoor with many walking opportunities and close to Bellever Forest and the River Dart.

OS 191 GR 668792

Sticklepath Halt

Sleeps: 16 ⊠ ▣ P ▣

ACCOMMODATION

The 'Old Bakery' now provides dormitory sleeping, large catering and separate recreation areas with good washing/shower facilities. Electric light, electricity on meter. Post office and pub adjacent.
Beneath the imposing Cosdon Beacon in the village of Sticklepath, the Halt offers direct access to spectacular walking routes over North Dartmoor and beyond. Also on the 180m Tarka Trail.

OS 191 GR 642941

Watercombe Farm

Sleeps: 20 ⊠ ▣ 2m P ▣

ACCOMMODATION

Large barn with five separate sleeping areas including one family/disabled room. Separate ladies and gents toilets and showers and large kitchen and recreation areas. Electric light. Nearest pub and post office 2m.
On the southern tip of Dartmoor with direct access to open moorland, and close to the Two Moors Way.

OS 202 GR 625613

Woodadvent

Sleeps: 12 ⊠ ▣ 1m P

ACCOMMODATION

Former cider barn in farmyard with sleeping for 12 upstairs and cooking/sitting area downstairs. Toilet within building. Electric light. Nearest post office and pub 1m.
In a quiet and unspoilt corner of Exmoor National Park, close to the picturesque village of Rondwater and with an excellent footpath network.

OS 181 GR 037373

Holne

Sleeps: 14 ⊠ ▣ ¼m ⚠ P ▣ ⚠

ACCOMMODATION

A converted barn, ideal base for groups with parking, and backing on to small camping field. Good facilities including showers and toilets, cooker, fridge and dryer. Woodburning stove and wood available. Electric light. Post Office and pub ¼m.
On southern slope of Dartmoor in attractive village of Holne. Only 4m from A38, on 'Two Moors Way' and close to River Dart.

OS 202 GR 706696

> **For further details and booking for Holne please ring: 01364 643920**

> For further information and booking please ring: 01271 24420
> More Barns will open during the year - please call for an update.

"I don't have enough money."
"$50 Restaurants?!"
"I have no place to stay."
"It's too much!"
"Travel's too expensive."

QUIT WHINING AND GO.

You are now officially out of excuses for not traveling. Because Hostelling International is the answer to all your problems. Like money. It costs just a few dollars a night to stay at any one of the 300 hostels across the U.S. and Canada. Plus with fully equipped do-it-yourself kitchens and numerous discounts on attractions, admissions and transportation tickets, you can save even more. If you're worried about meeting people, don't be. Hostels are the perfect places to meet travelers from all over the world. So quit making excuses and start making traveling plans.

HOSTELLING INTERNATIONAL

The new seal of approval of the International Youth Hostel Federation.

HOSTELLING INTERNATIONAL®

Northern Ireland (YHANI)

This is a land of blue mountains and forest parks, hazy lakes and windswept moors, white Atlantic sands and inland sea — in fact, it's just a country that's pretending to be small! Dozens of little towns are hidden away in the countryside and fishing villages spring out along the shores. The weather can be fickle but the rain keeps the land a magical emerald green and when the wind blows the clouds away to sea, the sky like the mountains is blue and the air is clean!

USEFUL PUBLICATIONS

Ireland the Youth Hostel way — send s.a.e to the address listed below.

Accommodation Guide of Northern Ireland — send s.a.e. to the address listed below.

Go as you please (the freedom of Northern Ireland by bus) — send s.a.e. to the address listed below.

For booking requirements and more information about hostelling in Northern Ireland contact: Youth Hostel Association of Northern Ireland, 22-32 Donegall Road, Belfast BT12 5JN. Tel: 01232 324733. Fax: 01232 439699.

48 BEDS	Open: 17.00hrs

Ballygally

Youth Hostel, 210 Coast Road, Ballygally, Co. Antrim BT40 2QQ ☎ **01574 583377 Fax: 01232 439699**

Overnight Charges: Under 18 £5.30 Adult £6.30

Parking available.

Larne-Stranraer/Cairnryan 5m

We regret that this Youth Hostel will no longer be open after 31 December 1994. The nearest Youth Hostels are Cushendall 25m and Belfast 26m.

126 BEDS	Open: All Day

Belfast International

Youth Hostel, 22 Donegall Road, Belfast BT12 5JN ☎ **01232 324733 Fax: 01232 439699**

Overnight Charges: Under 18 £7.50 Adult £9.00

Larne-Stranraer/Cairnryan and Belfast-Stranraer

Hostel is open 24 hours a day, 365 days a year.

ACCOMMODATION 36 2

Newly constructed purpose-built Hostel central to all city attractions. Good accesss point to explore Northern Ireland. Ulster Museum, Ulster Folk and Transport Museum (50% discount for members), Queens University, Crown Liquor Saloon, Grand Opera House.

TRAVEL INFO
Citybus No 89 (☎ 01232 246485) Belfast Central 1m

NEXT HOSTELS
Ballygally 26m, Newcastle 31m

HOW TO GET THERE
OS 15 GR 332732

55 BEDS   Open: 17.00hrs

Castle Archdale

Youth Hostel, Castle Archdale, Country Park, Irvinestown, Co. Fermanagh BT94 1PP
☎ 013656 28118

Overnight Charges: Under 18 £5.30 Adult £6.30

 Available for cars and coaches. (IBN).

Open every day of the year.
(Advance bookings only for Jan/Feb 1995)

ACCOMMODATION 🛏️2-4 2 🛏️9+ 2
Built in 1773 in the heart of Castle Archdale Country Park, the Hostel occupies a major wing of the old courtyard complex.

TRAVEL INFO
🚌Ulsterbus 194 from Enniskilen (with connections from Belfast).
ℹ️ ☎01365 323110

NEXT HOSTELS
Donegal 30m, Sligo 35m, Londonderry 50m

HOW TO GET THERE
11 miles N of Enniskillen on the Eastern shore of Lough Erne, signposted Castle Archdale Country Park.
OS 17 GR 176588 Bart 1

---

56 BEDS   Open: 17.00hrs

Cushendall

Youth Hostel, Layde Road, Cushendall, Co. Antrim BT44 0NQ ☎ 012667 71344

Overnight Charges: Under 18 £5.30 Adult £6.30

 (IBN)

Open every day of the year.
(Advance bookings only for Jan/Feb 1995)

ACCOMMODATION 🛏️3 🛏️5-8 1 🛏️9+ 2
A large building set in its own grounds on the hillside of the Antrim Coast overlooking Cushendall Bay and Garron Point.

TRAVEL INFO
🚌Ulsterbus 162, 252/4 from Larne (passing NIR Larne); 150 from Ballymena (passes close NIR Ballymena). On all, alight Cushendall, thence 1m
(☎01232 333000/320574) 🚆Ballymena 20 m.
ℹ️ ☎012657 62225

NEXT HOSTELS
Whitepark Bay 15m, Ballygally 25m

HOW TO GET THERE
Situated 1m N of Cushendall Village on the Layde Road towards Cushenddall. Bus service from Cushendall along Antrim Coast.
OS 5 GR 241286 Bart 1

---

40 BEDS   Open: 17.00hrs

Newcastle

Youth Hostel, 30 Downs Road, Newcastle, Co. Down BT33 0AG ☎ 013967 22133

Overnight Charges: Under 18 £5.30 Adult £6.30

 On street at Hostel or car park opposite. (IBN)

Open every day of the year.
(Advance bookings only for Jan/Feb 1995)

ACCOMMODATION 🛏️3-4 3 🛏️5-8 5
A large town house situated near the sea front in Newcastle. As well as the Hostel, a family apartment is available.

TRAVEL INFO
🚌Ulsterbus 18, 20 Belfast-Newcastle; 39, 240 from Newry (☎ 01232 333000/320574). Bus station 300m from Hostel. 🚆Newry 22m.
ℹ️ ☎013967 22222

HOW TO GET THERE
OS 29 GR 379314 Bart 1

---

44 BEDS   Open: 17.00hrs

Whitepark Bay

Youth Hostel, 157 Whitepark Road, Ballintoy, Ballycastle, Co Antrim BT54 6NH
☎ 012657 31745 Fax: 012657 32034

Overnight Charges: Under 18 £5.30 Adult £6.30

 For cars and coaches. (IBN)

Open every day of the year.

ACCOMMODATION 🛏️5-8 2 🛏️9+ 2
Beautifully located overlooking the National Trust property of Whitepark Bay on the North Antrim causeway coast between the famous Giant's Causeway and Carrick-a-Rede Rope Bridge.

TRAVEL INFO
🚌Ulsterbus 172, 252 from Portrush (☎ 01232 333000/320574). North/south coastal bus route.
🚆Portrush 12m.
ℹ️ ☎01265 823333

NEXT HOSTELS
Cushendall 25m, Londonderry 35m

HOW TO GET THERE
OS 5 GR 073436 Bart 1

The YHA Democracy

YHA is a registered charity and is not funded by the Government. We welcome you to join us in conservation work, Youth Hostel maintenance, voluntary Wardening, fund-raising and publicity work. YHA member-volunteers and YHA Local Groups often organise working parties and other activities which are both sociable and fun.

YHA is a membership organisation with 250,000 members. It wholly owns and controls the limited company, YHA (England and Wales) Limited (which is also a registered charity) which employs a team of full-time professional managers to run its operations. The policies they follow are decided by YHA members through the democratic structure shown below:

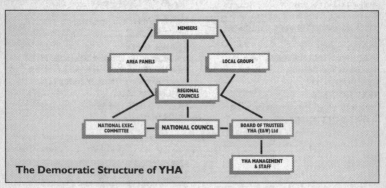

The Democratic Structure of YHA

Area Panels co-ordinate the activities of groups of volunteers. Your Area Panel is elected at an open Area AGM announced in **YHA News.** This meeting is a good place to find out what is happening in your area. Activities are organised on a 'Voluntary Area' basis (you are welcome to join us in any area) and YHA Voluntary Areas are shown on the opposite page.

Regional Councils are involved in developing policy, encouraging members to participate in YHA activities and monitoring the service provided to members.

There are four Regional Councils — Northern England, Central, Wales and South England. These are elected at an open Regional AGM and are drawn from members nominated at the meeting, together with representatives of Area Panels and Local Groups.

YHA NEWS is a newspaper for those who want to keep in close touch with the policies and activities of the YHA. Voluntary subscriptions are invited. Apply to YHA (address on p.1) if you would like to be put on the mailing list.

YOUR VOTE COUNTS! You are welcome to come along to your Regional AGM and ask questions, express opinions, propose motions (with appropriate notice), stand for elections and vote. For details, contact Sarah Burbridge on 01727 855215 ext.201 or see **YHA News.**

NATIONAL COUNCIL, which consists mainly of Regional representatives, meets annually and establishes the principles of YHA. It elects a National Executive Committee which determines policies within these principles and a Board of Trustees of the Company which has legal responsibility for managing all Youth Hostels. These policies are then implemented by the management and volunteers as appropriate.

YHA voluntary activities are organised on an area basis and the Voluntary Areas are indicated by the dotted lines on the map below. You can choose to participate in any area that suits you.

1	BORDER AND DALES	9	SOUTH ENGLAND 2
2	YORKSHIRE	10	SOUTH ENGLAND 1
3	EAST ENGLAND	11	MIDLAND
4	SOUTH ENGLAND 7	12	SOUTH WALES
5	SOUTH ENGLAND 6	13	NORTH WALES
6	SOUTH ENGLAND 5	14	PEAK
7	SOUTH ENGLAND 4	15	LAKELAND
8	SOUTH ENGLAND 3		

YHA

HOSTELLING INTERNATIONAL

AUSTRALIA OFFERS

 Complete travel packages which include accommodation, 12 month valid coach travel, entrance tickets to Australia's favourite tourist places and more.

Packages are from as little as AUD$25 a day - e.g. Aussie Explorer "Best of East" bus pass with Australian Coachlines with 60 night's accommodation for AUD$1,415.

 Stay in over 130 Australian YHA Hostels. There are also over 5,500 Hostels in over 65 countries, all with friendly, helpful hostel staff.

 No age limits in any Australian YHA Hostels with 24 hour access.

 A centralised booking system where YHA Hostels can be booked for your next destination throughout Australia.

 Sydney, Brisbane, Melbourne, Cairns, Adelaide and Perth can all be booked on the IBN Computer Reservation System.

 Access to over 600 discounts throughout Australia - a saving of thousands of dollars to YHA members only. Ask for the free YHA Discount Book.

 YHA Hostels that feature clean and comfortable accommodation at all of Australia's favourite tourist destinations.

 Self-catering facilities to help you save money.

 Travel Agencies in every State capital city as well as Alice Springs, Cairns, Airlie Beach and Canberra. Each Travel Office offers special discounts to YHA members on a wide range of travel products from international airline tickets, coach passes, travel insurance and local tours.

- ✂

Please send further information on the excellent travel packages available from YHA Australia

Name: _____

Address: _____

_____ Postcode: _____

Country: _____

Send to: Australia YHA, Level 3, 10 Mallett Street, Camperdown, NSW 2050 Australia. EW94/95

YHA Adventure Shops understand what **YOU** as a YHA member want from an outdoor clothing and equipment retailer.

That's why, as the UK's most dynamic specialists in their field, more YHA members use YHA Adventure Shops knowledge, information and quality products than any other outdoor retailer.

YHA Adventure Shops' buyers have travelled the world to assemble one of the most comprehensive ranges of clothing, equipment and travel accessories available. Each one of their 12,000 individual products offers quality and value for money. And each has a price promise that guarantees the lowest prices, plus a 10% discount for YHA members.

Amongst the international names you will find at YHA Adventure Shops are Berghaus, Karrimor, Line 7, Zamberlan, Coleman and Reef. They are also supporting the newly emerging economies of Czechoslovakia, Poland, Vietnam, Indonesia and Afghanistan.

The resulting range – including their exclusive own label Mountaincraft – offers an incredible diversity of products suitable for beginners and professionals alike.

In addition you will find a range of services unlike any other retailer in the outdoor world; an in-house travel agency, YHA membership information and enrolment, a pre and post customer sales service, a mail order department, a privileged client facility, a specialist cycling outlet – even a windsurfing and watersports retailer (in Brighton only).

All the services **YOU** have requested.

And with services like this on offer, you would expect that the product range just can't be beaten. Here are just some of the products you'll find:

- Rucsacs, Travel sacs, Daypacks and Accessories
- Adult and Childrens Footwear
- Mens, Womens and Childrens Clothing
- Tents and Tent Accessories
- Sleeping Bags, Sheet Bags and Accessories
- YHA Approved Items
- First Aid Kits and Survival Equipment
- Travel Accessories
- Cooking and Lighting Equipment
- Ski Clothing and Equipment
- Guide and Travel Books
- Foreign and Domestic Maps
- Climbing Equipment *(Covent Garden only)*
- Cycles, Cycle Clothing and Accessories *(larger stores only)*
- Windsurfing and Watersports *(Brighton Store)*
- Gift Vouchers
- 10% Discount for YHA members

But the best way to see just what YHA Adventure shops have to offer is by visiting one of their branches – **YOU** won't be disappointed.

Branches at: London – Covent Garden 0171 836 8541 • Victoria 0171 823 4739 • Kensington 0171 938 2948 • Manchester 0161 834 7119 • Birmingham 0121 236 7799 • Brighton 01273 821554 • Bristol 0117 929 7141 • Cambridge 01223 353956 • Cardiff 01222 399178 • Leeds 0113 246 5339 • Liverpool 0151 709 8063 • Nottingham 0115 947 5710 • Oxford 01865 247948 • Reading 01734 587722 • Salisbury 01722 422122 • Sheffield 0114 276 5935 • Southampton 01703 235847 • Staines 01784 452987 • Sunderland 0191 510 9060.

For full details of future store openings and any other facilities call 01784 458625 (24 hours).

WHAT IS A
YHA MEMBER..

Y O U

YOU love the great outdoors

YOU know you need the right clothing and equipment

YOU require the clothing and equipment you purchase to perform to the limits you set.

YOU want to be sure that you get value for money – and that you will not find the same products cheaper elsewhere.

YOU want a large selection of anything and everything you need. To browse the latest fabrics, innovations and technology.

YOU want to be sure that if you change your mind you can exchange or obtain a refund without any hassle.

YOU want your shopping experience to be an enjoyable part of your great adventure.

YOU need YHA Adventure Shops.

Stores throughout England and Wales. 12,000 individual products with guaranteed lowest prices – plus an additional 10% YHA members discount on all purchases.

Great Stores • Great Staff • The Best Products • The Lowest Prices

We look forward to being of service to **YOU**

Adventure S H O P S

CALL 01784 458625 (24 hrs)
for details of your nearest branch and mail order service.

One thing even a Barclays Connect card can't buy.

Money can't buy you love, they say.

Neither, to be honest, can a Barclays Connect card. But a card in your wallet is a lot more convenient than a cheque book in your pocket. And Barclays Connect is accepted at over 400,000 outlets in Britain as well as 10 million worldwide.

Anywhere, in fact, that displays the Visa or Delta sign. From Hong Kong to the High Street.

It's not a credit card though, it's a debit card. Any amount you spend is taken from your current account. Every transaction appears on your bank statement.

But, unlike a cheque, spending power is not restricted by a guarantee card, only by the amount available in your current account.

If you want cash, you can use Barclays Connect in our network of over 6,200 dispensers.

So what can't you get with a Barclays Connect card?

Well, one of the best things in life still can't be bought with it.

For further details call in to your nearest branch or phone the Barclays Information Line on 0800 400 100.

CALL THE BARCLAYS INFORMATION LINE ON 0800 400 100 FREE

BARCLAYS

YHA ENROLMENT FORM

To YHA, TREVELYAN HOUSE, ST ALBANS, HERTS, AL1 2DY

Please enrol me as a member of the Association.
I have been resident in England or Wales for at least 12 months.
PLEASE COMPLETE IN BLOCK CAPITALS

Title	Surname	First names	Date of Birth	Membership No. (if already a member)

Address

Postcode

I enclose £ _____ (Under 18: £3.00/Adult: £9.00). PLEASE MAKE CHEQUES PAYABLE TO YHA.

Please note that membership prices are valid from 1 Jan 95.

For applicants under 16 a signature from a parent or guardian is required.

Signature

We now offer our members the opportunity to receive mailings and offers from a few carefully selected companies, whose products and services are particularly appropriate to the interests of YHA members.

If you do not wish to receive such mailings, please indicate by placing a tick in the box provided. ☐

Date _____

Cancellations & Refunds

NOTICE OF CANCELLATION

In all cases, if you have to cancel your visit please let the Hostel staff know — even at the last minute — as someone else can then use your bed.

In mountain and remote areas, it is vital that you contact the Youth Hostel if you decide not to take up your reservation. Otherwise the police or rescue teams may be called out to look for you.

REFUNDS

Individuals and families

Individuals and family members of the YHA (England and Wales) and other Associations within the International Youth Hostel Federation network are covered by YHA's free Cancellation Refund Package.

Every claim will be subject to an administration fee of £5.

Under this scheme, YHA will refund members in respect of loss of charges paid to the Association for their accommodation and/or meals not taken up (up to £100 per individual) where the member is forced to cancel or curtail his or her journey provided three days notice of cancellation has been given to the Hostel concerned.

Activity Holidays

Activity Holidays run by the YHA are subject to separate insurance policies. Details are contained on the booking form and policies are sent to participants before the holiday.

Groups

A cancellation refund package is available to those making group bookings. This is strongly recommended and available for a nominal charge. See the reverse of the YHA Group Booking Form for full details, or contact our Customer Services Department on 01727 845047.

How to Apply

To apply for a refund, just complete an application form (available from Hostels or any YHA office) and send it, together with all supporting documentation — including appropriate copy booking forms, invoice and receipts, as well as any medical certificates — to YHA National Accounts Office (address on the form). Applications are normally processed within 28 days of receipt.

KEY (S)= Seasonal Price (July 1 – Aug 31)   * = See Hostel entry for overnight price

1995 YHA ACCOMMODATION GUIDE

EDITOR
Suzy Dubowski

DESIGN
Cover and Editorial pages: In-Touch Design Consultancy, Hatfield.
Hostel entries: Elanders (UK) Ltd.

PRINTING
Reproduced, printed and bound in Sweden by Elanders.

ISBN 0-904530-18-3

Published November 1994
by the Youth Hostels Association (England & Wales)

*All public transport information in this Guide is provided by Barry S. Doe of **Travadvice, 25 Newmorton Road, Bournemouth BH9 3NU.** Barry also publishes a travel guide giving bus times from stations to over 330 places not on the BR network, many of which have Youth Hostels. Published in February, June, August and October, it costs just £6 (sterling) post-free within Europe, or an annual subscription to any four consecutive copies is £21 (£19 to YHA members quoting this page). To addresses outside Europe add £1 per copy (£2 on subscription).*